I0755800

Uneven Rewards

MILESTONES IN LABOUR ECONOMICS

Uneven Rewards

MILESTONES IN LABOUR ECONOMICS

ALISON L BOOTH

ANU PRESS

GLOBAL THINKERS SERIES

ANU PRESS

Published by ANU Press
The Australian National University
Canberra ACT 2600, Australia
Email: anupress@anu.edu.au

Available to download for free at press.anu.edu.au

ISBN (hardcover): 9781760467296
ISBN (online): 9781760467302

WorldCat (hardcover): 1574508566
WorldCat (online): 1574508610

DOI: 10.22459/UR.2026

Cover design and layout by ANU Press

This book is published under the aegis of the Public Policy editorial board of ANU Press.

Contents

Section III: Gendered behavioural responses: Evidence from experiments

Introduction

Many of the requests that academics receive for copies of their published papers are from people who cannot gain access to academic journals without being charged too high a price, and open access is an important way of reaching these potential readers. Because I'm committed to the dissemination of ideas and to The Australian National University's open-access *Global Thinkers Series*, I was delighted when Andrew Kennedy of The Australian National University's Crawford School of Public Policy invited me to contribute. Published by the ANU Press, the *Global Thinkers Series* is an initiative of the Public Policy Editorial Board. This volume contains – and places in context – a sample of research papers that I have published in the four decades since I completed my PhD at the London School of Economics. Over this time, I have worked continuously in the higher education sector, mainly at universities in the UK and Australia, although I have spent periods of leave at the University of Amsterdam and at MIT in Cambridge, Massachusetts. Many of the papers in this volume were jointly written with academic collaborators, and I am grateful for their enthusiastic permission to reproduce our work in this volume. All chapters have been previously published in academic journals, the preferred publication outlet for academic scholars, and all have policy relevance today.

Scholars from other social science fields sometimes ask why there are so many collaborative papers in economics. The reason is that economic methodology is complex, requiring a number of different skills. These range from the analytical skills needed to formulate the research question of interest, to data-handling expertise, to econometric techniques, and to the ability to write it all up in as compelling a narrative as possible. The relevance of labour economics to society rests on understanding the analytical foundations of the policy under consideration, on drawing out the testable predictions of the analysis, and on confronting the predictions with the appropriate data. It is unusual to find all these skills in one person, and I have found it to be deeply rewarding to work with a co-author rather than alone.

In 1984, I completed my PhD thesis, entitled *The Microeconomics of the Trade Union*, supervised by the eminent economist Professor Sir Anthony Atkinson, who at that time was at the London School of Economics. I count myself lucky to have had his guidance. The analysis in my PhD thesis reflected the general importance of trade unions in modern developed countries. Over the period since then, there have been immense changes in politics and economics as the world began to grapple with neoliberalism, whose principal notion was that markets generally outperform governments in the allocation of resources. The growth of neoliberalism was associated with a weakening of the power of trade unionism in the UK, through a series of laws directed explicitly at trade unions (Booth 1995). At the same time, over the past decades, there have been developments in microdata collection – whether from surveys or experiments – and in the sophisticated statistical techniques needed to analyse microdata.[1]

The volume comprises three sections. The first covers selected issues in industrial relations and some concerns arising from the growth of neoliberalism. The second focuses on empirical issues arising from societal changes – including the growth of female participation in the labour market – and utilises quality data sets to analyse these changes, including data from a field experiment. The third section is devoted to papers using data from experiments to address the following questions: does nature or nurture affect the preferences of women and men in an economically meaningful way, and are their preferences malleable? The policy relevance of the analyses reported herein is clearly spelled out within each chapter.

1 The scope and relevance of labour economics as a discipline has developed, over my working lifetime, through better collection and availability of micro-level survey data. This began with cross-sectional surveys of a representative set of individual observations (for example, persons, firms, households), collected at a single point in time. These micro surveys facilitated more precise estimation of the effects of policy and demographics on economic and social outcomes, thereby widening the information set available to academics and policymakers. In due course, cross-sectional data were expanded by panel data collection. Here the same individuals from a representative cross-section are surveyed repeatedly across time. Panel data allow the researcher to undertake longitudinal analysis to see how individuals change their behaviour across time, in response to policies as well as to life events. Importantly, panel data and panel data statistical techniques also allow researchers to differentiate out unobservable factors like ability that would otherwise result in biased estimates of the parameters of interest.

Section I: Evolving industrial relations and neoliberalism

My initial interest in trade unions was triggered by a puzzle that presented itself in the analysis of trade union behaviour. The literature on public good provision by groups has traditionally emphasised the free rider problem. Suppose that a group, such as a trade union, forms to provide, or to lobby for the provision of, a good, such as a wage increase that is collective to potential members. Then the major conceptual problem with the formation of such a group is that individuals can enjoy the benefits of group action without incurring the costs (union dues). By doing this, they free ride. In small groups, the free rider problem is not generally considered insurmountable. However, the larger the number of potential beneficiaries, the more difficult it is to overcome the free rider problem, due to exclusion and surveillance difficulties. Consequently, optimal collective good provision, or any collective good provision in the extreme, is less likely.

The free rider hypothesis has a long history in economic thought. As early as 1848, the free rider potential of any group of workers was perceived by Mill. However, it appears that it was not until 1965 that an attempt was made to explain why *large* groups providing collective goods manage to exist despite the free rider problem. Olson (1965) proposed the following explanation. If a large group exists, it must have formed either because membership is compulsory or because the group provides private goods and services accessible only to its members, with ancillary provision of the collective good as a 'by-product.'

In Chapter 1, I developed a social custom model of trade union membership that explains the existence of union membership without compulsion, with the only incentive good being reputation from belonging to the group. That paper showed that a trade union can exist without compulsory membership and union closed shop legislation.[2] It also proved that, under certain conditions, the economic incentive to 'free ride' on trade union membership can be less than the economic incentive to join a large union, in the absence of compulsion. And finally, it incorporated sociological and psychological factors into the traditional utility-maximising model, in what

2 A closed shop trade union is where *all* workers covered by the agreements the union negotiates with employers have to be members of that union. An open shop union will allow *non-members* to be covered by the agreement the union negotiates.

is termed the 'social custom' theory of large union membership. In so doing, the analysis represents the first of my forays into behavioural economics, since it applies psychological insights into human behaviour to explain economic decision-making.

In Chapter 2, Jeff Frank and I investigated the productivity effects of individual performance-related pay (PRP). With the growth of neoliberalism and the weakening of trade union power from the early 1980s, there was a growing emphasis on incentives to increase individual worker productivity by payment mechanisms such as PRP, which can induce greater effort while also attracting more able workers. At the same time, there was an expanding interest in temporary and part-time work contracts, since workers were no longer benefiting to the same extent from permanent jobs. Moreover, women were entering the labour force in increasing numbers, feminism was continuing to grow, and it was no longer the case that labour market researchers could continue the past practice of leaving women out of their studies on the grounds that they were too hard to analyse because of selection issues.

The rationale for government encouragement of different forms of PRP was the belief that these would increase labour market flexibility and generate higher productivity or employment. For instance, the UK Government was in the lead in providing incentives for profit-related pay, one form of PRP. From 1991, up to 20 per cent of total pay could be fully exempt from income tax if received in an approved PRP scheme. As a result, the number of employees covered by approved schemes rose from 232,000 in March 1990 to 2,438,000 in March 1995. The large tax expenditure following from this growth led the Chancellor of the Exchequer to announce the phasing out of the scheme in his 1997 budget.

In investigating the productivity effects of individual PRP, Jeff Frank and I wished to see if jobs with PRP attracted workers of higher ability and induced workers to provide greater effort. We constructed an integrated model of effort and sorting that clarified the distinction between observable and unobservable ability and the relationship between earnings and productivity. We tested the predictions of this against new data from the British Household Panel Survey (BHPS), and found that PRP raised wages by nine per cent for men and six per cent for women. Our theoretical calculations showed that these estimated earnings differentials represented average productivity differentials net of monitoring costs at the marginal firm using PRP, but not of the disutility of additional effort expended by workers.

I turn now to another aspect of neoliberalism, the growth of temporary jobs, which is the focus of Chapter 3. Of policy interest is whether these could be viewed as stepping stones to more secure employment. (The data that my co-authors Marco Francesconi, Jeff Frank and I used for this analysis are British, but the same techniques can be applied to other countries that have comparable datasets to the BHPS.) This chapter was part of a symposium on temporary work that was published in 2002 in a special issue of the *Economic Journal* covering four countries.[3]

Temporary contracts are often regarded as an important component of labour market flexibility, for temporary workers can be laid off without incurring statutory redundancy payments or restrictions imposed by employment rights legislation. This may have explained the dramatic growth in temporary or fixed-term-contract jobs in France, Italy and Spain – countries characterised by high levels of employment protection. The proportion of temporary workers in these countries doubled between 1985 and 1997. In contrast, in the United States and the United Kingdom – which have relatively little employment protection regulation – the proportion of the workforce on fixed-term contracts has been relatively low and fairly stable.

While temporary contracts can avoid some labour market inflexibilities, there are potential costs. Some commentators have expressed concern about the quality of the stock of jobs and the lack of opportunities for career advancement associated with temporary or flexible work. In Britain, about seven per cent of male employees and 10 per cent of female employees were in temporary jobs in the 1990s, a proportion that was relatively stable over the decade. Using data from the BHPS, my co-authors and I confirmed the popular perception that temporary jobs are generally not desirable when compared to permanent employment. Temporary workers have lower levels of job satisfaction, receive less training and are less well-paid. There was some evidence that fixed-term contracts are a stepping stone to permanent work. Women who started in fixed-term employment and moved to permanent jobs fully caught up to those who started in permanent jobs.

3 See also the introduction by Booth, Dolado and Frank (2002) to this symposium.

It is ironic that just as neoliberalism with its free-market ethos gained traction across the developed world, economists were starting to highlight the imperfectly competitive nature of labour markets, and to develop important new models explaining wage determination and unemployment. These included search theory, efficiency wages, bargaining models and oligopsonistic competition.

Chapter 4 reproduces a paper that I wrote for the 25th anniversary of *Labour Economics*. The paper illustrated in a simple way two polar imperfectly competitive models of the labour market and their implications for modern economies. The chapter begins by describing the perfectly competitive benchmark model of the labour market. It then moves on to summarise wage determination under trade unions that hold market power in wage determination, and are thus able to extract some of the surplus arising from the employment relation between the firm and its employees, in the form of higher wages. One of the most interesting developments in wage determination theories of the past few decades has been the realisation that *employers* frequently have some market power in wage setting.[4] This is not only a plausible and reasonably tractable characterisation of the labour market, but it can also help explain certain labour market phenomena. An example of oligopsonistic competition is a situation where workers face monetary and/or psychic costs in moving across firms or locations. Since such job transitions involve costs, workers will move only if the observed wage gap between the destination firm and the origin firm is sufficiently large to cover the costs of moving. Thus, the presence of mobility costs may explain why workers choose to stay in low-wage local markets instead of migrating to markets that offer higher wages.

As an example of the policy relevance of oligopsony, consider the economics of work-related training. According to orthodox human capital theory, in a perfectly competitive labour market, workers should always finance work-related general training. If firms were to pay for it, they would be vulnerable to the hold-up problem: the worker could simply quit after being trained, taking with them the embodied general training, and the firm would get no return on the investment. However, in a labour market characterised by oligopsonistic wage setting, it can be shown that the

4 Monopsony (or oligopsony power) exists when one or more buyers of labour face little competition from other buyers for that labour, so they are able to set lower wages for the workers they are hiring than would be the case in a competitive market.

associated wage compression will increase the incentive for firms to invest in general training, provided that post-training productivity net of training costs is increasing in training at a faster rate than wages.

Empirical evidence for Britain has shown that employers do indeed finance work-related general training, as I show with Mark Bryan in Chapter 5. This chapter was inspired by Acemoglu and Pischke (1999), who demonstrated that, in oligopsonistic labour markets, some of the predictions of the human capital model are overturned. In particular, the wage returns to general training may be less than the productivity returns, and firms may therefore find it profitable to pay for training even though it is general. In our research, Mark Bryan and I summarised the main predictions of the various human capital theories for wages and cost sharing and confronted these with important new data from the BHPS for the period 1998–2000. We found that employer-financed training was associated with significantly higher wages at current and future firms, with a larger impact in future firms. This is consistent with human capital theory with credit constraints and with the new training literature assuming imperfectly competitive labour markets. It also suggests that an over-reliance on the basic human capital model that assumes a competitive labour market may be misleading for policy purposes.

If the labour market were perfectly competitive, the introduction of a minimum wage is predicted to reduce general training investment by covered workers who can no longer finance such training through lower wages. However, if the low-paid labour market is *imperfectly* competitive, firms will be more likely to pay for general training, as noted above. Intuitively, the monopsonistic character of the labour market compresses workers' returns to human capital, allowing the firm to keep some of the surplus.

In Chapter 6, my co-authors, Wiji Arulampalam and Mark Bryan, and I investigated the impact of a new national minimum wage on work-related training. A UK National Minimum Wage (NMW) was introduced on 1 April 1999. It followed a period of six years, from the abolition of the Wages Councils, during which there was no statutory wage-floor in any sector but agriculture. The UK Government viewed the NMW as an 'important cornerstone of Government strategy aimed at providing employees with decent minimum standards and fairness in the workplace'.[5] At the same

5 Department of Trade and Industry (n.d.) 'The national minimum wage', webarchive.nationalarchives.gov.uk/ukgwa/20060213213640/http:/www.dti.gov.uk/er/nmw/index.htm.

time, it emphasised the development of workforce skills – 'particularly the basic skills of some adults'.[6] Our analysis empirically investigated whether the two goals were compatible.

Using important new data from the BHPS, we estimated the impact of the new NMW on the work-related training of low-wage workers. We used two 'treatment groups' – those workers who explicitly stated they were affected by the new minimum and those workers whose derived 1998 wages were below the minimum. Using difference-in-differences techniques for the period 1998–2000, we found no evidence that the introduction of the minimum wage reduced the training of affected workers and some evidence that it increased it.

Section II: Men and women in the labour market

From the early 1970s, women in developed countries around the world were entering the labour force in increasing numbers. As the second wave of feminism gathered pace in the 1970s, it was no longer the case that labour market researchers could continue the past practice of leaving women out of their analyses, without facing pushback from increasingly vocal 'minorities'. Moreover, the improvement in data availability and statistical techniques to control for selection issues greatly facilitated researchers' studies of female participation, discrimination and wage determination. At the same time, theorists were increasingly expanding our understanding of the labour market by highlighting certain features of labour markets that give women reduced bargaining power in their wage determination.

In Chapter 7, Wiji Arulampalam, Mark Bryan and I investigated gender pay gaps by sector across wage distribution in 11 countries of the European Union. We used harmonised microdata for the years 1995–2001 from the European Community Household Panel. In estimations that controlled for the effects of individual characteristics at different points of the distribution, we calculated the part of the gap attributable to differing returns between men and women. The magnitude of the gender pay gap, thus measured, varied substantially across countries and across the public and private sector

6 Department of Education and Skills (n.d.) 'DfES research', www.dfes.gov.uk/research (site discontinued).

wage distributions. The gap typically widened towards the top of the wage distribution (the 'glass ceiling' effect), and in a few cases it also widened at the bottom (the 'sticky floor' effect).

In addition to this detailed exploration of gender pay gaps across the wage distribution, we extensively discussed policies – including gender-specific policies (for example, equal opportunity and anti-discrimination legislation, parental leave, provisions, and childcare availability) – that might affect mean wage gaps as well as the gaps across the distribution. These gaps are also likely to be influenced by wage-setting institutions that do not directly impinge on gender (for example, those governing collective bargaining and minimum wages). With only 11 observations, we could not make conclusive tests, but we did obtain some interesting and policy-relevant correlations. We suggested that differences in childcare provisions and wage-setting institutions across EU countries may partly account for the variation in patterns by country and sector.

We now turn to an analysis of the happiness of men and women in partnered households, focusing in particular on hours of work, both in the domestic and labour market spheres. In Chapter 8, Jan van Ours and I explored the gender divide in home production in partnered households and how it affected various measures of partners' satisfaction. Considering interdependence within the family, we investigated the relationship between part-time (PT) and other forms of work and various self-reported measures of happiness. Our data source was a sample of partnered men and women from the Household, Income and Labor Dynamics in Australia Survey, which closely followed the format of the BHPS. Our analysis indicated that PT women were more satisfied with working hours than full-time (FT) women. Partnered women's life satisfaction was increased if their partners worked FT. Male partners' life satisfaction was unaffected by their partners' market hours, but increased if they themselves were working FT.

Does this suggest that Australian families are characterised by complete specialisation, with one partner engaged predominantly in domestic work and the other in market-sector work? The answer is no. According to the specialisation hypothesis, there will be a negative monotonic relationship between the share of housework done by one partner and that same partner's share of market work. This prediction was not supported by the data; in households where the female does the majority of market work, the male's share of housework remains proportionately low. Thus, the degree of specialisation is partial and non-symmetric. Men doing a small share of market work were also doing a small share of housework. This finding is consistent with the gender identity hypothesis, and it may suggest a reason why Australian women are happier with PT work.

Over the past few decades, economists have become increasingly interested in designing and running experiments – either laboratory-based or in the field – to shed new light on patterns of individual behaviour that might not be picked up using survey data. As an illustration, consider the thorny question of how to measure ethnic discrimination. My co-authors Andrew Leigh, Elena Varganova and I addressed this in a large-scale field experiment designed to measure labour market discrimination in Australia, the results of which are included in Chapter 9.

Among economists, the most common approach to measuring ethnic discrimination has been to compare labour market outcomes across ethnic groups. But this method may not provide an accurate answer. If an individual's ethnicity is correlated with some unobserved productive trait, then differences in economic outcomes will reflect more than just discrimination. Similarly, social researchers have often used surveys to measure the degree of racism in a society. But if respondents know the socially correct response, then this approach will also provide a biased estimate of true attitudes towards ethnic groups. When studying labour market outcomes, the problem arises from the unobservable characteristics of ethnic minorities. When analysing social attitudes, the problem stems from unobservable biases in the reporting of ethnic attitudes.

In both cases, field experiments can help solve the unobservables problem by creating a context in which all other factors except ethnicity are held constant. Andrew Leigh, Elena Varganova and I conducted a large-scale field experiment to measure labour market discrimination in Australia, one-quarter of whose population was born overseas. To denote ethnicity, we used distinctively Anglo-Saxon, Indigenous, Italian, Chinese and Middle Eastern names. We compared multiple ethnic groups, rather than a single minority, as in most other studies at the time. In all cases, we applied for entry-level jobs and submitted a CV indicating that the candidate attended high school in Australia. We found significant differences in callback rates; ethnic minority candidates would need to apply for more jobs in order to receive the same number of interviews. We found that these differences varied systematically across ethnic groups.

Section III: Gendered behavioural responses: Evidence from experiments

Among labour and behavioural economists recently, there has been a growing interest in experiments addressing the extent to which gender gaps in labour market outcomes might be due to inherent differences in the economically significant preferences of men and women. My research agenda over the past few years has been directed to this issue. In particular, we explored whether it is nature or nurture that affects the preferences of women and men in an economically meaningful way. A selection of those papers is presented in the final five chapters of this volume. The experiments reported in these chapters were conducted in the UK, China, Taiwan, Japan and Korea. Our particular interest was not only in gender differences but also in exploring whether behaviour is malleable. In other words, can male and female behaviour be modified in response to environments that uphold women's values?

It is well known that women are underrepresented in high-paying jobs and in high-level occupations. Recent work in experimental economics has examined to what degree this under-representation may be due to innate differences between men and women. For example, gender differences in risk aversion, feedback preferences or fondness for competition may help to explain some of the observed gender disparities. If the majority of remuneration in high-paying jobs is tied to bonuses based on a company's performance, then, where men are less risk-averse than women, women may choose not to take high-paying jobs because of the uncertainty. Differences in risk attitudes may even affect individual choices about seeking performance feedback or entering a competitive environment.

Understanding the extent to which competitive preferences and risk attitudes are innate or shaped by the environment is important for policy. For instance, if attitudes to competition or risk are innate, under-representation of women in certain areas may be solved only by changing the way in which remuneration is rewarded. However, if these attitudes are primarily shaped by the environment, changing the educational or training context could help to address under-representation. Thus, the policy prescription for dealing with the under-representation of women in high-paying jobs will depend upon whether the reason for the absence is innate to an individual's gender.

Patrick Nolen and I embarked at the end of the first decade of this century on a series of experiments exploring these topics. Our interest was in whether economically relevant preferences such as risk-taking and willingness to compete might be affected by cultural and environmental influences. Chapter 10 in this volume reports the results from our controlled experiment using school children as subjects whose average age was just under 15 years, and designed to investigate if individuals' risk preferences are affected by (i) the gender composition of the group to which they are randomly assigned for the day of the experiment, and (ii) the gender mix of the school they attend. Our subjects, from eight publicly funded single-sex and co-educational schools, were asked to choose between a real-stakes lottery and a sure bet. We found that girls in an all-girls group or attending a single-sex school were more likely than their co-ed counterparts to choose a real-stakes gamble. This suggests that observed gender differences in behaviour under uncertainty found in previous studies might reflect social learning rather than inherent gender traits.

Subsequently, Patrick Nolen, Lina Cardona Sosa and I expanded our research to the university sector. The motivation, details and results of this experiment are reported in Chapter 11. Our goal was to examine the effect of single-sex classes on the educational attainment of students within a co-educational university. More women than men attend university, yet women are under-represented in technical fields like mathematics, the physical sciences and engineering (National Academy of Sciences 2007). They are also underrepresented in economics, the discipline on which we focused in this chapter.

Our field experiment was designed to examine the effects of single-sex classes on the performance of first-year university students in a highly ranked and publicly funded economics department. The novel features of our design were twofold. First, we randomly assigned students to a single-sex or a co-ed class environment, and hence selection was not an issue. Second, we implemented this random assignment to single-sex classes in the economics faculty of a co-educational university.

We examined whether single-sex classes within a co-educational environment have an effect on female test scores, pass rates and continuing to study at university, as well as longer-run outcomes such as degree class. We found that females assigned to all-female classes scored a quarter of a standard deviation higher in their Introductory Economics class and were 7.3 per cent more likely to pass the course. Furthermore, the benefits to females of single-sex classes appeared to carry over past the first year and led to a 57 per cent decrease in the likelihood that a female did not graduate with a degree in economics and a 61 per cent increase in the likelihood that she graduated with a 'good degree.' These results all occurred with no additional expenditure on the part of the university.

Chapter 12 reports the results of another experiment, this time one that Elliott Fan, Xin Meng and Dandan Zhang and I designed to address the following question: can the gender gap in competitive inclination be altered in a relatively short period by changing social norms induced by institutional changes? In this experiment, we were interested in two regions: Beijing in Mainland China and Taipei in Taiwan. People from both regions are descended from the same Confucian traditions, but their experiences from 1949 onwards dramatically diverged, as the chapter highlights.

Our Beijing-based laboratory experiment investigated gender differences in competitive choices across different birth cohorts experiencing, during their crucial developmental age, different institutions and social norms. To control for general time trends, we used Taipei counterpart subjects with identical original Confucian traditions. Our findings confirmed that exposure to different institutions or norms during crucial developmental ages significantly changed individuals' behaviour. In particular, Beijing females growing up during the communist regime were more competitively inclined than their male counterparts, their female counterparts growing up during the market regime, and Taipei females. For Taipei, there were no statistically significant cohort or gender differences in willingness to compete. Thus, we showed that some aspects of 'culture' can be formed or changed in a relatively short period. This suggests that policy intervention may contribute to the further narrowing of gender gaps in labour market outcomes.

In Chapter 13, Eiji Yamamura and I analysed unique performance data from a real-world activity – speedboat racing in Japan. This sport is by its very nature competitive, and the potential payoffs from winning are high. Women have been competing in this activity since the early 1950s under exactly the same conditions as men.

In speedboat racing in Japan, men and women are randomly assigned to mixed-sex or single-sex groups for each race. We used a sample of over 140,000 individual-level records obtained from the Japanese Speedboat Racing Association to examine how male-dominated circumstances affect women's racing performance. Our fixed-effects estimates revealed that women's race time is slower in mixed-sex races than in all-women races, whereas men's race time is faster in mixed-sex races than in men-only races. The same result is found for the place in the race. Moreover, in mixed-sex races, men are more aggressive than women, as demonstrated by lane changing, in spite of the risk of being penalised for rule infringement.

The first finding above is of particular interest. It shows that female competitive performance, even for women who have chosen a competitive career and are very good at it, is enhanced by being in a single-sex environment rather than in a mixed-sex environment in which they are a minority.

The gender proportion in the mixed-sex speedboat races is skewed towards men. Women racers assigned by lot to a mixed-sex race will typically face five male competitors or, rather infrequently, four. We suggest that this gender imbalance may trigger awareness of gender identity for both men and women, and that this might go some way to explaining observed differences in behaviour across mixed-sex and single-sex groups. For example, a man's gender identity may lead him to consider being defeated by women to be more dishonourable than by men, and he will try to avoid it.

Our findings may well have implications for other activities in which men and women compete with one another and where the gender balance is skewed in favour of men. One example is in the STEM disciplines, where being in a minority may well affect the performance of women in that situation.

Finally, we point out that sportspeople are likely to be particularly selected on willingness to compete, and to that extent, our effects of mixed-sex treatments may be relatively muted compared to other settings where selection is not as competitive. Alternatively, behaviour in repeated (daily) interactions may differ from that in a short race. We hope that future research will explore these issues further.

In Chapter 14, Jungmin Lee and I adopted a different but complementary approach to the experiments reported above by analysing unique performance data from a real-world activity that is competitive by its very nature – the South Korean television quiz show for young people, *Janghak!* (Scholar). We compared the performance of high-ability adolescent girls and boys who participated in this long-running television quiz show. Our aim was to gauge whether there are gender differences in the behaviour of girls and boys of high-school age in this extremely competitive environment.

We also wished to establish how contestants' behaviour alters as the game rules vary, imposing varying levels of psychological stress affecting girls and boys differently. We also examined how girls and boys behave differently as they advance to a higher round and get closer to winning the game when competitive pressure is escalated.

We found that there is a significant gender gap in performance – in favour of boys – when we pooled all Round 1 episodes of the quiz show. To investigate underlying mechanisms that might explain this, we explored how performance varies under different exogenously varied rules of the game. We found that there were no gender gaps in performance when stress was kept to a minimum – that is, in games without fastest-finger buzzer, knockouts or penalties. However, in games with some of these features, there were significant gender gaps. In addition, we examined performance in Round 2 of the shows, where we found larger gender gaps. Finally, we used question-by-question panel data to track performance in games where players stay in for 25 questions. Here, we found that girls are less likely to respond faster, especially when their winning probability is higher. Further, the gender gap is more salient at the end of the game. The results are consistent with gendered behavioural responses to psychological pressure.

As is obvious from the ideas presented in Section III of this volume, my research agenda with colleagues over the past few years has aimed to explore whether or not it is nature or nurture that affects the preferences of women and men in an economically meaningful way. The results show that nurture can have a powerful effect. In other words, culture matters, and this is something that policy can change, if those in charge are willing. Such change can be beneficial, but it can also be harmful, as the recent erosion of women's rights and the inflation of men's rights in some countries has shown.

Finally, I wish to draw some overall conclusions that I trust readers will consider as they read these chapters. The volume shows that culture and nurture associated with the raising of boys and girls can have profound implications for both educational and labour market performance and relative outcomes by gender. I hope that readers will be aware of the meaning and consequences of gender-based occupational bunching (women are much more likely to be employed, for example, in caring and low wage-variance occupations such as nursing, teaching, and child and aged care). And that they will be aware of the tendency for men to be in the highest risk occupations, such as senior company executives. And finally, that readers will also consider the implications for our understanding of the use of average remuneration, rather than a combination of mean and variance, in understanding the gender pay gap.

It should be remembered that there is no right or wrong place for young women and men to be. What matters is that they are given the opportunity to go where their talents lead them without being thwarted by cultural pressures.

References

Acemoglu, D., and Pischke, J.S. (1999). 'The structure of wages and investment in general training', *Journal of Political Economy,* 107(3):539–572.

Booth, A.L. (1995). *The Economics of the Trade Union*, Cambridge University Press. Reprinted 2002.

Booth, A.L., Dolado, J., and Frank, J. (2002). 'Introduction to the symposium on temporary work', *The Economic Journal*, 112(480):181–187.

Mill, J.S. (1848). *Principles of Political Economy*, John W Parker.

National Academy of Sciences. (2007). *Beyond Bias and Barriers: Fulfilling the Potential of Women in Academic Science and Engineering*, National Academies Press. doi.org/10.17226/11741.

Olson, M., Jr. (1965). *The Logic of Collective Action: Public Goods and the Theory of Groups,* Harvard University Press.

Section I: Evolving industrial relations and neoliberalism

1

The free rider problem and a social custom model of trade union membership

Alison L Booth

Introduction

The literature on public good provision by groups has traditionally emphasised the free rider problem. If it is assumed that a group forms to provide, or to lobby for the provision of, a good that is collective to potential members, then the major conceptual problem to the formation of such a group is that individuals can enjoy the benefits of group action without incurring the costs. By doing this, they free ride. In small groups, the free rider problem is not generally considered insurmountable. However, the larger the number of potential beneficiaries, the more difficult it is to overcome the free rider problem, due to exclusion and surveillance difficulties, and optimal collective good provision, or any collective good provision, in the extreme, is less likely.

The free rider hypothesis has a long history in economic thought. As early as 1848, the free rider potential of any group of workers was perceived by Mill (1891). However, it appears that it was not until 1965 that an attempt was made to explain why *large* groups providing collective goods manage to exist despite the free rider problem. Olson (1971) proposed the following explanation. If a large group exists, it must have formed either because membership is compulsory or because the group provides private goods and services accessible only to its members, with ancillary provision of the collective good as a 'by-product.'

The literature that developed from Olson's work has focused primarily on the suboptimal provision of the collective good, the difficulties of getting members to contribute in proportion to the benefits received, and preference revelation incentives. (See, for example, Groves and Ledyard (1977).)

However, there are problems with both of the solutions proposed by Olson to overcome the free rider problem facing large groups. First, if coercion is looked at as a solution to the free rider problem, the question arises as to how the coercion itself is financed (Guttman 1978). This is unlikely to be costless. The second problem concerns the 'by-product' solution. Private good provision, with collective good provision as an ancillary function of the group once its members have been 'captured,' is not a sufficient condition, as Olson thought. Unless the group has a monopoly in the provision of a private good, new firms can enter to provide the private good without the collective good, at a cheaper rate because the provision of the collective good is not costless by assumption.

The Olson by-product model, modified so that the group must possess a monopoly in the provision of a desired private good in the absence of compulsion, appears plausible for professional associations providing incentive private goods, such as technical journals, indemnity schemes, and certificates of skill. But the model, as it stands, does not immediately appear applicable to an important example of large groups in existence in the economy: trade unions. Olson suggested that 'In most cases it is compulsory membership and coercive picket lines that are the source of the union's membership' (Olson 1965, p. 5). His view that large modern unions exist only because membership is compulsory is not supported by statistical evidence in the United Kingdom, for example, where there are areas with a high proportion of employees in trade unions, but few closed shops.[1]

The aims of this chapter therefore are as follows: first, to show that a trade union can exist without compulsory membership and union shop legislation; second, to prove that under certain conditions the economic incentive to 'free ride' can be less than the economic incentive to join a large union,

1 Gennard, Dunn, and Wright (1980) estimated that closed shop arrangements affected only a quarter of UK employees, and that some 19 per cent of workers in areas with high union membership were not covered by closed shop provisions.

in the absence of compulsion; and third, to incorporate sociological factors into the traditional utility-maximising model, in what will be called below a 'social custom' theory of large union membership.

Social custom model of group formation

It is an argument of this chapter that social customs and sanctions of peer pressure are not confined to small groups, but may be found in whole communities. In any society, there may exist codes of behaviour or social customs that are not enforced by a police system, but by peer pressure or loss of reputation for disobedience. Following Akerlof (1980, p. 749), I shall define a custom as 'an act whose utility to the agent performing it in some way depends on the beliefs or actions of other members of the community.' Akerlof takes up an argument that is commonly put forward by sociologists and psychologists. This is that, within a community, there is a set of rules and customs that are obeyed by individuals because of the loss of reputation within the community (a sanction) if the custom is disobeyed. Reputation is assumed to be desired by individuals: each person's utility function includes his or her reputation within the community. Consider now any group. Individuals may follow a social custom of membership in the group. Adherence to the custom is reinforced by the sanction of loss of reputation if the individual does not conform. As utility is assumed to be a function of reputation, I argue that there is an economic incentive to join the group as long as the social custom exists.

It is hoped that the model used below clearly illustrates the potentially important effects of social custom and reputation on group behaviour. The model aims to show that equilibria derived from the maximising behaviour on the part of reputation-seeking individuals may diverge from those derived from the maximising behaviour of isolated individuals. Of course, the model assumes the existence of a social custom of joining a group: it is not supposed that this assumption holds everywhere in the economy. It is also not supposed that the model chosen precisely describes an individual's behaviour in deciding to join a large group. Rather, the analysis is directed towards extending the Olson model by providing an explanation of why individuals may join a large group in spite of the collective nature of the good the group forms to provide.

The model

Consider a trade union that exists to secure increased wages and fringe benefits, and assume that these are collective across the entire industry as the union bargaining process determines the minimum legal wage for all the industry. Suppose that the union provides a single excludable good for its members: reputation from belonging to the union and not being a 'scab.' This good is collective to the union; additional consumption by one unionised person does not imply reduced consumption by another. The good is not collective to the industry because access to it is available only through union membership. The union possesses a monopoly in its provision.

Assumptions

ASSUMPTION 1. Consider a closed sector or industry in which there is only one union, membership of which is not legally compulsory. There are only two goods available to individuals in the closed industry: reputation r and wages w. Suppose that reputation is achieved solely through membership of some group that forms within the sector, such that

(1) $r = r(M)\ r_M > 0;\ r_{MM} < 0;\ r(0) = 0$

The letter M denotes the proportion of the workforce belonging to the group, so that

(2) $0 \leq M \leq 1$

Wages w are assumed to be exogenous. In a two-good model, it is assumed that r and w are net substitutes. It may be supposed more generally that initially at a very low w, w_s (where the subscript denotes subsistence), only wages will enter the utility function. As w increases above w_s, the individual is able to derive utility from r as well as w, as this chapter assumes. It is a matter for observation as to how individuals rank r with w. The preference ordering is likely to vary with place, period and class. In a feudal society, for example, where r is relatively inflexible, there may be a high ranking for r: peasants may be 'poor but loyal.' In some societies, for some groups of individuals, r may be preferred to w at all levels of w except for w_s, as may be conceivable with revolutionaries, writers or academics.

In the model that follows, it is assumed that wages are above subsistence level, wages and reputation are normal goods, and that the social custom of trade union membership arises only with some $M > 0$. The sanction of loss of reputation if the custom should not be followed can therefore emerge only with the existence of a social custom; that is, when $M > 0$. The question of how a social custom may arise or how a trade union might form from zero membership is not addressed here, although an attempt has been made to make endogenous the initial emergence of a trade union in Booth (1982).

ASSUMPTION 2. There are positive costs to membership in the trade union, and these are subscription and organisation costs s. These costs consist of some fixed costs, plus a cost that decreases with the number of members. Thus, s can be written as:

(3) $s = \gamma + \dfrac{\delta}{M + \varepsilon}$ per member

or more generally, $s = s(M)$

$S_M < 0; S_{MM} > 0.$

Thus, s at $s(0)$ is $\gamma + \dfrac{\delta}{\varepsilon}$

ASSUMPTION 3. All individuals are identical and have identical preferences for the two goods.

ASSUMPTION 4. Utility is assumed to be a strictly increasing continuous, twice differentiable, concave function. When an individual joins the union, the utility function is:

(4) $U^j = U(r, w - s)$,

where the superscript j denotes joining, and $U_1 > 0$, and $U_2 > 0$, where the subscripts are the usual notation for the partial derivatives of the function with respect to its first and second arguments. When an individual does not join the group, the utility function is

(5) $U^{nj} = U(0, w)$,

where the superscript nj denotes not joining. However, the individual receives the union wage, so is 'free riding' in that respect. Here:

(6) $U_1 = 0$, and $U_2 > 0$.

An individual's choice set is to join, or not to join, the trade union. There is no compulsion and so no restriction on an individual's choice set. Individuals are rational, self-interested utility maximisers. There is an economic incentive to join the union if $U^j > U^{nj}$, and an economic incentive for the group *not* to form if $U^j. > U^{nj}$. The individual is indifferent between membership and non-membership, where $U^j = U^{nj}$.

A. Equilibrium

Equilibrium is where individuals cannot, by behaving differently, make themselves better off. Because union membership is not compulsory, the proportion of the sector unionised, M may in theory take any value in the interval (0,1] as a result of individual choice.

Define the function F as:

(7) $F = U^j - U^{nj}$

PROPOSITION 1. $F < 0$ at $M = 0$.

Proof. At $M = 0$,

$$U^j = U[r(0), w - \left(\gamma + \frac{\delta}{\varepsilon}\right)]$$

from equations (3) and (4), and

$U^{nj} = U\,(0,w)$.

As both the values of the utility functions are strictly increasing, and both are zero with respect to reputation, but $U^{nj} > U$ with respect to wages, then it must be the case that $F < 0$ at $M = 0$. For the existence of a unique, though not necessarily stable, interior equilibrium, it is necessary to prove that $F > 0$ only at the maximum, that is, where $M = 1$. Then continuity of the two functions implies that $F = 0$ for some M in the open interval M (0, 1). However, F may take three possible values at M=1:

Case 1: $F > 0$

Case 2: $F = 0$

Case 3: $F < 0$.

PROPOSITION 2. Given r=r(M), fixed wages, and identical individuals, a union will form if and only if preferences and membership costs s are such that $F > 0$ at the upper boundary. The free rider problem is unlikely to emerge.

Proof. The sector in this model is closed in the sense that no exchange occurs between it and the rest of the economy. Wages, and thus implicitly the behaviour of firms, are exogenous, as might be the case if workers are paid the value of their marginal product, and productivity is held constant. The values of the utility function are therefore:[2]

(8) $U^j = U\,[r(M), w - s(M)]$

and

(9) $U^{nj} = U\,(0, w)$.

Three possible cases for these values of the utility function, and for F at $M = 1$, are shown in Figure 1.1.

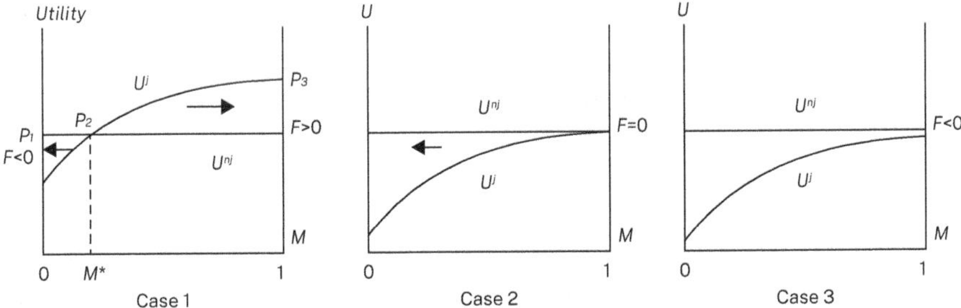

Figure 1.1: Social custom model of trade union membership

Case 1. $F > 0$ at $M = 1$. Assume that if subscription costs and preferences are of a certain configuration, joining the union is preferred to not joining. If one individual perceives that $U^j > U^{nj}$, then by Assumption 3, where all individuals have identical preferences, everyone will join the union and $M = 1$. If $U^j > U^{nj}$,, then $F > 0$ at $M = 1$. It has already been proven that $F < 0$ at $M = 0$. Continuity of the two functions then implies that $F = 0$ for some $M(0,1)$, by the intermediate value theorem. Figure 1.1, Case 1, shows that there are two stable boundary equilibria at $M = 0$ and $M = 1$, and one unstable interior equilibrium at M^*, where $U^j = U^{nj}$,. At this point, the individual, and by Assumption 3, the whole sector, is indifferent between joining and not joining. Indifference can occur only in the range $0 < M \leq 1$, and in Case 1, it occurs somewhere less than $M = 1$ because it has been assumed that $F > 0$ at $M = 1$. The interior equilibrium point P_2 is unstable. Even if M should by accident occur at M^*, after any disequilibrium, the

2 It is straightforward to show that the first and second order conditions of U^j are positive and negative respectively.

adjustment process will not return it to its initial position. Suppose that the adjustment process is $M = G(U^j > U^{nj},)$. In the interval M [0, M^*), $U^{nj} > U^j$ and individuals will leave the group. In the interval M [M^*, 1), $U^j > U^{nj}$ and individuals will all join the group. Clearly, any changes in the reputation and cost functions will alter the steepness of the slope of U^j, and any tax on union membership will shift U^j down, having different implications for the determination of P_2. However, this only becomes important in models with stable interior equilibria, such as might occur if wages were endogenous. Group *membership* in this model is unstable except at $M = 1$. Note that by definition, free riders are only found in the open interval M (0,1) although potential free riders may be found at $M = 1$. If $M = 1$, there are no actual free riders, and if $M = 0$, there is no group. The instability of P_2 is proof of the absence of the free rider in this model, except in the situation where, by chance, $M = M^*$ and the economy is in a long-run equilibrium; that is, the underlying functions do not vary.

Of course, where there is a stable interior equilibrium, union membership lies in the open interval M (0,1). The model can easily be extended to allow for this if wages are assumed to be a function of trade union size. However, the point of this analysis was not to demonstrate the existence of union membership of less than 1, but to show that unions can exist without compulsion or incentive for private goods of the usual nature. Thus, the simplest model of wage determination was chosen.

Case 2. $F = 0$ at $M = 1$. Assume that costs s and preferences are such that individuals are indifferent between joining and not joining the union at $M = 1$. There are two boundary equilibria, P_1 and P_3, but as the latter is unstable, the union will not form (See Figure 1.1).

Case 3. $F < 0$ at $M = 1$. Assuming that nowhere in the interval M (0,1] is $F > 0$, then not joining will always be preferred to joining, and the union will never form.

Conclusion

The social custom model of trade union membership presented here may explain the existence of trade union membership without compulsion, and with reputation being the only incentive good. However, observation suggests that in addition to unions fitting into this type of model, there are others characterised by compulsion in the form of pre-entry or post-entry closed shop requirements, and others characterised by apprenticeship schemes where the union card is a signal to the employer that the prospective employee possesses some minimum level of skill. Hence, this chapter explains only a facet of trade union membership.

Acknowledgements

This chapter was first published as Booth, A.L. (1985). 'The free rider problem and a social custom model of trade union membership', *The Quarterly Journal of Economics*, 100(1):253–261. doi.org/10.2307/1885744. Reprinted in Booth, A.L., ed. (2002). *The Economics of Labor Unions*, vol I, Edward Elgar Publishing.

I would like to express my thanks to Tony Atkinson for his many helpful suggestions on earlier drafts, and to David de Meza and Ray Richardson for their useful comments. Any mistakes are mine.

References

Akerlof, G.A. (1980). 'A theory of social custom, of which unemployment may be one consequence', *The Quarterly Journal of Economics*, 94(4):749–775. doi.org/10.2307/1885667.

Booth, A.L. (1982). 'Trade union membership and the free rider problems'. Unpublished manuscript, Mimeo.

Gennard, J., Dunn, S., and Wright, M. (1980). 'The extent of closed shop arrangements in British industry', *Employment Gazette*, LXXX:16–22.

Groves, T., and Ledyard, J. (1977). 'Optimal allocation of public goods: A solution to the "free rider" problem', *Econometrica*, 45(4):783–809. doi.org/10.2307/1912672.

Guttman, J. (1978). 'Interest groups and the demand for agricultural research', *Journal of Political Economy*, 86(3):467–484.

Mill, J.S. (1891). *Principles of Political Economy*, Longmans, Green & Company.

Olson, M., Jr. (1971). *The Logic of Collective Action: Public Goods and the Theory of Groups*, Harvard University Press.

2

The productivity effects of performance-related pay

Alison L Booth and Jeff Frank

Introduction

Performance-related pay (PRP) is one of a number of labour market institutions that have recently been encouraged by governments. The UK Government has been in the lead in providing incentives for profit-related pay, one form of PRP. Since 1991, up to 20 per cent of total pay can be fully exempt from income tax if received in an approved profit-related pay scheme. As a result, the number of employees covered by approved schemes has risen from 232,000 in March 1990 to 2,438,000 in March 1995. The large tax expenditure following from this growth led the Chancellor of the Exchequer to announce the phasing out of the scheme in his 1997 budget.

The rationale for government encouragement of different forms of PRP is the belief that these mechanisms increase labour market flexibility and generate higher productivity or employment.[1] An article in the Organization for Economic Cooperation and Development (OECD) Employment Outlook (1995), based upon Estrin et al. (1995), provides an extensive survey of profit sharing and concludes that there is strong evidence of productivity

1 See Beatson (1995) for a discussion of labour market institutions and flexibility.

gains in profit-sharing firms.[2] Profit sharing is likely to be associated with a free rider problem, and other forms of PRP, such as individual PRP, may have even larger productivity effects.

With the exception of Ewing (1996) and Lazear (1996), virtually all of the evidence in the literature about the productivity gains associated with PRP is based upon establishment or firm data.[3] However, there are considerable endogeneity problems in using establishment or firm data. Workforces with PRP may differ in significant ways from those without PRP. In this chapter, we examine the effects of PRP using individual panel data from the British Household Panel Survey (BHPS). The use of individual data allows adjustment for observable characteristics such as education. Panel data potentially also enable us to control for unobservable heterogeneity.

The BHPS individual panel data include earnings but not a direct measure of productivity. We develop the theoretical approach in Lazear (1986, 1996) to show the relationship between estimated earnings effects and underlying productivity differences. In Lazear's models, jobs with PRP attract workers of higher unobservable ability and also induce workers to provide greater effort. In our model, from the competitive equilibrium conditions, we find that the estimated earnings differential associated with PRP is the average total (ability and effort) productivity difference, taking account of the monitoring costs (at the marginal firm adopting PRP) needed to implement a PRP system, but not the disutility of the extra effort expended by workers on PRP.

Our model also shows that the major determinant of whether or not an individual is on PRP is unobservable individual ability. It is therefore not surprising that our empirical analysis finds few variables that are significant in predicting coverage by PRP, in spite of the rich set of controls in the BHPS. Interestingly, the BHPS individual data do lead to some different results about coverage than in the establishment data literature. Women are 8 per cent less likely to be on PRP. Union representation makes PRP more likely by about 22 per cent. Factors such as education have no predictive significance.

2 The benefits claimed for profit sharing can either be microeconomic in nature (for example, increased effort by workers) or macroeconomic (see Weitzman 1985) – greater wage flexibility over the business cycle. Studies in the literature focus upon microeconomic efficiency gains, owing to data availability.

3 Lazear (1996) studies the productivity effects of PRP with a unique single-firm data source. Ewing (1996) uses US individual data.

Our estimated earnings equations show that PRP raises wages by about 9 per cent for men and 6 per cent for women over the entire (union and non-union) sample. This is consistent with the US establishment data results in Brown (1992) and the recent US individual data results in Ewing (1996). It might be expected that, since unions can bargain for some of the surplus gain from instituting PRP, the return would be significantly higher in the union sector. In fact, our estimated earnings return to PRP in the union sector is only 5 per cent for men and 7 per cent for women. A potential explanation is that, since higher-quality workers would be attracted to the higher pay in the union sector under any system of remuneration, there is less of a sorting gain to PRP.

For a UK worker on average earnings, the tax relief on an approved profit-related pay scheme can represent approximately 5 per cent of earnings, which is not much less than our 6–10 per cent estimated earnings effect on any form of PRP. It is therefore not surprising that the take-up rate grew so dramatically, to the point where the Chancellor decided to phase out the scheme.

The chapter develops the model and its implications for measuring productivity effects. We consider the empirical determinants of the use of PRP and present earnings estimates, extending the theory and estimation to compare the union and non-union sectors.

The competitive model of payment mechanisms

Why do some jobs offer PRP? From Lazear (1986, 1996), two potential advantages to a firm adopting PRP are that it can induce greater effort and also that it attracts more able workers. We extend the Lazear approach in three major ways to facilitate our econometric analysis. First, we provide an integrated model that encompasses both sorting and effort effects. Second, we distinguish between observable and unobservable components of ability. The firm can reward observable ability factors such as education in its salary structure, and we therefore control for these in our estimation. Third, we examine the equilibrium conditions across heterogeneous firms as well as workers. This allows us to relate the estimated earnings effects of PRP to underlying productivity differences.

Assume that productivity in a given job depends upon an individual worker's ability I and upon the effort E applied. The worker's output is given by the strictly concave and increasing production function, identical across jobs, $Q(I, E)$.[4] This formulation allows for effort and ability to be either complementary or substitute factors in production. A firm is a combination of a large number of jobs, and the output associated with a particular worker cannot be observed costlessly. It can be ascertained exactly at a job-specific cost of k_j in job j. Effort E is not observable at any cost, but ability I divides into two components: freely observable ability I^o and unobservable (to the firm) ability I^n. Actual ability $I = I^o + I^n$. Unobservable ability is distributed over the support $I^u \in [0, I^{\wedge}]$, with a distribution function $\Phi(I^u)$ with the density $\Phi'(I^u) = \varphi(I^u) > 0$; the distribution of I^u is independent of I^o. Workers know their own observable and unobservable abilities. Each worker, indexed by i, gains utility from earned income Y_i and disutility from effort E_i: $U_i = Y_i - C(E_i)$, where $C(\cdot)$ is an increasing, strictly convex function. The minimum effort level is normalised as 0 with $C(0) = 0$.

We consider two possible forms of remuneration. Workers may be offered full PRP, where they are paid their output less a fixed profit for the firm, or a fixed salary.[5] In a competitive labour market, all PRP jobs must pay the same remuneration $Q(I, E) - p$, where p is the common 'markdown' retained by the firm. The fixed salary offered to workers will be conditioned on observable ability I^o and is written $S(I^o)$.

Given the availability of both salary and PRP jobs, which workers choose the salary jobs? A worker of type I^o and I^n will only accept a salary job over PRP if the salary exceeds the utility gained from PRP under an optimal choice of effort[6]:

(1) $S(I^o) \geq max_E[Q(I^o + I^u, E) - C(E) - p]$

By the envelope theorem, the right-hand side of (1) is increasing in I^u at the rate $Qi(\cdot) > 0$. The left-hand side is constant in I^n. The salary and PRP remuneration levels, for workers of given I^o but varying I^u, are shown in

4 For simplicity, we ignore the possibility that more able or harder working individuals are more suited for particular jobs.

5 We do not consider more general sharing rules of the form $\alpha . Qi + \beta$. These lie somewhere between a fixed salary and full PRP. Our data do not allow us to distinguish between different degrees of PRP.

6 In a salaried job, the worker chooses the minimum possible effort $E=0$ with $C(0)=0$.

Figure 2.1 as $S(I^o)$ and $Q(I, E) - p$. For observable ability level I^o, there is a marginal worker m, as illustrated in Figure 2.1, with unobservable ability $I^u = m$ such that remuneration is the same under either system:

(2) $S(I^o) = Q[I^o + m, E^*(I^o + m)] - C[E^*(I^o + m)] - p$

where $E^*(\cdot)$ is that worker's optimal effort choice. Workers of high unobservable ability $I^u \geq m$ choose the PRP remuneration. Write $m(I^o)$ to show the marginal unobservable ability for each observable ability level.

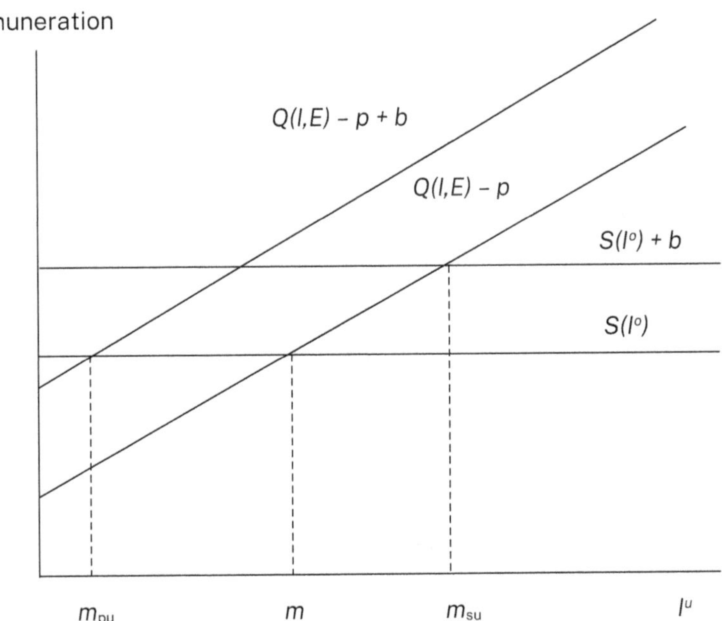

Figure 2.1: Determination of pay

Notes: The determination of the marginal unobservable ability level (for workers of given observable ability) such that a worker is indifferent to PRP or salary remuneration in the absence of a union (m); the marginal participant in a union workplace offering salaried remuneration (m_{su}); and the marginal participant in a union workplace with PRP (m_{pu}).

Firms differ only in their monitoring costs k_j. If a firm offers PRP, it gains profits $p - k_j$ from any worker taking up the offer and is indifferent to the worker's observable ability. Write k_M as the monitoring cost of the marginal firm M offering PRP; firms with higher k_j offer salaries. In any equilibrium where a salary $S(I^o)$ is offered to each observable type of worker, that salary must lead to the same expected profit as the marginal firm gains with PRP:

$$(3)\ \int_0^{m(I^o)} \frac{Q(I^o + I^u,0)\varphi(I^u)d(I^u)}{\{\Phi[m(I^o)]\}} - S(I^o) = p - k_M$$

where the expected profit on a salaried worker is average productivity less the salary.

Combining (2) and (3), the equilibrium is described by:

$$(4)\ \int_0^{m(I^o)} \frac{Q(I^o + I^*,0)\varphi(I^u)d(I^u)}{\{\Phi[m(I^o)]\}} = Q\{(I^o + m(I^o), E^*\{[I^o + m(I^o)]\} - C\{E^*[I^o + m(I^o)]\} - k_M$$

Salaried jobs are held by low unobservable ability workers at high monitoring cost firms. For each observable type, the average productivity of workers on salaried jobs equals the productivity of the marginal work on PRP, less the cost of monitoring at the marginal firm.

How do earnings differ between salaried and PRP jobs for workers of a given observable ability? From (3), the salary $S(I^o)$ equals:

$$(5)\ \int_0^{m(I^o)} \frac{Q(I^o + I^u,0)\varphi(I^u)d(I^u)}{\{\Phi[m(I^o)]\}} - p + k_M$$

In PRP jobs, average (over unobservable ability) earnings equal average productivity less p:

$$(6)\ \int_{m(I^o)}^{I^\wedge} \frac{Q\{I^o + I^u,E^*[I^o + m(I^o)]\}(\varphi(I^u)d(I^*)}{1 - \{\Phi[m(I^o)]\}} - p$$

Comparing (5) and (6), we observe that the difference in average earnings observed in the data, having controlled for observable characteristics I^o, is a good measure of average productivity differences across remuneration systems. It includes both the sorting and effort effects on productivity, allows for monitoring costs at the rate appropriate to the marginal firm, but it does not take into account the worker's disutility in supplying effort.

In the remainder of the chapter, we apply this model in our empirical analysis.

Empirical analysis of the determinants of PRP

From the discussion, the primary determinants of whether or not a particular worker is subject to PRP are the worker's unobservable ability and the cost of monitoring the worker's output. Since the first is by definition unobservable, and the second extremely hard to ascertain, we would expect empirical analyses of the use of PRP to display limited explanatory power. In this section, we present probit estimates of the determinants of PRP. These equations, as expected, have little explanatory power in spite of the fact that we have a rich set of controls. The individual data results do, however, show some interesting differences from establishment data studies in the literature.

The data source for the current study is the BHPS, a nationally representative survey of households conducted from September to December 1991 and annually thereafter (see Taylor 1996). We chose the BHPS since it not only contains standard data about individual and employer attributes but also information on individual coverage by PRP. It is a panel survey, and therefore potentially allows us to control for unobservable individual-specific factors. The BHPS asks the following question about PRP: 'Does your pay ever include incentive bonuses or profit-related pay? Note: Includes any extra payments, including performance bonuses and sales commissions, but not overtime.'

The current dataset includes waves 1–4 of the BHPS. The PRP question was only asked in waves after wave 1 if the individual changed jobs. For this reason, we use only wave 1 for our probit analysis of the determinants of PRP. In later waves, the individual may have changed their method of pay without changing jobs, so the individual's PRP status is unknown. The BHPS indicates that approximately 23 per cent of all female employees (full-time and part-time) and 37 per cent of male employees were paid by PRP in wave 1. A shortcoming of the BHPS question about PRP is that it does not distinguish between profit sharing and other forms of PRP, such as individual incentive payments. However, the big increase in take-up of profit-sharing schemes occurred after 1991, the year of wave 1, so it is reasonable to assume that most BHPS employees on PRP in wave 1 were in individual performance, rather than approved profit-sharing schemes.[7]

7 From UK Government figures reported in the Employment Gazette, 232,000 employees were in profit-sharing schemes in March 1990 (Beatson 1995). This increased to 350,000 in 1991, 718,000 in 1992, 1,167,000 in 1993, 1,794,000 in 1994, and 2,438,000 in 1995.

Table 2.1: Determinants of PRP, wave 1

	All		Men		Women	
Variable	**Marginal effect**	**SE**	**Marginal effect**	**SE**	**Marginal effect**	**SE**
Individual characteristics						
Female	-.076	(.018)**	–	–	–	–
Married	.036	(.019)	.066	(.031)*	.011	(.022)
Number of children	-.023	(.009)**	-.017	(.013)	-.028	(.012)*
Private sector	.169	(.056)**	.241	(.104)*	.131	(.059)*
Union coverage	.221	(.058)**	.323	(.110)**	.151	(.060)*
Union × private	-.102	(.059)	-.232	(.111)*	-.011	(.063)
Managerial worker	.187	(.047)**	.079	(.070)	.292	(.067)**
Sales worker	.107	(.047)**	.118	(.081)	.132	(.058)*
Highest educational qualification						
First degree and above	.067	(.040)	.093	(.058)	.023	(.051)
A-level	.038	(.028)	.032	(.040)	.036	(.037)
O-level	.044	(.021)*	.072	(.033)*	.011	(.025)
Establishment characteristics						
50–99 employees	-.010	(.025)	-.025	(.038)	.010	(.031)
100–199 employees	.034	(.025)	.029	(.038)	.024	(.032)
200–499 employees	.061	(.025)*	.053	(.037)	.065	(.032)*
500–999 employees	.058	(.032)*	.069	(.045)	.010	(.043)
Over 1,000 employees	.035	(.029)	.080	(.042)*	-.026	(.038)
N	4,045	–	2,010	–	2,035	–
Pseudo R^2	.131	–	.088	–	.173	–

Notes: PRP = performance-related pay; * Significant at 95% confidence level; ** Significant at 99% confidence level; The table reports marginal effects and standard errors. In addition to reported variables, a number of variables were included but not reported. These include industry classifications, age, experience, race, manual, shift and night working, and regional dummies. The base for establishment size is plants with fewer than 50 employees. Means of variables are reported in Table 2.2 for men and Table 2.3 for women. A-level denotes one or more 'advanced' level qualifications usually taken at the age of 18 at university entrance level; O-level denotes one or more 'ordinary' level qualifications usually obtained at the minimum school leaving age of 16. The base for highest educational qualification is qualifications lower than 'O' level or no qualifications.

Table 2.1 presents our probit estimates of the determinants of PRP for the full sample and separately for men and women.[8] Interestingly, the individual data results are in some ways opposite to the establishment-level effects shown in the literature. Establishment-level studies by Brown (1990) for the United States and Heywood et al. (1995) for the United Kingdom both find that unionisation leads to less use of PRP, while the percentage of female workers correlates with greater use of PRP, as does the size of establishment. In contrast, we find that women are less likely to be on PRP, while union status increases PRP coverage.[9] The size of the establishment has a modest positive effect, but only for men.

Our use of individual data allows us to examine the effects of education level on the use of PRP. The absence of a significant education effect in the results emphasises that PRP, compared to salary remuneration, rewards *unobservable* ability. Observable ability, such as that associated with education, can be rewarded in a salary structure.

The results in Brown (1990) and Heywood et al. (1995) suggest that PRP may be associated with 'bad' jobs in establishments where women represent a higher proportion of the workforce and where unions are absent. Our results differ. Not only are women less likely to be covered by PRP, and union workers more likely, but there is no relation between education and PRP. The difference may arise from our ability to control for individual characteristics. Alternatively, the difference may be due to the wording of the BHPS question, which emphasises incentive bonuses rather than the piece-rate systems that form a major part of the Brown, and Heywood et al. studies.

8 All our estimates are calculated using Stata. The sample size was determined by eliminating individuals with missing information.

9 Since the union can act as the workers' agent in resolving any disputes about output or profits, workers in the union sector may be more favourably disposed to PRP than in the non-union sector. Note also that the interaction term for union and private sector shows that, for men, the union effect is largely a public sector one since the interactive term is of opposite sign and almost as large as the union effect.

The effect of PRP on earnings

The model presented in this chapter implies that individuals under PRP have higher earnings, ceteris paribus, for two reasons: they are self-selected as those with higher unobservable ability, and they are induced to supply greater effort. Brown (1992) finds from US establishment data that incentive pay raises wages by about 3–6 per cent relative to standard pay.[10] This result is consistent with earlier US studies by Pencavel (1977) and Seiler (1984). The recent study by Ewing (1996) on US individual data finds an earnings effect of 5.5 per cent. Lazear (1996) studies the effects of introducing PRP in a single firm, the Safelite Glass Corporation. He finds that pay for a given employee rose by 9.6 per cent when PRP was introduced, while productivity rose by 20 per cent.

In Tables 2.2 and 2.3, we present our estimated earnings equations for men and women using wave 1 BHPS data.[11] Our dependent variable is the natural logarithm of the hourly wage rate constructed from the worker's usual gross pay per month. This includes the regular bonuses and commissions associated with PRP systems, but excludes one-off payments such as Christmas bonuses or redundancy payments. Unfortunately, the data do not distinguish how much of the total pay is due to bonuses, so we cannot measure the magnitude of PRP for different workers. We do, however, know the number of standard and overtime hours worked, and we convert monthly pay into hourly pay by assuming that overtime pay is at 1.5 times the standard hourly rate.[12] This is a standard method of adjusting for the different hours worked by individuals.

10 Brown uses a three-way division of pay methods. Incentive pay exceeds merit pay, an intermediate category, by 10–12 per cent. But standard rates of pay also exceed merit pay by 6–7 per cent.

11 The sample size here is smaller than in Table 2.1 due to missing earnings information on some individuals.

12 The logarithm of the hourly wage rate is given by $w_{it} = ln \frac{PAYGU_{it}}{4.33\,(HS_{it} + 1.5HOT_{it})}$, where *PAYGU* is the usual gross pay per month in the current job, *HS* is standard hours, *HOT* is paid overtime hours, *i* refers to the individual, and *t* to the time period.

Table 2.2: Male hourly wage rates, wave 1 BHPS

	Model 1 all		Model 2 union		Model 3 non-union		Mean all men
Variable	**Coefficient**	**SE**	**Coefficient**	**SE**	**Coefficient**	**SE**	
PRP	.093	(.022)**	.047	(.027)	.117	(.036)**	.373
Individual characteristics							
White	.100	(.052)	.173	(.065)**	–.019	(.074)	.969
Private school	-085	(.046)	.033	(.066)	.113	(.074)*	.047
Married	.106	(.022)*	.088	(.023)	.100	(.040)	.639
Number of children	–.004	(.010)	.005	(.011)	–.009	(0.17)	.650
Manual worker	–.140	(.040)**	–.212	(.049)**	–.052	(.062)	.475
Part-time	–.012	(.094)	–.124	(.188)	.086	(.109)	.027
Experience	.045	(.003)**	.040	(.004)**	.048	(.006)**	21
Experience^2	–.001	(.000)**	–.001	(.000)**	–.001	(.000)**	602
Tenure	.004	(.003)	.003	(.004)	.004	(.006)	5
Tenure^2	–.000	(.000)	–.000	(.000)	–.000	(.000)	74
Overtime proportion	–.084	(.056)	–.221	(.057)**	.049	(.095)	.143
Shift worker	.099	(.025)**	.085	(.027)**	.090	(.058)	.143
Night worker	.076	(.056)	.107	(.072)	.015	(.094)	.026
Incremental wage	.047	(.018)**	.056	(.022)*	.021	(.028)	.486
Union coverage	.034	(.021)	–	–	–	–	–
Resident in London	.070	(.036)	.112	(.039)**	.016	(.062)	.095
Resident in the south-east	.147	(.020)**	.112	(.025)**	.177	(.031)*	.319

	Model 1 all		Model 2 union		Model 3 non-union		Mean all men
Variable	**Coefficient**	**SE**	**Coefficient**	**SE**	**Coefficient**	**SE**	
Highest educational qualification							
Second degree and above	.360	(.094)**	.398	(.110)**	.314	(.163)	.021
First degree	.345	(.042)**	.339	(.049)**	.349	(.070)**	.093
Other higher qualification	.187	(.029)**	.179	(.033)**	.170	(.048)**	.220
A-level	.125	(.027)**	.128	(.033)**	.128	(.043)**	.147
O-level	.084	(.022)	.074	(.029)**	.092	(.042)	.214
Establishment characteristics							
50–99 employees	.143	(.026)**	.084	(.031)**	.195	(.044)**	.120
100–199 employees	.091	(.030)**	.048	(.034)	.117	(.051)*	.123
200–499 employees	.121	(.025)**	.102	(.030)**	.148	(.049)**	.145
500–999 employees	.154	(.031)**	.116	(.034)**	.259	(.065)**	.081
Over 1,000 employees	.167	(.026)**	.131	(.030)**	.265	(.052)**	.115
Constant	.738	(.106)**	.709	(.083)**	.417	(.163)*	–
N	2,010	–	1,125	–	885	–	2,010
Adjusted R^2	.55	–	.52	–	.57	–	–

Notes: PRP = performance-related pay; BHPS = British Household Panel Survey; * Significant at 95% confidence level; ** Significant at 99% confidence level; Industrial and occupational dummy variables were included but not reported.

Table 2.3: Female hourly wage rates, wave 1 BHPS

	Model 1 all		Model 2 union		Model 3 non-union		Mean, all men
Variable	**Coefficient**	**SE**	**Coefficient**	**SE**	**Coefficient**	**SE**	
PRP	.056	(.025)**	.073	(.030)	.082	(.040)*	.230
Individual characteristics							
White	.136	(.050)**	.178	(.064)**	–.017	(.067)	.969
Private school	.008	(.046)	.005	(.050)	.011	(.073)	.039
Married	.012	(.018)	.021	(.022)	–.000	(.029)	.620
Number of children	–.027	(.011)*	–.040	(.015)**	–.015	(.015)	.578
Manual worker	–.010	(.029)	.024	(.035)	–.059	(.043)	.186
Part-time	–.008	(.023)	–.018	(.029)	.022	(.034)	.359
Experience	.027	(.003)**	.024	(.004)**	.027	(.004)**	21
Experience^2	–.001	(.000)**	–.000	(.000)**	–.001	(.000)**	601
Tenure	.003	(.004)	.000	(.005)	.002	(.006)	4
Tenure^2	.000	(.000)	.000	(.000)	.000	(.000)	47
Overtime proportion	–.256	(.063)**	–.238	(.100)*	–.293	(.071)	.080
Shift worker	.018	(.031)	.009	(.036)	.042	(.054)	.067
Night worker	.024	(.039)	.033	(.055)	.040	(.047)	.077
Incremental wage scale	.069	(.018)**	.050	(.024)*	.075	(.025)**	.505
Union coverage	.131	(.019)**	–	–	–	–	.508
Resident in London	.174	(.032)**	.148	(.040)**	.196	(.048)**	.104
Resident in south-east	.088	(.021)**	.085	(.027)**	.085	(.030)**	.328

	Model 1 all		Model 2 union		Model 3 non-union		Mean, all men
Variable	**Coefficient**	**SE**	**Coefficient**	**SE**	**Coefficient**	**SE**	
Highest educational qualification							
Second degree and above	.574	(.097)**	.539	(.105)**	.664	(.221)**	.010
First degree	.391	(.050)**	.362	(.057)**	.420	(.093)**	.074
Other higher qualification	.264	(.033)**	.312	(.041)**	.190	(.052)**	.178
A-level	.115	(.031)**	.135	(.040)**	.107	(.047)*	.097
O-level	.101	(.021)**	.079	(.030)**	.114	(.030)*"	.294
Establishment characteristics							
50–99 employees	.091	(.026)**	.044	(.032)	.140	(.041)**	.108
100–199 employees	.094	(.025)**	.061	(.031)**	.129	(.038)**	.101
200–499 employees	.108	(.025)**	.032	(.030)	.202	(.042)**	.105
500–999 employees	.076	(.036)*	.026	(.039)	.261	(.080)**	.052
Over 1,000 employees	.153	(.030)**	.125	(.034)**	.180	(.087)*	.073
Constant	.537	(.105)**	.864	(.102)**	.082	(.040*	
N	2,035	–	1,033	–	1,002	–	2,035
Adjusted R^2	.52	–	.54	–	.43	–	–

Note: PRP = performance-related pay; BHPS = British Household Panel Survey; * Significant at 95% confidence level; ** Significant at 99% confidence level; Industrial and occupational dummy variables were included but not reported.

Model 1 in Table 2.2 shows the estimated wage equation for men over the entire (union and non-union) sample. The PRP raises earnings by 9.3 per cent. The rest of the equation is fairly standard, and the results are unsurprising. Following the BHPS earnings equations reported in Booth and Frank (1996), we allow for an incremental wage scale. That study establishes that, when automatic progression up a scale is in place, the efficiency gains lead to higher average earnings, as is the case here. Model 1 in Table 2.3 shows the estimated wage equation for women over the entire sample. The PRP raises female earnings by 5.6 per cent.

Since the determinants of the method of pay are largely unobservable, as predicted by the theory and established by the empirical results earlier in the chapter, switching regression techniques cannot be used to allow for the endogeneity of the choice of whether or not a worker has PRP.[13] However, by using all four waves of our panel data source, we can, in principle, adjust for the omitted variable bias created by unobservable individual-specific effects on wages. This is important for the econometric model:

(7) $w_{it} = \gamma + x'_{it}\beta + \alpha_i + \varepsilon_{it}$

where w is the logarithm of the hourly wage rate, γ is a constant, x' is a vector of exogenous characteristics affecting wages, i denotes the individual and t the time period, β is the vector of coefficients to be estimated, α_i is the individual-specific unobservable effect (assumed to be time invariant), and ε_{it} is a random error term. The estimated effects of PRP, based on several different assumptions about the individual-specific effects, are presented in Table 2.4. Note that the fixed-effects estimates suffer from a small sample problem. Only 2.7 per cent of those in the sample in wave 1 reported a later shift from no PRP to PRP, while only 2.98 per cent went in the reverse direction.[14] Moreover, the panel data models are likely to suffer from measurement error, since the question about PRP was asked in waves 2–4 only if respondents had changed jobs. To calculate the effect of PRP using the panel models, we assigned to job stayers over waves 2–4 their PRP status in wave 1.[15] Nonetheless, the estimated coefficients to PRP from the panel

13 Switching regression techniques depend upon a satisfactory selection equation. The study by Groot and Oosterbeek (1995), using the first wave of the BHPS, adopts a switching regression approach. This may explain why they estimate that incentive pay raises wages by 60 per cent.

14 Since information on PRP was only requested after wave 1 for people changing jobs, our fixed-effects estimates are measuring the effect of changes from one regime to another via job change. In contrast, Lazear (1996) estimates the effect of within-firm changes in regime from no PRP to PRP.

15 Wages in waves 2-4 were deflated to wave 1 wage levels using the consumer price index.

data models of hourly earnings provide support for the wave 1 cross-section results. For men, the cross-section estimate shows that PRP is associated with 9.3 per cent higher male hourly wage rates, while the panel estimates vary from 4.5–7.4 per cent; for women, the cross-section estimate is 5.6 per cent, and the panel estimates are 6.6–7.6 per cent.

Table 2.4: Comparison of panel and wave 1 cross-section estimates of PRP

	Men		Women	
Return to PRP	**Coefficient**	**SE**	**Coefficient**	**SE**
Wave 1 OLS	.093	(.022)**	.056	(.025)*
Between units	.074	(.016)**	.076	(.019)**
Fixed effects	.045	(.016)**	.066	(.018)**
Random effects	.070	(.012)**	.067	(.013)**

Note: PRP = performance-related pay; OLS = ordinary least squares; * Significant at 95% confidence level; ** Significant at 99% confidence level; The estimates reported in this table are of equation (7) in the text: $w_{it} = \gamma + x'_{it}\beta + a_i + \varepsilon_{it}$. The between units estimate of β is from OLS estimation of: $\bar{w}_i = \gamma + \bar{x}_i\beta + a_i + \varepsilon_{it}$, where the bar over a variable denotes the between units average. The fixed-effects estimate β is from OLS estimation of: $(w_{it} - \bar{w}_i) = \gamma + (x_{it} - \bar{x}_i)\beta + (\varepsilon_{it} - \bar{\varepsilon}_i)$. The random effects estimate is a matrix-weighted average of the between units and fixed-effects models: $(w_{it} - \theta\bar{w}_i) = (1 - 0)\gamma + (x_{it} - \bar{\theta}\bar{x}_i)\beta + (1 - \theta)a_i + (\varepsilon i_t - \theta\bar{\varepsilon}_i)$, where the weight θ is a function of σ^2_a and σ^2_ε (the variance of a and ε, respectively). For discussion, see Greene (1993, pp. 469–473).

Our overall conclusion is that the estimated return to PRP in our individual UK data is reassuringly similar to that of the studies using UK establishment data. Since the individual data allow us to adjust for observable characteristics, such as education, this is an important confirmation of the order of magnitude of these effects.

An issue that has received considerable attention in the US literature is the different pattern of PRP for men and women. Typically, women are found to have greater coverage by PRP, perhaps due to a shorter expected tenure that limits the firm's ability to determine and reward unobserved ability and effort over time in the salary structure (see Goldin 1986). Our results, controlling for individual characteristics, support a different hypothesis. The higher overall return to PRP for men compared to women may reflect an element of discrimination in the way firms award merit pay. If this is the case, women may avoid PRP remuneration. This is consistent with the result from the probit estimates that women are less likely to be covered by PRP. However, we would not wish to push this interpretation, since the differing effect of PRP on earnings for men and women is not significant; the difference between coefficients is (0.093–0.056)=0.037 with a standard error of 0.033.

PRP and trade unions

In Tables 2.2 and 2.3, it is seen that there is a lower return to PRP in union than in non-union workplaces. Men gain 4.7 per cent for PRP in the union sector versus 11.7 per cent in the non-union sector. Women gain 7.3 per cent in the union sector versus 8.2 per cent in the non-union sector. These results are surprising. If there are efficiency gains to PRP, unions should be able to bargain for a share of the surplus, and the earnings return to PRP should be higher in the union than in the non-union sector.[16]

A possible explanation is that, while union workers might anticipate a greater return to the higher effort induced by PRP, there is less of a sorting effect. Since unionised workplaces offer higher wages under any form of remuneration, they attract higher ability workers even in the absence of PRP, and the introduction of PRP does not raise the unobserved ability of workers to the extent that it does in the non-union sector.

Consider a firm facing a union of bargaining power b, where b represents the additional amount the firm must pay in either salary or PRP over the competitive level. We assume that the union sector is small. In this case, referring to Figure 2.1, the union firm can pay the salary $S(I^0) + b$ and attract workers of unobservable ability up to $m_{su} > m$ from the non-union sector. The salaried worker at the union firm is of higher average ability than at the non-union firm. If the union firm adopts the PRP system $Q(I, E) - p + b$, it attracts workers of unobservable ability down to $m_{pu} > m$ from the non-union sector. The PRP worker at the union firm is of lower average ability than at the non-union firm. It follows that there is a smaller difference in unobservable ability between salary and PRP workers in the union sector, and less of a sorting gain to using PRP. This may explain why the estimated return to PRP is smaller in the union sector.

16 We do not claim that the return is actually lower for the union sector, since the union-non-union differential in PRP effects is significant only at the 10 per cent level for men and is insignificant for women. For US establishment data, Brown (1992) finds that incentive payments have virtually the same return to wages in both sectors (9.8 per cent in the union and 9.3 per cent in the non-union). The surprise is that the return is not significantly higher in the union sector.

Conclusion

Previous studies, based upon establishment data, have considered the determinants of the use of PRP and its earnings effects. The current study uses individual panel data. This allows us to examine the relationship between individual characteristics – for example, education level – and the use of PRP. It also provides well-specified individual earnings functions that can potentially clarify the role of PRP in earnings and productivity.

The establishment data studies have found positive associations of PRP coverage with women and with non-union workplaces, suggesting that PRP is associated with bad jobs. Our results with individual data are very different, although this may be due to the wording of the BHPS question. Women are less likely to be in a PRP job, while union workers are more likely to be covered.

We confirm the findings of US establishment studies that there is an association of PRP with higher earnings. For men, there is a 9.3 per cent return to PRP (4.7 per cent in the union sector, 11.7 per cent in the non-union sector). For women, there is a 5.6 per cent return (7.3 per cent in the union sector, 8.2 per cent in the non-union sector).

The model relates the estimated earnings effects of PRP to productivity gains from PRP, net of monitoring costs at the marginal firm using PRP, but not of the disutility of effort. By definition, the marginal firm using PRP has higher monitoring costs than the average firm using PRP. The recent study by Lazear (1996), based upon the introduction of PRP by new management in a single firm, finds an earnings effect of 9.6 per cent and an actual productivity gain of 20 per cent. Insofar as 10 per cent is a plausible magnitude for marginal monitoring costs, our results on a large panel of individual UK workers are remarkably consistent with those of Lazear's single US firm.

Acknowledgements

This chapter was first published as Booth, A.L., and Frank, J. (1999). 'Earnings, productivity, and performance-related pay', *Journal of Labor Economics*, 17(3):447–463. doi.org/10.1086/209927.

This chapter was originally produced as part of a Centre for Economic Policy Research (CEPR) program on 'The UK Labour Market: Microeconomic Imperfections and Institutional Features,' supported by the UK Department for Education and Employment (DfEE). The views expressed in this chapter are not necessarily those of the CEPR or the DfEE. Marco Ercolani provided outstanding research assistance. Part of the chapter was written while Booth was visiting The Australian National University, whose hospitality is gratefully acknowledged. Earlier versions of this chapter were presented at the Employment, Education, and Earnings Group conference in Leeds, UK, and at the Society of Labor Economists meetings in Washington, DC. We are particularly grateful to Orley Ashenfelter, Mono Chatterji, Jim Rebitzer and John Pencavel for suggestions that have led to major improvements in the chapter. Helpful comments were also received at seminar presentations at The Australian National University and at the University of Sydney.

References

Beatson, M. (1995). 'Progress towards a flexible labour market', *Employment Gazette*, 103(2):55–66.

Booth, A.L., and Frank, J. (1996). 'Seniority, earnings and unions', *Economica*, 63(252):673–686. doi.org/10.2307/2555002.

Brown, C. (1990). 'Firms' choice of method of pay', *ILR Review*, 43(3):S165–S182. doi.org/10.2307/2523578.

Brown, C. (1992). 'Wage levels and methods of pay', *The Rand Journal of Economics*, 23(3):366–375.

Estrin, S., Perotin, V., and Wilson, N. (1995). 'Profit-sharing revisited: Miracle cure or mirage?', Labour Market and Social Policy Occasional Paper, OECD.

Ewing, B. (1996). 'Wages and performance-based pay: Evidence from the NLSY', *Economics Letters*, 51:241–246.

Goldin, C. (1986). 'Monitoring costs and segregation by sex: A historical analysis', *Journal of Labor Economics*, 4(1):1–27. www.jstor.org/stable/2534874.

Greene, W.H. (1993). *Econometric Analysis*, 2nd edn, Macmillan.

Groot, W., and Oosterbeek, H. (1995). 'Incidence and wage effects of incentive pay', Discussion Paper TI 95–83, Tinbergen Institute.

Heywood, J., Siebert, W.S., and Wei, X. (1995). 'The determinants of piece-rate payment schemes for manual workers in the UK', Royal Holloway College.

Lazear, E.P. (1986). 'Salaries and piece rates', *The Journal of Business*, 59(3):405–432. doi.org/10.1086/296345.

Lazear, E. (1996). 'Performance pay and productivity', NBER Working Paper No. 5672.

OECD. (1995). 'Profit-sharing in OECD countries'. *Employment Outlook*, OECD.

Pencavel, J. (1977). 'Work effort, on-the-job screening, and alternative methods of remuneration', in *Research in Labor Economics*, vol. 1, edited by Ronald Ehrenberg, pp. 225–258. JAI Press.

Seiler, E. (1984). 'Piece rate vs. time rate: The effect of incentives on earnings', *Review of Economics and Statistics*, 66(3):363–376.

Taylor, M., Brice, J., Buck, N., and Prentice, E., eds. (1996). *British Household Panel Survey User Manual*, vols. A and B, ESRC Research Centre on Micro-Social Change, Essex University.

Weitzman, M. (1985). 'The simple macroeconomics of profit-sharing', *American Economic Review*, 75:937–953.

3

Temporary jobs and neoliberalism

Alison L Booth, Marco Francesconi and Jeff Frank

Temporary contracts are often regarded as an important component of labour market flexibility. Temporary workers can be laid off without incurring statutory redundancy payments or restrictions imposed by employment rights legislation. This may explain the dramatic growth in temporary jobs in France, Italy and Spain, countries characterised by high levels of employment protection. The proportion of temporary workers in these countries doubled between 1985 and 1997. In contrast, in the United States and the United Kingdom, which have relatively little employment protection regulation, the proportion of the workforce on fixed-term contracts has been relatively low and fairly stable.

While temporary contracts can avoid some labour market inflexibilities (see, for example, Bentolila and Bertola (1990), Bentolila and Saint-Paul (1994) and Booth (1997)), there are potential costs. Some commentators have expressed concern about the quality of the stock of jobs and the lack of opportunities for career advancement associated with temporary or flexible work (Farber 1999; Arulampalam and Booth 1998). Purcell et al. (1999) have also found case study evidence from 50 British firms of decreasing employer enthusiasm for temporary contracts, owing to the low levels of retention and motivation of such staff.

The purpose of this chapter is to examine whether temporary jobs in Britain are 'dead-end' jobs with poor pay and prospects or 'stepping stones' to permanent employment in good jobs. Remarkably, little is currently known about temporary workers in Britain (Dex and McCulloch 1995). Discussion of flexibility in Britain has therefore tended to rely on popular perceptions rather than systematic analysis. In this chapter, we investigate three main issues. First, we describe who held temporary jobs in 1990s Britain. Second, we compare temporary jobs to permanent ones in terms of wages, and then estimate how satisfied temporary workers are with their jobs and how much training they receive. Third, we estimate how long it takes temporary workers to move into permanent jobs, which workers will be successful in this way, and how the wage profiles of workers who have ever held a temporary job compare with permanent workers over time. We address these issues using data from the first seven waves of the British Household Panel Survey (BHPS), conducted over the period 1991–7. The analysis is carried out separately for men and women in employment, and distinguishes between 'casual and seasonal workers' (where the nature of the job is temporary) and workers on 'fixed-term contracts' (where the job could, in principle, be held on a permanent basis). Since the second type is what advocates of greater labour market flexibility appear to have in mind, we explore how our results vary across the two forms of temporary work and if, indeed, fixed-term jobs are better than seasonal–casual employment.

Our results confirm the common – but hitherto undocumented – perception that temporary jobs are generally not desirable when compared to permanent employment. Temporary jobs typically pay less, are associated with lower satisfaction in some job components and provide less work-related training. However, we do find evidence that fixed-term contracts (but not casual/seasonal employment) are effective stepping stones to permanent jobs. Furthermore, women who start with a fixed-term job and then move to permanent work fully catch up to the wage level earned by women who start in permanent work. Men suffer a long-term 5 per cent loss in wages from starting with a fixed-term contract.

Our results look at temporary jobs from a microeconomic perspective. We believe an exploration of individual-level data is an appropriate way to look at the potential costs of temporary jobs. Further, we examine a largely unregulated labour market. In economies with greater employment protection for permanent workers, there are typically more temporary jobs with potentially higher marginal costs. Our results make two important points for policy. Even in a largely unregulated labour market, the use of temporary contracts has costs in terms of less training, lower job satisfaction, and lower wages, probably reflecting lower specific human capital investment. However, these costs are typically transitory, in the sense that workers on fixed-term contracts (and, to a lesser extent, in seasonal–casual work) move readily into permanent jobs and catch up either partially (for men) or fully (for women) to their counterparts who started in permanent jobs.

The chapter presents the main hypotheses underlying our analysis, describing the data and providing a picture of temporary work in 1990s Britain. In particular, we estimate who takes a temporary job, and the level of wages, satisfaction and work-related training of temporary workers compared to permanent workers. We examine the impact of an experience of a temporary job on subsequent employment and wages, and summarise our conclusions.

Hypotheses

Dolado et al. (2001) discuss the use of fixed-term contracts from a predominantly macroeconomic perspective. In our discussion, as in our empirical results, we emphasise the microeconomic aspects of such contracts. Although Britain may be viewed as a benchmark case, because of its relatively mild restrictions on dismissal for redundancy or cause, it is still costly to discharge long-serving employees.[1] There is currently no limit on the number of times a fixed-term contract can be renewed, although the Fixed Term Work Directive, to be implemented in July 2002, seeks to remedy this.

Other things being equal, in a competitive labour market, workers on temporary contracts should receive a higher wage that just offsets the value of the absent employment protection. In practice, however, temporary workers may receive lower wages due to lower investment in specific human capital or because they are of lower average ability.[2] The extent of these factors may differ across genders due to standard reasons in the economics of the family. Further, for some professional jobs, general human capital is more important than specific human capital, and temporary jobs in these fields may be high-wage jobs. In this section, we clarify these points to provide a basis for our empirical analysis.

1 Workers with sufficient length of service are entitled to statutory redundancy pay and can claim unfair dismissal. The length of service needed to obtain most of these employment rights has recently been lowered from two years to one year. The maximum sum awardable for unfair dismissal has also recently been increased to £50,000. For women and ethnic minorities, there is no limit on the sum.

2 Guell (2001) develops an efficiency wage model in which the wages of temporary workers may be low because they play no incentive role in reducing shirking. Booth (1997) raises the possibility that firing costs may be endogenous, and traces through their implications for wages and temporary employment.

First, consider temporary jobs where it is unlikely that the worker can eventually obtain a permanent contract for the job. This may be the case if the firm has a stable permanent workforce and maintains a buffer stock of temporary workers who can be readily dismissed to adjust to economic downturns. Alternatively, it may arise if the temporary job is a leave replacement for a permanent worker. In this situation, it is inefficient for workers in temporary jobs to invest in specific human capital or for the employer to provide this training. These jobs will therefore be relatively attractive to workers who have a lower probability of wishing to remain at the firm. This includes young, single individuals who might be disinclined to make a large investment in a particular job until they are sure of their career and regional preferences. For women, the higher probability of a move to non-market employment increases this effect. Older workers might – given the shorter period of return – also be less inclined to invest in specific human capital. However, since a permanent contract is at least as desirable as a temporary one (except for any costs of investing in specific human capital), wages in this sort of temporary job should be at least as high (net of investment costs) as wages in permanent jobs. Workers should voluntarily sort into these jobs, and levels of job satisfaction should be as high as in permanent jobs. Since early investments in specific human capital should have a limited impact on wages later in their career, wages should converge for those workers who start in temporary or permanent jobs.

However, firms may also use temporary contracts as a probation device, whether or not they wish to have a buffer stock of temporary workers to adjust to economic fluctuations or to fill in for permanent workers on leave.[3] Workers on initial temporary contracts who display high ability are later offered permanent employment at the firm.[4] If a firm knows a potential worker is of high ability, the firm might offer a permanent contract, encouraging the worker to immediately begin acquiring specific human capital.[5] If the firm is unsure, however, it may offer a temporary contract. There is an efficiency gain (in the ability to freely discharge low-ability

3 Recent literature (Autor 2000; Polivka 1996; Abraham and Taylor 1996; Houseman and Polivka 1999) makes the further point that firms can hire temporary workers from temporary help supply firms who have economies of scale in screening and training temporary workers. In view of this, firms might find it optimal to hire temporary workers only when there is an element of probation involved. Unfortunately, our data do not distinguish workers at temporary help supply firms.

4 Models of probation include Loh (1994) and Wang and Weiss (1998).

5 In Britain, whether or not a firm adopts a period of probation depends on individual company policy. While some companies accord permanent workers with full rights from the first day of their employment, others offer periods of probation from 3–12 months.

workers at the end of their temporary contract) to offset the efficiency loss of deferred specific human capital investment for those workers who progress to permanent employment. Under these circumstances, workers who start in temporary contracts are of lower expected ability than those who start in permanent contracts, and the expected wage differentials should persist through the individuals' careers. Further, these workers – who would have preferred the permanent job – will have low levels of job satisfaction.

These competing features of temporary jobs are likely to differ in significance between men and women. The desire to defer investment in specific human capital – even for high-ability individuals – is more likely to apply to women who may be deciding between market and home production (Weiss and Gronau 1981).[6] Therefore, the data should show that initial placement in a temporary job has less of a permanent effect on observed wages for women than for men. For men, an initial temporary job is a better signal of low ability than for women. There is another important possible gender difference. Some women may wish to retain career flexibility through a significant portion of their working lives. In this case, it can be optimal to invest in a high level of general, rather than specific, human capital, and to hold a succession of temporary posts. An important example is teaching. We would therefore expect the data to show differences in the effects of temporary work across occupations and its interaction with gender.

Our discussion to this point has concerned fixed-term contracts used either as a buffer stock of employment or for leave replacements, for the purposes of probation, or for allowing a high relative investment in general, rather than specific human capital. These explanations essentially apply to jobs that could, in principle, be held under permanent contracts. Seasonal/casual temporary jobs are very different. These jobs do not lend themselves to the high acquisition of specific human capital, and observation suggests that they are not concentrated in fields requiring high general human capital. Under these circumstances, these jobs would be held largely by individuals with low ability to acquire human capital, and would therefore (particularly insofar as ability to acquire human capital is correlated with general ability) be low paid as well as low in job satisfaction and training, with low probability of moving into good permanent jobs. However, a possible gender difference is that some high-ability women who seek high

6 Using BHPS data, Paull (1997) finds significantly positive returns to tenure (firm-specific human capital) that are greater for women than men. She suggests this may reflect differences in the types of contracts offered to men and women.

employment flexibility and – due to possible extended absences from the labour market – may not find it optimal to invest in general human capital, may participate in seasonal/casual jobs. We would therefore expect that the wage gap between seasonal–casual and permanent work would be greater for men than for women.

In summary, individuals holding temporary jobs are likely to do so either as voluntary sorting (while determining preferences over careers, location and market or home production) or involuntary (with the firm offering permanent jobs to individuals of higher perceived ability). In either case, it is inefficient to invest heavily in specific human capital, so these are likely to be lower wage jobs and – insofar as the sorting is involuntary – display low worker satisfaction. Depending on the extent to which the sorting is by ability, workers starting their careers in temporary jobs will suffer a permanent wage penalty. However, we suggest that voluntary sorting is more likely to occur for women than for men, so starting in a fixed-term job is likely to have a smaller long-term effect for women. Similarly, women should show a smaller wage differential in either fixed-term or seasonal–casual jobs than men.

The data

We use the first seven waves of the BHPS, 1991–7, a nationally representative random-sample survey of private households. Wave 1 interviews were conducted during the autumn of 1991, and annually thereafter. Our analysis is based on the subsample of white men and women who were born after 1936 (thus aged at most 60 in 1997), reported positive hours of work, provided complete information at the interview dates, had left school and were employed at the time of the survey, and were not in the armed forces or self-employed. We have a longitudinal sample of 1,740 male and 1,981 female workers.

The data allow us to distinguish two types of temporary work: the first refers to seasonal or casual jobs; the second refers to jobs done under contract or for a fixed period of time.[7] The percentages of men and women in these two types of temporary work are given in Table 3.1. Over 1991–7, the average percentage of male workers in all temporary jobs is 6.8 per cent, with 3.9 per cent in seasonal and casual jobs, and 2.9 per cent in jobs involving

7 The precise form of the question is: 'Is your current job: A permanent job; A seasonal, temporary or casual job; Or a job done under contract or for a fixed period of time?'

fixed-term contracts. The proportion of women in temporary work is higher, with 6.3 per cent of all women employees being in seasonal and casual jobs, and 3.3 per cent in fixed-term contracts.[8] The distinction in types of temporary jobs is important since labour market flexibility arguments are typically based on the use of short-term contracts in what might otherwise be permanent jobs, rather than the expansion of seasonal–casual work.

Table 3.1: Distribution of temporary work and mean hourly wages by type of contract and gender

	Men		Women	
	Unweighted	**Weighted**	**Unweighted**	**Weighted**
Temporary contract (%)				
Seasonal and casual	3.9	3.8	6.3	6.1
Fixed-term	2.9	2.9	3.3	3.1
N	11,186	11,167	12,821	12,830
Hourly wages (£)				
Permanent (p)	8.55	8.59	6.29	6.32
Seasonal and casual (s)	4.79	4.64	4.92	4.88
Fixed-term contract (f)	7.38	7.47	7.19	7.22
Wage differences (£)				
(p)–(s)	3.76*** (11.755)	3.95*** (12.023)	1.37*** (8.850)	1.44*** (8.867)
(p)–(f)	1.17*** (3.154)	1.12*** (2.942)	-0.90*** (4.306)	-0.90*** (4.020)
(s)–(f)	-2.59*** (4.823)	-2.83*** (5.592)	-2.27*** (7.761)	-2.34*** (7.768)

Notes: *** indicates that the wage difference is significant at 0.01 level; Weighted figures are obtained using the BHPS cross-sectional enumerated individual weights. *N* is the number of person-wave observations. Wages are in constant (1997) pounds. Absolute value of the t-test of the wage difference is in parentheses.

Source: British Household Panel Survey 1991–1997.

8 The proportion of male and female workers in seasonal and fixed-term contracts has remained fairly stable over the sample period. Data from the Labour Force Surveys (LFS) 1991–1997 show proportions of temporary male and female workers that are about 2–3 percentage points lower than those found with the BHPS data. However, the LFS figures confirm the relatively stable time trend. We are grateful to Tim Butcher for providing us with the LFS figures.

Table 3.1 reports the male and female average hourly wages disaggregated by type of contract (permanent, seasonal and casual, or fixed-term contract), the wage differences by contract and their significance.[9] In these raw data, men gain the highest wages in permanent work. The largest wage gap is between permanent and seasonal–casual workers, averaging £3.76 over the period, a highly significant 78 per cent wage gap. The hourly pay differential between permanent and fixed-term contract workers is also significant over the seven-year period, but it is only £1.17 (a 16 per cent wage gap). For women, the highest wages are actually earned by workers on fixed- term contracts, who receive a significant £0.90 per hour (a 13 per cent wage gap) more than permanent workers. The wage gap between seasonal–casual workers and workers in fixed-term contracts is a significant £2.27 (46 per cent wage gap). The two types of temporary work also differ in other ways. Seasonal–casual workers are concentrated in personal and protective services, sales, plant and machine operations and other low-skill occupations, as well as primary, distribution and catering industries. A sizeable group of seasonal–casual female workers are also in transport, banking and other service industries. The large share of male and female workers on fixed-term contracts, in contrast, is in professional and technical occupations across most industries. Effort – as measured by hours of work – also differs significantly between seasonal–casual workers and fixed-term contract workers. For men, mean normal weekly hours (and standard deviation) are: permanent, 45 (11); seasonal–casual, 28 (17); and fixed-term, 41 (15). For women, the mean normal weekly hours are: permanent, 32 (13); seasonal–casual, 21 (13); and fixed-term, 31 (14). For both men and women, hours of work are similar between permanent and fixed-term contracts, although the latter displays greater variance. Seasonal–casual jobs entail fewer hours of work.

In summary, the raw data show the need to distinguish between seasonal–casual temporary jobs (which are clearly low-wage and effort jobs concentrated in low human capital occupations) and fixed-term contracts. The latter appear much like permanent jobs and, for that reason, may be buffer stock or probationary posts that can be stepping stones into good

9 The hourly wage rate is given as w = PAYGU/[(30/7) (HS + κHOT)], where *PAYGU* is the usual gross pay per month in the current job (deflated by the 1997 Retail Price Index), *HS* is standard weekly hours, *HOT* is paid overtime hours per week, and κ is the overtime premium. We set κ at 1.5, the standard overtime rate, but all our results below are robust to alternative values of κ ranging between 1 and 2.

permanent jobs. The data also indicate that there are significant differences between men and women in the nature of temporary jobs, notably in the pay premium women receive under fixed-term contracts.

A picture of temporary work

We now look more closely at a number of characteristics of temporary workers, controlling for individual and workplace attributes. We examine who takes a temporary job, the levels of job satisfaction and training of temporary workers, and how wages compare to permanent jobs. Later in the chapter we examine the longer-run effects of holding a temporary job.

Who takes a temporary job?

To address this question, we perform multinomial logit regressions for men and women separately, in which the dependent variable distinguishes our three categories of employment.[10] These results are not shown but can be found in Booth et al. (2001). Men aged 45 and older are 2–3 times more likely to be in either form of temporary work, relative to the base of men aged 35–44 years. Men with more layoffs are more likely to be in temporary work. For an average male worker, an additional layoff increases the risk of being in a seasonal–casual job by 49 per cent and the risk of being on a fixed-term contract by 30 per cent.[11] Although not significant, there is a positive coefficient on young men aged 16–24 holding fixed-term contracts. These results are consistent with the hypotheses presented earlier in the chapter. Older individuals, those who are laid off and the young may not find it efficient to invest heavily in specific human capital in a new job or may be on probationary contracts.

10 We performed several pooled (men and women) regressions. Despite the higher raw percentages (see Table 3.1), the regression results show that women are less likely than men to be in any type of temporary work, after controlling for demographic and labour market characteristics. We always rejected pooling by gender. We also performed a test for pooling the two types of temporary work, a test for pooling permanent work and seasonal–casual work, and a test for pooling permanent work and fixed-term contracts using the procedure suggested by Cramer and Ridder (1991). The three tests strongly rejected pooling.

11 This finding is consistent with Stewart (2000) and Arulampalam (2001). Stewart (2000) argues that unemployment experience followed by low-paid unstable jobs contributes to observed low pay persistence.

How does the pattern differ for women? The primary difference in the results is that women in high-skilled occupations (professionals, technicians and teachers) are more likely to work under fixed-term contracts. The female probability of holding a fixed-term contract is greater in local government and other public and non-profit employment. Women with older children are also more likely to hold fixed-term contracts, while younger women are more likely to hold seasonal–casual jobs.

Job satisfaction

Despite its measurement problems, job satisfaction may offer a useful perspective on many aspects of the labour market, through its correlation with job separations, effort and productivity (Clark 1996).

Table 3.2: Job satisfaction of temporary workers

	Men (N = 11,186)		Women (N = 12,821)	
	Seasonal & casual	Fixed-term contract	Seasonal & casual	Fixed-term contract
Overall	−0.146** (2.173)	-0.042 (0.597)	-0.165*** (3.336)	-0.052 (0.872)
Promotion prospects	−0.359*** (6.437)	-0.251*** (3.923)	-0.188*** (4.516)	-0.144** (2.240)
Total pay	0.107 (1.636)	-0.172** (2.029)	0.082* (1.718)	-0.065 (0.971)
Relation with the boss	0.114* (1.732)	0.142** (2.010)	0.064 (1.396)	0.133* (2.065)
Security	−0.714*** (9.449)	-0.729*** (9.012)	-0.695*** (13.147)	-0.774*** (10.969)
Initiative	−0.410*** (6.251)	-0.118* (l.662)	-0.256*** (5.316)	-0.102 (1.620)
Work itself	−0.189** (2.783)	0.053 (0.779)	−0.174*** (3.700)	0.032 (0.476)
Hours worked	0.023 (0.351)	0.053 (0.687)	-0.062 (1.282)	-0.011 (0.159)

Notes: * significant at 0.10 level; ** significant at 0.05 level; *** significant at 0.01 level; N = person-wave observations; Coefficients are obtained from ordered probit regressions. For each row, the dependent variable is 'job satisfaction' measured on a scale from 1 to 7, where a value of 1 corresponds to 'not satisfied at all' and a value of 7 corresponds to 'completely satisfied'. The reported numbers are the coefficients (and absolute t-ratios from robust standard errors) on the two types of temporary work. Other variables included in each regression are: cohort of entry into the labour market (5 dummies), disabled, region of residence (6), industry (6), firm size (7), number of full-time and part-time jobs ever held at the start of the panel, marital status (2 dummies), age-marital status interactions (2), number of (marital or cohabiting) partnerships and cohort of partnership (3).

Table 3.2 reports estimates of an ordered probit model of seven different components of job satisfaction, as well as an overall measure, for men and women separately.[12] Each aspect of job satisfaction is measured on a scale from 1 to 7, where a value of l corresponds to 'not satisfied at all' and a value of 7 corresponds to 'completely satisfied'. The overall measure reveals that seasonal–casual men and women are significantly less likely to be satisfied with their jobs than permanent workers. However, no difference in overall job satisfaction emerges between workers in permanent jobs and workers on fixed- term contracts. When we consider the different aspects of job satisfaction separately, we find that workers in both types of temporary work are less satisfied than permanent workers with their promotion prospects and job security.

Training opportunities

In Table 3.3, the pooled probit regression estimates show that the male probability of receiving work-related training is 12 per cent lower for workers on fixed-term contracts and 20 per cent lower for men on seasonal–casual contracts, relative to permanent workers, ceteris paribus.[13] Female workers on fixed-term contracts have a 7 per cent lower probability than permanent workers of being trained, while seasonal–casual females have a 15 per cent lower probability. Training intensity measures the number of days of training, conditional on receiving training. Pooled tobit regressions indicate that seasonal–casual workers receive, on average, 9–12 fewer training days per year than permanent workers, but there is no differential training intensity between permanent workers and fixed-term workers. Controlling for unobserved heterogeneity reduces the effects on both training incidence and training intensity only marginally.

12 In the BHPS interviews, individuals report their satisfaction level for each of the seven aspects of their job first and then, in a separate question, they are asked about their overall satisfaction. The pooled (men and women) regressions reveal that women are significantly more satisfied than men in all but two aspects of their job (promotion prospects and initiative). Clark (1996) reports similar results and discusses a number of plausible explanations.

13 Our measure of training incidence takes the value of unity if the worker has received training in the past 12 months to increase or improve their skills in the current job. The measure of training intensity is the number of days spent in skill-enhancing training during the last 12 months in the current job. Using the same definition of training, Arulampalam and Booth (1998) find a similar result for the first five waves of the BHPS.

Table 3.3: Training receipt and training intensity of temporary workers

Training receipt	Men (N=11,186)		Women (N=12,821)	
	Pooled probit	RE probit	Pooled probit	RE probit
Seasonal & casual	−0.198*** (6.509)	−0.195*** (6.671)	−0.146*** (7.015)	−0.139*** (7.726)
Fixed-term contract	−0.122*** (4.010)	−0.095*** (3.658)	−0.070*** (2.588)	−0.062*** (2.964)
ρ	–	0.331*** [0.000]	–	0.298*** [0.000]
Log likelihood	-6,351	-6,003	-6,732	-6,445
Model χ^2	995.7 (0.000)	907.5 (0.000)	1397.2 (0.000)	1244.0 (0.000)
Mean of dependent variable	0.360		0.314	
Seasonal & casual	-12.435*** (5.485)	-12.212*** (5.459)	-9.384*** (6.787)	-9.245*** (6.725)
Fixed-term contract	-1.569 (0.846)	-1.262 (0.662)	-0.186 (0.135)	-0.116 (0.084)
ρ	–	0.020*** [0.0027]	–	0.012** [0.0214]
Log likelihood	-20,926	-20,875	-21,504	-21,478
Model χ^2	1256.2 (0.000)	988.3 (0.000)	1977.4 (0.000)	1515.0 (0.000)
Mean of dependent variable	3.839 11.262§		2.883 9.188§	

Notes: § Computed on positive values only (N=3,812 for men; N=4,023 for women); * significant at 0.10 level; ** significant at 0.05 level; *** significant at 0.01 level. N is the number of person-wave observations. The reported numbers are marginal effects for the two types of temporary work obtained from pooled and random-effects probit regressions (top) and from pooled and random-effects tobit regressions (bottom). Absolute t-ratios (obtained from robust standard errors in the pooled probit regressions and pooled tobit regressions) are in parentheses. Other variables included in each regression are all the variables used in Table 3.2, plus union coverage. The term p is the fraction of total variance contributed by the panel-level variance component. The p-value of the likelihood ratio test of ρ=0 is reported in square brackets. Model is χ^2 the Wald statistic for the goodness-of-fit test and is equal −2(LR–LU) where LR is the constant-only log-likelihood value and LU is the log likelihood reported in the table. The χ^2 statistic has 64 degrees of freedom and its p-value is in square brackets.

Wages in temporary jobs

The raw data in Table 3.1 showed that the permanent-temporary wage gap was between 16 per cent (fixed-term contract) and 78 per cent (seasonal–casual employment) for men. For women, we detected a 46 per cent wage penalty in the case of seasonal–casual workers and a 13 per cent wage premium for contract workers. Perhaps part of these differences is driven by differences in endowments of human capital or by differences in work motivation and other unobserved individual components. For this reason, we estimate ordinary least squares (OLS) and fixed-effects (FE) wage regressions to measure the effects of being in a seasonal–casual job (SCJ) and in a fixed-term contract (FTC) on the natural logarithm of real (1997 prices) hourly wages for men and women separately, after controlling for a large set of individual and job-specific characteristics.[14] These are reported in Table 3.4. The OLS estimates show that the gap (compared to permanent jobs) for a seasonal–casual male is 16 per cent and, for a fixed-term male, 17 per cent. For women, the seasonal–casual gap is 13 per cent, and the fixed-term gap is 14 per cent. Controlling for observable characteristics has brought the temporary-permanent gaps close together across gender and across the nature of the temporary work. The FE estimates show smaller (but always precisely determined) wage gaps of 11 per cent for men in seasonal–casual jobs and women on FTCs and 7 per cent for men on fixed-term contracts and women in seasonal–casual jobs.[15]

In summary, we find that temporary jobs are held disproportionately by the young and the old, for whom investment in specific human capital may be inefficient. There is a significant wage penalty in both types of temporary work. Seasonal–casual jobs have low job satisfaction, while fixed-term contract jobs have low satisfaction in particular components of the measure, specifically, job security and promotion prospects. There is less training in both types of temporary jobs. The main difference across gender is that some women seem to hold fixed-term professional jobs (e.g., in teaching) on a career basis.

14 The variables included in this estimation are linear and quadratic terms in years of job tenure, local unemployment rate, and dummy variables for region of residence, education, industry, occupation, sector, firm size, disability status, part-time employment, marital status, whether the worker has changed jobs because of promotion, quit or layoff, the number of previous jobs, whether the worker has received on-the-job training in the last 12 months, whether the worker is union covered and whether the worker receives performance-related pay. All wage equations for women are selectivity corrected to account for non-participation using a participation probit equation. This equation is performed on 2,844 women and 17,947 person-wave observations. It is identified by age, time trend dummy variables, cohort of entry in the labour market, age-marital status interactions, cohort of first partnership, number of partnerships, number of children by age group, housing tenure and individual attitudes about working women. The estimated coefficient of the selection term is always negative, marginally significant in the OLS regressions, and not significant in the FE regressions. The results are unaffected if the selection term is obtained from a random-effect probit model.

15 In a previous version of the chapter, we also estimated random-effects wage equations. Those estimates always lie between the OLS and FE estimates reported here for both men and women. They can be found in Booth et al. (2001).

The effects of temporary employment on career prospects

If temporary jobs are voluntarily chosen by individuals who are unsure of their career or location preferences, then taking a temporary job should have no long-run career implications. Given that mobility rates across permanent jobs are fairly high for the young, low investment in specific human capital early in the career should have little effect. In contrast, if permanent jobs are rationed to higher ability individuals, then an initial temporary job signals that an individual is of relatively low ability, and this effect should be permanent. The relative impact of these effects may differ by gender. If new female entrants are initially less committed to the workforce, placement in a temporary job may convey less of a negative signal about ability than for men. In this section, we examine what happens to temporary workers in terms of the duration of temporary jobs, whether such jobs lead to permanent work, and the long-term wage effects of holding temporary jobs.

Job duration and type of exit

How long do temporary jobs last compared to permanent jobs? The Kaplan–Meier estimator of job duration, including both completed and uncompleted spells, reveals that the median duration of seasonal–casual jobs over the 1990s is very short: it is about 3 months for men and 6 months for women.[16] The median duration of fixed-term contracts is around 12 months for both men and women. Permanent jobs have a median duration of almost 3½ years for men and 2½ years for women. By five years, almost all male and female temporary jobs have finished, as compared with 64 per cent of male and 73 per cent of female permanent jobs.

16 These estimates are reported in Booth et al. (2001).

Table 3.4: Ordinary least squares (OLS) and fixed-effects (FE) wage estimates (absolute *t*-ratio in parentheses)

	Men				Women			
	OLS		FE		OLS		FE	
	[1]	[2]	[1]	[2]	[1]	[2]	[1]	[2]
SCJ	−0.155*** (4.414)	−0.171*** (2.986)	−0.107*** (5.004)	−0.224*** (6.511)	−0.126*** (5.062)	−0.169*** (4.111)	−0.075*** (4.513)	−0.189*** (6.439)
SCJ × FT experience	–	−0.003 (0.297)	–	0.018*** (2.652)	–	0.003 (0.487)	–	0.023*** (4.657)
SCJ × FT experience^2	–	0.0002 (0.628)	–	-0.0003 (1.616)	–	−0.0001 (0.573)	–	−0.0006*** (3.494)
SCJ × PT experience	–	0.033 (0.328)	–	0.101** (2.140)	–	0.010 (0.734)	–	−0.004 (0.508)
SCJ × PT experience^2	–	−0.008 (0.638)	–	−0.016** (2.058)	–	-0.0001 (0.157)	–	0.0006 (1.569)
FTC	−0.171*** (3.956)	−0.426*** (5.443)	−0.069*** (3.110)	−0.247*** (6.008)	−0.144*** (3.899)	−0.444*** (5.468)	−0.109*** (5.010)	−0.373*** (7.771)
FTC × FT experience	–	0.035*** (3.379)	–	0.030*** (4.647)	–	0.031* (1.786)	–	0.034*** (3.533)
FTC × FT experience^2	–	−0.0007*** (2.536)	–	−0.0007*** (3.970)	–	-0.0009 (1.141)	–	−0.0009** (2.223)
FTC × PT experience	–	0.099** (2.456)	–	0.071*** (2.605)	–	0.063*** (3.248)	–	0.034** (3.214)
FTC × PT experience^2	–	−0.006*** (2.590)	–	−0.006*** (3.365)	–	−0.002** (2.331)	–	−0.001** (2.236)

	Men				Women			
	OLS		FE		OLS		FE	
	[1]	[2]	[1]	[2]	[1]	[2]	[1]	[2]
FT experience	0.042*** (16.683)	0.040*** (15.429)	0.111*** (30.328)	0.109*** (29.654)	0.022*** (8.053)	0.020*** (7.281)	0.112*** (25.034)	0.109*** (24.259)
FT experience^2	−0.0008*** (12.461)	−0.0007*** (11.562)	−0.001*** (13.241)	−0.001*** (12.627)	−0.0004*** (4.613)	−0.0004*** (4.090)	−0.001*** (8.504)	−0.001*** (7.784)
PT experience	−0.015 (1.125)	-0.023 (1.521)	0.032*** (5.933)	0.029*** (4.537)	0.003 (1.117)	0.0008 (0.297)	0.066*** (12.258)	0.065*** (11.982)
PT experience^2	0.0003 (0.296)	0.0009 (0.746)	−0.007*** (3.067)	−0.005** (1.988)	−0.00004 (0.332)	0.00002 (0.187)	−0.0004 (1.558)	-0.0003 (1.445)
R^2	0.544	0.546	0.216	0.214	0.539	0.542	0.170	0.169
N	11,186		11,186		12,821		12,861	
No. of individuals	1740				1981			

Notes: ** significant at 0.05 level; *** significant at 0.01 level; SCJ = seasonal–casual job; FTC = fixed-term contract; FT = full-time; PT = part-time; Each specification also includes linear and quadratic terms in years of job tenure, local unemployment rate, and dummy variables for region of residence (6), educational level (5), industry (9), occupation (8), sector (4), firm size (7), disability status, PT employment, marital status (2), whether the worker has changed jobs because of promotion, quit or layoff, the number of previous jobs, whether the worker has received on-the-job training in the last 12 months, whether the worker is union covered and whether the worker receives performance-related pay. Base is married or cohabiting workers with no educational qualification, without disabilities, who live in Greater London, who have received on-the-job training and PRP, work in unskilled occupations, in primary industries, in the private sector, in union-covered jobs and in firms with 1,000 or more employees. All wage equations for women are selectivity corrected using a participation probit equation. This equation is identified by age, time trend (6 dummy variables), cohort of entry in the labour market (5), age-marital status interactions (2), cohort of first partnership, number of partnerships, number of children by age group (5 age groups), housing tenure (2), and individual attitudes about working women (6). The t-ratios in the OLS regressions are obtained from standard errors that are robust to arbitrary forms of correlation within individuals. N is number of person-wave observations.

Where do workers go at the conclusion of a temporary job?[17] The destination patterns by gender are quite similar. About 71 per cent of men and 73 per cent of women in temporary jobs take another job with the same employer; another 26 per cent and 24 per cent, respectively, move to a job at a different employer; and another 3 per cent leave the labour force. We observe virtually no transitions from either of the two types of temporary work to unemployment (Boheim and Taylor 2000). Of those employed in a seasonal–casual job, 28 per cent of men and 34 per cent of women have become permanent between 1991 and 1997. About 1 in 7 workers did so within the first three months of their job. However, the median seasonal–casual job duration before exit into permanency is 18 months for men and 26 months for women. For workers on fixed-term contracts, the transition rate to permanency is significantly higher (compared to seasonal–casual jobs) for men (38 per cent) and almost the same for women (36 per cent). The median duration of fixed-term contracts before exit into permanent jobs is about 3 years for men and 3½ years for women. Finally, regardless of the type of temporary employment and gender, about 70 per cent of workers gaining permanency continue working for the same employer.[18]

Which temporary workers are most likely to exit into permanent jobs? To investigate the transition of workers from temporary to permanent employment in a multivariate setting, we specify a discrete-time proportional hazard model relating the exit process to a number of individual and job-specific characteristics. We exploit the time variation of job tenure by using a monthly measure. The time-varying regressors for which we have precise information (such as occupation, industry, sector and firm size) also differ by month, while other time-varying regressors (for example, union coverage and local labour market conditions) take the same value for all months between interviews. Because we condition the estimating sample on temporary workers, the number of transitions is too small to allow estimation of competing-risk models, in which the exit process into permanency gained in the same firm differs from that into permanency gained in another firm. We do, however, allow the determinants of exit behaviour to vary between spells starting in seasonal–casual jobs and

17 The transition from temporary to permanent jobs is also analysed inter alia by Blanchard and Landier (2001) for France, Guell and Petrongolo (2000) for Spain, and Holmlund and Storrie (2002) for Sweden.

18 Segal and Sullivan (1997) note that a majority of US temporary workers are employed in permanent jobs one year later, especially in clerical and technical occupations. In their analysis, however, they do not specify whether this transition occurs within the same firm.

spells starting in fixed-term contracts. The estimation is performed both with and without a Gamma mixture distribution that is meant to capture unobserved heterogeneity between individuals. Table 3.5 presents the estimation results, with columns [1] and [2] reporting the estimates without and with unobserved heterogeneity. For three out of the four exits, we find that including a mixing distribution is relevant and has significant effects on the coefficients of some of the covariates. It does not, however, improve the model fit in the case of the male exit from fixed-term contracts, for which the estimates in the two columns do not significantly differ from one another.

Our results show that the transition from fixed-term to permanent work differs for men and women. For men, but not for women, being younger than 35 years of age has a positive impact on exit to permanent work, suggesting that men on fixed-term contracts follow a natural career progression into permanency. Women in the public and non-profit sectors have a lower likelihood of exiting into permanent work. Interestingly, part-time (PT) men have a low exit rate, while PT women do not have a significantly different exit rate than full-time (FT) women.

The transition from seasonal–casual to permanent work also displays a differential public sector effect, with public sector women less likely to exit into permanent jobs. Part-time seasonal–casual workers, regardless of gender, are less likely to move to permanency. Local labour market conditions (as measured by the unemployment-vacancy ratio) also have a negative impact on exit.

Table 3.5: Exit from temporary work to permanent work: estimates from proportional hazard model – non-parametric baseline hazard specification

Variable	Men				Women			
	Exit from seasonal & casual to permanent work		Exit from fixed-term to permanent work		Exit from seasonal & casual to permanent work		Exit from fixed-term to permanent work	
	[1]	[2]	[1]	[2]	[1]	[2]	[1]	[2]
Age dummy								
16–24	0.144 (0.321)	0.788 (1.400)	1.205*** (2.842)	1.180*** (2.960)	−0.247 (1.116)	−0.832** (2.479)	0.301 (1.014)	−1.069*** (3.289)
25–34	0.317 (0.643)	0.673 (0.956)	1.094*** (2.856)	1.083*** (2.780)	0.029 (0.142)	−0.339 (0.759)	0.393 (1.331)	0.286 (0.880)
45–60	−0.706 (1.252)	−0.514 (0.554)	0.581 (1.326)	0.562 (1.302)	−0.661** (2.259)	−0.581 (1.530)	−0.127 (0.342)	0.938 (1.641)
Education								
Less than GCSE or O-level	0.167 (0.331)	−0.168 (1.370)	−0.935 (1.644)	−0.912 (1.569)	0.106 (0.369)	0.394 (0.369)	1.513*** (3.061)	−0.017 (0.436)
GCSE/O-level	−0.479 (1.169)	−0.746** (1.985)	−0.254 (0.532)	−0.238 (0.482)	−0.027 (0.111)	−0.531 (0.606)	1.1342*** (2.962)	0.573 (1.478)
A-level	−0.342 (0.799)	−0.664 (1.521)	−0.038 (0.075)	−0.027 (0.051)	−0.106 (0.379)	−0.433 (0.456)	1.191** (2.425)	0.447 (1.095)
Vocational degree	−0.099 (0.222)	−0.634 (1.037)	0.545 (1.095)	0.539 (1.094)	−0.126 (0.377)	−0.141 (1.197)	1.739*** (3.133)	0.454 (1.434)
University degree or more	0.259 (0.422)	−0.781 (0.617)	0.842 (1.426)	0.893 (1.547)	0.290 (0.830)	1.376 (1.030)	1.521** (2.439)	0.739*** (2.795)
Occupation								
Managerial	7.371*** (7.201)	6.849** (2.037)	0.248 (0.333)	0.319 (0.616)	1.085** (2.132)	0.134 (0.016)	−0.379 (0.568)	0.840 (0.240)
Professional	2.940*** (2.873)	0.836 (0.703)	−0.607 (0.913)	−0.568 (1.065)	−0.633 (1.154)	1.074 (0.869)	−1.305*** (2.598)	−0.715 (0.569)

Variable	Men				Women			
	Exit from seasonal & casual to permanent work		Exit from fixed-term to permanent work		Exit from seasonal & casual to permanent work		Exit from fixed-term to permanent work	
	[1]	[2]	[1]	[2]	[1]	[2]	[1]	[2]
Technicians	2.949*** (5.713)	2.523*** (2.566)	−0.428 (0.827)	−0.410 (0.854)	−0.095 (0.245)	−1.196 (1.244)	0.125 (0.265)	0.312 (0.667)
Clerks and secretaries	0.933** (2.204)	−0.039 (0.031)	0.072 (0.141)	0.079 (0.161)	0.308 (1.162)	−0.817 (1.144)	0.356 (0.883)	0.791 (0.215)
Craft	2.621*** (6.667)	2.308*** (3.347)	2.291*** (4.945)	2.278*** (5.034)	1.091** (2.383)	−1.189 (0.820)	−0.351 (0.848)	−0.531 (0.545)
Protection and pers. services	−0.682 (1.032)	−1.530** (2.315)	0.074 (0.128)	0.085 (0.154)	0.297 (1.116)	−1.373** (2.015)	0.039 (0.297)	0.217 (0.329)
Sales	1.032** (2.299)	1.457 (1.646)	1.231** (2.401)	1.243*** (2.576)	1.058*** (3.809)	−0.364 (0.498)	−0.041 (0.075)	0.325 (0.747)
Plant and machine operatives	−0.006 (0.014)	0.306 (0.262)	0.990** (2.175)	0.984** (2.182)	−1.413*** (3.411)	−1.795*** (5.071)	−1.071 (0.967)	−0.906*** (3.893)
Sector								
Civil service	0.314 (0.471)	0.657 (0.597)	−0.433 (0.528)	−0.455 (0.571)	−0.641 (0.986)	−0.817 (0.570)	−1.581** (2.047)	−1.678** (2.059)
Local gov	0.029 (0.054)	−0.294 (0.519)	−0.002 (0.006)	0.001 (0.001)	−0.340 (1.378)	−2.444*** (3.545)	−1.247*** (4.094)	−1.245*** (3.313)
Other public	−1.224 (1.506)	0.176 (0.089)	0.142 (0.355)	0.135 (0.331)	−0.854** (2.510)	−1.321 (1.607)	−(3.005)	−1.478*** (3.301)
Non-profit	2.050*** (3.547)	1.819* (1.771)	−1.495* (1.904)	−1.481* (1.887)	−0.297 (0.710)	−3.556*** (3.356)	−1.445*** (3.470)	−1.415*** (4.539)
Part-time job	−1.681*** (4.549)	−1.473*** (3.695)	−1.054*** (2.586)	−1.062*** (2.658)	−0.917*** (5.212)	−1.658*** (3.342)	−0.244 (0.915)	−0.039 (0.038)

Variable	Men				Women			
	Exit from seasonal & casual to permanent work		Exit from fixed-term to permanent work		Exit from seasonal & casual to permanent work		Exit from fixed-term to permanent work	
	[1]	[2]	[1]	[2]	[1]	[2]	[1]	[2]
Union coverage	−0.155 (0.592)	−1.006* (1.677)	0.341 (1.434)	0.327 (1.435)	0.817*** (4.939)	1.267*** (4,.215)	0.436* (1.918)	−0.569* (1.907)
Total layoffs number	0.137 (1.576)	0.661** (2.191)	0.158* (1.729)	0.160* (1.719)	0.304 (3.754)	0.650** (2.044)	0.442*** (3.478)	0.458*** (3.279)
Local unempl. to vacancies ratio	−0.023** (2.050)	−0.093** (2.481)	−0.014 (1.361)	−0.014 (1.438)	−0.011 (1.639)	−0.093*** (4.286)	−0.005 (0.533)	−0.069*** (5.678)
Unpaid overtime hours§	0.522** (2.493)	0.102 (0.202)	0.013 (0.121)	0.016 (0.185)	0.079 (0.987)	0.315*** (2.672)	0.234** (2.299)	0.277** (2.431)
σ^2	–	2.861*** (3.561)	–	1.14×10-4 (0.004)	–	2.415*** (4.894)	–	3.778*** (4.743)
Log likelihood	-382	-349	-406	-406	-989	-935	-549	-501
Model χ^2	395.6	412.1	348.6	352.7	471.2	494.0	230.3	236.5
	[0.0000]	[0.0000]	[0.0000]	[0.0000]	[0.0000]	[0.0000]	[0.0000]	[0.0000]
Person-month obs.	5,602	5,602	4,591	4,591	12,016	12,016	6,716	6,716

Notes: § Predicted from tobit regressions which include all the variables used in the hazard models plus number of children by four age groups, and dummy variables for cohort of entry in the labour market (5 dummies), region of residence (6), and whether the worker receives PRP. The tobit regressions contain nine rather than three industry dummies. The F-statistics (and *p*-values) of the variables identifying hours of unpaid overtime work are $F(11, 11{,}130)=9.36$ (p-value = 0.000) and $F(11, 12{,}763)=14.03$ (p-value=0.000) for men and women, respectively; * significant at 0.10 level; ** significant at 0.05 level; *** significant at 0.01 level; Absolute ratio of coefficient to standard error in parentheses. The term σ2 is the variance of the Gamma-distributed random variable that summarises unobserved heterogeneity between individuals. All regressions also include industry (3 dummies), firm size (7), and a constant. Base is workers aged 35–44, with no educational qualifications, and who work in unskilled occupations, in primary industries, in the private sector, in full-time union-covered jobs, and in firms with 1000 or more employees. For the definition of model χ^2, see note under Table 3.3. The χ^2 statistic has 35 degrees of freedom and its p-value is in square brackets.

A natural hypothesis is that workers' effort will be used by employers to screen out the more able or hard-working temporary workers for retention. We would therefore expect effort to be a crucial determinant of exit from a temporary into a permanent position at a firm. To proxy effort, we use the number of weekly unpaid overtime hours usually worked. Because of potential endogeneity, we use predicted (rather than actual) unpaid overtime hours, whose identification is achieved through exclusion restrictions. These estimates are reported at the bottom of Table 3.5.[19] The estimates show that, after controlling for unobserved heterogeneity, a higher number of hours of unpaid overtime work increases women's chances of exiting from any type of temporary work. This is, however, not the case for men.[20]

Wage profiles

We now examine wage dynamics to see if there are any longer-term income effects of having held temporary jobs. The general specification of the wage equation follows the approach used by Hausman and Taylor (1981), Altonji and Shakotko (1987) and Light and McGarry (1998), and can be written as:

$$(1)\ ln\ \omega_{ijt} = \beta_0 + \beta_1 X_{ijt} + \beta_2 Z_{ijt} + \mu_i + \emptyset_{ij} + \varepsilon_{ijt}$$

where $ln\ \omega_{ijt}$ is the real (1997 prices) hourly wage for individual i on job j at time t, and X denotes a standard set of variables that are often included in reduced-form wage regressions (e.g., highest educational qualification, PT and FT work experience, job tenure, union coverage, industry and occupation).[21] The vector X also contains dummy variables indicating the workers' region of residence, marital status and disability status, the sector and size of their employing organisation, whether they have received

19 The number of children by four age groups, dummy variables for cohort of labour market entry (5), region of residence (6) and receipt of performance-related pay are assumed to affect an individual's exit propensity only through their effect on unpaid overtime hours. Inclusion of actual unpaid overtime hours does not significantly change the results, and thus we do not report those estimates.

20 We explored the relationship between effort and exit rates by looking at two additional specifications, one that distinguishes the effect of total hours of overtime work from that of paid overtime hours, and another specification in which we only include the number of hours of overtime work. All the other covariates enter the regressions as in Table 3.5. Again, the exit into permanency for men on fixed-term contracts is insignificantly affected by any of the effort measures. For all the other temporary workers, though, effort matters. An increase in the number of overtime hours always leads to a higher hazard of exit (in both specifications), while an increase in the number of paid overtime hours reduces the rate of exit into a permanent job.

21 For individuals who have more than one job between one interview date and the next, we assign to that individual the hourly wage for the interview date.

PRP and on-the-job training in the last 12 months, job-mobility variables (indicating if they have changed jobs because of promotion, quit or layoff), and the average local unemployment rate. The vector Z includes the contract-related variables that are the focus of our study. Specifically, Z contains controls for the number of seasonal–casual jobs and the number of fixed-term contracts held over the seven years of the survey, NSCJ7 and NFTC7, respectively.[22] We also include interactions between NSCJ7 and NFTC7 and the linear and quadratic FT experience terms. This allows the returns to 'experience capital' to differ by contract type. We excluded from our reported specification the interactions between contract types and other human capital variables (PT experience and job tenure), because they had no additional explanatory power and did not alter the estimates of the other variables. The error term in (1) contains a time-invariant individual-specific component, μ_i, a time-invariant job-specific component, $\emptyset_{ij}$ and a white noise, ε_{ij}. We assume that the three error components are distributed independently of each other, have zero means and finite variances.

The estimation of (1) is performed using the instrumental variables generalised least squares (IV/GLS) procedure used by Light and McGarry (1998). We use an IV procedure because a number of wage regressors – including work experience, job tenure and, most notably, those related to the contract type – are likely to be correlated with individual and job-specific characteristics, which cannot be observed by the analyst and are captured by μ_i, and $\emptyset_{ij}$.[23] We treat as endogenous all the regressors in Z, along with PT employment status, PT and full-time experience and job tenure (and their squared terms), marital status, the job-mobility variables, and the dummy variables indicating training and PRP.[24] The instrumental variables used in estimation are given by: (i) the deviations from within-job means of both exogenous and endogenous time-varying variables, and (ii) the within-job

22 For men, the conditional mean (SD) for *NSCJ7* is 1.597 (0.920) while for women it is 1.632 (1.023). For *NFTC7*, the conditional mean (SD) for men is 1.591 (1.014) while for women it is 1.710 (1.198).

23 See Light and McGarry (1998) for a discussion of the advantages of using a random-effects GLS procedure over a fixed-effects (within-individual/within-job) procedure.

24 We have performed several sensitivity tests in which other variables in *X* were treated as endogenous (namely, part-time experience, job tenure, education, union coverage, disability status, occupation and sector). Adding these variables to the list of endogenous variables did not improve the statistical fit and did not have a statistically significant effect on *NSCJ7*, *NFTC7* and their interactions with full-time work experience.

means of all exogenous variables. Because ε_{ij} is a white noise, the deviations are uncorrelated with the composite error term by construction, and thus they are valid instruments.[25]

Table 3.6 reports the IV/GLS wage estimates of the contract-related variables (columns [1] and [2]) and their interactions with FT experience (column [2] only) for men and women separately. The column [1] estimates imply that men and women who had one seasonal–casual job between 1991 and 1997 experienced, respectively, a wage reduction of 8.9 per cent and 6 per cent as compared to those who always had a permanent job over the same period. The wage penalty associated with the experience of one FTC is half that for a seasonal-casual job, at 4.6 per cent but is significant for men, while it is insignificant and around 2.4 per cent for women. The fraction of the residual variance that is attributable to job-specific unobservables is quite large (particularly for women, for whom Var($\emptyset_{ij}$) is about 44 per cent of the total variance). This may help to reconcile the differences between the raw data presented in Table 3.1 and the estimates found with the OLS and FE regressions. In column [2], we control for the interactions of temporary work with FT experience. For both men and women, we note that the direct experience effects are always strongly significant but smaller than in the previous specification. For workers with one year of FT experience, the implied penalty to one seasonal–casual job over the first seven years of the career is, *ceteris paribus*, 11.5 per cent and 4.5 per cent for men and women, respectively. For workers with 10 years of FT experience, the penalty increases respectively to 12.3 per cent and 8.8 per cent, ceteris paribus. Turning to workers on FTCs, the wage penalty to one FTC is about 8.5 per cent and 4.7 per cent for men and women with one year of FT experience, respectively. The penalty decreases to 5 per cent and 0.4 per cent for men and women respectively, with 10 years of FT experience. The returns to experience capital differ strongly by contract type and gender.

25 In other regressions not reported here, we also used as instruments the number of children that each worker has during the seven-year period and the local unemployment rate (Light and McGarry 1998). The over-identifying-restrictions tests fail to reject the hypothesis that these two additional sets of variables are valid instruments at any conventional level of significance, and they slightly improve the R^2 in the first-stage regressions. However, the estimated parameters for the variables of primary interest (*NSCJ7*, *NFTC7* and their interactions with full-time experience) are not altered when these additional instrumental variables are used. Moreover, with these 'extra' instruments, the structure underlying model (1) relies on exclusion restrictions which are hard to justify. We therefore decided to exclude such instruments from the specifications discussed below.

Experience magnifies the differences between seasonal–casual workers and those who always have been in permanent jobs, while it reduces the differences between fixed-term workers and permanent workers. Both these effects are larger for women.[26]

To describe the effect of contract type on wages further, we compute predicted log-wages paths from the column [2] estimates of Table 3.6 for workers with four different employment patterns. The first pattern involves workers who are always in a FT permanent job for the first 10 years of their career. The second and third patterns are for workers who hold one FTC or one seasonal–casual job, respectively, in the first period (at the start of their career) and are in a permanent job for the remaining part of their career. The fourth pattern involves workers who hold three consecutive one-year fixed-term contracts in the first three years of their career and are employed on a permanent contract thereafter. The predicted wages are computed assuming that individuals work continuously FT for the first 10 years of their career, are not disabled, are unmarried and childless, live in Greater London, work in the private sector in a non-union job and begin their career in 1991.[27]

26 As a robustness check, we estimated two additional specifications for men and women. In the first specification, we introduced two dummy variables indicating current employment in a seasonal–casual job or current employment in a job with a fixed-term contract. The IV/GLS wage estimates are similar to those obtained from standard random-effects regressions. In the second specification, we tested for the presence of nonlinear effects in *NSCJ7* and *NFTC7* on (*ln*) hourly wages. We introduced two dummy variables, the first taking the value of one if the worker held only one seasonal–casual job or fixed-term contract over the panel years; the second taking the value one if the worker held two or more seasonal–casual jobs or fixed-term contracts over the panel years. For both men and women, we found no evidence of a wage penalty beyond the first fixed-term contract. We detected, however, a worsening of the wage penalty as the number of seasonal–casual jobs increases, especially for women.

27 We also assume that each individual's occupation, industry, education, firm size, training, performance-related pay, job-mobility patterns and local unemployment rate take the sample values for men and women respectively. Changing these assumptions would only alter the levels but not the relative rankings (and slopes) of the wage profiles in Figure 3.1.

Table 3.6: Temporary work and wages, selected estimates from IV/GLS regressions

	Men		Women	
	[1]	[2]	[1]	[2]
NSCJ7	-0.116*** (3.167)	-0.147*** (3.681)	-0.073*** (3.276)	-0.050** (2.522)
NSCJ7^2	0.027** (2.212)	0.033*** (2.737)	0.013** (2.409)	0.012** (3.509)
NSCJ7 × FT experience	–	-0.001 (0.298)	–	-0.007*** (2.786)
NSCJ7 × FT experience^2	–	0.000 (0.192)	–	0.002** (2.289)
NFTC7	-0.059** (2.195)	-0.104*** (2.873)	-0.030 (1.273)	-0.058* (1.706)
NFTC7^2	0.013** (2.183)	0.014** (2.098)	0.006 (1.418)	0.004 (0.910)
NFTC7 × FT experience	–	0.005 (1.324)	–	0.007 (1.193)
NFTC7 × FT experience^2	–	-0.0001 (1.109)	–	-0.0002 (0.850)
FT experience	0.045*** (5.079)	0.037*** (12.643)	0.031*** (4.021)	0.024*** (8.062)
FT experience^2	-0.001*** (4.259)	-0.0007*** (10.166)	-0.0006** (2.367)	-0.0004*** (4.775)
Var(μ_i)	0.086	0.085	0.076	0.074
Var(ϕ_{ij})	0.054	0.054	0.093	0.091
Var(ε_{ijt})	0.047	0.044	0.044	0.042
R^2	0.544	0.550	0.482	0.534
No. person-wave observations	11,186		12,821	
N	14,156		17,006	

Notes: * significant at 0.10 level; ** significant at 0.05 level; *** significant at 0.01 level; NSCJ7 = number of seasonal-casual jobs held over the seven years of the panel survey; NFTC7 = number of fixed-term contracts held over the seven years of the panel survey; FT = full-time; The terms Var(μ_i), Var(ϕ_{ij}) and Var(ε_{ijt}) are the estimated variances of the individual, job, and transitory components of the residual, respectively. The other variables used in estimation are those used in the OLS and FE regressions (see text). All wage equations for women are selectivity corrected. *N* = number of person-job-wave observations. Absolute *t*-ratios are in parentheses.

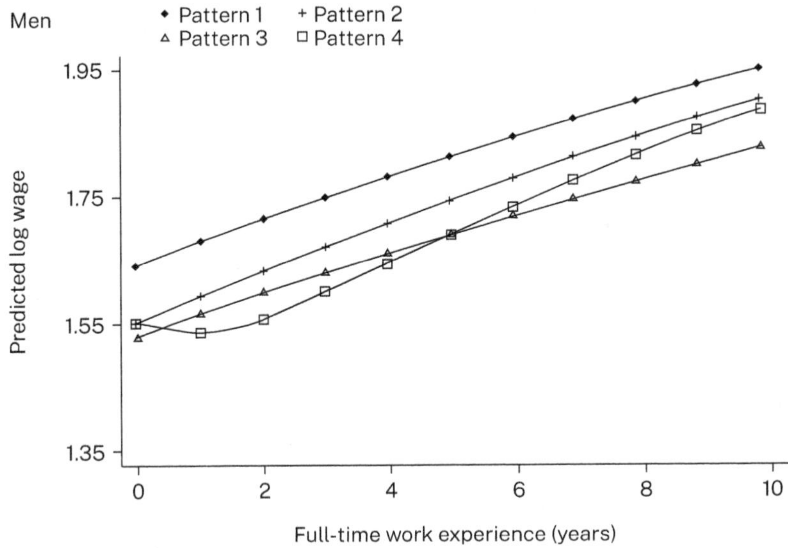

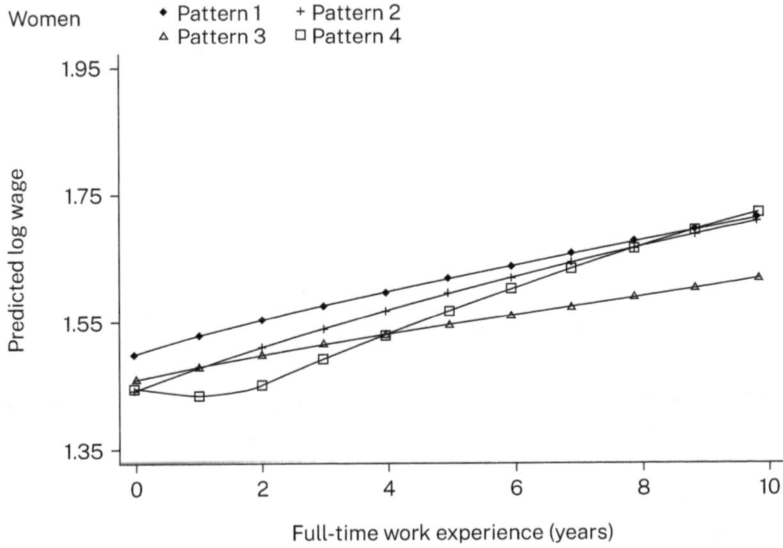

Figure 3.1: Predicted log wages by experience level and early employment patterns

Notes: Based on predictions from the estimates presented in Table 3.5. All jobs are full-time jobs. Pattern 1: worker is always employed in a permanent job. Pattern 2: worker holds one fixed-term contract in first period and is employed in permanent job thereafter. Pattern 3: worker holds one seasonal-casual job in first period and is employed in permanent job thereafter. Pattern 4: worker holds three fixed-term contracts in first three periods and then is employed in permanent job.

The results of this simulation are graphed in Figure 3.1. Having always had a permanent job is clearly the pattern delivering the highest real wage profile over the first 10 years of a man's career, with an average growth of 3 per cent per year. Men who have one or three fixed-term contracts at the beginning of their career display lower wage profiles (especially at the beginning of their work cycle) but a slightly higher wage growth. In fact, the wage gap among these three types of workers is larger at the start of the career and tapers off over time as they accumulate general work experience. Men who started off with a seasonal–casual job, though, have the lowest wage profile and the smallest wage growth. This leads to an increase in the wage gap in comparison with the other three types of workers, which is particularly clear when we contrast pattern 3 with patterns 2 or 4. This finding holds for women, too. However, for women, having had one or three fixed-term contracts at the start of their career does not permanently damage the wage profile. Indeed, women following pattern 2 or pattern 4 end up with the highest wage levels and the largest wage growth (approximately 2.5 per cent per year over a 10-year period). The wage gap for these two types of workers and those who have always been in a permanent job is very large at the start of the career, but it declines over time. It is the interaction between FT experience and fixed-term contracts that causes type 4 (and type 2) workers to overtake type 1 workers, for their productivity increases as they move to permanent jobs as a return to this 'experience capital'.

Conclusions

In Britain, about 7 per cent of male employees and 10 per cent of female employees are in temporary jobs. In contrast to much of continental Europe, this proportion has been relatively stable over the 1990s. Using data from the BHPS – which disaggregates temporary work into seasonal or casual jobs and FTC jobs – we found that, on average, temporary workers report lower levels of job satisfaction (at least in some components), receive less work-related training than their counterparts in permanent employment and receive lower wages. This holds for both seasonal–casual workers and workers on fixed-term contracts, and for both men and women. Therefore, the creation of temporary jobs as a substitute for permanent jobs – in the desire to increase labour market flexibility – comes at a cost.

However, we also found evidence that temporary jobs are a stepping stone to permanent work. The median time in temporary work before such a transition is between 18 months and three and a half years, depending on contract type (seasonal or fixed-term) and gender. Our wage growth models (which allow for potential endogeneity of many of the explanatory variables, including contract type) show that the wage growth penalty associated with experience of seasonal–casual jobs is quite high for both men and women. Even with 10 years of FT experience, having held one seasonal–casual job has a wage penalty of 12.3 per cent for men and 8.8 per cent for women. In contrast, men with experience of one FTC suffer a much lower wage penalty, 5 per cent, after 10 years of experience. Interestingly, we find evidence that women who start off their career on fixed-term contracts may experience high wage growth and, within a period of 7–10 years, have fully caught up with their permanent counterparts.

Overall, our results are consistent with theories of temporary work. Particularly, in seasonal–casual jobs (where there is little possibility of moving to a permanent job), there will be little training. Wages and job satisfaction will be low. For fixed-term temporary jobs, there is greater potential for moving into permanent jobs. There is evidence for this in our study. Fixed-term temporary jobs may well be stepping stones to a future career, although men who begin in jobs with fixed-term contracts suffer a permanent earnings loss compared to men who begin their careers in permanent jobs. This is consistent with the idea that these men are less able than those who immediately acquire a permanent job on entering the workforce. In contrast, women who start with fixed-term contracts fully catch up with those who began on permanent contracts. This is consistent with a view that some women, on entering the labour force, may take longer to decide on their career choices. Under this hypothesis, women who begin in temporary work are as able as those who begin in permanent jobs, and these women eventually make up for the lack of specific human capital acquisition during the period of temporary work.

The important policy conclusion from our work is that the expansion of temporary work, as a way of increasing labour market flexibility, comes at a cost. However, the cost may be transitory, and workers can effectively use fixed-term jobs (and, to a lesser extent, seasonal–casual jobs) as stepping stones to permanent work.

Acknowledgements

This chapter was first published as Booth, A.L., Francesconi, M., and Frank, J. (2002). 'Temporary jobs: Stepping stones or dead ends?', *The Economic Journal*, 112(480):F189–F213. doi.org/10.1111/1468-0297.00043.

We are grateful to the ESRC for financial support under 'The Future of Work: Flexible Employment, Part-time Work and Career Development in Britain', Award No. L212 25 2007. We thank for their helpful comments Mark Beatson, Tim Butcher, David Card, Erica Groshen, Juan Jimeno, Boyan Jovanovic, Wilbert van der Klaauw, Alan Krueger, Donald Storrie and seminar participants at the 2000 British Association Conference (Imperial College, London), the EEEG Labour Workshop at the University of Southampton, the Department of Trade and Industry, FEDEA (Madrid), the LABORatorio Riccardo Revelli Second Conference (Turin), and the Universities of Bilbao, Essex, Newcastle, Princeton, Rome (La Sapienza) and York, and The Australian National University. We also thank Steve Machin and the referees for their comments.

References

Abraham, K.G., and Taylor, S.K. (1996). 'Firms' use of outside contractors: Theory and evidence', *Journal of Labor Economics*, 14(3):394–424. doi.org/10.1086/209816.

Altonji, J.G., and Shakotko, R.A. (1987). 'Do wages rise with job seniority?', *Review of Economic Studies*, 54:437–459.

Arulampalam, W. (2001). 'Is unemployment really scarring? Effects of unemployment experiences on wages', *The Economic Journal*, 111(475):F585–606. doi.org/10.1111/1468-0297.00664.

Arulampalam, W., and Booth, A.L. (1998). 'Training and labour market flexibility: Is there a trade-off?', *The British Journal of Industrial Relations*, 36(4):521–536. doi.org/10.1111/1467-8543.00106.

Autor, D.H. (2000). 'Why do temporary help firms provide free general skills training?', NBER Working Paper No. w7637.

Bentolila, S., and Bertola, G. (1990). 'Firing costs and labour demand: How bad is Eurosclerosis', *The Review of Economic Studies*, 57(3):381–402. doi.org/10.2307/2298020.

Bentolila, S., and Saint-Paul, G. (1994). 'A model of labour demand with linear adjustment costs', *Labour Economics*, 1(3–4):303–326. doi.org/10.1016/0927-5371(94)90015-9.

Blanchard, O., and Landier, A. (2001). 'The perverse effects of partial labour market reform: Fixed term contracts in France', *The Economic Journal*, 112(480):F214-244. doi.org/10.1111/1468-0297.00047.

Boheim, R., and Taylor, M.P. (2000). 'The search for success: Do the unemployed find stable employment?', ISER Working Paper Series No. 2000-05.

Booth, A.L. (1997). 'An analysis of firing costs and their implications for unemployment policy', in D. Snower and G. de la Dehesa (eds), *Unemployment Policy*, Cambridge University Press, pp. 359–388.

Booth, A.L., Francesconi, M., and Frank, J. (2001). 'Temporary jobs: Who gets them, what are they worth, and do they lead anywhere?', ISER Working Paper No. 00-13.

Clark, A.E. (1996). 'Job satisfaction in Britain', *British Journal of Industrial Relations*, 34(2):189–217. doi.org/10.1111/j.1467-8543.1996.tb00648.x.

Cramer, J.S., and Ridder, G. (1991). 'Pooling states in the multinomial logit model', *Journal of Econometrics*, 47(2–3):267–272. doi.org/10.1016/0304-4076(91)90102-J.

Dex, S., and McCulloch, A. (1995). 'Flexible employment in Britain: A statistical analysis', Equal Opportunities Commission, Research Discussion Series No. 15.

Dolado, J.J., García-Serrano, C., and Jimeno, J.F. (2001). 'Drawing lessons from the boom of temporary jobs in Spain', *The Economic Journal*, 112(480):F270–F295. doi.org/10.1111/1468-0297.00048.

Farber, H.S. (1999). 'Alternative and part-time employment arrangements as a response to job loss', *Journal of Labor Economics*, 17(S4):S142–S169. doi.org/10.1086/209946.

Guell, M. (2001). 'Fixed-term contracts and unemployment: An efficiency wage analysis', Princeton University IRS Working Paper No. 433.

Guell, M., and Petrongolo, B. (2000). 'The transition of workers from temporary to permanent employment: The Spanish case', London School of Economics CEP Discussion Paper No. 438.

Hausman, J.A., and Taylor, W.E. (1981). 'Panel data and unobservable individual effects', *Econometrica*, 49(6):1377–1398. doi.org/10.2307/1911406.

Holmlund, B., and Storrie, D. (2002). 'Temporary work in turbulent times: The Swedish experience', *The Economic Journal*, 112(480):F245–F269. doi.org/10.1111/1468-0297.00042.

Houseman, S.N., and Polivka, A.E. (1999). 'The implications of flexible staffing arrangements for job stability', Upjohn Institute Staff Working Paper No. 99-056.

Light, A., and McGarry, K. (1998). 'Job change patterns and the wages of young men', *The Review of Economics and Statistics*, 80(2):276–286. doi.org/10.1162/003465398557519.

Loh, E.S. (1994). 'Employment probation as a sorting mechanism', *Industrial and Labor Relations Review*, 47(3):471–486. journals.sagepub.com/doi/10.1177/001979399404700307.

Paull, G. (1997). 'Low pay and wage growth in Britain: The returns to experience and tenure', [Unpublished manuscript]. Mimeo, Institute for Fiscal Studies.

Polivka, A.E. (1996). 'Are temporary help agency workers substitutes for direct hire temps? Searching for an alternative explanation of growth in the temporary help industry', [Unpublished manuscript]. Mimeo, Bureau of Labor Statistics, Washington, DC.

Purcell, K., Hogart, T., and Simm, C. (1999). *Whose Flexibility? The Costs and Benefits of Non-standard Working Arrangements and Contractual Relations*. Joseph Rowntree Foundation, York Publishing Services.

Segal, L.M., and Sullivan, D.G. (1997). 'The growth of temporary services work', *Journal of Economic Perspectives*, 11(2):117–136. doi.org/10.1257/jep.11.2.117.

Stewart, M.B. (2000). 'The inter-related dynamics of unemployment and low pay', [Unpublished manuscript]. Mimeo, University of Warwick.

Wang, R., and Weiss, A. (1998). 'Probation, layoffs, and wage-tenure profiles: A sorting explanation', *Labour Economics*, 5(3):359–383. doi.org/10.1016/S0927-5371(97)00019-5.

Weiss, Y., and Gronau, R. (1981). 'Expected interruptions in labour force participation and sex-related differences in earnings growth', *The Review of Economic Studies*, 48(4):607–619. doi.org/10.2307/2297200.

4

Wage determination and imperfect competition

Alison L Booth

Introduction

How have labour economists' perspectives about theories of wage determination altered over the past quarter of a century? In the anniversary issue of *Labour Economics*, celebrating 20 years since the journal's inception and 25 years since the establishment of the European Association of Labour Economists, it seems particularly appropriate to consider this question.

It would be fair to say that even a quarter of a century ago, many economists viewed the labour market as intrinsically perfectly competitive. Of course, there were earlier exceptions to this perfectly competitive approach. From our 2014 vantage point, two examples seem especially insightful. These are Joan Robinson's 1933 monopsony theory and Alfred Marshall's 1920 summary of the features of labour that distinguish it from other inputs.

There are a number of different models of wage determination in the labour economics literature, all deviating from perfect competition in various ways. These include search theory, efficiency wages and others, some of which are covered in this volume. Here I shall look only at two. These are my own personal favourites, partly because they can be viewed as representing two polar extremes but also because they are intuitively appealing and tractable.

The first considers a situation with few sellers of labour (wage determination under trade unions), while the second considers a situation in which there are few buyers (wage determination under oligopsony).

In the 20th century, no analyst of the labour market could have failed to be aware of the importance of trade unions. They were typically viewed as operating within an otherwise perfectly competitive labour market and having harmful effects on the economy through their control over the supply of labour. This monopoly power forced up wages, generating rents for those workers fortunate enough to be in employment, and causing allocative inefficiencies. The magnitude of these rents depended crucially on the elasticity of labour demand. The more elastic labour demand is, the smaller is the size of any surplus that could be appropriated.

While there were some rare dissenting voices claiming that trade unions could, in some instances, be efficiency-enhancing, the dominant opinion in the late 1970s was that they caused allocative inefficiencies. From the late 1970s through to the 1990s, there was a tremendous growth in the economics of the trade union. This focused on the wage-setting behaviour of unions as well as measuring their impact on other outcomes. Initially, the models viewed trade union behaviour as a modification of perfect competition in which trade unions represented workers and were characterised by monopoly power. As the years rolled by, the notion that union workers possess monopoly power and expropriate all the surpluses gave way to the idea that the surpluses might be shared between union workers and the firm. Insights from bargaining theory were employed to show how this would be managed. It came as no surprise that the share each party received depended on their relative bargaining power. Moreover, the size of the surplus also mattered. And in time, it became clear that the size of the surplus was positively related to the degree of imperfect competition in the product market.

Paralleling these developments in theories of union wage determination and employment were innovations in macroeconomic thinking. Here, researchers were beginning to utilise models of, for instance, monopolistic competition to explain how small adjustment costs could give rise to large business cycle fluctuations that could happen without any trade union presence. Increasingly, labour economists began to take on board these ideas. Other approaches, such as heterogeneous job characteristics that Salop (1979) incorporated into the theory of the firm, were also to filter into labour economics.

Perhaps the most interesting development in wage determination theories of the past decade or so has been the realisation that employers have some market power in wage setting.[1] This is not only a plausible and reasonably tractable characterisation of the labour market, but it can also help explain certain labour market phenomena. An early example of an oligopsonistic competition model is that of Stevens (1994). Another example is Bhaskar and To (1999), who assume asymmetric information in analysing the impact of minimum wages. Their starting point was that workers have idiosyncratic preferences over employment at different firms, and that these preferences are private information. Manning (2003) further develops this in the context of other characterisations (including search theory, which is the subject of Pierre Cahuc's (2004) paper).

There are a number of other sources of rents in the employment relation. Not only do individuals have heterogeneous preferences for jobs, but they also have differences in mobility costs, and they face imperfect information. Because of this, it takes time for a worker to find an alternative employer who is a perfect substitute for their current one. Moreover, it is expensive for the firm to find another worker who is perfectly substitutable for their current one. This heterogeneity, and search and mobility costs, imply that there are rents in the employment relationship.

The remainder of the chapter describes the perfectly competitive benchmark and wage determination under trade unions. There has been a dramatic decline in research in this area since the early 2000s. I shall discuss whether this happened because of fashion or irrelevance and will argue that unions remain relevant, but that fashion has moved away. I will also explore wage determination under oligopsonistic competition. This is currently the flavour of the decade, and I shall give the reasons why. At the end of the chapter, I will examine where imperfect competition/monopsony theory and trade union economics have helped us better understand wage determination and the workings of labour markets.

This chapter gives only a brief overview. It is not a survey of all the wage determination literature, nor does it touch on the extensive empirical literature on wages and wage inequality. Rather, it simply presents my own view, an idiosyncratic one perhaps, but all as requested by the founding editors of *Labour Economics,* Joop Hartog and Jules Theeuwes. It is to Jules's memory that I dedicate this chapter.

1 Of course this had been realised by many economists years earlier, but the idea has only relatively recently been embraced more widely by labour economists.

The perfectly competitive labour market

Perfectly competitive markets are described in economic theory as those in which no participants (buyers or sellers) have the market power to set the price of a homogeneous product. The conditions for perfect competition are strict; for example, an infinite number of agents, no barriers to entry or exit, perfect factor mobility, perfect information and no transaction costs. While the assumptions underlying perfect competition might sometimes be applicable for auction markets for certain commodities, they are rather less applicable for labour markets.

Labour has several features distinguishing it from other inputs, and that means that labour markets cannot be considered in the same way as the markets for other factor inputs (Marshall, 1920). The two principal distinguishing characteristics of labour are (1) that workers retain ownership of their human capital (in the absence of slavery) and (2) that workers must be present in the workplace for the delivery of their skills. The fact that workers retain ownership of their human capital has the implication that any education or skills associated with employment are the property of the worker, who can therefore exercise some control over the use of the skills, and perhaps extract any surplus associated with them. The fact that workers must be present for the delivery of their skills means that they must live near the workplace.[2] This may constrain the opportunities of other family members and make workers vulnerable to opportunistic behaviour. (We shall return to this point later in the chapter.) This embodiment of human capital within a person also means that the social aspects of the work environment are important.

In spite of these caveats, perfect competition may sometimes serve as a useful benchmark against which to measure imperfectly competitive labour markets and also to measure allocative inefficiency. However, once one accepts that there are rents in the employment relationship, then there is more of a role for policy.

2 This may well change in the future in occupations in which homeworking may become more feasible.

Wage determination under trade unions

Do trade unions still matter?

Although the bargaining models used in trade union theory have a wider application than to unionised labour markets, I shall confine my discussion here to trade unions and union wage setting. The reader may well ask why. After all, we regularly read in the media about the declining power of trade unions, so should we as labour economists forget about the union wage-setting models? In my opinion, we should not. This is not only because the modelling framework is applicable to other non-union situations, but also because union power is not declining across OECD countries to the extent suggested by the union membership figures alone.

Table 4.1: Trade union density and collective bargaining coverage

	Trade union density		Collective bargaining coverage	
	1990	Latest year[i]	1990	Latest year[i]
Australia	39.5	18.0	80	40
Austria	46.9	28.1	98	99
Belgium	53.9	52.0	96	96
Canada	34.0	31.6	38	31.6
Czech Republic	43.5	17.3	–	42.5
Denmark	75.3	68.8	84	80
Estonia	–	8.0	–	19
Finland	72.5	69.9	81	90
France	9.9	7.6	92	90
Germany	31.2	18.5	72	62
Great Britain	38.2	25.8	54	32.7
Greece	34.1	24.0	70	65
Hungary	49.1	16.8	–	33.5
Iceland	92.9	79.3	96.4	88
Ireland	48.5	33.4	60	44
Italy	38.8	35.1	83	80
Japan	25.4	19.0	23	16
Luxembourg	46.4	37.3	60	58
Mexico	22.4	13.2	–	7
Netherlands	24.3	18.2	82	82.3
New Zealand	49.5	20.8	61	17

	Trade union density		Collective bargaining coverage	
	1990	Latest year[i]	1990	Latest year[i]
Norway	58.6	54.6	70	74
Portugal	27.9	19.3	79	45
Slovakia	64.2	17.2	–	40
Spain	12.5	15.9	82.2	84.4
Sweden	80.0	67.7	89	91
Switzerland	22.7	17.8	48	48
United States	15.5	11.3	18.3	13.6
OECD	40.1	28.0	70.3	62.1

Notes: [i] refers to the latest year for which data were available when searched in May 2013.

Source: OECD.

While in the 1990s trade union density averaged 40.1 per cent across OECD countries, by 2009 it had declined to 28 per cent.[3] (Trade union density refers to the number of trade union members as a percentage of wage and salary earners.) This is indeed a large drop, but the averages conceal an extraordinary degree of heterogeneity across countries, as inspection of Table 4.1 reveals. For example, of the 28 countries listed in the table, six have union density exceeding 50 per cent, and four have union density exceeding two-thirds (these are Denmark, Finland, Iceland and Sweden). On the other hand, 14 countries have union density of less than one-fifth of the workforce. Can we conclude from this that unions are a dead institution? I think the answer is no. Union presence is still very important for some countries, especially European ones.

For European countries, Australia and New Zealand, the influence of trade unions at the macroeconomic level is better indicated by the extent of collective bargaining coverage of the workforce, rather than by union density. (The definition of the collective bargaining coverage rate, or coverage rate for short, is the number of workers covered by wage bargaining agreements as a proportion of all wage and salary earners.) Across OECD countries, union coverage averaged 70 per cent in 1990 and declined to 62 per cent two decades later.

3 The figures given in this paper come from the OECD database on trade unions and from Visser (2011).

France provides an interesting example of how misleading focusing on union membership alone can be. With just under 8 per cent of the workforce union members, nonetheless, union coverage is high, at 90 per cent. Clearly, a lot of French workers are taking a free ride on union membership. Elsewhere, others and I have argued that union coverage is a better measure of union influence than density, and that the level at which union bargaining occurs is also important (see, for example, Booth, 1995; Boeri et al., 2001; Fitzenberger et al., 2013).

However, there are still some countries in Table 4.1 in which both density and coverage are low. For example, in the US, only 11 per cent of the workforce belongs to a union, and only 14 per cent are covered by union collective bargaining. Mexico is another example of a low coverage country. Britain has a union density of 26 per cent and coverage of 33 per cent. Given that union density is declining in most industrialised countries, and that in many countries only a minority of the workforce is covered by unions, do we really need to worry about providing appropriate models of trade union behaviour? Or might we be better advised to adhere to other theories of wage setting and worker behaviour?

One answer, which we mentioned above, is that union bargaining models are generalisable and hence more widely applicable. Not only may they characterise explicit labour contracts between the union and management, but the models are also relevant to a broader class of situations than those in which a union explicitly represents workers.[4]

Moreover, trade union influence in a particular economy extends beyond the direct measure of union power suggested by the union density and coverage figures. For example – and this is especially appropriate to the US institutional framework – the threat of union organisation of a non-union sector may provoke management to provide wages and working conditions that mimic those negotiated in union firms.

The idea is that the non-union workers will be less prone to unionise, therefore, because there is little difference between their welfare in the union firm and another non-union firm providing matching benefits. Furthermore, modelling the behaviour of trade unions in partially unionised economies is

4 Indeed, union contracts may be viewed simply as an explicit formulation of a wider variety of labour contracts that are found in many labour markets. Where non-union firms face an incumbent workforce with a degree of bargaining power, management and workers may be in a situation of bilateral monopoly that can be characterised by a union-firm bargaining model (Booth 1995).

obviously of importance for sectoral analysis of the parts of the economy that are heavily unionised or where a powerful sector is unionised, and there are knock-on effects for the rest of the economy through particular institutional aspects of wage setting. In addition, the threat of union organisation may provoke management into directing resources into anti-union activities and resource allocation in the non-union sector unless it is indirectly affected by trade unions (Pencavel 1991).

Why has labour economists' interest in trade unions declined despite the fact that trade unions are still important agents in many OECD countries? Is it due to fashion? Or does it perhaps reflect irrelevance – to the largest and most powerful economy, the US – of trade unions? The answer is probably a bit of both. The US dominates research agendas with its prestigious journals and its huge population. And unions are extremely weak in the US; trade union coverage was only 13.6 per cent in 2008, having declined from 18.3 per cent in 1990, while US union density was a mere 15.5 per cent in 1990 and dropped to 11.4 per cent in 2010.

Is there another possible reason for the declining interest of labour economists in trade unions? Could it be that economists have already said everything they usefully can about unions? The bulk of labour economists seem to think so, given the decline in published papers on this topic over the past decade since two edited volumes in the early 2000s.[5] In addition, other interesting areas and methodologies have arisen, attracting researchers into less well-trodden areas where they hope to make a bigger contribution. We shall be discussing one of these alternative approaches to wage determination later in the chapter. But first we will briefly consider the economics of the trade union.[6]

An overview of the analytical framework

How do economists define trade unions? A trade union is an organised association of workers formed for the protection and promotion of their common interests. The standard view of unions is that they are monopoly organisations that improve the welfare of members, principally by raising wages above the competitive level. For a trade union to be able to increase wage rates above the competitive level, there must be some surplus that can be shared between the firm and the union, and the union must have some

5 See Boeri et al. (2001) and Addison and Schnabel (2003).

6 Readers who wish to follow a more technical exposition are referred to Booth (1995) and Cahuc and Zylberberg (2004: Chapter 7), while a European overview can be found in Boeri et al. (2001).

bargaining power to induce the firm to share this surplus. How can a union achieve such power? One way is to try to organise all workers in an industry, thereby acting as a monopolist over the supply of labour.[7]

Even if a union controls labour supply, it will not necessarily be able to negotiate a large wage increase relative to the competitive level. The magnitude of the union wage depends crucially on the elasticity of labour demand in that sector as well as union bargaining strength. There can be little doubt that, if unions emerge in competitive markets, high union wages introduce allocative inefficiencies into the economy through the distortion of factor prices. Without unions, allocative efficiency is associated with the equalisation of the marginal products of identical factor inputs across sectors. With higher wages in the union sector, union firms employ fewer workers. Displaced union workers crowd into the non-union sector, lowering wages there. As a result, too few workers are employed in the union sector where output falls, while too many workers are employed, and too many goods are produced, in the non-union sector. There is a deadweight efficiency loss, because the value of marginal products in the two sectors is not identical. In addition, there are distributional issues to consider, and longer-run effects due to the substitution of capital for labour. Furthermore, in unionised sectors, there may be underinvestment in capital through the hold-up problem (see, for example, Grout 1984).

Even within this framework, there are arguments suggesting that, in the presence of imperfect information and uncertainty, unions may enhance efficiency. To the extent that unions reduce labour turnover and negotiating costs, they may increase the available surplus to be shared between parties (Freeman and Medoff 1984). Of course, there may be interdependence between the monopoly and efficiency roles of trade unions: unless the union has some bargaining power, it may be unable to increase efficiency.[8]

7 The earliest successful unions were craft unions, which became established because of a combination of high demand for skilled labour during industrialisation, and the control of trained labour by skilled workers through the apprenticeship system. The emergence of general or industrial unions followed a different path. During industrialisation, the huge surplus of unskilled displaced agricultural labour made manipulation of labour supply impossible. A depression, coupled with a readily available pool of substitute workers, could destroy a union. To ensure survival, a general union needed political support or very high levels of membership. Obtaining the latter was difficult in the early stages of unionisation, when there were no immediately obvious wage benefits because the union had not yet obtained any power (see Booth (1995)).

8 The most commonly used bargaining models for wage determination are the game theoretic approaches. These are widely used in labour economics theory regardless of the particular modelling framework.

This discussion of allocative inefficiency assumes that the union has emerged in an economy characterised by competitive product and labour markets. But there is considerable evidence that, in modern industrialised countries, many product markets are characterised by imperfect competition. Moreover, non-union firms may also face an incumbent workforce with a degree of bargaining power. Thus, even in the absence of unionisation, management and workers may be in a situation of bilateral monopoly. An important question arises as to whether or not the replacement of individual bargaining by collective bargaining generates additional inefficiencies and misallocation of resources in situations where markets were previously not functioning in accordance with the textbook model of perfect competition. The majority of formal trade union models in the literature assume a perfectly competitive product market to allow the models to focus on wage and employment determination in the simplest environment. Nonetheless, it is an empirical regularity that imperfections in product and labour markets are correlated (see inter alia Stewart, 1990; Dobbelaere and Mairesse, 2013).

As noted above, the existence of a potential surplus is a necessary condition for union success in its goal of improving union workers' welfare. The surplus may arise from a variety of sources, the most obvious being market imperfections or regulation of the particular industry. In non-competitive firms and industries where firms are making surpluses, unions with sufficient power can insist that management increases wages without threatening the demise of the firm. Thus, one would expect a higher probability of union organisation in non-competitive industries than in competitive product markets.

As noted, a condition for a union to achieve wage gains is that the union has the necessary power to force the firm to share any surplus with the union. An alternative view is that the firm may be willing to grant higher wages in return for increases in productivity that increase the surplus available from the firm. And although unions may cause wages to increase in the union sector, neither employment nor the firm's profitability need necessarily be greatly affected, since the firms' higher labour costs may be offset by improved productivity. Since there are a variety of theories suggesting opposing union effects on productivity, it is ultimately an empirical issue as to whether unions are associated with increased or decreased productivity.

Next, we consider an alternative approach to modelling wage determination that has captured the interest of labour economists – especially European ones – over recent years. This approach assumes that the labour market is characterised by oligopsony and monopsonistic competition. I shall use these terms interchangeably in what follows.

Oligopsony in the labour market

An intuitively appealing framework for modelling oligopsony is based on the assumption that workers with identical skills and abilities have heterogeneous preferences over the non-wage job characteristics associated with a job. What might these be? These might be working hours, the distance of the firm from home, the people working at the firm and the like. Bhaskar and To (1999) argued that a useful metaphor for heterogeneous preferences is in terms of the costs of travel to work (Hotelling 1929, Salop 1979). Of course, these costs can be interpreted not only as travel costs but also as a measure of a worker's idiosyncratic preferences over job characteristic space. Hence, the costs represent both physical and psychological aspects, which vary across workers and result in some being willing to work at a particular establishment for a lower wage than at another.

What is the evidence for oligopsony?

The current thinking about oligopsony is based on the following incontrovertible assumptions. Not only do individuals have idiosyncratic preferences for jobs, but they also have different mobility costs and face imperfect information. Because of this, it takes time for a worker to find an alternative employer who is a perfect substitute for their current one. Moreover, it is expensive for the firm to find another worker who is perfectly substitutable for their current one. This heterogeneity, coupled with mobility and search costs, implies that there are rents in the employment relationship. The larger the rents accruing to an employer and worker from an ongoing employment relationship, the more important imperfect competition is to labour markets.

It is all very well to agree that these arguments are intuitively appealing. (And after all, they do find support in casual empiricism and one's own experiences.) But what do empirical studies have to say about heterogeneous preferences and mobility costs? The answer is not very much, and this is an area that would benefit from further research. While McCue and Reed (1996) provide some evidence, this is for the US, which may not be typical of other economies, including those in Europe.[9] Manning (2011, p. 983) provides some evidence about hiring costs. To summarise, although those cover a broad range of estimates, hiring costs seem to be around 5 per cent of total labour costs. Manning argues that we do not yet know enough about the hiring process, including the costs associated with hiring, and how these vary across worker types and firm types.

A simple analytical framework

A popular model used to capture the essence of imperfectly competitive labour markets is an equilibrium search framework. Since this is discussed extensively in Manning (2011), I will not replicate that discussion here. To a large extent, it is a matter of taste which modelling framework one wants to use. I find the monopsony framework as described in Bhaskar and To (1999) appealing, as it provides a simpler equilibrium framework than the search theoretical approach. As noted in Booth and Coles (2007, p. 1664):

> Like the Nash bargaining approach, the Bhaskar and To (1999) framework implies equilibria and wage compression; that wages need not increase one-to-one with an increase in labour market productivity. The central advantage of this framework is that we need not specify matching functions, free entry conditions and so on or describe equilibria wage dispersion. The discussion is consequently clearer, as there are no thick market or congestion externalities to complicate matters.

Bhaskar and To (1999) simply assume that workers have idiosyncratic preferences over employment at different firms, and that those preferences are private information. Thus, a firm's wage offer depends on how much they believe the employee prefers working there rather than elsewhere. This assumption usefully summarises the variety of reasons for imperfect competition in the labour market.[10]

9 McCue and Reed (1996) utilise survey evidence in which workers were asked about their willingness to accept different low-wage jobs at various wages and they found a significant heterogeneity in tastes.

10 The market structure is analogous to a Hotelling pricing game with at least two competing firms who differ in their non-pecuniary attributes such as location and other non-wage job characteristics. Workers have heterogeneous preferences: the more distant the firm's characteristics from the worker's preferred characteristics the larger the worker's disutility cost associated with employment at that firm. See also Rosen's (1974) related article on product differentiation.

How does this framework help us to understand labour markets?

How have these models of oligopsony and monopolistic competition helped us understand labour markets? Perhaps the most analysed area in which oligopsony has improved our understanding of the labour market is minimum wages. Stigler (1946) showed that a minimum wage can increase employment under monopsony. But the situation is more realistic where there might be a few employers with market power. Bhaskar and To (1999) make an important theoretical contribution in this regard. In addition, there is a whole raft of papers looking empirically at whether or not the introduction of a minimum wage will affect employment. Examples are the influential work by Card and Krueger (1995) and, in the European context, the comprehensive research by Dolado et al. (1996). Holmlund (2014) also discusses this extensively. Other instances where monopoly and oligopsonistic competition have improved our understanding relate to the gender pay gap. (See Manning (2011) for a survey.)

There is an additional area in which oligopsony has increased our understanding of the workings of the labour market, and this relates to the economics of work-related training. According to orthodox human capital theory, workers should always finance work-related general training. If firms were to pay for it, they would be vulnerable to the hold-up problem: the worker could simply quit after being trained, taking with them the embodied general training, and the firm would get no return to the investment.

And yet empirical evidence has demonstrated that employers do finance work-related general training (see, for instance, the findings of Booth and Bryan 2005). In a labour market characterised by oligopsonistic wage setting, it can be shown that the associated wage compression will increase the incentive for firms to invest in general training, provided that post-training productivity net of training costs is increasing in training at a faster rate than wages. Important papers in this area are by Stevens (1994) and Acemoglu and Pischke (1999a, 1999b). However, as those authors indicate, the equilibrium amount of training provided may be suboptimal from society's viewpoint. The empirical predictions of these models involving wage compression are that the firm may finance general training and that the training firm's wages will be less than the net marginal product.[11]

11 Acemoglu and Pischke (1999a, 1999b) considered only absolute wage compression. Booth and Zoega (2004) extended their approach to consider relative wage compression and show that the latter approach encompasses a wider range of institutional arrangements and is therefore more general.

Why are these models important for labour economics? Because they are able to explain survey evidence showing that firms pay for the acquisition of general training by their workforce in contradiction to what would be predicted under perfect competition. Moreover, in a study estimating the impact on training of the introduction in the UK of a national minimum wage, Arulampalam et al. (2004) also find evidence in support of these models. A perfectly competitive minimum wage would reduce the training of affected workers, but these authors found evidence that training increased.

Finally, we must mention direct evidence of labour market power that can be obtained by estimating the elasticity of the labour supply curve to an individual establishment. Manning (2003, 2011) utilises a dynamic monopsony model based on Burdett and Mortensen (1998) to obtain a formal estimate of the elasticity of labour supply, which can then be confronted with the data. Manning (2003) provides an extensive discussion of this, encompassing both the elasticity of the labour supply curve to an individual establishment as well as the sensitivity of separations. The essence of monopsonistically competitive labour markets is that labour supply to a firm is imperfectly elastic with respect to the wage rate. The intuition is that, where workers have heterogeneous preferences or face mobility costs, firms can offer lower wages without immediately losing their workforce. This is in stark contrast with the perfectly competitive extreme, in which the elasticity is infinite. Monopsony suggests that the lower the ability of a worker to exploit outside options and move from job to job, the further a worker's wage is below their marginal product, and the greater the share of rents that the employer can appropriate from the worker.

A simple test of whether labour markets are imperfectly or perfectly competitive involves estimating the wage elasticity of labour supply to a firm. Studies that have done this using individual-level data find that wage elasticities of labour supply are typically very small (see the summary table in Manning 2011). Indeed, these estimates of the wage elasticity of labour supply to a firm are so far from the perfectly competitive prediction of an infinite elasticity that it would be difficult to make a case that labour markets are perfectly competitive. This has implications for policy based on simplistic modelling of the labour market as perfectly competitive. It is interesting that a parallel stream of labour economics literature, focusing on employer-provided training and the conditions under which firms will finance it, has reached similar conclusions.

A final example of how models of oligopsony and monopolistic competition help us to understand labour markets is in the field of education. Booth and Coles (2007) show how, in a model with heterogeneous workers and home production, increasing returns to education interact with imperfectly competitive labour markets. Increasing returns to education are exacerbated by frictional labour markets because of an increasing wage competitiveness effect. This arises because, in a frictional labour market, firms bid more competitively for workers' services as the value of employment increases. And since, in frictional labour markets, wage compression decreases at higher productivity levels, the marginal returns to education are further increased as education increases. This has policy implications; the authors suggest an employment subsidy that could be efficiently targeted as a public childcare program.

Conclusion

A striking feature of the past 20 years since the foundation of *Labour Economics* has been the expansion in the development and application of models that explicitly deal with imperfectly competitive labour markets, be they based on bargaining models or models of oligopsonistic competition. These are proving to be rich avenues of research.

Another striking feature of the past 20 years has been the overall drop in interest in the economics of the trade union (although there are notable individual exceptions). I believe this is a shame for the following reasons. First, labour markets are typically not competitive. Second, while union membership has been declining, collective bargaining coverage is far more important than density, because of institutional arrangements within Europe and in some other OECD countries. Third, the US has unusually low density and coverage, but even there, the threat of unionisation imparts some relevance to the union model. Fourth, as I have suggested in this chapter, labour economists' research on unions has diminished not only because of fashion but also in part because of US dominance of the academy. *Labour Economics*, a European-based journal, provides some counterbalance to this. It will be interesting to see what the literature looks like another 20 years hence.

Finally, should imperfectly competitive models be used whenever researchers are modelling the labour market? Some people would argue only in cases when the predictions and comparative statics of the imperfectly competitive model differ from those of the competitive model. Of course, to know this, one needs to know precisely what the predictions and comparative statics of the respective models are. However, there is now a growing –and some would suggest, lamentable – trend for labour economists not to use any analytical framework. The syllabi of some labour economics courses I have seen include little about imperfectly competitive models. Moreover, atheoretic randomised experiments are increasingly being used in labour economics and represent an alternative methodology that can reveal the effect of an intervention without the need for any analytical framework. Nonetheless, for policymakers to be able to determine if an intervention is required in the first place, there does need to be some analytical framework to act as a guide. In the perfectly competitive model of labour markets, for example, typically no intervention or regulation would be justified. However, labour economics has moved far beyond this position, with new ideas being incorporated into modelling wage determination in imperfectly competitive labour markets and with the availability of better datasets.

Acknowledgements

This chapter was first published as Booth, A.L. (2014). 'Wage determination and imperfect competition', *Labour Economics*, 30:53–58. doi.org/10.1016/j.labeco.2014.06.010.

This chapter was originally prepared for the 20th anniversary issue of *Labour Economics* and the 25th anniversary celebration of the European Association of Labour Economists (EALE), held in Turin in September 2013. Thanks to Joop Hartog for his helpful suggestions, and also to my discussant, Bernd Fitzenberger.

References

Acemoglu, D., and Pischke, J.-S. (1999a). 'Beyond Becker: Training in imperfect labour markets', *The Economic Journal*, 109(453):F112–F142. www.jstor.org/stable/2565588.

Acemoglu, D., and Pischke, J.-S. (1999b). 'The structure of wages and investment in general training', *Journal of Political Economy*, 107(3):539–572. doi.org/10.1086/250071.

Addison, J.T., and Schnabel, C. (2003). *International Handbook of Trade Unions*, Edward Elgar.

Arulampalam, W., Booth, A.L., and Bryan, M.L. (2004). 'Training and the new minimum wage', *The Economic Journal*, 114(494):C87–C94. doi.org/10.1111/j.0013-0133.2003.00197.x.

Bhaskar, V., and To, T. (1999). 'Minimum wages for Ronald McDonald monopsonies: A theory of monopsonistic competition', *The Economic Journal*, 109(455):190–203. www.jstor.org/stable/2565930.

Boeri, T., Brugiavini, A., and Calmfors, L., eds. (2001). *The Role of Unions in the Twenty-First Century*, Oxford University Press.

Booth, A.L. (1995). *The Economics of the Trade Union*, Cambridge University Press.

Booth, A.L., and Bryan, M.L. (2005). 'Testing some predictions of human capital theory: New training evidence from Britain', *Review of Economics and Statistics*, 87(2):391–394. doi.org/10.1162/0034653053970357.

Booth, A.L., and Coles, M.G. (2007). 'A microfoundation for increasing returns in human capital accumulation and the under-participation trap', *European Economic Review*, 51(7):1661–1681. doi.org/10.1016/j.euroecorev.2006.12.004.

Booth, A.L., and Zoega, G. (2004). 'Is wage compression a necessary condition for firm-financed general training?', *Oxford Economic Papers*, 56(1):88–97. www.jstor.org/stable/3488914.

Burdett, K., and Mortensen, D.T. (1998). 'Wage differentials, employer size, and unemployment', *International Economic Review*, 39(2):257–273.

Cahuc, P., and Zylberberg, A. (2004). *Collective Bargaining, in Labour Economics*, MIT Press.

Card, D., and Krueger, A.B. (1995). *Myth and Measurement: The New Economics of the Minimum Wage*, Princeton University Press.

Dobbelaere, S., and Mairesse, J. (2013). 'Panel data estimates of the production function and product and labour market imperfections', *Journal of Applied Econometrics*, 28(1):1–46. doi.org/10.1002/jae.1256.

Dolado, J., Kramarz, F., Machin, S., Manning, A., and Margolis, D. (1996). 'The economic impact of minimum wages in Europe', *The Economic Policy*, 319:1–50.

Fitzenberger, B., Kohn, K., and Lembcke, A.C. (2013). 'Union density and varieties of coverage: The anatomy of union wage effects in Germany', *Industrial Relations Research Journal*, 66(1):169–197. doi.org/10.1177/001979391306600107.

Freeman, R.B., and Medoff, J.L. (1984). *What Do Unions Do?*, Basic Books.

Grout, P.A. (1984). 'Investment and wages in the absence of binding contracts: A Nash bargaining approach'. *Econometrica*, 52(2):449–460. doi.org/10.2307/1911498.

Hotelling, D.H. (1929). 'Stability in competition', *The Economic Journal*, 39(153): 41–57. doi.org/10.2307/2224214.

Manning, A. (2003). *Monopsony in Motion: Imperfect Competition in Labour Markets*, Princeton University Press.

Manning, A. (2011). 'Imperfect competition in the labour market', in *Handbook of Labour Economics*, vol. 4b, pp. 973–1041, Elsevier.

Marshall, A. (1920). *Principles of Economics: An Introductory Volume*, 8th ed., Macmillan.

McCue, K., and Reed, W.R. (1996). 'New evidence on workers' willingness to pay for job attributes', *Southern Economic Journal*, 62(3):647–653. doi.org/10.2307/1060884.

OECD and AIAS. (2021). *Institutional Characteristics of Trade Unions, Wage Setting, State Intervention and Social Pacts*, OECD Publishing.

Pencavel, J. (1991). *Labour Markets under Trade Unionism*, Blackwell.

Robinson, J. (1933). *The Economics of Imperfect Competition*, Macmillan.

Rosen, S. (1974). 'Hedonic prices and implicit markets: Product differentiation in pure competition', *Journal of Political Economy*, 82(1):34–55. www.jstor.org/stable/1830899.

Salop, S.C. (1979). 'Monopolistic competition with outside goods', *The Bell Journal of Economics*, 10(1):141–156. doi.org/10.2307/3003323.

Stevens, M. (1994). 'A theoretical model of on-the-job training with imperfect competition', *Oxford Economic Papers*, 46(4):537–562. doi.org/10.1093/oxfordjournals.oep.a042147.

Stewart, M.B. (1990). 'Union wage differentials, product market influences and the division of rents', *The Economic Journal*, 100:1122–1137.

Stigler, G. (1946). 'The economics of minimum wage legislation', *American Economic Review*, 36:358–365.

5

Testing some predictions of human capital theory: New training evidence from Great Britain

Alison L Booth and Mark L Bryan

Introduction

Acemoglu and Pischke (1999a, 1999b) show that, in oligopsonistic labour markets, some of the predictions of the human capital model are overturned. In particular, the wage returns to general training may be less than the productivity returns, and firms may find it profitable to pay for training even though it is general. In this chapter, we summarise the main predictions of the various human capital theories for wages and cost sharing and confront these with important new data from the British Household Panel Survey (BHPS) for the period 1998–2000.

Hypotheses

The main predictions of the various human capital theories for wages and cost sharing are summarised in Table 5.1

Table 5.1: Predictions of human capital theory

Row	Model	Who pays	Divergence between wages (w) and net marginal productivity (MP) at Training Firm	Transferability of training
[1]	Perfect competition, general training	Worker	None	Fully transferable
[2]	As above, but with credit constraints	Sharing	$w > \text{MP}$ during training, and $w < \text{MP}$ after training	Transferable, but wage returns elsewhere greater than returns at firm providing training
[3]	Perfect competition, specific training	Sharing	$w > \text{MP}$ during training, and $w < \text{MP}$ after training	Nontransferable
[4]	Perfect competition, mix of general and specific training	Sharing	$w > \text{MP}$ during training, and $w < \text{MP}$ after training	Partially transferable; wage returns elsewhere less than returns at firm providing training
[5]	Oligopsonistic labor market, general training	Firm	$w < \text{MP}$ during and after training, implying rents for the firm	Fully transferable; wage returns elsewhere greater than returns at firm providing training

According to human capital theory – row [1] of Table 5.1 – workers in competitive labour markets will invest in general work-related training by receiving low training wages and will reap the returns by receiving higher wages afterwards (Becker, 1964). Workers who cannot afford to accept low wages during general training will be adversely affected by credit market constraints, barring them from borrowing to finance their investment. However, should the firm be willing to act as a lender, it can pay workers more than their marginal product (net of training costs) during training and less afterwards – see row [2]. The firm will only agree to such a contract if some mechanism can be devised, such as an apprenticeship contract or a minimum employment guarantee, to bind workers to the firm until repayment of the loan. The magnitude of the wedge between wages and productivity reflects the degree of cost sharing. Because training is transferable across firms, trained workers changing employers should get a greater return than they received in the firm providing the training and the loan.

In the specific training model, it is efficient for the firm and worker to share both the costs and the net returns of the training investment (Hashimoto, 1981). Consequently, workers' wages will be above net productivity during training and below after training, and the magnitude of this wedge will reflect the degree of cost sharing – see row [3] of Table 5.1. By definition, the training will not be transferable across firms.

If training comprises a mix of general and specific components, workers will finance their general training, and firms will share the costs of the specific training. Because there will be some cost sharing, wages at the training firm will be greater than net productivity during training and less than productivity after training – see row [4]. Wages at subsequent firms will reflect returns only to the general component of training, and consequently will be less than wages at the training firm (in which there is some return to the worker to the shared investment in specific training).

However, in a labour market characterised by oligopsonistic wage-setting – as in the new training literature – it can be shown that the associated wage compression may increase the incentive for firms to invest in general training, provided that post-training productivity net of training costs is increasing in training at a faster rate than wages.[1] However, the equilibrium amount of training provided may be suboptimal from society's viewpoint. The predictions are that the firm may finance general training and that the training firm's wages will be less than the net marginal product. According to the contracting model of Loewenstein and Spletzer (1998), there may be a greater wage return to training in future firms than in the current firm if a minimum-wage guarantee binds in the current job. If it does, the employer can extract rents from providing general training. According to the model of Acemoglu and Pischke (1999a, 1999b) – based on mobility costs – although all workers receive a positive return to their training, the current employer has monopsony power over the worker because of the mobility costs. Consequently, wages will increase more with the future employer than with the current employer. These predictions are summarised in row [5].

Finally, consider the effects of asymmetry of information about the value of firm-provided training, where the firm providing general training knows its value, but other firms do not. This can affect training transferability in an otherwise competitive labour market. For example, according to the asymmetric information model of Acemoglu and Pischke (1998), training is rewarded more in the current firm than in outside firms. This is because the current firm will pay higher wages to retain high-ability workers, whereas

1 For examples of the new training literature, see inter alia, Katz and Ziderman 1990), Stevens (1994), Chang and Wang (1996), Loewenstein and Spletzer (1998), and Acemoglu and Pischke (1999a, 1999b).

low-ability workers will be dismissed. Some of the high-ability workers who need to leave their jobs will be treated as low-ability workers in the outside market. Because training and ability are complements, training will be valued less for workers who have been laid off or who have quit. Consequently, in the outside market, these workers will receive lower returns on their training. The predictions of this model are as for row [4].

A formal qualification associated with a training course might be viewed as a means of conveying to the outside market the value of the employer-provided general training and of the worker's ability. For this reason, one might expect accredited training to have a larger effect on wages in future firms than non-accredited training, ceteris paribus. One might also expect it to be financed by the individual, because it is transferable. Provided the qualification is a good signal of worker ability, the predictions of the model with accreditations for training are therefore the same as for row [1] – the individual will pay and will get all the pay returns. The predictions of some hypotheses are observationally equivalent. For example, two models predict that transferable training might have bigger returns to subsequent firms than to the firms at which training actually takes place – see rows [2] and [5]. However, some predictions are quite distinct. For example, the models in rows [I] and [5] predict that training is transferable, but the first predicts that workers pay for it, whereas the fifth predicts that firms do.

The data and estimates

Our data are from the BHPS, a nationally representative survey of private households in Britain. The training questions were expanded from wave eight – conducted in 1998 – onward, and we use data from waves eight to 10. Respondents are asked how many training schemes they started in the past year, and detailed information is collected on the longest three events (or all events if fewer than three). This information includes the duration of each training event, its type, where it took place, how it was financed and if it led to a qualification. We do not know the date at which the training event occurred within a given year, or the wages an individual received during training. We have wage data only for the annual survey points.

Our estimating sample comprises private sector full-time (FT) employees aged 16-65 years, with valid information on our main variables and who did not report more than a calendar year of training. This gives 8,316 person-years, for which training was received in 2,575 (or 31 per cent of) cases.

Our training variable measures any training schemes or courses (whether employer-provided or not) received by individuals since September 1 in the previous year to increase or improve their skills in the current job.[2] It excludes spells of FT education and leisure courses.

For each wave of data, approximately 30 per cent of individuals received training. The (conditional) mean number of training events is 2.05. Over half those receiving training (52 per cent) experienced one event, 24 per cent two events, 12 per cent three events, and 12 per cent more than three events. The vast majority of training (85 per cent) is regarded by recipients as general. An even larger proportion (89 per cent) is viewed as employer-financed, and respondents report almost no explicit cost sharing.[3]

We estimate a fixed-effects (FE) model of the natural logarithm of the real (1998 prices) hourly wage w_{ijt}, of individual i in job j at time t:

2 The survey asks for details of up to three training events received since September I last year. The precise question is:

> Was this course or training: (i) To help you get started in your current job? (ii) To increase your skills in your current job? (iii) To improve your skills in the current job? (iv) To prepare you for a job or jobs you might do in the future? (v) To develop your skills generally?

The categories are not mutually exclusive. We redefined the first category as induction training, which is reported for only 12 per cent of events. Because it is difficult to see any distinction between (ii) and (iii), we combined training to increase/improve skills in the current job into a single type – skills in the current job. Training events are viewed as increasing/improving current skills in nearly 85 per cent of cases, and future skills in 59 per cent of cases. Some 85 per cent of events are viewed as improving general skills. There is comparatively little variation across gender. There is overlap of the training categories, particularly current job skills and general skills, where the correlation coefficient is 0.75. Only 5.7 per cent of events are described as general skills training only. Because it is not possible to construct meaningful separate variables for each of these types (as respondents typically view their training as falling into a number of different categories), we dropped the separate general training indicator. We focus on current job skills training because we are primarily interested in skills investments intended to have a direct effect on productivity and in the subsequent portability of these skills.

3 Respondents were asked 'Which statement or statements on this card describe how any fees were paid, either for the course or for the examinations?' The non-mutually exclusive categories include: no fees; the respondent or family paid; the employer or future employer paid; or it was financed in some other way. Booth and Bryan (2002) report this in detail. The raw data indicate that the employer is reported as financing just over 60 per cent of events. The substantial proportion of individuals reporting *no fees* may suggest economic naiveté on the part of respondents, for it is unlikely that any training activity is truly costless. At a minimum, there will be some loss of production while individuals train (in the absence of pure learning by doing, which is not captured in the BHPS training questions). Individuals not self-financing training, and who see no direct evidence of the employer paying, may report that no one pays. We found that individuals tend to report no fees when the training location is internal to the employing organisation, and in our view, this suggests the costs are borne by the employer. In our multivariate analysis, we therefore combine the *no fees* and *employer finance* categories, which together account for nearly 90 per cent of training finance. We experimented with disaggregating these categories and found it made little difference to our results, so we report the aggregated measure because of the larger cell sizes.

$$(1)\ w_{ijt} = x'_{ijt}\beta + T'_{it}\alpha + D'_{t}\gamma + \mu_i + v_{ij} + \varepsilon_{ijt}$$

where x'_{ijt} is a vector of characteristics influencing the wage, T'_{it} denotes measures of training accumulated from the start of the sample period, and D_t denotes year-specific dummy variables. Unobservable characteristics comprise a fixed effect μ_i, an employer match-specific component v_{ij}, and a transitory effect ε_{ijt}. We approximate v_{ij} by an employer-specific effect v_j, captured by a dummy variable taking the value 1 throughout the duration of a new job (if an individual changes jobs), and 0 otherwise; and another dummy capturing any second new job (a maximum of two job changes can be observed). The base is the first job observed in the panel.[4] Our approach follows Loewenstein and Spletzer (1998); the main empirical difference is that they estimated a first-differenced version of the wage equation, whereas we estimate the FE wage equation (1) using within-group methods.[5] We did this to exploit more fully the three-year span of data.

We distinguish between training undertaken with the current employer to increase or improve skills in the current job and similar training undertaken with previous employers. We separate training into three types – employer-financed current job skills training, self-financed current job skills training, and a residual category of other forms of training. In an additional specification, we distinguish between training leading to qualifications – accredited training – and training that does not. Some 1,269 individuals received employer-financed training during the three waves, and only 127 undertook self-financed training. We investigated different functional forms for the accumulated training measures, to allow current training to have a different effect from previously acquired training, but were unable to find robust results that distinguished the various models.[6] Therefore, our training measures are simple cumulative totals of training received.

4 The individual FE in equation (1) controls for individual, and therefore gender-specific, heterogeneity in the returns to time-invariant characteristics. We tested if male and female observations could be pooled, and could not reject the hypothesis (P-value 0.36). Therefore, equation (1) is estimated on men and women combined. The FE model also allows for non-random female participation insofar as it is due to time-invariant characteristics.

5 Thus, the employer-specific effect in Loewenstein and Spletzer's differenced equation is represented by a simple impulse dummy variable taking the value 1 when the employer changes, and 0 otherwise. We did this to exploit more fully the 3-year span of data.

6 We experimented with linear, quadratic, log and square-root functions in an equation for wage growth between waves eight and 10 in which training received in each wave was entered separately. The lack of precision in the estimates appeared to stem from the smaller cell sizes and larger effect of measurement error in the disaggregated training measures.

Table 5.2: The effect of training incidence and events on wages: Fixed-effects model

Variable	Mean	[1]	[2]	[3]	[4]
Dependent variable: *ln*(wage)	1.771	–	–	–	–
Employer-financed current skills training – incidence and counts					
Current emp. – incidence	0.327	0.0122 (0.97)	0.0240** (2.28)	–	–
Current emp. – count	0.694	0.0079* (1.70)	–	0.0104*** (2.69)	–
Previous emp. – incidence	0.028	0.1014** (2.51)	0.0779*** (3.38)	–	–
Previous emp. – count	0.051	-0.0117 (0.65)	–	0.0243** (2.41)	–
Employer-financed current skills training, by accreditation status – counts					
Current emp. – accredited	0.231	–	–	–	0.0191** (2.55)
Current emp. – nonaccredited	0.463	–	–	–	0.0075* (1.66)
Previous emp. – accredited	0.021	–	–	–	0.0529*** (2.91)
Previous emp. – nonaccredited	0.030	–	–	–	0.0115 (0.94)
Self-financed current skills training – incidence and counts					
Curr. and prev. emp. – incidence	0.031	0.0168 (0.35)	0.0245 (0.80)	–	–
Curr. and prev. emp. – counts	0.040	0.0041 (0.13)	–	0.0148 (0.72)	0.0142 (0.69)
Other training – incidence and counts					
Current emp. – incidence	0.100	-0.0045 (0.16)	0.0227 (1.33)	–	–
Current emp. – counts	0.133	0.0221 (1.27)	–	0.0190* (1.77)	0.0189* (1.76)
Previous emp. – incidence	0.011	0.0754 (1.22)	0.0759** (2.22)	–	–
Previous emp. – counts	0.016	0.0019 (0.05)	–	0.0408** (2.08)	0.0396** (2.02)
Other characteristics					
Employer match 1	0.090	0.0202 (1.49)	0.0170 (1.26)	0.0295** (2.24)	0.0287** (2.18)
Employer match 2	0.010	0.0537** (2.18)	0.0470* (1.92)	0.0660*** (2.73)	0.0646*** (2.67)
Observations	–	7,167	7,167	7,167	7,167

Variable	Mean	[1]	[2]	[3]	[4]
Number of individuals	–	3,333	3,333	3,333	3,333
R^2-within	–	0.16	0.15	0.15	0.15
R^2-between	–	0.07	0.07	0.07	0.06
R^2-overall	–	0.05	0.05	0.05	0.05

Notes: [1] t-statistics in parentheses. [2] * significant at 10%; ** significant at 5%; *** significant at 1%. [3] Other controls: experience, experience squared, tenure, tenure squared, local unemployment rate, dummies for charity sector, and one-digit industry. region, marital status, firm size, fixed and temporary contracts, union coverage, highest educational qualification lagged one year, one-digit occupation and year dummies.

Table 5.2 reports the FE training estimates. Though the individual and employer-specific effects in equation (1) will remove time-invariant ability bias and control for the average return to job mobility, there are possible selectivity effects not allowed for in the FE framework. Therefore, our estimated training coefficients should be interpreted not as causal but as correlations between wages and past/current job training events. The first specification, given in column [1], includes incidence and count variables for training events. Only employer-financed training has a statistically significant positive association with wages, mainly through the incidence of training with previous employers, which is associated with nearly 10 per cent higher expected current wages.[7]

Inasmuch as, by construction, the incidence and count variables are highly correlated, we present, in columns [2] and [3], estimates when these are included separately.[8] The two tell similar stories. Employer-financed training received with former employers has a larger positive association with current wages than does training undertaken with the current employer, and both coefficients are statistically significant. Having received any employer-financed training with previous employers is associated with 7.8 per cent higher expected wages subsequently, whereas the incidence of training with the current employer is associated with only 2.4 per cent higher expected wages. The difference in impact is significant at the 5 per cent confidence level.[9] Both specifications indicate that training in the residual category

7 We also estimated all our specifications substituting training intensity (measured in days) for the training measures reported in Table 5.2, and the results show a similar pattern (for details, see Booth & Bryan, 2002).

8 The correlation coefficient of incidence and counts of employer-paid skills training is 0.78 for training with the current employer and 0.88 for training with the previous employer.

9 As we discuss further below, the fact that the returns to training with future employers exceed the returns with the current employer suggests that a large part of the training is transferable.

('other training') is associated with higher wages, but only when received with previous employers. There is no evidence that self-financed training has any effect on wages.

Column [4] reports the estimates when employer-financed training is disaggregated by accreditation (included as event counts). The results indicate that only accredited training has a statistically significant positive association at the 5 per cent level. Again, the point estimate for training acquired with previous employers is substantially larger than that with the current employer (although the difference is just statistically insignificant at the 5 per cent confidence level). An additional accredited training event with a previous employer is associated with 5.3 per cent higher wages, whereas a similar event with the current employer has only a 1.9 per cent increase.

Self-financed training to develop current skills has a statistically insignificant association with wages (the cell sizes for this relatively uncommon form of training are small). Finally, note that the estimated coefficients on the employer match dummy variables indicate that an employer change is generally associated with an improved unobserved match of 2.5–3.0 per cent.

Conclusions

The BHPS raw data indicate that most training is viewed by its recipients as general. However, such training could comprise both specific and general components, and respondents might simply not have perceived this. If so, we would expect – see row [4] of Table 5.1 – that the direct training costs would be shared by both parties and that the wage returns elsewhere would be less than the returns at the training firm. This is not what the estimates show.

The fact that employers finance training that is transferable across employers, as our results show, is inconsistent with orthodox general human capital theory but consistent with the hypotheses summarised in rows [2] and [5] of Table 5.1. First, consider row [2]. Our evidence that the returns to training between employers exceed the returns with the current employer is consistent with the perfectly competitive general human capital model with credit constraints. Our findings are also consistent with Loewenstein and Spletzer (1998) and Acemoglu and Pischke (1999a, 1999b) – see row [5] and our earlier discussion. Our results for Britain corroborate those of Loewenstein and Spletzer (1998), a finding that is particularly interesting in that we have more detail on individual training spells (including whether or not training is accredited) and a higher training frequency in Britain (almost three times that of the United States).

We also find that accredited employer-financed training is more strongly associated with higher wages at both current and future employers than is non-accredited training, and that only accredited training is transferable between employers. This result perhaps vindicates policy initiatives to encourage accreditation of training where appropriate. The fact that employers pay for highly portable accredited training is again inconsistent with simple human capital theory in the absence of credit constraints.

Acknowledgements

This chapter was first published as Booth, A.L., and Bryan, M.L. (2005). 'Testing some predictions of human capital theory: New training evidence from Britain', *The Review of Economics and Statistics*, 87(2):391–394.

We are grateful to the Leverhulme Trust for financial support under Award F/00213C 'Work-related Training and Wages in Britain.' For helpful comments, we thank the editor Daron Acemoglu, an anonymous referee, Wiji Arulampalam, Bruce Chapman, Bob Hart and seminar participants at the University of Essex and The Australian National University.

References

Acemoglu, D., and Pischke, J.-S. (1998). 'Why do firms train? Theory and evidence', *The Quarterly Journal of Economics,* 113(1):78–118. www.jstor.org/stable/2586986.

Acemoglu, D., and Pischke, J.-S. (1999a). 'Beyond Becker: Training in imperfect labour markets', *The Economic Journal,* 109(453):112–142. doi.org/10.1111/1468-0297.00405.

Acemoglu, D., and Pischke, J.-S. (1999b). 'The structure of wages and investment in general training', *Journal of Political Economy*, 107(3):539–572. doi.org/10.1086/250071.

Becker, G.S. (1964). *Human Capital: A Theoretical and Empirical Analysis, With Special Reference to Education,* National Bureau of Economic Research, New York. doi.org/10.1177/000271626536000153.

Booth, A.L., and Bryan, M.L. (2002). 'Who pays for general training? New evidence for British men and women', IZA discussion paper No. 486, docs.iza.org/dp486.pdf.

Chang, C., and Wang, Y. (1996). 'Human capital investment under asymmetric information: The Pigovian Conjecture revisited', *Journal of Labor Economics*, 14(3):505–519. www.jstor.org/stable/2535364.

Hashimoto, M. (1981). 'Firm-specific human capital as a shared investment', *The American Economic Review*, 71(3):475–482. www.jstor.org/stable/1802794.

Katz, E., and Ziderman, A. (1990). 'Investment in general training: The role of information and labour mobility', *The Economic Journal*, 100(403):1147–1158. doi.org/10.2307/2233964.

Loewenstein, M.A., and Spletzer, J.R. (1998). 'Dividing the costs and returns to general training', *Journal of Labor Economics*, 16(1):142–171. doi.org/10.1086/209885.

Stevens, M. (1994). 'A theoretical model of on-the-job training with imperfect competition', *Oxford Economic Papers*, 46(4):537–562. www.jstor.org/stable/2663510.

6

Work-related training and the minimum wage

Wiji Arulampalam, Alison L Booth and Mark L Bryan

Human capital theory predicts that the introduction of a minimum wage in competitive labour markets will reduce general training investment by covered workers who can no longer finance such training through lower wages (Rosen 1972). However, if the low-paid labour market is imperfectly competitive, firms will be more likely to pay for general training, although under-provision may result; see inter alia Stevens (1994); Acemoglu and Pischke (1999). Intuitively, the monopsonistic character of the labour market compresses workers' returns to human capital, allowing the firm to keep some of the surplus. By compressing wages further, the introduction of a minimum wage can increase training.

Early empirical studies that looked at the effect of training on wage growth found that minimum wages lowered wage growth (Leighton and Mincer, 1981; Hashimoto, 1982). However, more recent studies – all using US microdata – perform more direct tests with better data but with mixed results. While Schiller (1994) and Neumark and Wascher (2001) found that workers subjected to a minimum wage received less training, Grossberg and Sicilian (1999) and Acemoglu and Pischke (2003) found no clear evidence either way.

A UK National Minimum Wage (NMW) was introduced on 1 April 1999. It followed a period of six years, from the abolition of the Wages Councils, during which there was no statutory wage-floor in any sector but agriculture. The government views the NMW as an 'important cornerstone of Government strategy aimed at providing employees with decent minimum standards and fairness in the workplace' (DTI 2006). At the same time, it emphasises the development of workforce skills – 'particularly the basic skills of some adults' (DfES n.d.). Our analysis empirically investigates whether the two goals are compatible.

Our study provides the only investigation of the training effects of minimum wages in Britain. Moreover, it utilises important new data from the British Household Panel Survey (BHPS) – on both training and whether or not individuals' wages were increased to comply with the NMW – facilitating a comparison of training evolution across various groups. We use individuals' responses as to whether or not they were affected by the NMW to identify groups 'affected' and 'not affected'. We compare these results to those derived using an alternative definition based on hourly wages. Our methodology is similar to that of Stewart (2004), who uses the BHPS to analyse the employment effect for low-wage workers of the NMW.

Empirical framework

We estimate the mean impact of the NMW on training for those affected by this policy intervention using the difference-in-differences estimator in the context of a linear probability model (LPM).

Let $T_{it} = 1$ if individual i received any training (to increase or improve skills in the current job during the past 12 months) in period t and zero otherwise. Then:

$$(1)\ \Delta T_{it} = \Delta X_{it}\beta + \alpha + \gamma A_i + \Delta\varepsilon_{it}$$

where $A_i = 1$ if individual i is in the affected group and zero otherwise; X_{it} is a vector of individual and job characteristics influencing the outcome variable; and is our parameter of interest. Differences in training experiences common across individuals due to, say, business cycle effects, are captured by α. The equation implicitly allows for individual-specific unobservable effects that may be correlated with some of the regressors. $\Delta\varepsilon_{it}$ is allowed to have an arbitrary heteroscedastic covariance matrix in the LPM estimation. We stress that all our analyses are conditional on employment.[1]

1 Stewart (2004), using the BHPS, finds no statistically significant evidence of employment effects of the NMW. It should be emphasised that our estimated model accounts for selection biases arising from correlation with unobserved individual-specific characteristics.

The data

Our data are from waves 8 to 10 of the BHPS. The pre-NMW data are from wave 8, and the post-NMW data are from wave 10, conducted in 1998 and 2000, respectively.[2]

The BHPS is a nationally representative panel survey of private households in Britain. From wave 8, a new format was introduced for work-related training. The new questions cover up to three training events since September of the previous year, and provide information on where training occurred, how it was financed, its duration and if it led to qualifications. Our sample of individuals was interviewed in wave 8 between August 1998 and March 1999 about training received since 1 September 1997. In wave 10, they were interviewed between September 2000 and May 2001 about training experienced since 1 September 1999. Reported training, therefore, falls unambiguously before and after the introduction of the NMW. We do not use training data from wave 9 since we cannot determine if reported training occurred before or after the NMW was introduced.

The NMW was introduced at three levels: a main rate of £3.60 per hour, a youth rate of £3.00 for 18–21-year-olds and a special development rate of £3.20 for workers over 21 years old undertaking specific types of approved training. The existence of the development rate potentially distorts the training decision since employers can pay a lower wage in return for providing training. Although we are unable to identify explicitly individuals covered by this provision, in principle, we can identify them indirectly by using a reported hourly wage measure, which was introduced to the BHPS in wave 9 (for hourly paid employees only). We found no such cases.

Our analysis covers employees aged between 18 and 60 years in wave 8, who are not in the army, farming or fisheries, and with valid training information. Individuals reporting over 100 working hours per week (hours are used to derive hourly wages) were dropped. Where there were many missing observations on control variables, we created dummy variables indicating

2 We use the data from 1998 onwards because major changes to the training questions were introduced in 1998. See Booth and Bryan (2005) for a discussion about the differences in the questionnaires and training responses before and after this change. Bryan (2002) analysed training changes over 1995–7, when no minimum wage was in place, finding no significant differential effect for workers who would have been covered by the minimum wage. The government introducing the NMW came to power in May 1997, so one might have expected to see any 'announcement effect' reflected in reported training in 1997.

their status to maintain reasonable sample sizes. Individuals must satisfy the selection criteria in at least waves 8 and 10. For one of the treatment control groups discussed below, they must also be present in wave 9.

The outcome variables and the treatment/control groups

We use two outcome variables: changes in training incidence ΔT_{it} and training intensity: ΔT^{*}_{it}. These are identical unless training incidence is positive in both periods: then $\Delta T^{*}_{it} = 1$ if intensity increases, $\Delta T^{*}_{it} = -1$ if intensity decreases and $\Delta T^{*}_{it} = 0$, if intensity remains the same.

We define two alternative treatment and control groups, summarised in Table 6.1. Treatment group 1 contains individuals whose derived hourly wage was below the NMW for their age in wave 8. These individuals' wages should have been raised to the NMW in April 1999 (assuming their derived wages are free of measurement error and would not have increased in real terms between waves 8 and 9). Control group 1 comprises individuals earning between the NMW and 15 per cent more than the NMW in wave 8. To investigate spillover effects, we include the group of individuals ('high-wage') from the rest of the wage distribution above 115 per cent minimum wage in 1998.

Individuals replying positively to the new question, 'Has your pay or hourly rate in your current job been increased to bring you up to the national minimum wage (NMW) or has it remained the same?' were categorised as belonging to Treatment group 2. Since this question was only asked of individuals who did not change jobs between 1st April 1999 and the date of interview (from August 1998 to March 1999), this definition will exclude some workers who were subject to the NMW in a new job.[3]

3 The treatment group will therefore tend to over-represent job stayers. However, insofar as individuals remain in their jobs because of characteristics, which are constant over time, the differencing estimator will eliminate potential selection bias.

Table 6.1: Means of training incidence, training intensity and the derived wage

Treatment/ control group definition	Wave	Treatment group				Control group				High-wage group[§]			
		Training incidence	Training intensity	Derived wage	*N*	Training incidence	Training intensity	Derived wage	*N*	Training incidence	Training intensity	Derived wage	*N*
		Derived wage[†] < NMW				NMW ≤ Derived wage < 1.15 NMW				Derived wage ≥ 1.15 NMW			
1 (based on derived wage in wave 8)*	8	0.160	2.551	2.818	259	0.189	6.465	3.818	221	0.290	5.212	8.942	2,777
	9	–	–	3.947	–	–	–	4.452	–	–	–	9.274	–
	10	0.243	4.779	4.422	259	0.180	2.824	4.814	221	0.317	5.310	9.555	2,777
2 (based on whether wage increased to NMW)[‡]	8	0.101	2.257	3.837	99	0.280	4.951	8.451	2,405	–	–	–	–
	9	–	–	4.353	–	–	–	8.833	–	–	–	–	–
	10	0.172	6.508	4.583	99	0.303	4.882	9.109	2,405	–	–	–	–

Notes: * Wave 8 refers to pre-NMW period and wave 10 to post-NMW period; [†] Wave 8 derived wage calculated as: $(\frac{12}{52})[\frac{PAYGU}{JBHRS + 1.5PDOT}]$, where PAYGU is usual gross pay per month, JBHRS is usual standard weekly hours and PDOT is usual paid overtime weekly hours; [‡] 'Has your pay or hourly rate in your current job been increased to bring you up to the national minimum wage or has it remained the same?' Variable INMWPACH (wave 9 only, asked if respondent did not change jobs between 1/4/99 and interview); [§] Since the second definition of what constitutes a treatment group and a control group is not based on information on wages, we do not define a 'high-wage' group here; Of the 189 individuals in Treatment group 1 who did not change jobs between 1/4/99 and interview, 53 were also in Treatment group 2.

However, the question provides a treatment group that is arguably less prone to measurement error than the derived wage used for Treatment group 1. Our Control group 2 is corresponding individuals who were job stayers and who answered no to the above question. Since the question was only asked in wave 9, this selection requires individuals to be present in all three waves (8, 9 and 10). The sample size is therefore smaller than for Treatment group 1. Since the definition is based entirely on a question that does not use the wage information, we do not include any other groups in this specification.

Table 6.1 reports the mean training for the pre- and post-NMW periods. Training incidence typically increased in all groups, with a particularly marked proportionate increase in the treatment groups. For example, incidence in Treatment group 2 increased from 0.10 in wave 8 to 0.17 in wave 10; in Control group 2, incidence went from 0.28 to 0.30. Despite the increases, training is much less prevalent among workers earning close to the minimum wage than in the higher-paid groups.

The pattern is less clear when we consider (unconditional) training intensity. In Treatment group 1, mean intensity rose from 2.6 days in wave 8 to 4.8 days in wave 10. In Control group 1, intensity fell sharply from 6.5 days to 2.8 days. An increase over the period, from 2.3 days to 6.5 days, is observed in Treatment group 2. In the two groups of higher-paid workers ('High-wage' group 1 and Control group 2), intensity, like incidence, is quite stable at around 5 days a year. The volatility in the smaller groups is possibly caused by their sizes or by the noisiness of training intensity. If so, incidence change ΔT may be the preferred dependent variable. In the next section, we present results for both ΔT and ΔT^* and highlight the differences in the model estimates.

Results

Table 6.2: The effect of the NMW on training

	Raw differences-in-differences				Regression-adjusted			
	ΔT		ΔT*		ΔT		ΔT*	
	Treatment/ control group		Treatment/ control group		Treatment/ control group		Treatment/ control group	
	1	2	1	2	1	2	1	2
	[1]	[2]	[3]	[4]	[5]	[6]	[7]	[8]
Treatment group	0.0901 (1.98)**	.0503 (1.18)	0.1004 (1.97)**	0.1046 (2.19)**	0.0785 (1.72)*	.0422 (1.00)	.0876 (1.71)*	0.0984 (2.02)**
High-wage group	0.0343 (0.98)	-	0.0187 (0.47)	-	0.0392 (1.12)	-	.0242 (0.61)	-
Intercept	−0.0090 (0.27)	.0204 (1.83)*	−0.0000 (0.00)†	0.0166 (1.24)	−0.0706 (1.41)	−0.0418 (0.94)	−0.0790 (1.36)	−0.0663 (1.26)
Observations	3,257	2,504	3,257	2,504	3,257	2,504	3,257	2,504

Notes: Absolute robust *t*-statistics in parentheses; * significant at 10%; ** significant at 5%; Regression-adjusted estimates have the following first-differences controls: age-squared, part-time status, whether the job is fixed-term or temporary, whether the worker changed employers, marital status, union coverage, sector, firm size, 1-digit industry, local unemployment rate, and dummies for missing values; Table 6.1 defines dependent variables ΔT and ΔT*; † The estimated standard error for this coefficient is 0.04.

The raw difference-in-differences estimates of [1] with no additional controls are reported in Table 6.2, columns [1]–[4]. Columns [1] and [2] show the results for ΔT (incidence-changes), and columns [3]–[4] the results for ΔT^* (intensity-changes). Column [1] indicates that the training probability in Treatment group 1 increased by about 9 percentage points more than it did in the control group. This increase is statistically significant at the 5 per cent level. The training probability also increased in the high-wage group relative to the control group, but the coefficient is not statistically significant. This suggests no spillover effect of the NMW into this group. From column [2], where we use treatment and control groups 2, we see that, although training incidence increased more in the treatment group (by 5 percentage points) than in the control group, the estimate of the effect of the NMW on the training probability is not statistically significant at conventional levels. In this equation, however, the constant, capturing the trend increase in incidence, is significant at 10 per cent. The differences between columns [1] and [2] may be because Control group 1 comprises workers just above the NMW, whereas Control group 2 contains higher-paid workers as well.

However, the results in columns [3] and [4] show that a similar result is obtained when information on changes in intensity is incorporated into the definition of training. More specifically, affected workers appear to be 10 percentage points more likely to experience an increase in training than workers in the control group. The increases are statistically significant. These results suggest that the NMW may have resulted in increased training.[4]

Columns [5]–[8] of Table 6.2 show the regression-adjusted difference-in-differences estimates of equation (1) incorporating individual and job characteristics. We exclude potentially endogenous variables like tenure and occupation. Insofar as the additional variables change significantly over time, they help control for individual differences in training growth. Regression-adjusted estimates of the treatment effect are slightly lower than the estimates in columns [1]–[4]. Thus, for Treatment group 1, the NMW increases the training probability by 8.0 percentage points ceteris paribus, significant at the 10 per cent level. The training probability in the high-wage group increases by 4.0 percentage points, but this is not significant at conventional levels. Both figures are relative to the base of control group 1. When the dependent variable is redefined to incorporate the information on intensity, the estimate, shown in column [7], is slightly higher at 8.8 percentage points.

In the specifications comparing Treatment group 2 with Control group 2 (columns [6] and [8]), the estimates are again similar to those without additional control variables (columns [2] and [4]). The NMW does not appear to significantly affect the training incidence probability (the coefficient is positive), while it significantly increases intensity by 9.8 percentage points.

Overall, we interpret these results as providing support for the hypothesis that the NMW increased work-related training against the null hypothesis of no effect.[5]

4 We model the sign of changes in training intensity rather than the magnitude, since this relates directly to relevant theory. Modelling the exact change in training intensity would require us to address the issue that a change from eight to 10 days is not necessarily the same as a change from four to two days or even a change from two to zero days. Such analysis is beyond the scope of our current study.

5 In companion papers, we describe extensions of the analysis (Bryan 2002; Arulampalam et al. 2003). These alternative models (that also investigate the sensitivity of our estimates to changes in the definitions of Treatment group 1 and its control group) produced similar results to those reported here and our conclusions are unchanged.

Conclusions

We estimated the impact of the new NMW on the work-related training of low-wage workers using two 'treatment groups'. These were workers whose wages derived in 1998 were below the minimum, and those workers explicitly stated they were affected by the new minimum. Using difference-in-differences techniques and information on training incidence and intensity, we found no evidence that the minimum wage introduction reduced the training of affected workers and some evidence that it increased it. In particular, we found that the training probability increased by 8 to 11 percentage points for affected workers. Our findings provide little evidence supporting the human capital model as it applies to training and weak evidence of new theories based on imperfectly competitive labour markets. Finally, our estimates suggest that two of the UK Government's goals – improving wages of the low-paid and developing their skills – have been compatible, at least for the introductory rates of the minimum wage.

Acknowledgements

This chapter was first published as Arulampalam, W., Booth, A.L., and Bryan, M.L. (2004). 'Training and the new minimum wage', *The Economic Journal,* 114(494):87–94. doi.org/10.1111/j.0013-0133.2003.00197.x.

This research was supported by the Leverhulme Trust Award F/00213C 'Work-related Training and Wages of Union and Non-union Workers in Britain'. For helpful comments, we thank an anonymous referee, Mark Stewart and seminar participants at the University of Essex, The Australian National University, the Policy Studies Institute and the Centre for Economic Performance.

References

Acemoglu, D., and Pischke, J.-S. (1999). 'The structure of wages and investment in general training', *Journal of Political Economy,* 107(3):539–572. doi.org/10.1086/250071.

Acemoglu, D., and Pischke, J.-S. (2003). 'Minimum wages and on-the-job training', *Research in Labor Economics,* 22:159–202.

Arulampalam, W., Booth, A.L., and Bryan, M.L. (2003). 'Work-related training and the new national minimum wage in Britain', Working Papers of the Institute for Social and Economic Research, No. 2003–5, University of Essex.

Booth, A.L., and Bryan, M.L. (2005). 'Testing some predictions of human capital theory: New training evidence from Britain', *The Review of Economics and Statistics*, 87(2):391–394. www.jstor.org/stable/40042912

Bryan, M.L. (2002) 'The effect of the national minimum wage on training', PhD thesis, University of Essex.

DfES (Department for Education and Skills). (n.d.). www.dfes.gov.uk/research (page discontinued).

DTI (Department of Trade and Industry). (2006). 'Employment relations: The national minimum wage'. *The National Archives*. webarchive.nationalarchives.gov.uk/ukgwa/20060213213640/http://www.dti.gov.uk/er/nmw/index.htm.

Grossberg, A.J., and Sicilian, P. (1999). 'Minimum wages, on-the-job training and wage growth', *Southern Economic Journal*, 65(1):539–556.

Hashimoto, M. (1982). 'Minimum wage effects on training on the job', *American Economic Review*, 72:1070–1087.

Leighton, L., and Mincer, J. (1981). 'The effects of minimum wages on human capital formation', in S Rottenberg, ed. *The Economics of Legal Minimum Wages*, pp. 155–173, American Enterprise Institute, Washington, DC.

Neumark, D., and Wascher, W. (2001). 'Minimum wages and training revisited', *Journal of Labor Economics*, 19(3):563–595. doi.org/10.1086/322073

Rosen, S. (1972). 'Learning and experience in the labor market', *The Journal of Human Resources*, 7(3):326–342. doi.org/10.2307/145087

Schiller, B.R. (1994). 'Moving up: The training and wage gains of minimum-wage entrants', *Social Science Quarterly*, 75(3):622–636. www.jstor.org/stable/42863374.

Stevens, M. (1994). 'A theoretical model of on-the-job training with imperfect competition', *Oxford Economic Papers*, 46(4):537–562. www.jstor.org/stable/2663510.

Stewart, M.B. (2003). 'The impact of the introduction of the U.K. minimum wage on the employment probabilities of low-wage workers', *Journal of the European Economic Association*, 2(1):67–97. www.jstor.org/stable/40004869.

Section II: Men and women in the labour market

7

Is there a glass ceiling over Europe? Exploring the gender pay gap across the wage distribution

Wiji Arulampalam, Alison L Booth and Mark L Bryan

Although the mean gender wage gap has been extensively studied in the labour economics literature, only relatively recently has attention shifted to investigating the degree to which the gender gap might vary across the wage distribution and why. Albrecht et al. (2003), using 1998 data for Sweden, showed that the gender wage gap was increasing throughout the wage distribution and accelerating at the top, and they interpreted this as evidence of a glass ceiling in Sweden. De la Rica et al. (2005) undertook a similar analysis using 1999 data for Spain. They stratified their sample by education group and found that the gender wage gap was expanding over the wage distribution only for the group with college/tertiary education. For less educated groups, the gender wage gap was wider at the bottom than at the top. Thus, it appears that in Spain, there was a glass ceiling for the more educated but not for the less educated. Using a different decomposition methodology in the quantile regressions framework and Spanish data for 1995, del Rio et al. (2005) obtained results similar to those of De la Rica et al.

The purpose of our chapter is to investigate these issues further in order to see if the glass ceiling phenomenon was prevalent across pre-enlargement Europe (the European Union before the admission of 10 new countries in

2004). Using harmonised data from the European Community Household Panel, we analyse gender pay gaps across the wage distribution for 11 countries using the quantile regression (QR) framework. We investigate the extent to which gender affects the location (conditional mean), scale, and shape of the conditional wage distribution, and whether or not these patterns differ across the public and private sectors.

We first chart the gender pay gap using raw data. We then compare the raw gender gaps with estimates that control for men's and women's attributes using the QR framework. This enables us to see how the gender pay gaps would have differed if women had kept the same distribution of characteristics but had been rewarded like men. Unlike ordinary least squares (OLS), QR methods allow for the possibility that characteristics have different returns at different points of the distribution. Following Albrecht et al. (2003), we interpret a widening gender wage gap at the top of the wage distribution as a glass ceiling. We refer to the situation in which the gender pay gap widens at the bottom of the wage distribution as a sticky floor.[1] Towards the end of the chapter, we discuss various hypotheses that could explain our empirical findings.

The data, variables and raw gender wage gap

Our data are from the European Community Household Panel (ECHP), a large-scale survey conducted annually from 1994 to 2001. The ECHP was specifically designed to be harmonised at the input stage: in most countries, a standard questionnaire was used, with harmonised definitions and sampling criteria. Although a standardised questionnaire does not overcome the nuances of interpretation and meaning between different languages, the harmonised format greatly facilitates cross-country comparisons. We include in our analysis the 11 European countries listed in Table 7.1. We omit Greece and Portugal owing to apparent gaps in the training data and because of the small estimating subsamples with usable information for those two countries. The ECHP data for Britain and Germany were

1 Booth et al. (2003) first defined a sticky floor as the situation arising when otherwise identical men and women might be appointed to the same pay scale or rank, but the women are appointed at the bottom and the men further up the scale. Such a strategy can evade some discrimination laws, since the appointment rank is the same. Here we use the term more generally to describe the situation in which the gender pay gap widens at the bottom of the wage distribution, as will be further explained below.

adapted from those countries' existing national household surveys, while data from the full harmonised questionnaire are available for the other countries. Sample sizes are reported in column [5] of Table A7.1.

The education, industry and occupation variables are all coded according to standard, internationally comparable definitions. Education levels are defined according to the UNESCO International Standard Classification of Education (ISCED). ISCED was intended for education policy analysis and was designed to be invariant to differences in national education systems.[2] The ECHP distinguishes between education completed to the lower secondary stage (ISCED 0-2), upper secondary education (ISCED 3) and post-secondary or tertiary education (ISCED 5-7). The data on the industrial sector are categorised according to the European Union's Classification of Economic Activities in the European Community (NACE), and occupation is defined using the International Standard Classification of Occupations (ISCO-88). The Data Appendix lists the occupation and industry groups.

We initially estimated the gender pay gap separately for waves 2 and 8, in order to chart any changes that might have occurred between 1995 and 2001. Since there was little difference between the two sets of estimates, in our main model, we estimate the gender gap over the entire sample of waves 2 to 8 inclusive,[3] pooling all the waves and also including wave dummies as explanatory variables in addition to the usual set of exogenous variables. For the pooled sample, we do not require individuals to be present in all waves or in consecutive waves. We therefore have new entrants across waves, and we lose some individuals through attrition. Thus, we have a changing composition of individuals. As reported in the final column of Table A7.1, respondents were typically present in the panel for four waves. As we discuss below, we account for multiple observations on the same individuals in the calculation of the standard errors.

Because we wish to avoid conflating issues having to do with gender and early educational enrolments, we exclude from our analysis individuals under the age of 22 years, as well as paid apprentices and those on special

2 For details, see International Standard Classification of Education (ISCED): ISCED 1997 (fields) and ISCED-F 2013, *Eurostat*, ec.europa.eu/eurostat/statistics-explained/index.php?title=International_Standard_Classification_of_Education_(ISCED)#ISCED_1997_.28fields.29_and_ISCED-F_2013.

3 We omitted Wave 1 for two reasons. First, it does not contain information about whether or not the respondent's employment contract was fixed-term/casual. If temporary contract coverage varies between men and women, temporary contracts could be an important determinant of the gender wage gap. Second, the deflator used (the EU Harmonised Index of Consumer Prices, from Eurostat) is only available from Wave 2. Also note that Austria did not join the ECHP until Wave 2 and that Finland did not join until Wave 3 (following its accession to the EU in 1995). Thus, we have seven waves of data for all countries except Finland, for which we have six waves.

employment-related training schemes (who account for less than 1 per cent of the sampled age group). Among older workers, there may also be differential withdrawal from the labour force, depending, for example, on how early retirement schemes operate. We therefore exclude workers aged 55 years and over. For each country, our estimating subsamples stratified by gender comprise full-time and part-time public and private sector employees who were (i) between the ages of 22–54 years inclusive, (ii) working at least 15 hours per week, (iii) not employed in agriculture, and (iv) with valid observations on all the variables used in the wage equations. The 15-hour-per-week cut-off was necessary because of the nature of the ECHP data, where, in the first two waves, we were unable to distinguish individuals regularly working fewer than 15 hours from those out of the labour force. In addition, for those working fewer than 15 hours, the ECHP across all waves provides no information on firm size, public/private sector, or tenure. Thus, our estimating subsamples will under-represent low-hour part-timers.[4]

The dependent variable is the log of the average hourly wage, including overtime payments, in the respondent's main job, deflated to 2001 prices.[5] The deflators are the European Union's harmonised indices of consumer prices (HICP) (see Eurostat Yearbook 2003). The ECHP provides a rich set of controls, which are listed in the notes under Table 7.2. Unfortunately, the ECHP does not collect any information on either union status or union coverage, and so we are unable to control for those variables in our estimation. The data do not contain information on labour market experience, but we do include tenure (6 categories) and a binary indicator denoting whether the individual has had a spell of unemployment since 1989, which should capture some of the variation in workers' labour market attachment.

Throughout, we estimate our models for three subsamples of data: first, a combined sample comprising both public and private sector workers, and then two disaggregated subsamples, comprising public and private sector workers, respectively. In the remainder of this section, we discuss the estimates of the raw gender wage gap for all three samples and then briefly present the methodology used to estimate the gender wage gap.

4 For most countries, low-hours part-timers represent only a tiny fraction of workers. Exceptions are Britain (6.4 per cent of the subsample), Denmark (3.2 per cent), the Netherlands (9.8 per cent), and Ireland (4.0 per cent). In all other countries the proportion of low-hours part-timers is under 3 per cent.

5 The log wage was calculated from the ECHP variables as log (wage) = log (PI211MG × (12/52) / PE005A) = log (normal gross monthly earnings from main job including overtime × (12/52) / weekly hours in main job including overtime). No specific information is provided on overtime hours and premia.

Table 7.1: The raw gender wage gap in 11 European countries, 1995–2001

	Men (proportion)	Mean	10th percentile	25th percentile	Median	75th percentile	90th percentile
Country	[1]	[2]	[3]	[4]	[5]	[6]	[7]
Pooled							
Austria	0.580	0.234	0.268	0.236	0.210	0.194	0.201
Belgium	0.538	0.100	0.100	0.100	0.074	0.080	0.150
Britain	0.505	0.246	0.238	0.248	0.234	0.248	0.252
Denmark	0.508	0.132	0.107	0.091	0.099	0.155	0.248
Finland[a]	0.496	0.184	0.112	0.119	0.170	0.243	0.266
France	0.541	0.142	0.136	0.127	0.113	0.122	0.139
Germany	0.570	0.204	0.230	0.189	0.178	0.206	0.227
Ireland	0.551	0.201	0.253	0.233	0.209	0.166	0.129
Italy	0.593	0.063	0.089	0.072	0.054	0.037	0.028
Netherlands	0.597	0.183	0.151	0.146	0.155	0.196	0.232
Spain	0.622	0.138	0.154	0.127	0.114	0.071	0.044
Public sector							
Austria	0.519	0.135	0.153	0.122	0.087	0.093	0.115
Belgium	0.478	0.073	0.061	0.058	0.033	0.065	0.136
Britain	0.349	0.212	0.213	0.185	0.216	0.197	0.217
Denmark	0.336	0.114	0.128	0.085	0.105	0.119	0.175
Finland[a]	0.350	0.259	0.164	0.196	0.260	0.316	0.307
France	0.451	0.116	0.112	0.095	0.110	0.128	0.139

	Men (proportion)	Mean	10th percentile	25th percentile	Median	75th percentile	90th percentile
Country	[1]	[2]	[3]	[4]	[5]	[6]	[7]
Germany	0.432	0.128	0.105	0.098	0.146	0.157	0.157
Ireland	0.521	0.110	0.133	0.140	0.079	0.040	0.093
Italy	0.513	*0.006*	*-0.002*	*0.010*	*0.001*	*-0.021*	0.046
Netherlands	0.481	0.200	0.144	0.187	0.191	0.196	0.232
Spain	0.527	0.054	0.083	0.068	0.058	*-0.005*	0.065
Private sector							
Austria	0.606	0.292	0.286	0.286	0.275	0.273	0.266
Belgium	0.577	0.137	0.121	0.135	0.120	0.140	0.199
Britain	0.564	0.306	0.269	0.304	0.309	0.326	0.311
Denmark	0.636	0.134	0.104	0.115	0.091	0.167	0.240
Finland[a]	0.600	0.167	0.121	0.135	0.146	0.199	0.242
France	0.588	0.202	0.180	0.156	0.170	0.201	0.228
Germany	0.624	0.262	0.294	0.253	0.231	0.247	0.282
Ireland	0.566	0.273	0.264	0.267	0.263	0.267	0.313
Italy	0.638	0.153	0.145	0.111	0.130	0.146	0.194
Netherlands	0.643	0.208	0.177	0.176	0.176	0.217	0.278
Spain	0.654	0.230	0.252	0.206	0.205	0.244	0.207

Notes: [a] Cover 1996–2001 only; The raw wage gap is measured as the difference between the log male and log female hourly wage. The log wage was calculated from the ECHP variables as log (wage)=log (PI211MG × (12/52) / PE005A)=log (normal gross monthly earnings from main job including overtime × (12/52) / hours in main job including overtime). It was then deflated to 2001 prices using HICP from the Eurostat Yearbook 2003; Except for the coefficients in italics, all coefficients are significantly different from zero at the 5 per cent level.

Table 7.1 reports estimates of the raw gender wage gap by country. Column [1] of Table 7.1 indicates the male percentage of the various subsamples by country. Men formed the majority of the workforce in all countries except Finland (pooled). Britain and Denmark had a very similar gender composition, at 50.5 per cent and 50.8 per cent, respectively. The male proportion was highest in Spain (62.2 per cent of employees), closely followed by the Netherlands (59.7 per cent) and Italy (59.3 per cent). The mean raw gender gap is presented in column [2]. Inspection of columns [3]–[7] reveals that in three countries – Ireland, Italy, and Spain – the raw gender gap is decreasing as we move from the 10th to the 90th percentiles. In contrast, there is a striking increase of 15–16 percentage points as we shift from the 10th to the 90th percentiles in Finland and from the 50th to the 90th percentiles in Denmark. In Britain, while the raw gender wage gap was rather large (its mean was 24.6 per cent), it was relatively constant across the distribution.

This simple comparison suggests the presence of considerable heterogeneity across our EU countries. It also shows that measuring the gender pay gap at the mean of each distribution (that is, comparing an 'average' woman with an 'average' man) can produce a misleadingly simple picture of how men's and women's wages differ. This mean gap can hide larger or smaller gaps between high-paid men and women, or between low-paid men and women.[6]

Next, consider the raw gaps for the public sector. We were interested in stratifying our sample by sector because institutions in the public sector typically differ greatly from those in the private sector. In the public sector, organisations are largely non-profit and thus isolated from the rigours of the market economy. Thus, in principle, they could more easily follow 'tastes for discrimination' in their wage-setting behaviour. However, they are also subject to government objectives and policies. The European Union countries have adopted strong regulations in favour of equal opportunities, and it is likely that these are more stringently enforced in the public sector

6 Overall wage inequality differs substantially across countries. In our data, the country with the most compressed raw log hourly wage distribution (public and private sectors combined) is Denmark, followed by Italy, the Netherlands, Finland, Belgium and Austria. The country with the most unequal wage distribution is Ireland, followed by Spain, Britain, France and Germany. The 90th–10th percentile differentials of the raw log wage distributions are as follows: Austria, 0.94 log points; Belgium, 0.90; Britain, 1.20; Denmark, 0.72; Finland, 0.90; France, 1.13; Germany, 1.01; Ireland, 1.32; Italy, 0.88; Netherlands, 0.89; and Spain, 1.30. Although calculated from our samples of prime-aged workers, these figures are reasonably close to the 90-10 log wage differentials reported by Blau and Kahn (1996), whose sample included four of the countries considered here, and in OECD (1996). Both of these studies used datasets different from ours.

than in the private sector. Simple OLS pooling tests reject joint equality of the public–private sector coefficients in every country, confirming that this is a valid separation.

As column [1] shows, the public sector had a majority female workforce in seven of our 11 countries. Only in Austria, Ireland, Italy and Spain were men in the majority in the public sector, and even in these countries, the majority was slim (the highest proportion of men was 52.7 per cent in Spain). In the private sector, on the other hand, men predominated across all countries, and in six countries they accounted for over 60 per cent of the private sector workforce.

The raw wage gap measured at the mean (column 2) was generally higher in the private sector than in the public sector. While the raw average gender wage gap in the public sector was in excess of 20 per cent in Britain, Finland and the Netherlands, in Belgium, Italy and Spain it was under 10 per cent, and indeed in Italy it was found to have been insignificantly different from zero. In contrast, in the private sector, the raw average gender gap exceeded 13 per cent in all countries, and in Britain and Austria, it was close to 30 per cent. In France, Germany, Ireland, the Netherlands and Spain, the gap was around or over 20 per cent.

How does the raw gender wage gap vary across the unconditional distribution? In the public sector, Italy is the only country where the raw gender gap is found to have been statistically insignificant in all parts of the distribution except at the top (see column [7]), where it was still very much smaller (at about 5 per cent) than in other countries. In Finland and the Netherlands, the raw gap increases monotonically as we move up the unconditional wage distributions, and in Belgium, Denmark and Germany, the gap is also higher towards the top of the distribution. In Ireland and Spain, the gap moves in the opposite direction. In Britain, a remarkably level raw gap of about 20 per cent occurs across the distribution.

Measures of the raw gap exhibit similar patterns in the private sector (Table 7.1). The gender wage gap varies little over the distribution in Britain. The gap increases moving up the wage distribution in Finland and the Netherlands, and is also higher towards the top in Belgium, Denmark, France, and Ireland. In contrast to what is found in the public sector in Italy, the wage gap is now significantly different from zero and is U-shaped. We find a similar pattern in Germany.

In summary, we find that in both the public and the private sectors, there was a tendency in some countries for the gender wage gap to be higher at the top of the wage distribution than in the middle region, hinting at a possible 'glass ceiling' effect. However, the gender wage gap was wider at the bottom end, too, for public sector workers in five countries (Austria, Britain, Denmark, France, and Spain) and for private sector workers in four countries (France, Germany, Italy, and Spain). This hints at a 'sticky floor' effect in some countries. But these are only raw gender gaps. In order to find out how much of the observed raw wage gap can be explained by the differences in the returns to various characteristics, we next turn to the QR results.

Wage gap estimates from QRs

The econometric model

Instead of looking at the effects of gender and other covariates on the conditional mean of the log wage distribution, we look at the effects of gender and other covariates on different quantiles of the log wage distribution.[7] The effects of covariates on the location, scale and shape of the conditional wage distribution can be easily estimated using a QR framework. Since the QR framework allows the characteristics to have different returns at different quantiles, at each point of the distribution, it can control more fully for differences between men's and women's wages that are attributable to their characteristics.

Following Buchinsky (1998), we specify the θth $(0 < \theta < 1)$[8] conditional quantile of the log wage (w) distribution for the i-th individual (i=1, …, N) in wave t (t=1, …, T), as:

(1) $\text{Quant}_\theta (w_{it} \mid \mathbf{x}_{it}) = \alpha(\theta) + \mathbf{x}'_{it} \beta(\theta)$, implying:

(2) $w_{it} = \alpha(\theta) + \mathbf{x}'_{it} \boldsymbol{\beta}(\theta) + \varepsilon_{\theta it}$,

with $\text{Quant}_\theta (\varepsilon_{\theta it} \mid \mathbf{x}_{it}) = 0$.

7 The linear conditional quantile regression model was first introduced by Koenker and Bassett (1978). For a recent survey of these models, see Buchinsky (1998).

8 $\theta = 0.5$ refers to the median.

For each sector, we estimate this model for men and women separately. Note that if the underlying model were truly a location model – in the sense that the changes in explanatory variables caused only a change in the location of the distribution of w and not in the shape of the distribution – then all the slope coefficients would be the same for all θ.[9] We use Stata 9 to estimate the coefficients of our QR model.

We do not use the conventional method of estimating gender pay gaps in a linear regression framework that was first introduced by Blinder (1973) and Oaxaca (1973). Instead, we use a different method to calculate the gender gap at the θth quantile due to differing returns adjusted for characteristics as detailed below. That is the gap measured as the difference in pay that women would have faced at the θth quantile if their labour market characteristics had been rewarded as men's were.[10]

Estimation strategy and the decomposition method

As noted above, we initially estimate the models separately by gender and country, and thus have 22 sets of estimations for each specification (Table 7.2 samples). Then we disaggregate by sector, and estimate the models separately by gender, sector, and country, yielding 44 sets of estimations for each specification (Table 7.4 subsamples). In the interest of space, and given the focus of our chapter, we do not provide the complete set of estimates for each country. Instead, we move straight to the calculations of the gender wage gap obtained from the QR model. Full details of all estimated effects for each country can be obtained from the authors on request. The calculations enable us to evaluate whether a glass ceiling, a sticky floor, or both are present.

9 Quantile regression models are more general than simple linear regression models allowing for heteroskedastic errors, since they allow for more general dependence of the distribution of w (the dependent variable) on the x's instead of just the mean and the variance of the conditional mean alone.

10 We also calculated the gap using men's characteristics as the reference, which answers the question of what the gender wage gap would be if women had men's characteristics but were still rewarded as women (or equivalently if men were rewarded as women). The results were qualitatively similar, the main difference being that for some countries the estimates of the gap were somewhat smaller in the higher parts of the wage distribution. For example, the estimated gap at the 90th percentile (using pooled data) was appreciably smaller in six countries (typically by about 6 percentage points). The practical effect of this is to reduce the glass ceiling effect and increase the sticky floor effect. To some extent, the choice of base is arbitrary, and these changes do not modify our conclusions.

Table 7.2: Estimated wage gap: Pooled model without industry and occupational dummies

Country	OLS		10%		25%		50%		75%		90%	
Austria	0.268	[114]	0.230	[86]	0.213	[90]	0.222	[106]	0.261	[135]	0.304	[151]
Belgium	0.146	[146]	0.102	[102]	0.118	[118]	0.133	[179]	0.165	[206]	0.214	[143]
Britain	0.233	[95]	0.196	[83]	0.204	[82]	0.223	[95]	0.250	[101]	0.286	[114]
Denmark	0.104	[79]	0.050	[47]	0.061	[68]	0.091	[92]	0.150	[97]	0.213	[86]
Finland	0.238	[129]	0.154	[138]	0.179	[151]	0.230	[135]	0.284	[117]	0.304	[114]
France	0.215	[151]	0.189	[139]	0.177	[139]	0.183	[162]	0.215	[176]	0.279	[201]
Germany	0.148	[73]	0.124	[54]	0.126	[67]	0.132	[74]	0.150	[73]	0.197	[87]
Ireland	0.248	[123]	0.236	[93]	0.260	[112]	0.263	[126]	0.250	[151]	0.232	[179]
Italy	0.146	[232]	0.146	[164]	0.127	[176]	0.115	[214]	0.137	[367]	0.183	[649]
Netherlands	0.131	[72]	0.047	[31]	0.072	[49]	0.107	[69]	0.173	[89]	0.242	[104]
Spain	0.185	[134]	0.236	[114]	0.213	[136]	0.180	[135]	0.147	[164]	0.124	[227]

Notes: Percentage of the raw gap explained by different returns. The model includes dummies for whether training was received in the last year, age, education, tenure, marital status, health status, any experience of unemployment since 1989, part-time status, fixed-term and casual contracts, region (where possible), sector, and year. Dummies were also included for cases with a very large number of missing values. All wage gaps were statistically significant at the 1% level; See the Appendix for further details.

All models include the full set of other controls listed beneath Tables 7.2 and 7.4 (including wave dummies). Table 7.2 shows the results from the wage gap calculations obtained from the pooled model, excluding controls for occupation and industry but including a dummy variable for the private sector. Table 7.4 gives the results disaggregated by sector, without and with occupation and industry dummy variables.

We now provide more details on our calculations of the wage gaps. First, we estimated the QRs for each gender (and by sector where necessary). Then we calculated the predicted wage at different parts of the wage distributions by gender (and sector). The wage gap in which we are interested measures the effect of different returns to men and women when women's characteristics are used in the counterfactual calculations. A positive wage gap implies that the returns to women's characteristics are lower than those of men, and a negative wage gap implies the reverse. Instead of using average characteristics of the female sample to calculate the counterfactuals, we follow the bootstrap procedure suggested by Machado and Mata (2005) and use the distribution of women's characteristics to calculate the decompositions directly at particular quantiles of interest.[11] The procedure involves estimating the marginal density of wages that are consistent with the estimated conditional densities given by (2) and the hypothesised distribution of characteristics. In practical terms, this was carried out as follows:

Step 1: Generate a random sample of size n=5,000 from a uniform distribution $U[0,1]$: $\theta_1, \ldots, \theta_n$. This will yield a series of numbers telling us which quantiles are to be estimated.

Step 2: For each θ from step 1, estimate the coefficients $\beta_m(\theta)$ and $\beta_f(\theta)$ in equation (2), using the male dataset and the female dataset, respectively.

Step 3: Randomly draw 5,000 women (with replacement) and use their characteristics to predict the wages using the estimated coefficients $\beta_m(\theta)$ and $\beta_f(\theta)$ from step 2, generating two sets of predicted wages covering the whole distribution. Note that because the block-bootstrapping procedure is used to account for clustering at the individual level, there are more than 5,000 observations in practice (see footnote 14). This enables us to calculate (i) the marginal distribution of women's wages and (ii) the marginal distribution of men's wages that would obtain if their characteristics were distributed as women's are.

11 A similar procedure was used by Albrecht et al. (2003) and De la Rica et al. (2005). Machado and Mata (2005, Section 2.4) provided a detailed discussion of various methodologies that have been used to calculate counterfactual densities.

Step 4: Using the distributions calculated in step 3, we estimate the wage gap as the difference between the predicted wage at each quantile using the newly generated wage distribution for women and the counterfactual distribution for men.[12]

Although we realise that individuals might self-select into a particular sector/industry/occupation, limitations of the dataset prevent us from addressing the issue of self-selection. However, in order to see how the results change, we first present the results from the estimation that pools the sectors, then separately estimate the wage gaps for each sector with and without the industry and occupational controls. We discuss the latter estimates towards the end of the next subsection.

Estimates for the combined sample (public and private sectors)

The wage gap estimates obtained following the method just described are reported in Table 7.2, together with the percentage of the raw gap that is explained by different returns.[13] To facilitate comparison with the usual procedure, in the first column of Table 7.2, we report the gender wage gap estimated from OLS using average female characteristics.

The first interesting point to note from this table is that all the estimated gender wage gaps from the model are positive. Thus, in all countries, even assuming that men and women have identical distributions of characteristics, there is a gender pay gap across the wage distribution (due to differing returns). Notice also that these estimates are all significantly different from zero at the 1 per cent level.[14]

12 An alternative procedure to the above would be to make use of the raw female wage distribution in the comparison. Although the simulated female wage distribution using the female characteristics and returns is very similar to the raw female wage distribution, we have chosen to use the former because the comparisons are made using wage distributions that have been simulated using the same procedure.

13 The controls included in the equations are listed under Table 7.2. In addition to human capital variables and job characteristics, they include year dummies to allow for cyclical effects on the gender wage gap at each quantile. Unfortunately, the ECHP contains no information about in individual union membership or coverage by collective bargaining.

14 A bootstrap sample of size 200 was used for the calculation of the standard errors. The sampling procedure used in the calculation also used the block- sampling method to account for clustering at the individual level because of the panel nature of the dataset (Fitzenberger 1998).

Table 7.3: Summary of Table 7.2 quantile regression results-pooled model

	Glass ceiling measured by[a]			Sticky floor measured by[b]		Estimated profile of wage gap along distribution	Estimated range of wage gap
	90–all gaps	90–75 difference	90–50 difference	10–50 difference	10–25 difference		
Country	[1]	[2]	[3]	[4]	[5]	[6]	[7]
Austria	✓	✓	✓	–	–	–	23–30
Belgium	✓	✓	✓	–	–	Increasing	10–21
Britain	✓	✓	✓	–	–	Increasing	20–29
Denmark	✓	✓	✓	–	–	Increasing	5–21
Finland	✓	✓	✓	–	–	Increasing	15–30
France	✓	✓	✓	–	–	–	18–28
Germany	✓	✓	✓	–	–	Increasing	12–20
Ireland	–	–	–	–	–	–	23–26
Italy	✓	✓	✓	✓	–	–	12–18
Netherlands	✓	✓	✓	–	–	Increasing	5–24
Spain	–	–	–	✓	✓	Decreasing	12–24

Notes: [a] A glass ceiling is defined to exist if the 90th percentile wage gap exceeds the reference gap by at least 2 points; [b] A sticky floor is defined to exist if the l0th percentile wage gap exceeds the reference wage gap by at least 2 points.

To facilitate comparison, we summarise in Table 7.3 the results from the QR model estimates. We first define a glass ceiling as existing if the 90th percentile wage gap is higher than the estimated wage gaps in other parts of the wage distribution by at least two percentage points. The sticky floor phenomenon is defined to exist if the 10th percentile wage gap is higher than the 25th percentile wage gap by at least two percentage points. The results are summarised in columns [1] and [5]. Column [1] of Table 7.3 shows that there was a glass ceiling in nine countries (Ireland and Spain are the exceptions). Alternative definitions of a glass ceiling – see columns [2] and [3] – produce similar conclusions. Note also that the estimated wage gap is found to increase in Belgium, Britain, Denmark, Finland, Germany and the Netherlands all along the wage distribution. In contrast, the estimated wage gap decreases as one moves up the wage distribution in Spain.

There is also some evidence of sticky floors, but in only two countries (Italy and Spain) using the 10–50 difference, and in only one country (Spain) using the 10–25 difference. Here, women at the bottom (the 10th percentile) are found to have been more disadvantaged than those at the 25th percentile. In general, the wage gap at the mean is found to provide a very incomplete picture of the differing returns faced by women and men at various points of the wage distribution.

The proportion of the observed raw wage gap that is explained by the differences in returns to characteristics is shown in square brackets for each country in Table 7.2. A value greater than 100 per cent implies that women had characteristics that compensated them for any 'discrimination' – defined here as different returns to the same characteristics – that they faced in the labour market. For example, in five countries – Belgium, Finland, France, Italy and Spain – women typically had better characteristics than men. The same was also true for Irish women whose earnings placed them in the top parts of the distribution. Next, we turn to the estimates obtained from the disaggregated subsamples, where public and private workers are examined separately.

Table 7.4: Estimated wage gap (industry and occupation excluded)

Country	OLS		10%		25%		50%		75%		90%	
Industry and occupation excluded												
Public sector												
Austria	0.227	[168]	0.153	[100]	0.140	[115]	0.190	[219]	0.239	[258]	0.289	[250]
Belgium	0.122	[167]	0.065	[105]	0.072	[124]	0.099	[304]	0.141	[218]	0.209	[154]
Britain	0.176	[83]	0.109	[51]	0.138	[75]	0.182	[84]	0.192	[98]	0.241	[112]
Denmark	0.089	[78]	0.058	[45]	0.063	[71l	0.084	[80]	0.122	[102]	0.181	[104]
Finland	0.255	[98]	0.158	[96]	0.192	[98]	0.247	[95]	0.298	[94]	0.313	[102]
France	0.172	[148]	0.145	[129]	0.130	[138]	0.146	[133]	0.189	[148]	0.273	[197]
Germany	0.099	[78]	0.058	[55]	0.072	[73]	0.102	[70]	0.137	[87]	0.167	[106]
Ireland	0.177	[161]	0.167	[125]	0.153	[109]	0.161	[205]	0.163	[407]	0.186	[199]
Italy	0.086	[1431]	0.031	[−1823]	0.037	[361]	0.072	[5490]	0.125	[−593]	0.169	[365]
Netherlands	0.142	[71]	0.049	[34]	0.088	[47]	0.131	[69]	0.183	[93]	0.235	[101]
Spain	0.077	[142]	0.102	[122]	0.096	[140]	0.082	[142]	0.040	[−844]	0.062	[96]
Private sector												
Austria	0.251	[86]	0.212	[74]	0.207	[72]	0.215	[78]	0.233	[85]	0.269	[101]
Belgium	0.144	[105]	0.090	[75]	0.120	[88]	0.144	[120]	0.174	[124]	0.218	[110]
Britain	0.247	[81]	0.201	[75]	0.224	[74]	0.246	[80]	0.272	[83]	0.302	[97]
Denmark	0.118	[88]	0.045	[44]	0.081	[71]	0.110	[122]	0.163	[98]	0.209	[87]
Finland	0.211	[126]	0.134	[111]	0.165	[122]	0.207	[142]	0.250	[126]	0.284	[117]

Country	OLS		10%		25%		50%		75%		90%	
France	0.234	[116]	0.197	[110]	0.174	[112]	0.189	[111]	0.236	[117]	0.294	[129]
Germany	0.162	[62]	0.139	[47]	0.142	[56]	0.146	[63]	0.159	[64]	0.200	[71]
Ireland	0.230	[84]	0.185	[70]	0.215	[81]	0.240	[91]	0.256	[96]	0.269	[86]
Italy	0.172	[112]	0.156	[108]	0.138	[124]	0.146	[112]	0.169	[116]	0.205	[106]
Netherlands	0.127	[61]	0.029	[16]	0.068	[38]	0.107	[61]	0.172	[79]	0.249	[90]
Spain	0.211	[92]	0.214	[85]	0.211	[102]	0.207	[101]	0.202	[83)	0.205	[99]
Industry and occupation included												
Public sector												
Austria	0.227	[168]	0.191	[125]	0.163	[133]	0.191	[220]	0.221	[239]	0.266	[230]
Belgium	0.090	[124]	0.046	[74]	0.050	[85]	0.070	[215]	0.109	[169]	0.169	[125]
Britain	0.134	[63]	0.091	[43]	0.116	[63]	0.135	[63]	0.144	[73]	0.205	[95]
Denmark	0.070	[62]	0.058	[45]	0.051	[58]	0.059	[56]	0.086	[72]	0.136	[78]
Finland	0.216	[83]	0.115	[70]	0.140	[71]	0.203	[78]	0.269	[85]	0.319	[104]
France	0.096	[83]	0.092	[82]	0.077	[81]	0.078	[71]	0.108	[85]	0.167	[121]
Germany	0.122	[95]	0.111	[105]	0.110	[112]	0.118	[81]	0.140	[89]	0.147	[93]
Ireland	0.184	[167]	0.186	[139]	0.169	[120	0.177	[225]	0.165	[413]	0.181	[194]
Italy	0.097	[1611]	0.041	[−2425]	0.047	[463]	0.081	[6182]	0.138	[−653]	0.169	[365]
Netherlands	0.121	[61]	0.039	[27]	0.070	[38]	0.112	[59]	0.160	[81]	0.218	[94]
Spain	0.083	[154]	0.090	[109]	0.079	[116]	0.095	[166]	0.069	[−1445]	0.076	[118]

Country	OLS		10%		25%		50%		75%		90%	
Private sector												
Austria	0.214	[73]	0.182	[64]	0.177	[62]	0.188	[68]	0.210	[77]	0.247	[93]
Belgium	0.132	[96]	0.100	[83]	0.121	[90]	0.131	[109]	0.148	[106]	0.185	[93]
Britain	0.190	[62]	0.155	[58]	0.172	[56]	0.188	[61]	0.213	[65]	0.227	[73]
Denmark	0.088	[66]	0.032	[31]	0.065	[56]	0.088	[97]	0.123	[74]	0.161	[67]
Finland	0.151	[91]	0.068	[56]	0.112	[83]	0.154	[105]	0.188	[95]	0.205	[85]
France	0.163	[81]	0.146	[81]	0.126	[81]	0.132	[77]	0.152	[76]	0.190	[83]
Germany	0.143	[55]	0.088	[30]	0.109	[43]	0.137	[59]	0.166	[67]	0.213	[75]
Ireland	0.163	[60]	0.081	[31]	0.143	[54]	0.184	[70]	0.195	[73]	0.206	[66]
Italy	0.173	[113]	0.148	[102]	0.135	[122]	0.152	[117]	0.179	[123]	0.220	[114]
Netherlands	0.131	[63]	0.059	[33]	0.091	[51]	0.123	[70]	0.168	[77]	0.222	[80]
Spain	0.181	[78]	0.173	[69]	0.178	[86]	0.184	[90]	0.189	[78]	0.176	[85]

Notes: Percentage of the raw gap explained by different returns. All models include dummies for whether training was received in the last year, age, education, tenure, marital status, health status, any experience of unemployment since 1989, part-time status, fixed-term and casual contracts, private sector firm size, region (where possible), and year. Dummies were also included for cases in which there was a very large number of missing values. See the Appendix for further details; All estimated wage gaps are statistically significant at the 1 per cent level.

The wage gap estimates obtained from the separate public and private sector subsamples are reported in Table 7.4, together with the percentage of the raw gap that is attributable to differing returns.[15] To facilitate comparison with the usual procedure, we report in the first column the gender wage gap estimated from OLS using average female characteristics. The findings we focus on, shown on the left-hand side of Table 7.4, are the results from estimations without industrial and occupational controls.

As for the pooled model, Table 7.4 shows that all the estimated gender wage gaps are positive, in both the public and the private sectors. Thus, in all countries, even if women had had the same returns as men, they still would have received lower pay across the wage distribution. All the gaps are significantly different from zero at the 1 per cent level. With the exception of Finland and the Netherlands, the estimated wage gaps are also generally higher in the private sector than in the public sector. In Finland, the OLS public sector gender gap was 25 per cent, versus 21 per cent in the private sector; and the gender gap in the public sector also exceeded that in the private sector over the whole distribution. In the Netherlands, the OLS gender wage gap was 13–14 per cent in both sectors, with a similar increasing gap across the wage distribution.

We next discuss in more detail how the wage gap varies across the wage distribution.

To facilitate comparisons, we summarise in Table 7.5 the results from the QR model estimates reported in Table 7.4 using the same definitions as before (see Table 7.3). We focus on the models excluding the industry and occupation dummies.

15 See Footnote 13.

Table 7.5: Summary of Table 7.4 quantile regression results-pooled model

	Glass ceiling measured by[a]			Sticky floor measured by[b]		Estimated profile of wage gap along distribution	Estimated range of wage gap
	90–all gaps	90–75 difference	90–50 difference	10–50 difference	10–25 difference		
Country	[1]	[2]	[3]	[4]	[5]	[6]	[7]
Industry and occupation included							
Public sector							
Austria	✓	✓	✓	–	–	–	14–29
Belgium	✓	✓	✓	–	–	Increasing	7–21
Britain	✓	✓	✓	–	–	Increasing	11–24
Denmark	✓	✓	✓	–	–	Increasing	6–18
Finland	–	–	✓	–	–	Increasing	16–31
France	✓	✓	✓	–	–	–	13–27
Germany	✓	✓	✓	–	–	Increasing	6–17
Ireland		✓	✓	–	–	–	15–19
Italy	✓	✓	✓	–	–	Increasing	3–17
Netherlands	✓	✓	✓	–	–	Increasing	5–24
Spain	–	✓	–	–	–	–	4–10
Private sector							
Austria	✓	✓	✓	–	–	Increasing	21–27
Belgium	✓	✓	✓	–	–	Increasing	9–22
Britain	✓	✓	✓	–	–	Increasing	20–30

	Glass ceiling measured by[a]			Sticky floor measured by[b]		Estimated profile of wage gap along distribution	Estimated range of wage gap
	90–all gaps	90–75 difference	90–50 difference	10–50 difference	10–25 difference		
Country	**[1]**	**[2]**	**[3]**	**[4]**	**[5]**	**[6]**	**[7]**
Denmark	✓	✓	✓	–	–	Increasing	5–21
Finland	✓	✓	✓	–	–	Increasing	13–29
France	✓	✓	✓	–	✓	–	17–29
Germany	✓	✓	✓	–	–	Increasing	14–20
Ireland	–	–	✓	–	–	Increasing	19–27
Italy	✓	✓	✓	–	–	–	14–21
Netherlands	✓	✓	✓	–	–	Increasing	3–25
Spain	–	–	–	–	–	Flat	21
Industry and occupation included							
Public sector							
Austria	✓	✓	✓	–	✓	–	16–27
Belgium	✓	✓	✓	–	–	Increasing	5–17
Britain	✓	✓	✓	–	–	–	9–21
Denmark	✓	✓	✓	–	–	Increasing	5–14
Finland	✓	✓	✓	–	–	Increasing	12–32
France	✓	✓	✓	–	–	–	8–17
Germany	–	–	✓	–	–	Increasing	1–15
Ireland	–	–	–	–	–	–	

	Glass ceiling measured by[a]			Sticky floor measured by[b]		Estimated profile of wage gap along distribution	Estimated range of wage gap
	90–all gaps	90–75 difference	90–50 difference	10–50 difference	10–25 difference		
Country	**[1]**	**[2]**	**[3]**	**[4]**	**[5]**	**[6]**	**[7]**
Italy	✓	✓	✓	–	–	Increasing	4–17
Netherlands	✓	✓	✓	–	–	Increasing	4–22
Spain	–	–	–	–	–	–	7–10
Private sector							
Austria	✓	✓	✓	–	–	–	23–30
Belgium	✓	✓	✓	–	–	Increasing	15–20
Britain	–	–	✓	–	–	Increasing	20–22
Denmark	✓	✓	✓	–	–	Increasing	10–16
Finland	–	–	✓	–	–	Increasing	20–22
France	✓	✓	✓	–	✓	–	14–17
Germany	✓	✓	✓	–	–	Increasing	20–21
Ireland	–	–	✓	–	–	Increasing	17–26
Italy	✓	✓	✓	–	–	–	16–21
Netherlands	✓	✓	✓	–	–	Increasing	14–19
Spain	–	–	–	–	–	Flat	21–24

Notes: [a] A glass ceiling is defined to exist if the 90th percentile wage gap exceeds the reference gap by at least 2 points; [b] A sticky floor is defined to exist if the 10th percentile wage gap exceeds the reference wage gap by at least 2 points.

First, consider the public sector estimates, shown in the top panel of Table 7.4. In nine of the 11 countries – Austria, Belgium, Britain, Denmark, Finland, France, Germany, Italy, and the Netherlands – the gender wage gap was higher at the 90th percentile of the wage distribution than at any of the lower percentiles we examined, pointing to a wide-spread glass ceiling effect across Europe. Following our precise criterion for the existence of a glass ceiling – that the 90th percentile wage gap must exceed the estimated wage gaps in other parts of the wage distribution by at least two percentage points – Finland drops out of the set. However, it rejoins this group of countries when the glass ceiling is defined by the 90–50 differential (column [3]). Across the countries, the highest wage gap at the 90th percentile is found in Finland, where it increases monotonically from about 16 per cent at the 10th percentile to about 31 per cent at the 90th percentile. The estimated wage gap is also found to increase monotonically along the wage distribution in six other countries – Belgium, Britain, Denmark, Germany, Italy, and the Netherlands – although not as dramatically as in Finland.

We find no evidence of sticky floors, as previously defined, in the public sector: that is, the results indicate that the wage gap at the 10th percentile did not exceed the wage gap at the 25th percentile by 2+ percentage points in the public sector in any of the 11 countries. In general, Belgium, Denmark, Germany, Italy, and Spain were countries with relatively low wage gaps. Once again, the wage gap at the mean is found to provide a very incomplete picture of the differing returns faced by women and men at various points of the wage distribution.

Second, consider the private sector estimates, shown in the bottom panel of Table 7.4 and also summarised in the bottom panel of Table 7.5. In contrast to the public sector, the private sector exhibits very large wage gaps. Furthermore, a glass ceiling effect is found in almost all of the 11 countries. The only exceptions are Spain, which had a fixed gap of about 20–21 per cent along the wage distribution, and Ireland, which had a glass ceiling only under the column [3] definition. The only evidence of sticky floors is in France, where the gap at the 10th percentile was just over two percentage points higher than at the 25th percentile.

We next turn to the proportion of the observed raw wage gap that is explained by the differences in returns to characteristics, shown in square brackets for each country in Table 7.4. Since the wage distributions are simulated using a single distribution of (women's) characteristics, differences over the quantiles represent interactions between the characteristics and returns. In the public sector in six countries –Austria, Belgium, France, Ireland, Italy and Spain – women typically had better characteristics than men, and at the top of the distribution, this was true for women in all countries except Spain.[16] In the private sector, Finland, France and Italy are the only countries in which women's superiority to men in productive characteristics was sufficient to compensate them for different returns across all parts of the distribution.

The estimates just discussed exclude controls for occupation and industry. We have focused on these results because of the possibility that industry and occupation are endogenous. An additional reason for omitting these controls is that employers' or trade unions' discriminatory or exclusionary practices could be highly correlated with occupation and industry. However, the occupational and industry controls might also reflect otherwise unmeasured human capital, and for this reason, we may wish to include them. The estimates of the gender pay gap without such controls – and which thereby ignore the potential effect of unobserved human capital – could be viewed as an upper bound for the extent of 'discrimination'. Conversely, the estimates of the gender pay gap with such controls could be viewed as a lower bound for the extent of 'discrimination.'

For comparison with our main results, the right-hand side of Table 7.4 presents estimates including occupation and industry. The right-hand panel of Table 7.5 summarises the pattern of glass ceilings and sticky floors according to the various definitions. Table 7.5 shows that using occupation and industry to try to account for the gender wage gap does not greatly change the previous conclusions that glass ceilings are widespread, especially in the public sector, and that two countries also have sticky floors. This may suggest that these occupational and industry controls are not picking up heterogeneity in discriminatory practices towards women. However, there are some notable exceptions: with the inclusion of industry and occupation, the private sector glass ceilings in Britain and Finland disappear using the column [1] and [2] definitions. This could indicate that the glass ceilings in these countries primarily reflect occupational or industrial segregation, but we do not push this interpretation too far, given the possible endogeneity issues and potential unobserved productivity effects. Finally, notice that a public sector sticky floor using the 25–10 differential is now found for Austria and a private sector sticky floor remains in France.

16 The very large values in, for example, the public sector in Italy merit comment. They arise because there is essentially no gap in the raw data (Table 7.1), but a large gap when characteristics are controlled for, resulting in a high percentage figure due to differing returns.

Discussion and conclusions

The European institutional setting

Our estimated gender pay gaps show that even if the distribution of characteristics were the same across gender, men and women would receive different returns across the wage distribution. We now speculate as to why the estimated gender pay gaps in Europe are (i) larger at the top of the wage distribution (glass ceilings) in most countries, and (ii) larger at the bottom of the wage distribution (sticky floors) in two countries.

Gender-specific policies – such as equal opportunity and anti-discrimination laws, parental leave provisions and the availability of childcare – are likely to affect gender wage gaps, including both mean gaps and gaps across the wage distribution. Gender wage gaps are also likely to be influenced by wage-setting institutions that do not directly impinge on gender, such as those governing collective bargaining and minimum wages. Cross-country differences in such policies and institutions across the 11 European Union countries for which we have data may well contribute to observed variations in gender wage gaps. While clearly, with just 11 observations, we cannot hope to provide a conclusive test of the impact of different institutions on the gender pay gap, we are able to provide some interesting correlations between summary measures of various important institutions and our observed gender pay gaps. In what follows, we use our estimated gaps (taken from Table 7.2) for the combined samples (in which public and private sector workers were pooled). We do so because our summary measures of various institutions are only available countrywide and are not disaggregated by sector.

Gender-specific policies

First, we consider how gender-specific policies might affect pay. Member states of the European Union prohibit discrimination based on gender, race (including nationality and citizenship), and – in Northern Ireland only – religion.[17] Nonetheless, although discrimination may be proscribed by legislation, whether or not it is still practised may depend on the effectiveness of the law's implementation and the willingness of individuals

17 In light of the European Framework Directive, categories covered by anti-discrimination legislation were extended in 2003 to include religion and sexual orientation, and in 2006 to include the additional categories of age and disability.

to take violations to the courts. To the extent that only the more articulate and better educated are willing to take legal action against breaches of the law, we might expect the impact of these policies to work against glass ceilings as defined above.

Parental leave provisions and state provision of childcare for under-school-age children vary considerably across countries (OECD 2001; Jaumotte 2003).[18] These institutions are likely to influence the behaviour of men and women differently and hence affect gender wage gaps. Blau and Kahn (2003) noted that the expected impact of these policies is unclear a priori. On the one hand, women who are not subject to parental leave provisions might give up – or lose – their jobs on having a child, and might re-enter subsequently at lower-level jobs providing shorter hours and lower pay, while women who do have access to parental leave might enjoy higher relative earnings through the fact that these policies preserve their ties with the firm and thereby increase incentives to invest in specific human capital. These factors will lead to a correlation between parental leave policies and higher female pay. We will term this the positive effect of parental leave policies. On the other hand, however, generous leave policies could increase women's time out of the workforce for childbearing, thus exacerbating the average gender pay gap for that group. This is the potential negative effect of parental leave policies.

Empirical research tends to find a positive effect of short leaves on women's wages but a negative effect for long leaves (Ruhm 1998; Waldfogel 1998). But why should these leave policies affect gender wage gaps across the wage distribution? We might expect, a priori, that women at the bottom will be less attached to the workforce, and so the positive impact of leave policies increasing women's attachment to firms might dominate the negative effect outlined above. Ultimately, however, which effect dominates – and in which countries – is an empirical question.

What is the extent of statutory parental leave policies in the EU countries for which we have data? According to the OECD (2001, Table 4.7), the country with the highest total duration of maternity/ childcare leave (weeks) is Finland, followed by Spain, France, Germany and Austria; the country with the lowest is the United Kingdom, followed by Ireland. There is also some evidence of extra-statutory provision of similar family-friendly arrangements by firms. According to the OECD (2001, p. 147) and Evans (2001), the

18 Paternity leave entitlements are still relatively uncommon, and where they are found are typically of short duration (OECD 2001:145). Of our 11 countries, Spain, the Netherlands, Belgium and France mandate three or fewer days' paternity leave, while Denmark mandates 14 days.

countries with the highest coverage of extra-statutory provisions are Austria and West Germany, followed by Italy, Greece and Spain, and coverage is lowest in the Nordic countries, Ireland and the United Kingdom.[19]

We now consider formal childcare policies. These are likely to have a positive effect on women's wages, not only because they are likely to increase women's attachment to firms, thereby increasing incentives to make investments in firm-specific skills, but also because they may enable women to return to work earlier than would otherwise be possible. We would therefore expect childcare provision to reduce the gender pay gap, ceteris paribus. However, an additional possibility is that the presence of subsidised childcare attracts into the workforce those women who are the least committed to market production. The associated selectivity effect may then actually increase the gender wage gap at the bottom of the wage distribution.

According to the OECD (2001), the countries with the largest proportions of children under three years old using formal childcare are Denmark at 64 per cent, followed by Ireland at 38 per cent, Britain at 34 per cent, France at 29 per cent, and Finland at 22 per cent. In four other countries, in contrast – Italy, the Netherlands, Spain and Austria – the figure is below 7 per cent.

Figure 7.1 presents three scatter plots (a, b and c) illustrating the cross-country correlation between the OECD (2001) work–family reconciliation index and (i) sticky floors defined as the 10=50 pay difference, (ii) glass ceilings defined as the 90–50 pay difference, and (iii) the mean gender pay gap. The OECD work–family reconciliation index is the sum of indicators for the coverage of children under three years of age in formal childcare, maternity leave, flexi time, voluntary part-time and half of the extra-statutory leave by firms indicator (see OECD 2001, p. 152). The plots show that, across countries, the work–family index is negatively correlated with sticky floors and positively correlated with glass ceilings, with *t*-statistics of -2.7 and 3.2, respectively. Thus, countries with more 'generous' work–family policies have a lower wage gap at the bottom of the wage distribution and a wider gap at the top. For example, Denmark and the Netherlands have the most liberal work–family policies, and they have a big pay gap at the top and a small pay gap at the bottom of the wage distribution.

19 Evans (2001) identified four main types of family-friendly arrangements by firms: leave from work for family reasons; changes to work arrangements for family reasons; practical help with childcare and eldercare; and the provision of training and information. OECD (2001) summarises these extra-statutory provisions along two dimensions: average percentage of female employees reporting extra family leave, and percentage of female employees reporting provision/subsidies for child daycare. The Netherlands has especially high levels of firm-provided daycare relative to the amount of extra-statutory leave.

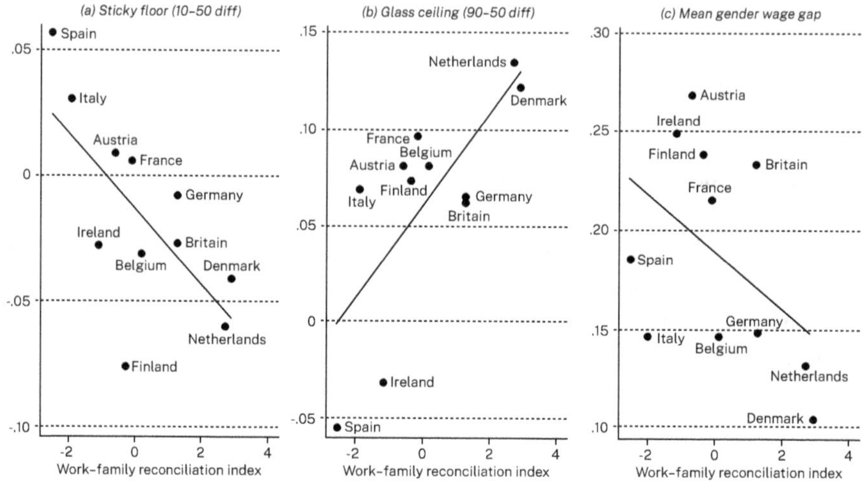

Figure 7.1: Work–family reconciliation
Source: OECD 2001 index.

We noted above that family-friendly policies could be a double-edged sword. On the one hand, they might raise women's relative earnings by preserving their ties with the firm, thereby increasing incentives to invest in specific human capital and leading to higher female pay. But on the other hand, family-friendly policies could increase women's time out of the workforce for childbearing, thus widening the average gender pay gap for that group. Our scatter-plot in Figure 7.1b – showing that the gender pay gap is higher at the top of the wage distribution in countries with generous family-friendly policies – suggests that the negative effect dominates at the top of the distribution in our sample of 11 European countries.

What about women at the bottom of the wage distribution? If such women are, on average, less attached than other women to the workforce, it is plausible that generous family-friendly policies might increase their attachment to firms. Our data are certainly consistent with that hypothesis. The scatter-plot in Figure 7.1a – showing that the gender pay gap is lower at the bottom of the wage distribution in countries with generous family-friendly policies – suggests that the positive effect of family-friendly policies dominates at the bottom of the distribution.

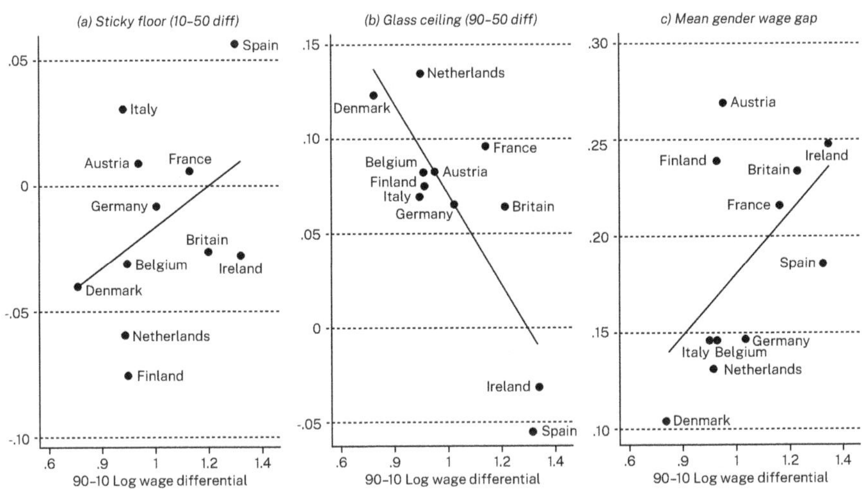

Figure 7.2: Wage dispersion

Albrecht et al. (2003, p. 172), using a QR framework, charted the extent of the Swedish glass ceiling and speculated as to its causes. They found that gender differences in returns were the primary factor. They rejected the notion of a 'taste-based explanation … [whereby] Swedish women prefer to work in family-friendly but low-wage jobs,' on the grounds that gender differences arise from differences in rewards even when the analysis controlled for occupation. A more likely explanation, they wrote, is one based on the 'work environment faced by Swedish women,' especially 'the Swedish parental leave policy and the daycare system,' which provide strong incentives to participate but not to commit strongly to a career.

Albrecht et al.'s conjecture is interesting and is supported by our results for Denmark.[20] But the fact that we find the same glass ceiling effect across the majority of other EU countries, with their very different parental leave policies and daycare systems, suggests that this cannot be the primary explanation. For example, Italy has low levels of 'work-family reconciliation policies' – and it too exhibits a glass ceiling.

A second reason put forward by Albrecht et al. (2003) for the Swedish glass ceiling phenomenon is the relatively high wages at the bottom of the wage distribution, making it 'very difficult for career-oriented women to hire household help or help with child-care', especially for the very

20 See Pylkkanen and Smith (2004) for a detailed analysis of the impact of family-friendly policies on women's parental leave behaviour in Sweden and Denmark.

young children under 12 months who cannot be admitted into daycare. For this reason, women might wind up in less demanding jobs and thus fall substantially behind men towards the top of the distribution. Thus, cross-country evidence should show a negative correlation between the magnitude of the glass ceiling and the dispersion of the wage distribution. This relationship is illustrated in Figure 7.2b for our sample of 11 countries, where we have measured wage dispersion by the 90th–10th percentile differential of log wages in the full sample of workers in each country. There is indeed a statistically significant negative correlation that is consistent with this hypothesis: the *t*-statistic on the log wage dispersion measure in the glass ceiling regression is –4.1.

Pay-bargaining institutions

Next, we consider pay-bargaining institutions that may not directly impinge on gender. While collective bargaining institutions and the degree of coordination and centralisation of wage bargaining might not have direct gender effects, they could well have important indirect effects. For example, trade unions may be less likely to represent the interests of their female electorate – who may be perceived as having a marginal attachment to the workforce – than of the male electorate (Booth and Francesconi, 2003).

In addition, collective bargaining and associated institutions affect the wage structure in general. To the extent that the wage distribution is compressed, these institutions may thus impinge indirectly on women's wages and, through this mechanism, affect the gender pay gap. Figure 7.2 suggests that this may indeed be the case. It shows that sticky floors are increasing, while glass ceilings are declining, in the 90:10 log wage differential. For those countries with greater wage dispersion, in particular Spain, the gender pay gap is relatively high at the bottom of the distribution and relatively low at the top of the distribution compared to the median. However, only the latter relationship is statistically significant (the former has a *t*-statistic of only 1.3, while the latter has a *t*-statistic of –4.1). Quite why the glass ceiling should be declining in wage dispersion is unclear. One hypothesis already mentioned is that high-wage dispersion may mean that high-skilled career-focused women can obtain cheaper domestic services.

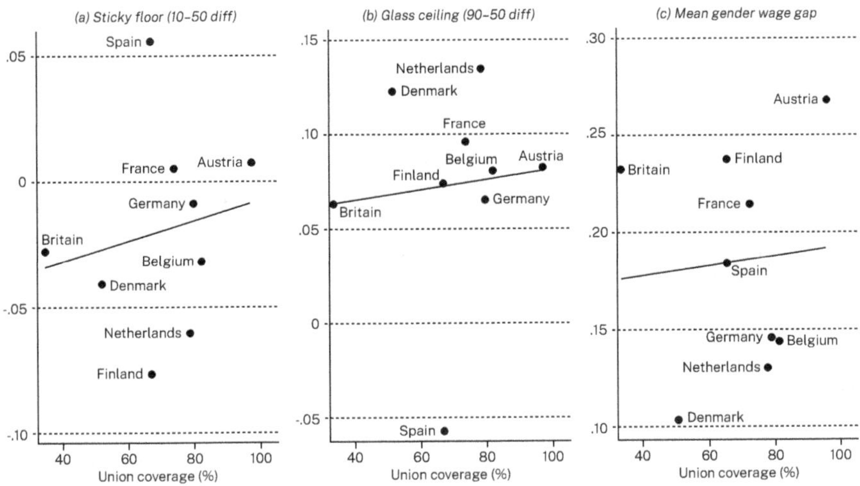

Figure 7.3: Union coverage

Countries with higher levels of unionisation and more centralised or coordinated bargaining also tend to have the lowest wage dispersion (Blau and Kahn 1992, 1996, 2003; Boeri, Brugiavini, and Calmfors 2001). Centralised bargaining – and more coordinated bargaining – results in lower wage dispersion, and is thus likely to lower the gender pay gap, ceteris paribus, perhaps especially at the bottom of the wage distribution. Moreover, in all the countries for which we have data, the female wage lies below the male wage across the entire distribution. Hence, centralised pay-bargaining systems that raise the minimum level of pay regardless of gender are also likely to lower the gender pay gap, ceteris paribus.

Although we can group our countries by both the extent of union density and the extent of union coverage, we choose to focus only on coverage.[21] The countries in which at least 75 per cent of the workforce is covered are Austria, Germany, Belgium, the Netherlands and France (Boeri et al. 2001, p. 92). The countries with the highest levels of coordination of bargaining – both of unions and employers – are Austria and Norway, followed by Germany and Finland. The lowest levels of coordination are found in the United Kingdom and Ireland. Of course, it is impossible with so few observations to tease out the direct and indirect effects of unions on our estimated gender

21 The extent of union recognition or coverage is a better measure of union power than is union density, as argued in Booth (1995). In addition, the degree of coordination between unions, and between unions and employers, can also be crucial, as well as the degree of centralisation of bargaining. See Boeri et al. (2001) for a discussion and for detailed tables indicating the variation of these measures across the EU.

gaps. We have only 11 observations for the wage dispersion measure, and for the union measure, we have only nine observations, as there were no data available for Ireland and Italy. However, Figure 7.3a does reveal a positive correlation between the magnitude of the sticky floor and union coverage. Figure 7.3b reveals a positive correlation between the magnitude of the glass ceiling and union coverage, and Figure 7.3c also shows that the mean wage gap increases with union coverage. However, none of these estimated relationships is statistically significant (the *t*-statistics for Figures 7.3a–c are 0.5, 0.3, and 0.2). Perhaps it is unsurprising that the data here are not very informative, given that we have only nine observations.

Statutory minimum wages compress the bottom of the pay distribution, and so are likely to reduce the gap between men and women at the bottom (Dolado et al. 1996). Institutional pay compression – whether through unions or through minimum wages – may distort skills investment incentives. However, recent studies suggest that, in the presence of labour market imperfections inducing wage compression, firms may be willing to finance work-related training (see, inter alia, Stevens 1994; Acemoglu and Pischke 1999, 2003; Arulampalam et al. 2004). If pay returns are reduced by pay compression, women have less incentive to stay in the workforce when engaged in child-rearing. Conversely, high wage floors might increase the likelihood that women stay in the workforce, because of the higher opportunity cost of time out, and women might therefore have higher levels of work experience and skills acquisition. Whether these effects on the gender pay gap vary across the wage distribution is ultimately an empirical issue. Certainly, Figures 7.2a and b show that countries with low wage dispersion have lower gender pay gaps at the bottom of the wage distribution and higher pay gaps at the top. This correlation is consistent with the hypothesis that women in countries with low pay dispersion are more likely to stay attached to firms at the bottom of the distribution.

Other factors

Of course, other factors are also likely to be at work. Many labour markets are hierarchical, and promotion and appointment procedures can exacerbate gender pay gaps across the pay distribution. While promotions are typically subject to well-defined procedures, especially in larger organisations, exactly where in the rank-specific salary scale a successful candidate is appointed can depend on individual negotiation skills or bargaining power, or employer discretion, in addition to experience. Booth et al. (2005), using data on promotions from the BHPS, showed that women gained less from promotion than men did, ceteris paribus.[22] If promotion procedures favour men over women towards the top of the wage distribution, then the gender pay gap might be bigger towards the top. Landers et al. (1996) showed, in their study of US law firms, how such criteria for promotion as excessively long hours of work can exacerbate gender pay gaps towards the top of the lawyers' wage distribution.

Individuals are frequently appointed at a particular rank level of the relevant scale for their occupation or industry and then aim to work their way up the hierarchy. While both promotions and pay are covered by anti-discrimination legislation and equal opportunities policies, there is scope for discretion – or discrimination – in the choice of the particular level within a rank to which an individual is appointed. Thus, if men are initially appointed at a higher starting salary (a higher rung) within a particular scale than are comparable women, then the gender pay gap might be bigger towards the bottom of the wage distribution – the sticky floor. Another hypothesis is that women towards the bottom might have less bargaining power or be more likely to be subject to firms' market power than comparable men, due perhaps to unobservable family commitments or social custom whereby the man's career takes precedence. Although we are unable to explore these hypotheses with our data, we mention them in passing because it is possible that such mechanisms partly explain our findings.

Conclusions

The analysis in this chapter shows that, across our sample of 11 European Union countries in 1995–2001, women were paid less than men, even when the analysis holds the distribution of characteristics constant. The magnitude of the gaps – which can be attributed to differing returns – varied substantially across the different countries and across the wage distributions. We suggest that the considerable heterogeneity in EU countries' institutions is likely to contribute to these differences, as illustrated by the simple correlations in Figures 7.1–7.3.

22 Blackaby et al. (2005), using data on the labour market for academic economists in the United Kingdom, produced further evidence that promotions might exacerbate gender pay inequality.

Acknowledgements

This chapter was first published as Arulampalam, W., Booth, A.L., and Bryan, M.L. (2007). 'Is there a glass ceiling over Europe? Exploring the gender pay gap across the wage distribution', *ILR Review*, 60(2):163–186. doi.org/10.1177/001979390706000201.

The authors gratefully acknowledge the support of the Leverhulme Trust. For helpful comments, they thank Bernd Fitzenberger, Jose Machado, Blaise Melly, Jeremy Smith, and participants in the 7th Labour Econometrics Conference, Auckland, 13–14 August 2004, the 2nd SOLE/EALE World Conference, San Francisco, 2–5 June 2005, and the 2005 Conference of the European Panel Users Network, Colchester, UK, 30 June – 2 July 2005.

Data from the ECHP Survey 1994–2001 are used with the permission of Eurostat.

References

Acemoglu, D., and Pischke, J.-S. (1999). 'The structure of wages and investment in general training', *Journal of Political Economy*, 107(3):539–572. doi.org/10.1086/250071.

Acemoglu, D., and Pischke, J.-S. (2003). 'Minimum wages and on-the-job training', *Research in Labor Economics*, 22:159–202.

Albrecht, J., Björklund, A., and Vroman, S. (2003). 'Is there a glass ceiling in Sweden?', *Journal of Labor Economics*, 21(1):145–177. doi.org/10.1086/344126.

Arulampalam, W., Booth, A.L., and Bryan, M.L. (2004). 'Training and the new minimum wage', *Economic Journal*, 114(494):C87–C94.

Blackaby, D., Booth, A.L., and Frank, J. (2005). 'Outside offers and the gender pay gap: Empirical evidence from the UK academic labour market', *The Economic Journal*, 115(501):F81–F107. doi.org/10.1111/j.0013-0133.2005.00973.x.

Blau, F.D., and Kahn, L.M. (1992). 'The gender earnings gap: Learning from international comparisons', *American Economic Review*, 82(2), pp. 533–538.

Blau, F.D., and Kahn, L.M. (1996). 'Wage structure and gender earnings differentials: An international comparison', *Economica*, 63(Supplement):S29–S62.

Blau, F.D., and Kahn, L.M. (2003). 'Understanding international differences in the gender pay gap', *Journal of Labor Economics*, 21(1):106–144.

Blinder, A. (1973). 'Wage discrimination: Reduced form and structural estimates', *Journal of Human Resources*, 8(4):436–455.

Boeri, T., Brugiavini, A., and Calmfors, L., eds. (2001). *The Role of Unions in the Twenty-First Century*. Oxford: Oxford University Press.

Booth, A.L. (1995). *The Economics of the Trade Union*. Cambridge: Cambridge University Press.

Booth, A.L., and Francesconi, M. (2003). 'Union coverage and non-standard work in Britain', *Oxford Economic Papers*, 55(3):383–416. doi.org/10.1093/oep/55.3.383.

Booth, A.L., Francesconi, M., and Frank, J. (2003). 'A sticky floors model of promotion, pay, and gender', *European Economic Review*, 47(2):295–322. doi.org/10.1016/S0014-2921(01)00197-0.

Buchinsky, M. (1998). 'Recent advances in quantile regression models', *Journal of Human Resources*, 33(1):88–126.

De la Rica, S., Dolado, J.J., and Llorens, V. (2005). 'Ceiling and floors: Gender wage gaps by education in Spain'. IZA Discussion Paper No. 1483, Bonn.

Del Rio, C., Gradin, C., and Canto, O. (2005). 'The measurement of gender wage discrimination: The distributional approach revisited'. Working Paper No. 25, ECINEQ (Society for the Study of Economic Inequality).

Dolado, J.J., Kramarz, F., Machin, S., Manning, A., Margolis, D., and Teulings, C. (1996). 'The economic impact of minimum wages in Europe', *Economic Policy*, 23:319–372.

Eurostat. (2003). *Eurostat Yearbook 2003. The Statistical Guide to Europe: Data 1991–2001*. Luxembourg: Office for Official Publications of the European Communities.

Evans, J.M. (2001). 'Firms' contribution to the reconciliation between work and family life'. Labour Market and Social Policy Occasional Papers No. 45, OECD, Paris.

Fitzenberger, B. (1998). 'The moving blocks bootstrap and robust inference for linear least squares and quantile regressions', *Journal of Econometrics*, 82:235–287.

Jaumotte, F. (2003). 'Female labour force participation: past trends and main determinants in OECD countries'. Economics Department Working Paper No. 376, OECD, Paris.

Koenker, R., and Bassett, G. (1978). 'Regression quantiles', *Econometrica*, 46(1): 33–50. doi.org/10.2307/1913643.

Landers, R.M., Rebitzer, J.B., and Taylor, L.J. (1996). 'Rat race redux: Adverse selection in the determination of work hours in law firms', *American Economic Review*, 86(3):329–348.

Lucifora, C., and Meurs, D. (2004). 'The public sector pay gap in France, Great Britain, and Italy'. IZA Discussion Paper No. 1041, Bonn.

Machado, J., and Mata, J. (2005). 'Counterfactual decomposition of changes in wage distributions using quantile regression', *Journal of Applied Econometrics*, 20(4):445–465.

Oaxaca, R.L. (1973). 'Male-female wage differentials in urban labor markets', *International Economic Review*, 14(3):693–709.

OECD. (1996). 'Earnings inequality, low-paid employment and earnings mobility'. In *Employment Outlook*. Paris: OECD.

OECD. (2001). 'Balancing work and family life: Helping parents into paid employment'. In *Employment Outlook*. Paris: OECD.

Pylkkiinen, E., and Smith, N. (2004). 'The impact of family-friendly policies in Denmark and Sweden on mothers' career interruptions due to childbirth'. IZA Discussion Paper No. 1050, Bonn.

Ruhm, C.J. (1998). 'The economic consequences of parental leave mandates: Lessons from Europe', *The Quarterly Journal of Economics*, 113(1):285–317. doi.org/10.1162/003355398555586.

Stevens, M. (1994). 'A theoretical model of on-the-job training with imperfect competition', *Oxford Economic Papers*, 46(4):537–562. doi.org/10.1093/oxford journals.oep.a042147.

Waldfogel, J. (1998). 'The family gap for young women in the United States and Britain: Can maternity leave make a difference?', *Journal of Labor Economics*, 16(3):505–545. doi.org/10.1086/209897.

Appendix

Selection of estimating samples and sample sizes

The selection criteria are outlined in the text and result in sample sizes as given in column [5] of Appendix Table A7.I. The pooled, economy-wide models use the combined public and private sector samples for each gender. In the separate private and public sector analyses, which include occupation and industry, the various industry and occupation dummies were combined in the following cases: (i) where there were small cell sizes (less than 1 per cent of observations for both sexes); and (ii) where there was strong gender segregation (less than 1 per cent of one sex in a cell).

For the industry dummies, the base case in the public sector is administration, and the base case in the private sector is manufacturing. The table below shows how dummies were combined for each sector and country. For the public sector (where industry structure varies substantially across countries), the table lists the dummies combined and those included separately. Note that when energy is combined with manufacturing, it is simply left in the base case. For the private sector, the table lists only combined dummies. The others are all included separately. The full industry list is as follows: agriculture (all observations dropped), energy, manufacturing, construction, retail, hotels, communications, finance, property, administration, education, social services, other and missing industry.

For the occupational dummies, the base case is unskilled. The most common form of occupational segregation is in the public sector, where there are very few female craft workers or operatives. These categories were combined with service and shop workers (this was preferred to combining them with the unskilled category). The full occupational list is as follows: manager, professional, associate professional, clerical worker, service worker, agricultural worker (all observations dropped), craft worker, operative, unskilled/other and missing occupation.

Germany: to account for differences in wage determination between east and west in post-unification Germany, following a pooling test, we interacted the following variables with a dummy variable for Eastern Germany: age, education, health status, any experience of unemployment since 1989, fixed-term contract, occupation, firm size (private sector) and year.

Table A7.l: Sample selection and industry/occupation definitions

Country	Sector	Industry dummies	Occupation dummies	Final no. of pooled observations (men, women)	Mean waves per individual (men, women)
[1]	[2]	[3]	[4]	[5]	[6]
Austria	Public	Combined: energy, mfg, constr, retail, hotel, finance. Separate: comms, property, educ, socs, other	Combined: service worker, craft, operative	2,389, 2,214	4.3, 4.2
	Private	Combined: (1) energy, mfg; (2) admin, educ, socs	–	6,469, 4,205	4.1, 3.6
Belgium	Public	Combined: energy, mfg, constr, retail, hotel. Separate: comms, finance, property, education, socs, other	Combined: service worker, craft, operative	2,257, 2,466	4.2, 4.0
	Private	Combined: (1) energy, mfg; (2) admin, edu	–	4,271, 3,137	3.8, 3.6
Britain	Public	Combined: energy, mfg, constr, retail, hotel, finance. Separate: comms, property, education, socs, other	Combined: service worker, craft, operative	2,099, 3,918	4.4, 4.1
	Private	Combined: admin, edu	–	8,980, 6,934	3.8, 3.6
Denmark	Public	Combined: energy, mfg, constr, retail, hotel, finance. Separate: comms, property, education, socs, other	Combined: service worker, craft, operative	1,984, 3,922	4.1, 4.0
	Private	Combined: (1) energy, mfg; (2) admin, educ, socs	–	5,169, 2,955	4.0, 3.8
Finland	Public	Combined: energy, constr, retail, hotel, finance. Separate: mfg, comms, property, education, socs, other	Combined: service worker, craft, operative	2,240, 4,153	3.7, 3.5
	Private	Combined: (1) energy, mfg; (2) admin, educ, socs	–	5,413, 3,616	3.3, 3.2
France	Public	Combined: constr, retail, hotel. Separate: energy, mfg, comms, finance, property, education, socs, other	Combined: service worker, craft, operative	4114, 5017	4.2, 4.1
	Private	Combined: (1) energy, mfg;(2) admin, educ	–	10,309, 7,227	3.8, 3.6

Country	Sector	Industry dummies	Occupation dummies	Final no. of pooled observations (men, women)	Mean waves per individual (men, women)
[1]	[2]	[3]	[4]	[5]	[6]
Germany	Public	Combined: energy, mfg, constr, retail, hotel, property. Separate: comms, finance, education, socs, other	Combined: service worker, craft, operative	3,572, 4,698	4.6, 4.2
	Private	Combined: (1) energy, mfg; (2) admin, educ, socs	–	13,335, 8,031	4.3, 4.8
Ireland	Public	Combined: energy, mfg, constr, retail, hotel. Separate: comms, finance, property, education, socs, other	Combined: service worker, craft, operative	2,113, 1,945	3.9, 3.6
	Private	Combined: (1) energy, mfg; (2) admin, edu, socs	–	4,684, 3,597	3.2, 3.0
Italy	Public	Combined: constr, retail, hotel, finance, property. Separate energy, mfg, comms, education, social srvcs, other	Combined: (1) mgr, professional; (2) service worker, craft, operative	4,638, 4,404	4.2, 4.5
	Private	Combined: admin, edu, socs	Combined: mgr, professional	10,255, 5,812	3.7, 3.4
Netherlands	Public	Combined: energy, mfg, constr, retail, hotel, comms, finance. Separate: property, education, socs, other	Combined: service worker, craft, operative	3,125, 3,378	4.8, 4.3
	Private	Combined: admin, edu	–	10,491, 5,821	4.6, 3.9
Spain	Public	Combined: energy, mfg, constr, retail, hotel, finance. Separate comms, property, education, socs, other	Combined: (1) mgr, professional; (2) service worker, craft, operative	3,155, 2,837	4.1, 3.9
	Private	Combined: admin, edu, socs	–	11,790, 6,241	3.4, 2.9

Notes: comms = communication; constr = construction; edu = education; mfg = manufacturing; mgr = managerial; socs = social services.

8

Hours of work and gender identity: Does part-time work make the family happier?

Alison L Booth and Jan C van Ours

Introduction

In this chapter, we investigate the relationship between part-time (PT) work and working hours satisfaction, job satisfaction and life satisfaction. We account for interdependence within the family and use new panel data for partnered men and women.

Our chapter makes three contributions to the existing literature. First, we investigate explicitly the degree to which PT work may affect family subjective wellbeing. While there is a large and growing economics literature on the determinants of various components of satisfaction and happiness, few studies have explicitly investigated how PT work status might affect individual life satisfaction, and none have looked at how PT work affects family life satisfaction.[1] Second, following Ferrer-i-Carbonell and Frijters (2004), we use a fixed-effects ordered logit to estimate our

1 See for example Bardasi and Francesconi (2004). Some other studies examining individual life satisfaction include part-time work status as a control, but do not comment on the estimated coefficients. Frijters et al. (2004a, b), using the German Socio-Economic Panel (GSOEP) data find that life satisfaction is higher for full-time and part-time women – and for non-participating women – relative to the base of unemployed women. In job satisfaction studies, hours of work are frequently included as controls, and typically have a negative effect on job satisfaction (see inter alia Clark 1997; Clark and Oswald 1994), apart from overtime hours see Van Praag and Ferrer-i-Carbonell (2004, pp. 56–57).

models. This allows us to exploit more of the data than is usually done in the satisfaction literature, which typically uses a fixed-effects binary logit model. Finally, we utilise the time-use module available in our dataset to illuminate our findings about partnered life satisfaction by investigating the relationship between the male shares of housework and market work. The distribution of working hours within a household may be driven by partners specialising in either market work or housework, as argued by, for example, Becker (1965).[2] However, social custom and conditioning – in particular gender identity as argued by Akerlof and Kranton (2000) – may influence the distribution of time spent on childcare and housework, and preferences for FT and PT jobs.

Although many women prefer to work PT (OECD 2004), it is not clear a priori that PT work contributes to the happiness of the family. To explore this empirically, we use the first four waves of the Household, Income and Labour Dynamics in Australia (HILDA) Survey to investigate the relationship between PT work and various indicators of satisfaction. We use three indicators: satisfaction with working hours, overall job satisfaction and life satisfaction. Since we are especially interested in the effects of PT work on family life, we take into account that, for married or cohabiting couples, the distribution of paid work may not be unrelated to the distribution of home work. By studying the cross-partner effects of working PT, we can determine whether or not PT work makes families happier.

The setup of the chapter is as follows. We give a brief overview of the literature on PT work and job satisfaction, and relate this to the gender identity and specialisation hypotheses. We then describe the data and examine the degree to which workers are satisfied with their current hours of work, before using a fixed-effects ordered logit model to estimate whether or not PT work affects our three satisfaction indicators – hours, jobs and life. Our results show a gendered difference in the impact of PT and FT work on hours and life satisfaction. Since this suggests that Australian households are characterised by traditional gendered roles, we exploit time-use data to estimate the relationship between the male shares of housework and market work. We find that men doing a small share of market work are also doing a small share of housework. This finding is consistent with the gender identity hypothesis of Akerlof and Kranton (2000), but inconsistent with a gender neutrality hypothesis.

2 See also Rosen (1983), who emphasises how nonlinear production functions could lead to incomplete specialisation. We return to this later in the chapter.

Background

While there is a large and growing economics literature on the determinants of various components of satisfaction and happiness, few studies have explicitly investigated the degree to which PT work status might affect individual life satisfaction, as we noted in the Introduction. And none has looked at how PT work affects family life satisfaction. In contrast, numerous studies have focused on unemployment status and individual happiness.[3] These studies have typically found that it is the experience of unemployment itself, rather than the loss of income through unemployment, that reduces life satisfaction. This finding has been rationalised by appealing to work as a source of social connection and self-esteem that is not found in unemployment. But these same arguments might also apply to individuals choosing to work PT in the market sector rather than choosing home production or leisure. Moreover, a large – and in many countries growing – proportion of the workforce is in PT work, and it would therefore seem important to know whether or not this work pattern is welfare-enhancing to the individuals and couples concerned.

Although many young people may choose to work PT in order to finance educational investments or gain pocket money while at school, most PT workers have family responsibilities. And family responsibilities involve partners in difficult choices, such as whether to buy in from the market sector goods and services that might alternatively be produced by one partner at home. Theories of household behaviour, such as that put forward by Becker (1965), predict that partnered households will be characterised by specialisation of labour, whereby in the extreme case one partner engages in home work and the other in market-sector work. Incomplete specialisation, in which both partners perform part of the home work and part of the market work, may arise because of nonlinear production functions or because cost functions associated with skills investment are characterised by economies of scope. Nonlinear production functions might arise if there is activity-specific fatigue or boredom, implying diminishing marginal productivity in each activity. Cost functions characterised by economies of scope occur if investment in market skills reduces the cost of investing in home skills. (See Rosen 1983 for a nice exposition of these.) Under incomplete

3 For studies using panel data explicitly to investigate the relationship between happiness and unemployment, see Carroll (2007), Clark and Oswald (1994), Clark (2003), Clark et al. (2001), Gerlach and Stephan (1996) and Winkelmann and Winkelmann (1998).

specialisation, there will be a monotonically declining relationship between the share of housework done by one partner and that same partner's share of market work.

Notice that Becker's theory is gender-neutral. If it is the male partner who does the lion's share of market work, his partner's share of housework should be larger; but if he does the minority share of market work, according to the specialisation hypothesis, he should do the majority share of housework.

Part-time jobs provide a means of combining domestic and market production, while maintaining workforce skills or experience capital for the future. Part-time work, therefore, facilitates incomplete specialisation by either gender. The specialisation hypothesis predicts gender differences in working hours because partners within a household specialise (completely or incompletely) in either market work or housework. However, the prediction is symmetric; if one partner specialises in market work, the other will specialise in home production, and in principle, there is no a priori reason why the partner specialising in market work should be female or male. We term this the gender neutrality hypothesis.

In contrast, the gender identity hypothesis of Akerlof and Kranton (2000) is based on the idea that gender matters. Here, the distribution of household work and market work is determined by gender-specific 'utility'. According to this approach, since individuals operate within society's constraints, their happiness and the gender division of labour could be powerfully affected by social customs and conditioning. It is possible that, controlling for income, PT jobs could make partnered women happier than either FT work or no work, because such jobs allow them to gain esteem through working, while obtaining social and self-approbation from being with and caring for their families and their homes. Indeed, as argued by Akerlof and Kranton (2000), society's prescriptions about appropriate modes of behaviour for each gender might result in women and men experiencing a loss of identity should they deviate from the relevant code. If this is the case, men might be happier in FT work and women in PT work, since both are then adopting modes of behaviour dictated by social custom. Of course, these prescriptions are endogenous to a society, as noted by thinkers such as John Stuart Mill (1869). Prescriptions might arise and continue because it is in the dominant group's interest to maintain them. They can be weakened or removed when this group loses power. For example, the female suffragette movement can be viewed as a movement aiming to remove the presumption that women were not capable of voting responsibly. Akerlof and Kranton (2000) also note that the women's movement has reduced the gender associations of particular tasks and made it more acceptable for women to work in the market sector. Whether or not this applies to men engaging in housework is a topic to which we return later in this chapter. An empirical prediction of this gender identity model is that the average male share of housework will always be smaller than the female share, regardless of how the couple share their total hours of market work. (Later in the chapter, we will use the HILDA survey time-use module to discriminate empirically between the gender neutrality and gender identity hypotheses.)

How does the gender identity model affect life satisfaction? If women do feel a loss of identity by deviating from a particular prescription of responsibility for home production, we might expect PT work to increase life satisfaction, *ceteris paribus*, since PT work might be preferred simply because there is a finite amount of time in each day. If the responsibility for housework rests with the woman, then there are fewer hours available for market work, and for this reason, women might prefer PT commitments. Although some partnered couples no longer follow the conventional gendered division of labour, the bulk of the evidence suggests that in the average household, it is women who work PT and assume the main domestic care role while the men work FT.

In summary, if women prefer PT work because it satisfies their hours preferences, given their constraints, we should observe a positive correlation between PT work and hours satisfaction. But although PT work might increase hours satisfaction, it might not necessarily increase job satisfaction. (Part-timers may be doing more menial and less satisfying work than if they were working FT.) So if PT jobs are bad jobs, overall job satisfaction may be lower. The effect of PT work on overall life satisfaction is unclear a priori. It is likely to provide flexible working hours while maintaining an individual's self-esteem and social connection. On the other hand, PT jobs may be intrinsically unsatisfying and dead-end, and therefore may reduce life satisfaction through this avenue. Part-time jobs are often viewed as bad jobs with poor pay and promotion prospects. However, Rodgers (2004) and Booth and Wood (2008), also using the HILDA Survey data, show that there is a *ceteris paribus* PT pay premium in Australia for women and men. Ultimately, it is an empirical issue as to which effect dominates.

To our knowledge, no studies have yet explored the nexus between the happiness of the partnered couple and their work status. Yet the observed patterns of higher female participation over the life cycle, and the combination of market and household production engaged in by couples, would suggest that the relationship between work status and happiness is an important issue to address.

While happiness research in the economics literature has been underway for over a decade, only relatively recently have panel data techniques been employed to control for unobserved individual heterogeneity. Cross-sectional equations facilitate the establishment of correlation rather than causation. This is because unobservables, for example, an extrovert personality type, can be correlated both with the propensity to report happiness and with the explanatory variables of interest. Thus, the coefficients to the latter are possibly biased in cross-sectional work.[4] The use of panel data can overcome this problem, to the extent that personality traits are fixed over time and can be differenced out.

To our knowledge, only a few studies, apart from our own, look at interdependence within the family. Van Praag and Ferrer-i-Carbonell (2004, Chapter 6) investigate gender differences in happiness and explore covariances between satisfaction of the two partners in a household, using random effects from a cross-section of the BHPS. Winkelmann (2005) uses the German Socioeconomic Panel (GSOEP) to examine interdependence across generations, using random effects estimation.[5]

In contrast to those two studies, we use fixed-effects ordered logit estimation on a panel of partnered men and women. This is in contrast to the bulk of the empirical literature on satisfaction analysis, in which the categorical satisfaction scale is typically reduced to a (0,1) scale, permitting fixed-effects estimation of a binomial logit model using Chamberlain's (1980) method. But unfortunately, that method comes at a high cost, since only those individuals moving across the cut-off point can be used in the estimation. Instead of adopting that procedure, we follow Ferrer-i-Carbonell and Frijters (2004) and use an ordered logit model. This introduces individual-specific

4 Studies using panel data techniques to examine the determinants of satisfaction include Carroll (2007), Clark (2003), Ferrer-i-Carbonell and Frijters (2004), Frijters et al. (2004a, b) and Hamermesh (2001).

5 Plug and Van Praag (1998) compare partners' responses to subjective wellbeing questions. While they find little difference, this is not the case with our variable of interest. In a companion paper (Booth and van Ours 2007), we use the BHPS to explore the determinants of partnered wellbeing in Britain. We find that life satisfaction of men and women is not affected by how many hours they work. Men have the highest hours-of-work satisfaction if they work full-time without overtime hours; women have the highest hours-of-work satisfaction if they work part-time, irrespective of whether the part-time jobs are small or large.

fixed-effects and individual-specific thresholds, a simple reformulation that allows Chamberlain's method to be used, removing both individual-specific effects and thresholds from the likelihood specification. Moreover, the number of observations used in this approach is significantly greater relative to the binomial logit method. This is because all changes in satisfaction are exploited, and not just those across some arbitrary cut-off point.

Data

The empirical analysis is based on the first four waves of the HILDA Survey, a nationally representative random-sample survey of private households in Australia spanning the period 2001–04. The survey is a longitudinal study of representative households in Australia. (For details, see Appendix A; this appendix also gives an overview of the definitions of the variables used in the analysis.) We restrict our estimating subsample to married or cohabiting couples, because we are interested in the relationship between PT work and family welfare. Since prime-age women in particular are confronted with choices concerning family life and paid work, we further restrict our analysis to couples in which the female partner was aged 25–50 in 2001, the first year of the HILDA Survey. In addition, we dropped a few couples in which the male partner was over 60 in 2001, because such males are much less likely to participate in the labour market. We use an unbalanced panel, in which selected couples are present in at least two consecutive waves. These restrictions yield a sample of 2,326 couples. For females in these couples, 29 per cent have no job, 37 per cent have a PT job, and 34 per cent have an FT job. For males in these couples, 9 per cent have no job, 7 per cent have a PT job, and 84 per cent have an FT job.

In our analysis, we focus on three satisfaction variables: hours of work satisfaction, overall job satisfaction and life satisfaction. The hours and overall job satisfaction variables were obtained from the following question about the individual's main job:

> I now have some questions about how satisfied or dissatisfied you are with different aspects of your job … If not currently employed, these questions refer to the most recent job you were working in.

Respondents were then prompted for hours of work, and then for jobs. The precise question was: 'All things considered, how satisfied are you with your job?'

The responses could run from 0 to 10, with higher numbers denoting higher levels of satisfaction. The life satisfaction variable was obtained from the following question: 'All things considered, how satisfied are you with your life? Again, pick a number between 0 and 10 to indicate how satisfied you are.'

Our measure of PT work is based on individuals' usual hours of work in their main job (including any paid or unpaid overtime for work done at the workplace or at home). Part-time status is assigned to individuals reporting working fewer than 35 hours per week. This is also the definition of PT work used by Rodgers (2004) and Booth and Wood (2008), and is common in classifications of work status in Australia.

The distribution of each of the satisfaction variables across different groups is presented in Table 8.1. As shown, satisfaction ranges from 0 to 10, with most individuals being in the upper part of this scale. If we use the share of individuals in the two top grades as an indicator of satisfaction, it is clear that PT working women and men are both more satisfied with their hours of work than FT working individuals. The same holds for overall job satisfaction, although here the difference between part-timers and full-timers is smaller. If we use mean satisfaction as an indicator (see bottom of Table 8.1), FT working men have a slightly higher overall job satisfaction than PT working men.

Figure 8.1 gives the distribution of usual weekly hours worked in the main job for women and men, respectively (where observations are pooled across waves and more than 60 hours is the top category). For both men and women, there is a spike at 40 hours per week. However, female hours are also more dispersed across the lower part of the distribution, while men are more dispersed across the upper part. In addition, there are spikes at five hourly intervals, as is usual in reported hours per week.

Table 8.1: Satisfaction indicators by groups of individuals, 2000–2004 (%)

	Hours of work satisfaction				Overall job satisfaction				Life satisfaction					
	Women		Men		Women		Men		Women			Men		
	PT	FT	PT	FT	PT	FT	PT	FT	0	PT	FT	0	PT	FT
0	0.6	1.0	1.0	0.6	0.3	0.2	0.7	0.3	0.3	0.0	0.0	0.3	0.2	0.1
1	0.8	1.[illegible]	2.3	1.2	0.7	0.3	1.0	0.6	0.1	0.1	0.0	0.4	0.0	0.1
2	1.6	2.5	3.7	2.8	0.8	0.8	1.9	1.1	0.5	0.1	0.3	1.3	0.5	0.2
3	2.6	4.7	4.2	4.3	1.3	1.7	1.9	1.6	1.0	0.2	0.4	2.7	0.4	0.3
4	3.5	5.0	5.1	5.1	1.9	1.7	3.7	2.0	1.3	0.8	0.9	2.4	1.6	1.2
5	8.0	11.6	11.4	10.9	5.6	6.5	8.6	6.4	4.9	2.9	3.5	8.5	4.5	3.0
6	5.9	10.3	7.3	11.3	6.6	7.9	7.7	8.0	4.9	4.3	6.2	10.3	7.3	5.3
7	11.1	18.5	13.8	19.0	14.3	19.0	19.0	20.7	15.8	18.3	20.2	19.4	21.1	20.4
8	20.3	20.4	19.9	22.7	26.7	28.6	25.3	30.3	29.5	35.0	34.4	25.0	33.4	38.2
9	19.0	13.4	14.2	12.4	23.3	21.8	16.1	19.0	24.0	26.1	22.8	15.2	19.7	21.6
10	26.6	11.0	17.1	9.7	18.5	11.5	14.1	10.0	17.7	12.2	11.3	14.5	11.3	9.6
>8	45.6	24.4	31.3	22.1	41.8	33.3	30.2	29.0	41.7	38.3	34.1	29.7	31.0	31.2
Mean	7.78	6.86	6.98	6.86	7.90	7.67	7.36	7.54	8.03	8.09	7.95	7.45	7.80	7.92
N	3031	2750	581	6855	3032	2750	582	6854	2384	3034	2750	730	583	6853

Notes: PT = part-time; FT = full-time. Concerning life satisfaction, we distinguish between part-timers, full-timers and non-working individuals. The highest mean life satisfaction for women is associated with PT work, while for men it is associated with FT work. However, the differences are not large.

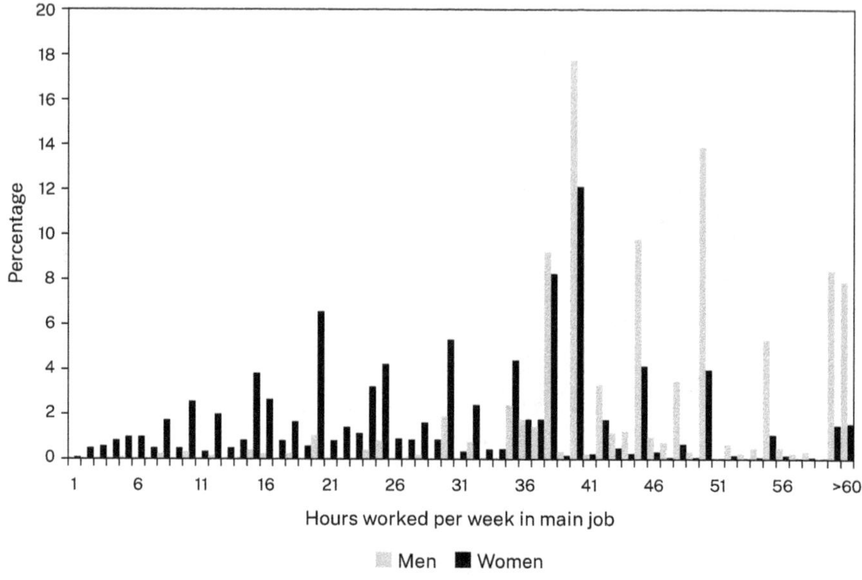

Figure 8.1. Weekly working hours, Australian women and men

Although partnered labour supply is not the focus of this chapter, in Appendix B we briefly report our estimates of the main determinants of each partner's employment probability and hours of work. Cross-sectional and fixed-effects results show that, for a woman, having young children is associated with a significantly lower employment probability and a greater PT employment probability, while having a partner in work significantly increases the employment and PT work probabilities. For men, having a partner in work and being in good health are associated with a significantly higher employment probability. However, the fixed-effects estimates show that male hours of work are unaffected by these variables.

Hours, job and life satisfaction

Pooled cross-section satisfaction estimates

We start our analysis of the satisfaction indicators – hours of work satisfaction, overall job satisfaction and life satisfaction – using an ordered logit model estimated on pooled cross-sectional data. (In the following section, we will discuss the panel estimates.) In the ordered logit model, j represents the response category (j=0, …, 10 for the satisfaction variables) and Pr = ($y_{it} = j$) = $\Lambda(\mu_j - \beta' x_{it}) - \Lambda(\mu_{j-1} - \beta' x_{it})$, with $\mu_0 = -\infty$, $\mu_1 = 0$, $\mu_{10} = \infty$. Here Λ is an indicator of the logistic cumulative distribution function, y indicates whether or not individual i is satisfied with working hours, t refers to the year, x is a vector of explanatory variables, and β is a vector of parameters to be estimated. Thus, the probability that the observed dependent variable y_{it} equals j is the probability that the latent variable y^*_{iy} is between the boundaries j–1 and j_{it}. The μ_j are unknown parameters that are estimated jointly with β. (These are not reported in the interests of space but are available from the authors on request.)

The parameter estimates for hours satisfaction are shown in the first pair of columns in Table 8.2a.[6] Women are more satisfied with their hours of work if they have recently given birth, if family income is higher, if they are in good health and if they work PT. The health and working hours of their partner do not affect their own satisfaction with their working hours. Observe that the estimated coefficient to the PT dummy variable is 0.87 (t-statistic 12.7). This is the largest coefficient of all, and is over twice as large as the next biggest coefficient of 0.41 (*t*-statistic 2.5) for the recent birth of a child. For men, hours of satisfaction are significantly increasing in their own health and working PT.

The third and fourth columns of Table 8.2 show the parameter estimates for job satisfaction. For women, these are by and large similar to the parameter estimates for hours satisfaction, which indicates that hours of work are an important attribute of job satisfaction. However, note that the estimated coefficient for PT work is around a quarter of the estimated effect in the hours satisfaction regression. This is unsurprising, since hours satisfaction is but one facet of job satisfaction. Note also that female job satisfaction is increasing with the health of their partner. The estimates for men indicate that men are more satisfied with their job if family income is higher and if they are in good health, but are unaffected by partner characteristics.

6 In an earlier version of the present chapter, we also estimated the determinants of whether or not individuals would be happier working about the same hours as currently, or working more or fewer hours (for details, see Booth and van Ours 2005).

Table 8.2: Parameter estimates: Hours satisfaction, job satisfaction and life satisfaction[a]

	Hours of work satisfaction		Overall job satisfaction		Life satisfaction		
	Women	Men	Women	Men	Women	Men	Sum
a. Pooled cross-section[b]							
Child born	0.41 (2.5)**	0.02 (0.2)	0.42 (2.8)**	−0.16 (1.6)	0.17 (1.9)*	0.20 (2.1)**	0.22 (2.5)**
Family income	0.18 (2.9)**	0.01 (0.1)	0.14 (2.2)**	0.21 (3.4)**	0.27 (4.9)**	0.22 (4.0)**	0.25 (4.6)**
Health women	0.30 (3.4)**	0.03 (0.4)	0.29 (3.0)**	−0.02 (0.3)	0.62 (7.3)**	0.02 (0.3)	0.42 (5.0)**
PT job women	0.87 (12.7)**	0.07 (1.0)	0.21 (3.1)**	−0.02 (0.3)	−0.04 (0.2)	0.02 (0.3)	0.03 (0.1)
FT job women	–	0.02 (0.3)	–	−0.12 (1.5)	−0.26 (1.3)	−0.07 (0.9)	−0.15 (0.7)
Health men	0.01 (0.2)	0.16 (2.1)**	0.21 (2.5)**	0.21 (2.8)**	0.08 (1.2)	0.37 (4.6)**	0.27 (3.5)**
PT job men	−0.09 (0.5)	0.28 (2.5)**	−0.27 (1.6)	−0.04 (0.3)	0.09 (0.7)	0.17 (1.0)	0.19 (1.4)
FT job men	−0.06 (0.4)	–	−0.15 (1.0)	–	0.20 (1.8)*	0.24 (1.6)	0.30 (2.4)**
Observations	5757	7401	5758	7401	8131	8129	8127
b. Panel analysis[c]							
Child born	0.09 (0.5)	−0.02 (0.2)	0.24 (1.2)	0.04 (0.3)	0.11 (0.9)	0.09 (0.8)	0.15 (1.3)
Family income	0.16 (1.7)*	0.05 (0.7)	0.18 (1.9)*	0.06 (0.7)	0.12 (1.6)	0.08 (1.0)	0.10 (1.3)
Health women	0.11 (0.8)	0.03 (0.3)	0.24 (1.8)*	0.11 (1.0)	−0.02 (0.2)	−0.06 (0.5)	0.01 (0.1)
PT job women	0.60 (6.2)**	−0.09 (0.9)	0.10 (1.0)	−0.05 (0.5)	−0.04 (0.4)	−0.06 (0.6)	−0.05 (0.5)
FT job women	–	−0.15 (1.2)	–	−0.04 (0.3)	−0.25 (2.2)**	−0.06 (0.5)	−0.19 (1.7)*
Health men	−0.07 (0.6)	−0.11 (1.2)	−0.10 (0.8)	−0.01 (0.2)	−0.07 (0.8)	0.10 (1.0)	−0.08 (0.9)
PT job men	0.09 (0.5)	0.03 (0.2)	−0.20 (0.9)	−0.13 (1.0)	−0.00 (0.0)	0.17 (1.0)	0.24 (1.4)
FT job men	0.04 (0.2)	–	−0.27 (1.4)	–	0.27 (1.8)*	0.37 (2.5)**	0.38 (2.6)**

	Hours of work satisfaction		Overall job satisfaction		Life satisfaction		
	Women	Men	Women	Men	Women	Men	Sum
Log likelihood	1910.8	2638.9	1815.0	2460.5	2600.5	2561.6	2953.3
Individuals	1510	1950	1433	1828	6848	6737	7658
Observations	5014	6795	4793	6404	1906	1875	2149

Notes: FT = full-time; PT = part-time; [a] Absolute *t*-values in parentheses (in the pooled cross-section estimates, corrected for clustering of observations across individuals); **(*) Parameter estimate significant at the 5% (10%) level; [b] ordered logit specification; the life satisfaction estimates also include other personal and family characteristics; in addition to this the other estimates also include other job characteristics (see Table A8.1 for an overview); [c] fixed-effects ordered logit specification; all estimates included dummies for year of survey.

Finally, the last three columns of Table 8.2a present parameter estimates for life satisfaction – our indicator for the degree of happiness. The estimating sample now also includes women and men who do not have a job. Women are happier if a child is born. Furthermore, their happiness increases with family income and their own health. However, their life satisfaction is unaffected by PT working, although the coefficient is negative. Notice also that happiness in women is not affected by their partner's health, but is affected by the labour market position of their partner. When we experimented with removing family income as an explanatory variable, this latter result becomes stronger, suggesting that it is the contribution of male FT working to family income that explains a large part of females' life satisfaction. This appears at first blush to provide some corroboration of the income-pooling hypothesis (see, for example, Lundberg and Pollak 1996).

Men, too, are happier if a child is born, if they have a high family income and if they themselves are healthier. The health and labour market position of their spouse, as well as their own labour market position, is irrelevant to their life satisfaction.

The last column of Table 8.2 presents the estimates obtained when the *LHS* variable is the sum of both partners' happiness scores. These confirm the findings discussed above. Finally, we interacted the PT variable with 'child born' and 'kids04' (estimates not reported in the table), but the interaction terms were never significantly different from zero. Moreover, the coefficient of the *PT* variable was hardly affected by the introduction of the interaction terms. This suggests that the effect of PT working on the various satisfaction variables is independent of the family situation.

But do these cross-sectional estimates coincide with those obtained from fixed-effects estimation methods? Cross-sectional estimates are likely to be biased, as we argued at the start of this chapter, and we therefore next report the results obtained from using fixed-effects estimation. As will be seen, we employ a less restrictive estimation method than that found in most of the panel data satisfaction literature.

Panel satisfaction estimates

In the empirical literature on satisfaction analysis, a categorical scale is usually reduced to a (0, 1) scale – choosing an arbitrary common cut-off point – so that, instead of an ordered logit model, a binomial logit model may be used. This allows for the introduction of fixed-effects and the estimation of the parameters using Chamberlain's method. However, this benefit comes at the cost of a large loss of observations, since only individuals who move across the cut-off point can be used in the analysis. This large loss of data may also mean that measurement errors become an important source of residual variation.

Instead of following that procedure, we use an ordered logit model, in which we introduce individual fixed-effects and individual specific thresholds: $\Pr(y_{it} = j) = \Lambda(\mu_{ij} - \alpha_i - \beta' x_{it}) - \Lambda(\mu_{ij-1} - \alpha_i - \beta' x_{it})$. Ferrer-i-Carbonell and Frijters (2004) show that, by choosing for every individual a specific barrier k_i, the fixed-effects ordered logit specification can be reformulated as a fixed-effects binomial logit. So instead of a common cut-off point, individual specific cut-off points are chosen. This reformulation allows Chamberlain's method to be used and removes the individual specific effects α_i, as well as the individual specific thresholds μ_{ij} from the likelihood specification.[7]

We start with the fixed-effects ordered logit estimates of hours of work satisfaction, reported in Panel b of Table 8.2. The results are broadly consistent with those in Panel a. Working hours satisfaction is highest for women working PT. It is also increasing in family income, although this is significant only at the 10 per cent level. Compared with the cross-sectional estimate, the magnitude of the PT work dummy variable drops by over one-

7 In our estimates, we use $k_i = \Sigma_t y_{it} / n_i$, where n is the total number of observations of individual i. All observations for which $y_{it} > k_i$ is transformed into z_{it}=1, and all observations for which $y_{it} \leq k_i$ is transformed into z_{it}=0. Alternatively, we used z_{it}=1 if $y_{it} \leq k_i$ and z_{it}=0 if $y_{it} < k_i$. This hardly affected the parameter estimates.

third to 0.60. However, this is still precisely estimated (the *t*-statistic is 6.2). Observe that male hours satisfaction is no longer affected by own health or PT status, in contrast to the cross-sectional estimates. Later, we shall report the results of the sensitivity analysis in which we further disaggregate the work status variables.

We next turn to the fixed-effects ordered logit estimates of overall job satisfaction, reported in the middle set of columns in the bottom panel of Table 8.2. It is striking that for neither partnered women nor men does PT work affect job satisfaction, in contrast to the cross-sectional estimates reported in the top panel of Table 8.2. For women, the fixed-effects estimates show that job satisfaction is increasing in family income and in own health, and the magnitude of these estimates is quite similar to the cross-sectional results.

Finally, consider the estimates of life satisfaction reported in the last three columns of Table 8.2b. Female life satisfaction increases if the partner gets an FT job, but declines if the woman herself moves into FT work. Male life satisfaction is also increased if the man moves into FT work. However, whether or not the spouse gets a job is irrelevant for the life satisfaction of Australian males.

How do the life satisfaction panel estimates compare with the cross-sectional ordered logits? We would expect that unobserved heterogeneity could be important, since, as we argued above, unobservables such as personality type may be correlated both with the propensity to report happiness and with the explanatory variables of interest.[8] Table 8.2a shows that the coefficient to FT work women in the female cross-sectional life satisfaction equation, in which family income is included, is –0.26 with a *t*-statistic of 1.3. Table 8.2b reveals that the coefficient for the same variable in the fixed-effects ordered logit is –0.25 with a *t*-statistic of 2.2. The coefficient for PT work for women barely changes across estimation methods.

A comparison of the results for life satisfaction between panels a and b of Table 8.2 is striking in that, once the fixed-effects are introduced, the only variables that remain statistically significant are those for hours of work. The cross-sectional estimate of the coefficient to family income in the female life satisfaction equation was 0.27 (*t*-statistic 4.9), suggesting that

8 To investigate the relevance of fixed effects formally, we performed Hausman tests for each satisfaction category. This compares the panel analysis estimates with those from the pooled cross-section. In all cases the chi-squared statistic indicates rejection of the null hypothesis that the difference in coefficients is not systematic. Hence the fixed-effects estimates are preferred.

women are happier if they have a high family income. But since this is not confirmed in the fixed-effects model (the coefficient drops to 0.12 with a *t*-statistic of 1.6), the implication is that intrinsically more satisfied women are found in households with higher family income. The fixed-effects estimate does not corroborate the income-pooling hypothesis.

Earlier in the chapter, we noted that if women prefer PT work because it satisfies their hours preferences given their constraints, we should observe a positive correlation between PT work and hours satisfaction. This is indeed what we find. We also noted that, if PT jobs were actually bad jobs, job satisfaction might be lower. But instead, we found no correlation between various hours of work patterns and job satisfaction for women and men. Finally, earlier we suggested that the impact of PT work on life satisfaction is unclear a priori. On the one hand, it provides a connection to the world of market work, allowing individuals to maintain human capital and some identity in that sphere. But on the other hand, the work might be a dead-end and hence reduce life satisfaction. We found that for men, life satisfaction was unaffected by PT work and increased by FT work. For women, life satisfaction was increased by PT work. Since we also controlled for family income, these findings are consistent with the hypothesis that, for women, PT hours increase self-esteem or identity through work, while FT hours do the same for men. We also found that men did not mind what their partners did with respect to market-sector work hours, but women's life satisfaction was increased if the men worked FT. Such a gendered difference in responses is suggestive of households with traditional gender divides.

Sensitivity analysis, fixed-effects estimates

Table 8.3 reports the estimates obtained when we disaggregated the two working-hours dummy variables (PT job and FT job) into six separate variables. These are 1–10 hours, 11–20 hours, 21–34 hours, 35–40 hours, 41–50 hours and 450 hours. The results in the table confirm our broad findings. First, own-hours of work are statistically significant determinants of hours satisfaction and job satisfaction for both women and men.[9] Women's hours satisfaction and job satisfaction are reduced by FT work, especially for FT jobs with longer hours. In contrast, male hours satisfaction is highest if they are working 35–40 hours, and their job satisfaction is greatest in jobs involving 35–50 hours.

9 We do not comment in the text on the other coefficient estimates, since they are very similar to those reported in Table 8.2b, except that for women hours satisfaction and job satisfaction is increasing in family income. Female job satisfaction is also increased by own health.

Table 8.3: Parameter estimates: Panel analyses, sensitivity analysis[a]

	Hours of work satisfaction		Overall job satisfaction		Life satisfaction		
	Women [1]	**Men [2]**	**Women [3]**	**Men [4]**	**Women [5]**	**Men [6]**	**Sum [7]**
Child born	0.09 (0.5)	−0.02 (0.2)	0.19 (1.0)	0.05 (0.4)	0.10 (0.8)	0.09 (0.8)	0.16 (1.4)
Family income	0.20 (2.1)**	0.09 (1.1)	0.20 (2.0)**	0.05 (0.7)	0.13 (1.6)	0.05 (1.1)	0.10 (1.4)
Health women	0.09 (0.7)	0.02 (0.2)	0.24 (1.8)*	0.11 (1.1)	−0.02 (0.2)	−0.05 (0.5)	0.01 (0.2)
Hours (women)							
1–10	–	−0.07 (0.6)	–	−0.03 (0.2)	−0.01 (0.1)	−0.09 (0.7)	−0.07 (0.5)
11–20	0.34 (2.5)**	−0.09 (0.8)	−0.24 (1.7)*	−0.10 (0.9)	0.03 (0.3)	0.00 (0.0)	0.07 (0.7)
21–34	0.16 (1.1)	−0.09 (0.8)	−0.50 (3.4)**	0.01 (0.1)	−0.11 (0.9)	−0.08 (0.6)	−0.11 (1.0)
35–40	−0.30 (2.0)**	−0.15 (1.2)	−0.48 (3.1)**	−0.06 (0.5)	−0.21 (1.7)*	−0.07 (0.5)	−0.18 (1.5)
41–50	−0.97 (5.4)**	−0.07 (0.4)	−0.58 (3.2)**	0.16 (1.0)	−0.34 (2.2)**	−0.09 (0.6)	−0.15 (1.0)
>50	−1.40 (5.9)**	0.06 (0.3)	−0.87 (3.7)**	0.13 (0.6)	−0.75 (3.6)**	0.24 (1.2)	−0.39 (2.0)**
Health men	−0.06 (0.5)	−0.11 (1.1)	−0.10 (0.8)	−0.01 (0.24)	−0.06 (0.6)	0.10 (1.0)	−0.07 (0.8)
Hours (men)							
1–34	−0.04 (0.2)		−0.01 (0.1)		−0.03 (0.2)	0.09 (0.6)	−0.17 (1.2)
35–40	−0.14 (0.9)	0.62 (4.8)	−0.02 (0.1)	0.28 (2.2)**	0.28 (2.1)**	0.37 (2.7)**	0.36 (2.8)**
41–50	−0.04 (0.3)	−0.03 (0.2)	−0.02 (0.1)	0.24 (1.8)*	0.28 (2.0)**	0.31 (2.2)**	0.34 (2.6)**
>50	−0.31 (1.7)*	−0.77 (5.4)**	−0.05 (0.3)	0.12 (0.8)	0.25 (1.7)*	0.09 (0.5)	0.24 (1.5)
Log likelihood	1879.6	2561.1	1806.8	2456.1	2595.1	2557.6	2950.3
LR test[b]	62.4**	155.6**	16.4**	8.8	10.8	8.0	6.0
Individuals	1510	1950	1433	1828	6848	6737	7658
Observations	5014	6795	4793	6404	1906	1875	2149

Notes: [a] Fixed-effects ordered logit specification; all estimates include dummies for year of survey; absolute t-values in parentheses; **(*) Parameter estimate significant at the 5% (10%) level; [b] Likelihood ratio test statistic on whether the more detailed hours-per-week specification differs from the simple distinction between PT and FT jobs; $\chi^2_{0.05} = 15.15$, $\chi^2_{0.10} = 13.4$.

Second, female life satisfaction is significantly lower in jobs that are FT and in FT jobs with overtime, bringing the total to 41–50 hours. It is even lower in jobs of over 50 hours per week. (The coefficient to '41–50 hours' is – 0.34 with a *t*-statistic of 2.2, while the coefficient to '450 hours' is – 0.75, *t*-statistic 3.6.) On the other hand, while female life satisfaction is higher if their men are working FT, women do not mind if their husbands work overtime hours: the estimated coefficients to the three male FT hours dummies in the female life satisfaction equation are of very similar magnitude. The impact of hours of work on life satisfaction is quite large. Using the parameter estimates of Table 8.3, we simulated the response categories for life satisfaction using an ordered logit model. Average life satisfaction goes down by 0.16 when women work FT, while average life satisfaction goes up by 0.20 if their partner works FT. Similarly, if men work FT, their satisfaction goes up by 0.26. Given that about half of all individuals have a life satisfaction of 8 or 9, we think these effects are substantial.

Third, male life satisfaction is significantly higher in jobs that are FT with or without overtime hours involving up to a 50-hour work week. This mirrors the result found for male job satisfaction, although the magnitude of the coefficients is larger here. Their partners' working hours do not affect male life satisfaction.

To summarise, our results yield a gendered difference in the impact of PT or FT work on hours and life satisfaction.[10] This remains even when account has been taken of unobserved heterogeneity using fixed-effects ordered logit estimation. This finding is suggestive of Australian households with traditional gender divides.

We next try to extract more information from the data by exploiting the time-use module.

10 We also formally tested if the panel estimates of life satisfaction are significantly different for men and women. For the estimates presented in Table 8.3 (columns [5] and [6]) we find that the likelihood ratio (LR) test statistic for equal parameter estimates = 25.0, which is significant at the 10 per cent level (the critical value = 23.5). This result is to a large extent driven by the many insignificant parameter estimates. If we re-estimate the model with a limited number of explanatory variables (hours women: 35–40, 41–50, 50 +; hours men: 35–40, 41–50, 50+, year dummies) we find the LR test statistic = 22.4, which is significant at the 5 per cent level (critical value = 15:5).

What explains these findings?

What might explain these observed gender differences in partners' satisfaction with PT work? We noted earlier that theories of household behaviour predict specialisation of labour in partnered households (see, for example, Becker 1965). In the extreme case, one partner will engage only in home work and the other only in market-sector work. We also pointed out that under incomplete specialisation (Rosen 1983), there will be a monotonically declining relationship between the share of housework done by one partner and that same partner's share of market work. Moreover, we noted that Becker's specialisation theory is gender-neutral. If the male does the lion's share of market work, his partner's share of housework should be larger; conversely, if he does the minority share of market work, he should do the majority share of housework. In contrast, the gender identity hypothesis of Akerlof and Kranton (2000) is based on the idea that gender matters. Here, the distribution of household work and market work is determined by gender-specific 'utility'.

Following the approach of Akerlof and Kranton, we next investigate the relationship between the male share of both partners' hours spent on housework (denoted by $hrwk_{it}$) and the male share of both partners' hours spent in market work (denoted by hit). We use data on housework from the time-use module in the HILDA Survey. The time-use information was obtained from each partner's responses to the following question: 'How much time would you spend on each of the following activities in a typical week? (Please do not count any activity twice).'

There then followed a list of activities, including 'Housework, such as preparing meals, washing dishes, cleaning house, washing clothes, ironing and sewing'. The information is given as hours per week, and the male share is calculated as the hours spent by men doing housework as a proportion of the combined hours of both partners. We have 6,214 observations for 2,175 families. The number of cases is somewhat smaller than for the regression results presented above, because we had to drop those observations with missing information on time use. Women spend, on average, 20.3 hours per week in housework compared with 5.8 hours for men. Average hours of market work for women are 21.6, while for men they are 42.0. In our sample, there are 874 observations in which women do the majority of market work, which accounts for approximately 14 per cent of the subsample. However, there are only 260 observations of households (4.2 per cent) in which men do less than 20 per cent of market work. We distinguish three types of family: those without children below age 14, those with the youngest child aged 0–4, and those with the youngest child aged 5–14.

Figure 8.2 presents men's share of housework in each decile of *h* for the three groups of families. As shown, there are not many differences between the groups, provided the men's share of working hours is above 0.3. Below this, there are differences between the groups, but note also that the number of observations is very small here; in fact, in the second decile, there are only three observations for families with children, of which the youngest child was aged 0–4.

The results show quite unambiguously that there is incomplete specialisation in market work and housework. Households in which the male partner does the majority of market work do provide some evidence of specialisation, since in those households the male share of housework is monotonically declining as their share of market work grows (see all points on the curve to the right of 0.5 on the horizontal axis). However, in households where the female does the majority of market work, the male's share of housework remains proportionately low. Thus, the degree of specialisation is partial and non-symmetric.[11]

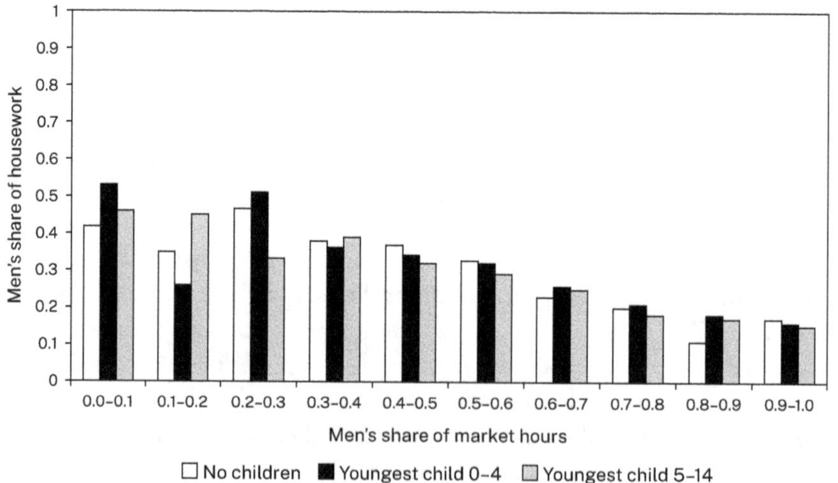

Figure 8.2. Men's share of housework hours versus their share of market work hours

Note: Average values per decile in men's share of market hours.

11 We also distinguished between those families in which the female partner had a high level of education (college and above) and those in which she had lower levels of education. Although in all cases the male share of housework was higher in those households with more highly educated females, the differences were small, and in no cases was the male share of housework as high as 50 per cent.

A simple test for gender neutrality is whether or not the slope of a regression of $hrwk_{it}$ on h_{it} equals −1. This is clearly not the case. In a pooled regression, the slope is given by −0.21 (t-statistic 13.1). In a fixed-effects estimate, the slope is −0.33 (22.6). This slope implies that a one-percentage-point decrease in men's share of market hours increases men's share of housework by only 0.33 per cent.

Another simple test for gender neutrality is based on the symmetry of Figure 8.2. In case of incomplete specialisation but gender neutrality, if the right-hand corner of Figure 8.3 is $(1, a)$, with a being small but positive, the left-hand corner of Figure 8.2 should be $(0, 1-a)$. If men do all market work and still have a share of the housework, symmetry requires that if women do all the market work, they too should do a share of the housework. The same holds for intermediate positions in Figure 8.2; gender neutrality requires the average share of housework for men who have a share in market work higher than any arbitrary value to be equal to 1 minus the average share of housework for men who have a share in market work lower than 1 minus that arbitrary value. More concisely: $(\overline{hrwrk}|h > x) = ((1 - \overline{hrwrk})|h < 1 - x)$ for values of $0.5 \leq x \leq 1$. This obviously is not the case. If we take x = 0.5, we find $(\overline{hrwrk}|h > 0.5) = 0.217$, significantly different from $((1 - \overline{hrwrk}|h < 0.5) = 0.629$. If we take x=0.25, these numbers are 0.238 and 0.559. Clearly, the distribution of household work and market work is not gender-neutral.

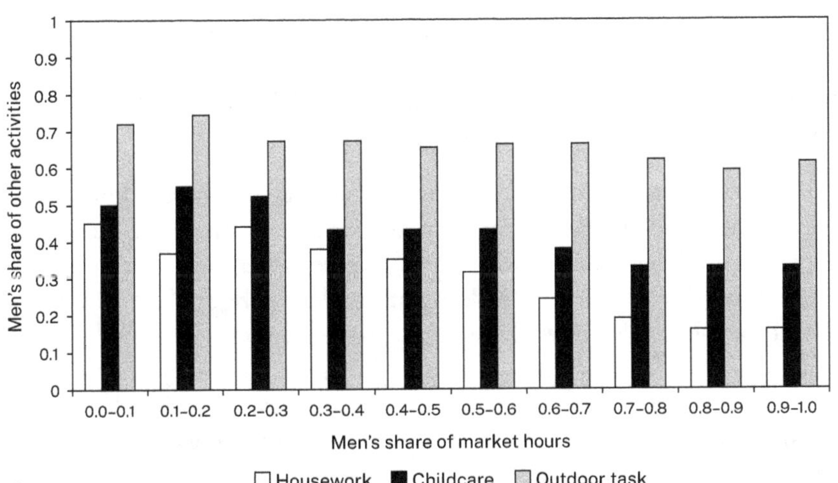

Figure 8.3: Men's share of housework hours, childcare hours and outdoor task hours versus their share of market work hours

Note: Average values per decile in men's share of market hours.

But perhaps men who do a low share of market work do a larger share of other household-related activities, such as outdoor tasks or childcare. To investigate this, we use responses to the time-use questions about these other activities. The outdoor activities and childcare responses were obtained from the listing following the question: 'How much time would you spend on each of the following activities in a typical week? (Please do not count any activity twice).'

The outdoor tasks question asked respondents to include time spent on 'home maintenance (repairs, improvements, painting, etc.), car maintenance or repairs and gardening'. The childcare question asked respondents to include time spent on 'playing with your children, helping them with personal care, teaching, coaching or actively supervising them, or getting them to childcare, school and other activities'. On average, women spend 3.4 hours a week on outdoor activities, while men spend 5.9 hours. Childcare activities absorb, on average, 17.3 hours of women's time and 8.3 hours of men's time. Figure 8.3 shows a breakdown of the male share of various household activities across the distribution of the male share of market hours. Thus, the figure gives average values per decile of men's share of market hours. The figure shows that outdoor tasks seem to be unrelated to market work. Men do a higher share of these tasks across the distribution. This suggests a gendered division of labour for outside work that is invariant to market hours shares. For childcare, there is a trade-off between the male share of childcare and the male share of market work, but it is not large. Men who do 90–100 per cent of market work do about 30 per cent of childcare, while men doing 0–10 per cent of market work do about 50 per cent of childcare. This suggests incomplete specialisation. The figure also confirms that the most striking finding is for housework.

In summary, we find a declining relationship between the share of housework done by men and their share of market work, and this is unaffected by the presence of dependent children. But there is certainly not complete specialisation, for even the men doing all market work are also still doing some home work. Nor does there appear to be gender neutrality, since in households in which women spend more time making money, they are also still doing more housework. This finding is inconsistent with the gender neutrality hypothesis, but is consistent with the gender identity hypothesis about time use within the household.[12]

12 This result was also found using US data by Akerlof and Kranton (2000).

Conclusions

This chapter investigates the relationship between PT work and three indicators of satisfaction: satisfaction with working hours, overall job satisfaction, and life satisfaction. The data used are from the first four waves of the HILDA Survey, spanning the period 2001–2003, and we focus on a sample of partnered men and women.

Our fixed-effects ordered logit results indicate that, conditional on observed characteristics, PT women are more satisfied with their hours of work than FT women. For men, hours of work satisfaction are greatest for those working 35–40 hours a week. However, for job satisfaction, there is no such relationship. Indeed, for both men and women, job satisfaction seems to be independent of hours of work.

Finally, we found that partnered women's life satisfaction is reduced by working FT, especially if their weekly hours are greater than 40. However, female life satisfaction is increased if their partners are working FT, and they are particularly happy if their partners are working 35–50 hours per week. In contrast, male partners' life satisfaction is unaffected by their partners' market hours but is significantly increased if they themselves are working FT, especially so if they are working 35–50 hours per week. Thus, it seems that FT work for men in the region of 35–50 hours is the major contributor to both partners' life happiness, but that female PT work has an asymmetric effect. Men do not mind how many hours per week their partners work, but women are happiest with PT work.

Does this suggest that Australian families are characterised by complete specialisation, with one partner engaged predominantly in domestic work and the other in market-sector work? The answer is no. According to the specialisation hypothesis, there will be a negative monotonic relationship between the share of housework done by one partner and that same partner's share of market work. This prediction is not supported by the data. In households where the female does the majority of market work, the male's share of housework remains proportionately low. Thus, the degree of specialisation is partial and non-symmetric. Men doing a small share of market work were also doing a small share of housework. This finding is consistent with the gender identity hypothesis, and it may suggest a reason why women are happier with PT work.

Acknowledgements

This chapter was first published as Booth, A.L., and van Ours, J.C. (2009). 'Hours of work and gender identity: Does part-time work make the family happier?', *Economica*, 76(301):176–96. www.jstor.org/stable/40071775.

We thank the Melbourne Institute of Applied Economic and Social Research for making available the HILDA Survey data, Hiau Joo Kee and Margi Wood for creating the partnered dataset, and the Australian Research Council for financial support under the Discovery Project Grant no. DP0449887. Helpful comments were received from two anonymous referees and participants of presentations to the HILDA Annual Conference, the Society of Labor Economists 2006 Boston meetings and the European Society of Population Economists 2006 conference in Verona.

References

Akerlof, G.A., and Kranton, R.E. (2000). 'Economics and identity', *The Quarterly Journal of Economics*, 115(3):715–753. doi.org/10.1162/003355300554680.

Bardasi, E., and Francesconi, M. (2004). 'The impact of atypical employment on individual wellbeing: Evidence from a panel of British workers', *Social Science & Medicine*, 58(9):1671–1688. doi.org/10.1016/S0277-9536(03)00400-3.

Becker, G.S. (1965). 'A theory of the allocation of time', *The Economic Journal*, 75(299):493–517. doi.org/10.2307/2228949.

Booth, A.L., and Van Ours, J.C. (2005). 'Hours of work and gender identity: Does part-time work make the family happier?' IZA Discussion Paper No. 1884.

Booth, A.L., and Van Ours, J.C. (2007). 'Job satisfaction and family happiness: The part-time work puzzle', IZA Discussion Paper No. 3020.

Booth, A.L., and Wood, M. (2008). 'Back-to-front down-under? Part-time/full-time wage differentials in Australia', *Industrial Relations*, 47(1):114–135. doi.org/10.1111/j.1468-232X.2008.00507.x.

Carroll, N. (2007). 'Unemployment and psychological well-being', *Economic Record*, 83(262):287–302. doi.org/10.1111/j.1475-4932.2007.00415.x.

Chamberlain, G. (1980). 'Analysis of covariance with qualitative data', *The Review of Economic Studies*, 47(1):225–238. doi.org/10.2307/2297110.

Clark, A.E. (1997). 'Job satisfaction and gender: Why are women so happy at work?', *Labour Economics*, 4(4):341–372. doi.org/10.1016/S0927-5371(97)00010-9.

Clark, A.E. (2003). 'Unemployment and social norms: Psychological evidence from panel data', *Journal of Labor Economics*, 21(2):323–351. doi.org/10.1086/345560.

Clark, A.E., and Oswald, A.J. (1994). 'Unhappiness and unemployment', *The Economic Journal*, 104(424):648–659. doi.org/10.2307/2234639.

Clark, A.E., Georgellis, Y., and Sanfey, P. (2001). 'Scarring: The psychological impact of past unemployment', *Economica*, 68(270):221–241. doi.org/10.1111/1468-0335.00243.

Dickens, R., and Ellwood, D.T. (2003). 'Child poverty in Britain and the United States', *The Economic Journal*, 113(488):F219–F239. doi.org/10.1111/1468-0297.00132.

Ferrer-i-Carbonell, A., and Frijters, P. (2004). 'How important is methodology for the estimates of the determinants of happiness?'. *The Economic Journal*, 114(497): 641–659. doi.org/10.1111/j.1468-0297.2004.00235.x.

Frijters, P., Hasken-DeNew, J.P., and Shields, M.A. (2004a). 'Money does matter! Evidence from increasing real incomes in East Germany following reunification', *American Economic Review*, 94(3):730–741. doi.org/10.1257/0002828041464551.

Frijters, P., Hasken-DeNew, J.P., and Shields, M.A. (2004b). 'Investigating the patterns and determinants of life satisfaction in Germany following reunification', *The Journal of Human Resources*, 39(3):649–674. doi.org/10.2307/3558991.

Gerlach, K., and Stephan, G. (1996). 'A paper on unhappiness and unemployment in Germany', *Economics Letters*, 52(3):325–330. doi.org/10.1016/S0165-1765(96)00858-0.

Hamermesh, D.S. (2001). 'The changing distribution of job satisfaction', *Journal of Human Resources*, 36(1):1–30.

Lundberg, S., and Pollak, R.A. (1996). 'Bargaining and distribution in marriage', *Journal of Economic Perspectives*, 10(4):139–158. doi.org/10.1257/jep.10.4.139.

Mill, J.S. (1869). *The Subjection of Women*. London: Longmans, Green.

OECD. (2001). 'Balancing work and family life: Helping parents into paid employment'. In *Employment Outlook*. Paris: OECD, pp. 129–166.

OECD. (2004). *Employment Outlook*. Paris: OECD.

Plug, E., and Van Praag, B.M.S. (1998). 'Similarity in response behaviour between household members: an application to income evaluation', *Journal of Economic Psychology*, 19(4):497–513.

Rodgers, J.R. (2004). 'Hourly wages of full-time and part-time employees in Australia', *Australian Journal of Labour Economics*, 7:231–254.

Rosen, S. (1983). 'Specialization and human capital', *Journal of Labor Economics*, 1(1):43–49. doi.org/10.1086/298003.

Van Praag, B.M.S. and Ferrer-i-Carbonell, A. (2004). *Happiness Quantified.* Oxford: Oxford University Press.

Winkelmann, L., and Winkelmann, R. (1998). 'Why are the unemployed so unhappy? Evidence from panel data', *Economica*, 65(257):1–15. doi.org/10.1111/1468-0335.00111.

Winkelmann, R. (2005). 'Subjective well-being and the family: Results from an ordered probit model with multiple random effects', *Empirical Economics*, 30:749–761. doi.org/10.1007/s00181-005-0255-7.

Appendix A: The HILDA data

The new HILDA Survey began in 2001. It is a nationally representative random-sample panel survey of private households in Australia. We use data from all four available waves, which span the period 2001–04.

All members of households providing at least one interview in the first wave form the basis of the panel. The sample has been gradually extended to include any new household members resulting from changes in the composition of the original households. The survey is a longitudinal study of representative households in Australia.[13] HILDA contains four survey instruments: the household form, a household questionnaire, a person questionnaire and a self-completion questionnaire. The household-level information can be provided by any adult member of the household, preferably a person with knowledge of the household finances. The person-level questionnaires are for all persons aged 15 years and over in the household.

13 For details, see 'Hilda survey', *Melbourne Institute of Applied Economic and Social Research*, melbourne institute.unimelb.edu.au/hilda.

Table A8.1: Definitions of variables and means

Variable	Definition	Women	Men
Personal characteristics			
Age	Respondent's age	39.3	41.8
Postgrad	Postgraduate degree (master's or doctorate)	0.03	0.05
Graddip	Graduate diploma or certificate	0.08	0.06
Bachelor	Bachelor degree	0.16	0.15
Advdip	Advanced diploma, diploma	0.10	0.10
Cert	Certificate	0.13	0.32
Year	Year 12 (base is year 11)	0.16	0.09
Born-oz	Australian-born	0.76	0.75
Born-engsp	Born in English-speaking country (not Oz)	0.10	0.12
Health	Dummy: in good health	0.85	0.81
Part-time job	Usual hours per week in main job < 35	0.37	0.07
Full-time job	Usual hours per week in main job ≥ 35	0.34	0.84
Hours of work[a]			
Housework	Hours spent on housework in typical week	20.3	5.8
Childcare	Hours spent on own childcare in typical week	17.3	8.3
Outdoor	Hours spent on outdoor activities per week	3.4	5.9
Home production	Total hours spent on home activities per week	41.0	19.9
Market work	Total hours spent in main job per week	21.6	42.0
Total hours of work		62.6	61.9
Job characteristics[b]			
Hours	Usual hours per week in main job	30.5	46.1
Casual	Casual contract	0.19	0.07
Contract	Fixed-term contract	0.08	0.06
Permanent	Ongoing permanent employment	0.55	0.61
Siz20–99	Firm has 20–99 employees	0.27	0.24
Siz100–499	Firm has 100–499 employees	0.16	0.17
Siz500up	Firm has 500 or more employees	0.09	0.10
Industry dummies	One-digit industrial classification	–	–
Family characteristics			
Family income	Log (total annual family gross income) – AU$1,000	Log(84.9)	
Child born	Dummy: whether or not household had a new birth	0.05	
Child 0–4	Dummy: kids 0–4 years of age	0.27	

Variable	Definition	Women	Men
Child 5–14	Dummy: kids 5–14 years of age	0.50	
Urban	Living in major city	0.59	
Inner	Inner regional	0.26	
Outer	Outer regional (base is remote/very remote)	0.10	

Notes: [a] Hours of work refer to the main job; [b] 10.4% of the females and 7.7% of the males had more than one job.

Table A8.1 provides an overview of the variables used in the analysis. There are five types of variable: personal characteristics, hours of work, job characteristics, family characteristics and the time-use information that was obtained from the self-completion questionnaire. We restrict our estimating subsample (for reasons given in the text) to married or cohabiting couples in which the female partner was aged 25–50 in 2001. We use an unbalanced panel in which selected couples are present in at least two consecutive waves. These restrictions yield a sample of 8,170 observations of 2,326 couples, of which 1,601 were observed four times, 316 three times and 409 twice.

Partnered women and men are very much alike in terms of personal characteristics, as shown in Table A8.1, but there are substantial differences in their hours of work. While women on average spend about 20 hours per week on housework and 17 hours per week on childcare, men spend about 6 hours per week on housework and 8 hours on childcare. Of the women in our sample, 37 per cent have a PT job, and 34 per cent have an FT job. Of the men, 7 per cent have a PT job, and 84 per cent have an FT job. These differences materialise in the usual hours per week in the main job, which is about 30 hours for women and 46 hours for men. In terms of job characteristics, the main difference between men and women concerns the share of workers with a casual contract, which is 19 per cent for women and 7 per cent for men.

Appendix B: Partnered labour supply

To get some idea about the determinants of employment, we estimate discrete choice models using pooled cross-section data as well as exploiting the panel character of the data. To investigate the way in which the decisions of one partner affect the other, we also allow some individual characteristics to affect the partner's employment position. Thus, we ignore joint decision-making and assume that the decision of the partner is exogenous to the decision of the individual. The probability of having a job is analysed using a logit specification. We use the logit specification since it is a natural starting point for the introduction of fixed effects. In a bivariate probit model (not reported), we investigate to what extent there is correlation in the behaviour of partnered men and women conditional on their observed characteristics. We find that the estimated parameters are hardly affected by the introduction of possible correlation in the unobserved characteristics, whereas the correlation itself is positive and significantly different from zero. This indicates either joint decision-making or perhaps selective matching (individuals who are more likely to work match with similar individuals) that is orthogonal to observed characteristics. Thus, $Pr = (y_{it} = 1) = \Lambda(\beta x_{it})$ and $Pr\ (y_{it} = 0) = \Lambda(-\beta x_{it})$, where Λ is an indicator of the logistic cumulative distribution function, y indicates whether or not an individual has a job, i refers to the individual, and t refers to the year of the survey. Furthermore, x is a vector of explanatory variables, and β is a vector of parameters.

The principal explanatory variables used in the analysis are: age, health, whether or not a household had a new birth in the period since the previous interview (or in the previous 12 months in the case of wave 1), whether the household has children in the age group 0–4 or 5–14, and the year of survey. Other variables included are education, country of birth and degree of urbanisation. However, since these variables are time invariant, they drop out of the panel analysis. In the interests of space, we do not report the estimated coefficients to these variables in the pooled cross-sectional models.

Column [1] of Table A8.2 reports the parameter estimates, where the upper panel gives the results for women and the lower panel, those for men. Age has a statistically significant effect for men-only. Older men are less likely to have a job. For both women and men, being in good health has a positive effect on the probability of having a job. Having young children or teenage children has a negative effect only on the female probability of having a job. As shown, having a partner with a PT or FT job is positively related to an individual's own job probability. This association is consistent with studies showing the presence of work-rich and work-poor households (see, for example, Dickens and Ellwood 2003).

Table A8.2: Parameter estimates: Employment, PT work and hours of work

	Pooled cross-section estimates			Panel estimates		
	Job [1]	PT [2]	Hours [3]	Job [4]	PT [5]	Hours [6]
Women						
Age	−0.00 (0.5)	0.03 (4.9)**	−0.12 (2.7)**	–	–	–
Health	0.84 (8.5)**	−0.12 (1.1)	0.50 (0.6)	0.43 (1.7)n	0.44 (2.0)**	-0.64 (1.2)
Child born	-1.20 (9.8)**	0.22 (1.2)	-2.15 (1.8)*	-2.43 (7.1)**	-0.02 (0.1)	-1.82 (2.2)**
Child 0–4	-1.26 (13.0)**	1.26 (10.6)**	-8.71 (11.8)**	-1.33 (4.2)**	1.91 (7.3)**	-6.73 (10.9)**
Child 5–14	-0.36 (4.4)**	0.91 (10.8)**	-5.59 (10.0)**	-0.08 (0.3)	0.42 (1.6)	-1.65 (2.6)**
Partner FT	1.38 (10.9)**	0.46 (2.6)**	-0.97 (0.9)	0.93 (3.0)**	0.60 (1.7)*	-0.06 (0.1)
Partner PT	1.36 (8.0)**	0.54 (2.6)**	1.74 (1.4)	1.11 (2.8)**	0.90 (2.3)**	-1.20 (1.3)
Observations	8170	5785	5639	1291	1770	5639
Individuals	–	–	–	448	519	1896
Men						
Age	-0.03 (3.3)**	0.02 (2.0)**	0.30 (0.8)	–	–	–
Health	1.95 (6.7)**	-0.73 (5.7)**	2.30 (3.9)**	0.78 (3.1)**	0.16 (0.6)	0.16 (0.4)
Child born	0.27 (1.2)	0.07 (0.3)	-0.16 (0.2)	0.16 (0.5)	0.21 (0.6)	-0.02 (0.5)
Child 0–4	0.24 (1.5)	-0.12 (0.8)	1.00 (1.9)*	-0.03 (0.1)	0.01 (0.0)	-0.36 (0.8)
Child 5–14	0.36 (2.8)**	-0.20 (1.6)	1.14 (2.5)**	-0.14 (1.4)	0.37 (1.2)	-0.18 (0.4)
Partner FT	1.08 (6.9)**	-0.11 (0.7)	0.91 (1.5)	0.53 (1.7)*	0.02 (0.1)	-0.06 (0.1)
Partner PT	1.56 (10.8)**	-0.06 (0.4)	0.20 (0.4)	0.87 (3.3)**	0.06 (0.2)	0.05 (0.2)
Observations	8170	7439	7273	872	913	7273
Individuals	–	–	–	243	270	2206

Notes: **(*) Parameter estimate significant at the 95% (90%) level; PT = part-time; [a] 'PT' and 'Hours' concern choices conditional on having a job. 'Job' and 'PT' logit model specification, 'Hours' linear specification and the pooled cross-section estimates also contain other personal characteristics and family characteristics (see Table A8.1 for details); The panel estimates include individual fixed effects; All estimates contain dummy variables for survey years. Absolute *t*-values in parentheses (in the pooled cross-section estimates corrected for clustering of observations).

If we introduce fixed effects in a logit model, the specification becomes $\Pr(y_{it} = 1) = \Lambda(\alpha_i + \beta x_{it})$ and $\Pr(y_{it} = 0) = \Lambda(-\alpha_i - \beta x_{it})$, where the α_i represent individual fixed-effects. The parameters of this fixed-effects logit model are estimated using Chamberlain's conditional likelihood method. This means that the parameters are identified on the subset of observations where the dependent variable changes at least once over time.

As shown in column [4] of Table A8.2, the number of observations reduces substantially if fixed effects are introduced. In total, 448 women and 243 found a job or lost a job at least once. However, by and large, the results are not much different from the estimates based on pooled cross-sections. Note that in a fixed-effects setting, we cannot identify the effects of age, since there is perfect correlation between age and calendar years. The results show, first, that the birth of a child increases the female probability of moving out of work. This is unsurprising – especially in view of the fact that Australia is one of the few OECD countries without a statutory maternity leave provision (OECD 2001). Second, if a child moves from the age category 0–4 years to a higher age category, the female probability of finding a job increases; however, for men, these changes in family situation do not affect their labour market position. Third, an improvement in health significantly increases the probability of finding a job.

Column [2] of Table A8.2 shows the pooled cross-sectional estimates of the determinants of the individual probability of having a PT job conditional on being in work. For both men and women, this probability increases with age. Females are less likely to have a PT job if there are preschool children. We also find this result in the fixed-effects estimates reported in column [5]. Furthermore, a woman is more likely to work PT if her partner works, a result that we do not find if fixed effects are included. This suggests that the partner effect may be due to unobserved characteristics rather than being a causal effect. For males, apart from age, only health has an effect on the probability of their working PT; but again, from the fixed-effects estimates, it seems as if this is not a causal effect.

Finally, columns [3] and [6] of Table A8.2 show the determinants of the hours of work decision from the pooled cross-sections and the fixed-effects estimation, respectively. In both, the presence of preschool children significantly reduces female but not male hours of work.

9

Does ethnic discrimination vary across minority groups? Evidence from a field experiment

Alison L Booth, Andrew Leigh and Elena Varganova

> After completing TAFE [technical and further education] in 2005, I applied for many junior positions where no experience in sales was needed – even though I had worked for two years as a junior sales clerk. I didn't receive any calls, so I decided to legally change my name to Gabriella Hannah. I applied for the same jobs and got a call 30 minutes later.
>
> (Gabriella Hannah, formerly Ragda Ali, Sydney)

Introduction

How should we measure ethnic discrimination? Among economists, the most common approach has been to compare labour market outcomes across ethnic groups. But this method may not provide an accurate answer. If an individual's ethnicity is correlated with some unobserved productive trait, then differences in economic outcomes will reflect more than just discrimination. Similarly, social researchers have often used surveys to measure the degree of racism in a society. But if respondents know the socially correct response, then this approach will also provide a biased estimate of true attitudes towards ethnic groups. When studying labour market outcomes, the problem arises from the unobservable characteristics of ethnic minorities. When analysing social attitudes, the problem stems from unobservable biases in the reporting of ethnic attitudes.[1]

In both cases, field experiments can help solve the unobservables problem by creating a context in which all other factors except ethnicity are held constant. In a context where the subject is unaware that he or she is participating in an experiment – or in which it is difficult for the subject to provide a socially acceptable response – it is more likely that the outcome will provide an accurate measure of racism than with more traditional approaches. The strengths of field experiments of this type are that they are randomised experiments that establish causality and provide strong evidence for the existence of discrimination. Explanations of employer motives generally call for other methods.[2] So too do explanations as to why some particular ethnic groups might be discriminated against more than others.

In this chapter, we present the results of a field experiment that we conducted in order to estimate discrimination against ethnic minorities in Australia, a country whose immigration policy is based on a points system that has been admired and adopted by other countries, including New Zealand and the UK. Unlike many field experiments, looking only at a single minority group, we take a broader focus: comparing attitudes to Anglo-Saxon Australians with attitudes to Indigenous Australians (the original inhabitants of the continent), Italian Australians (a relatively established migrant group), Chinese Australians (a more recent migrant group), and Middle Eastern Australians (another recent migrant group). By comparing across these groups, we hope to shed light on how the process of immigrant assimilation might change over time. However, we would not wish to push too hard the use of our experiment as a measure of how time in the country matters for discrimination rates, for there are other conjectures as to how stereotypes

1 We define an ethnic group as comprising individuals who are perceived as having a common heritage consisting of a common language, culture and ancestry.

2 As Arrow (1998, p. 96) notes, without explicit measures for the individual's marginal productivity, it is impossible to distinguish between taste-based and statistical forms of discrimination. While in our experiment all applicants attended school in Australia, and we hold constant their education and experience, it is likely that stereotypes about productivity still remain. For example, employers might view ethnic minority workers as less productive because of poor language skills that are not manifest in the application. This might be so even though such beliefs receive little support in, for example, the HILDA data. Among HILDA respondents who were born in Australia, but whose parents were born overseas, 98–99 per cent report speaking English 'very well' (the highest category in the survey). Since we cannot give in our fictional CVs precise measures of the applicant's productivity, we are unable in this study to separately identify the extent of statistical discrimination.

are formed. For instance, Eagly and Kite (1987, p. 452) hypothesise that individuals form stereotypes of people from particular countries based not so much on direct forms of interaction but rather on 'newsworthy events that draw these nations to their attention', often unfavourably. This might explain some of our results below (for example, for people from the Middle Eastern countries), although we cannot formally test this in our analysis.

With one in four residents born overseas, Australia is often regarded as something of a poster child for its ability to absorb new migrants into its social and economic fabric.[3] Skilled migrants are selected through a points system, which gives preference to applicants with high qualifications and workers in high-demand occupations.[4] Perhaps because of this, most research has found little discernible impact of migrants on the labour market conditions of Australian natives.

Yet recent events suggest that the Australian melting pot may not be so successful after all. In the late 1990s, Pauline Hanson's One Nation Party, with its policy of reducing Asian immigration to Australia, polled well in a number of federal and state elections. At the time of the 2000 Sydney Olympics, many journalists drew attention to the poor social indicators among Indigenous Australians. And in 2005, anti-Muslim riots on Sydney's Cronulla Beach drew international attention. As a series of reports have shown, some minority groups in Australia suffer extreme forms of persecution at work and in public places (see, for example, Walker 2001, Kabir and Evans 2002, Poynting and Noble 2004, Berman and The Victorian Equal Opportunity & Human Rights Commission 2008, and Forrest and Dunn 2007).

Moreover, the fact that firms specialising in helping migrants find work in Australia counsel clients to disguise their identity also raises concern. For example, a commercial firm that specialises in assisting migrants find work in Australia advises its clients that:

> if the job absolutely specifically requires second language skills, then include your proficiency with that language only. Otherwise, do not write anything about your other language skills. Especially never write anything about your English language proficiency.

3 The 2006 Census indicates that 28 per cent of the foreign-born in Australia are from 'Anglo' countries, namely the UK, New Zealand, South Africa, USA, Ireland and Canada (listed in order of numerical importance).

4 See Hatton (2005).

Jobseekers are also told 'never include your country of birth', and 'shorten and or Anglicise names where possible and appropriate'.[5]

Against this background, our experiment aims to estimate ethnic discrimination by employers. To do this, we conduct a correspondence discrimination study. In audit or correspondence studies, fictitious individuals who are identical in all respects apart from the one of interest (typically gender or ethnicity) apply for jobs. Audit studies, relying on actor pairs who apply for jobs, have been criticised on numerous grounds, including whether or not the applicants from different groups actually appear identical to employers. In response to these criticisms, correspondence studies substitute fictitious online or paper applications for fictitious personal candidates, thereby reducing potential heterogeneity in unobservables.

In our correspondence study conducted over six months in 2007, we randomly submitted over 4,000 fictional applications for entry-level jobs, varying only the name as an indicator of ethnicity. In terms of the number of applications submitted, ours is one of the largest correspondence studies ever conducted. This allows us to look at multiple ethnic groups, and to see if our effects differ by the gender of the fictitious applicant, the type of job advertised and the city in which the job is located. Relative to other work on discrimination, our correspondence study is novel in that we compare across multiple ethnic groups.[6] This allows us to learn more about the assimilation process than is possible with studies that focus on just one minority. In addition, we are the first to test discrimination against an Indigenous group compared with immigrant minority groups. Indeed, to our knowledge, we are the first to consider discrimination against an Indigenous group.

The rest of the chapter is structured as follows: we present background information on the share of Australians falling into the four ethnic categories, and review the available evidence on labour market outcomes and attitudinal surveys. We then discuss the experiment and the various discrimination hypotheses that our research proposes to test, and present the results of our experiment and compare our findings with those from other similar studies.

5 See www.migrantjobsservices.com.au (site discontinued).

6 While a comparison across three ethnic groups – black, white and Latino – was conducted by Pager, Western and Bonikowski (2009), theirs was an audit study, in which they recruited college-educated individuals to role-play and apply for 340 entry-level jobs in New York City. Since we conducted our correspondence study, Oreopoulos (2009) carried out a similar field experiment with 6,000 CVs in Canada.

Background

We briefly outline the characteristics of the ethnic groups that are the focus of this study by reviewing the literature on their population share, employment outcomes and levels of surveyed discrimination. Figure 9.1 depicts the share of Australian residents in each of the four ethnic minority groups, based on data from the Australian census, which was conducted in 1901, 1911, 1921, 1933, 1947, 1954, and every five years from 1961 onwards. Until the 1960s, the share of Australians reporting their ethnicity as Indigenous was about 1 per cent of the population. Since then, the share has risen steadily and was over 2 per cent in 2006. This change has been driven by two factors: higher fertility rates and a growing willingness of respondents to self-identify as Indigenous.

For Italian, Chinese and Middle Eastern Australians, our estimates are based upon country of birth (thereby ignoring second-generation immigrants). As the graph shows, Australia experienced a large influx of Italian migrants immediately after World War II. From the late 1970s, the share of Australians who are Italian-born has steadily declined. By contrast, immigration from China and the Middle East only began to expand in the 1970s and 1980s. By 2006, the share of Australians born in Italy, China and the Middle East was about 1 per cent each.

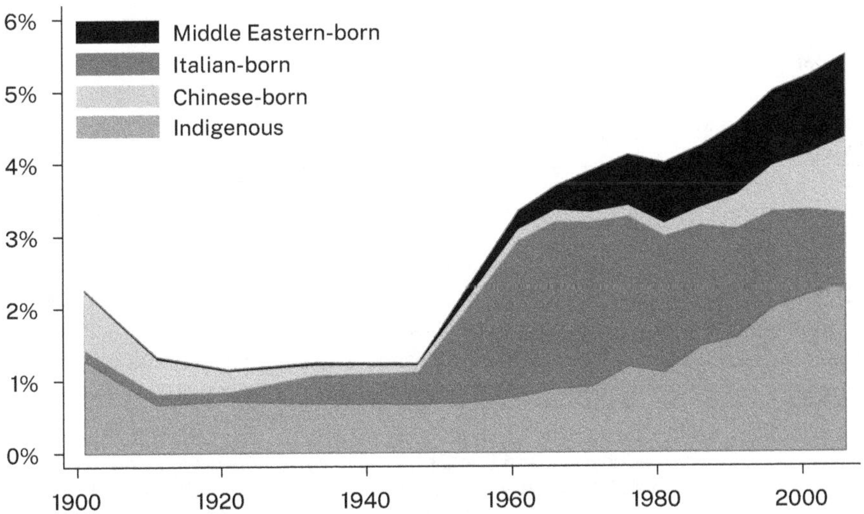

Figure 9.1: What share of the population do our minority groups comprise?

Since our experiment will focus on ethnicity rather than country of birth, a more appropriate comparator might be ancestry. However, the Australian census has not consistently asked respondents about their ancestry. Therefore, it is only possible to look at recent data, and not to construct a time series of ancestry shares. We focus here on respondents' first answer to the ancestry question in the 2006 census (it was possible to give multiple ancestries). The ancestries that are relevant to our analysis are Italian (4 per cent), Chinese (3 per cent) and Arab (1 per cent). By comparison, the most common ancestries are Australian (27 per cent) and British (35 per cent). It is not possible to distinguish Indigenous ancestry. While the country of birth figures suggest that Italians, Chinese and Middle Easterners are about equally represented among first-generation migrants, the ancestry data indicate that Italians are substantially more numerous among second-generation (and higher generation) migrants.

Table 9.1: Observed labour market differences by ethnicity

Dependent variable	[1]	[2]	[3]	[4]	[5]	[6]
	Employed		Log annual hours		Log hourly wage	
Indigenous (self-identified)	-0.102** (0.044)	-0.066 (0.046)	-0.055 (0.051)	-0.019 (0.054)	-0.069 (0.044)	-0.010 (0.033)
Italian (by birth or parentage)	-0.052* (0.031)	-0.005 (0.026)	-0.005 (0.033)	0 (0.035)	-0.060** (0.027)	-0.029 (0.025)
Chinese (by birth or parentage)	-0.119*** (0.041)	0.013 (0.035)	-0.107** (0.054)	-0.08 (0.060)	-0.028 (0.060)	0.033 (0.052)
Middle Eastern (by birth or parentage)	-0.137*** (0.042)	-0.032 (0.030)	-0.089 (0.068)	-0.063 (0.066)	-0.001 (0.037)	-0.01 (0.033)
Control for education, experience, and English proficiency?	No	Yes	No	Yes	No	Yes
Person-year observations	19,515	19,515	13,832	13,832	13,832	13,832
Individuals	4,979	4,979	3,989	3,989	3,989	3,989
R^2 or pseudo R^2	0.05	0.25	0.09	0.13	0.04	0.19

Notes: Robust standard errors, clustered at the individual level, in brackets; *, ** and *** denote statistical significance at the 10%, 5% and 1% levels respectively. All regressions control for survey year indicators, a quadratic in age, and a gender dummy. Employment results are marginal effects from a probit model, while results for annual hours and hourly wages are OLS coefficients. Experience is actual labour market experience, education is years of education, and English proficiency is measured by indicators for the four options on a self-assessed scale (very well, well, not very well, not at all). Those who do not speak a language other than English are assumed to speak English very well. Sample is major city respondents aged 21–64 in columns [1] and [2], and employed respondents aged 21–64 in columns [3]–[6].

Source: HILDA Survey, waves 1–6.

Table 9.1 shows how these four minority groups perform in the Australian labour market.[7] We estimate three outcome measures – participation, log annual hours and log hourly wages – with the omitted group being Australian-born non-Indigenous respondents. For this analysis, we require a large dataset with good information on employment participation and hourly wages. Although the census samples are relatively large, earnings and hours are coded in bands, leading to very imprecise measures of hourly wages.[8] We therefore opt to use the 2001–06 Household, Income and Labour Dynamics in Australia survey (HILDA), pooling all six waves and clustering standard errors at the person level. The sample is restricted to those who are aged 21–64, with non-missing information for all covariates.

Indigenous respondents are coded according to whether or not they self-identified as Aboriginal or Torres Strait Islander (HILDA respondents are not asked whether their parents are Indigenous). Respondents are coded as Italian, Chinese or Middle Eastern if they – or either of their parents – were born in one of those countries/regions.[9] We exclude first-generation or second-generation migrants from other regions, so that the omitted group comprises respondents who were born in Australia and whose parents were both born in Australia. Because our field experiment focuses on three large Australian cities, we similarly restrict the HILDA sample to those living in major cities. Across this particular sample, 2 per cent of respondents are Indigenous, 6 per cent are Italian, 3 per cent are Chinese and 4 per cent are Middle Eastern.[10]

In columns [1], [3] and [5] of Table 9.1, we include only a parsimonious set of controls – a survey year indicator, a gender indicator and a quadratic in age. In this specification, all the coefficients are negative, and five are

7 Naturally, we are not the first to use standard surveys to analyse migrant performance in the Australian labour market. For studies that have looked at various aspects of the labour market performance of migrants in Australia, see e.g. Cobb-Clark (2003); Mahuteau and Junankar (2008).

8 An alternative approach would have been to simply look at unemployment rates, using data on country of birth from the August 2006 *Employee Earnings and Hours* Survey (representative of all employees in the labour force), and data on ethnicity from the August 2006 census. The unemployment rates by country of birth in 2007 were: born in Australia 4.0 per cent, born in Italy 3.7 per cent, born in China 7.2 per cent, and born in North Africa/Middle East 9.5 per cent. The unemployment rate by ethnicity in 2006 was 5.0 per cent for non-Indigenous people, and 15.6 per cent for Indigenous people.

9 We include Hong Kong and Taiwan as part of China. Countries defined as Middle Eastern are Algeria, Egypt, Libya, Morocco, Sudan, Bahrain, Iran, Iraq, Israel, Kuwait, Lebanon, Oman, Syria and Turkey. Because of the way we code ethnicity, the categories are not mutually exclusive. Dropping respondents who are in more than one minority ethnic category makes no tangible difference to the results.

10 Cell sizes are still reasonably large. For example, in the employment regressions, the restricted HILDA sample still includes 432 person-year observations for Indigenous respondents, 1,085 Italian observations, 666 Chinese observations and 713 Middle Eastern observations.

statistically significant at the 95 per cent level. Specifically, Indigenous respondents are 10 percentage points less likely to be employed, Chinese respondents are 12 percentage points less likely to be employed, and Middle Eastern respondents are 14 percentage points less likely to be employed. Conditional on being employed, Chinese respondents work 11 per cent fewer hours, while Italian respondents earn wages that are 6 per cent lower. Note that for the other three minority groups, the hourly wage coefficients are negative but statistically insignificant. If employers (or customers or co-workers) have a distaste for associating with workers from ethnic minorities, or if there is statistical discrimination, we would expect to see lower wages being offered for these groups. Yet this is not observed in the HILDA data. This may reflect the fact that the Australian minimum wage is one of the highest in the developed world (Leigh 2007). Other features of the Australian employment system also lead to wage rigidity – for example, 17 per cent of employees have their wages set by industrial awards, while a further 39 per cent have their wages set through registered collective agreements (ABS 2009).[11] Given this institutional framework, the principal margin on which employers can adjust is likely to be through hiring (Becker 1971). We would therefore expect to see lower employment rates for ethnic minorities. This is indeed what is observed in column [1].

But what happens when additional observables are added to the specification? In columns [2], [4] and [6] of Table 9.1, we include controls for years of actual labour market experience, years of education and self-assessed English proficiency. In this specification, the coefficients tend to be closer to zero, and none are statistically significant at the 95 per cent level. However, the standard errors in Table 9.1 are sufficiently large that we cannot rule out modest ethnic differences in employment and wages, even controlling for observable productivity differences. Moreover, there are potentially important productivity differences that are unobservable, including school quality, interpersonal skills and work ethics. To the extent that these are correlated with a respondent's ethnicity, they could help explain (or confound) estimates of labour market discrimination. In addition, any observed negative effects of immigrant status on the outcomes reported in Table 9.1 might reflect discrimination at one or more of the different

11 Registered collective agreements are defined by the ABS as:

> An agreement between an employer (or group of employers) and a group of employees (or one or more unions or employee associations representing the employees). A collective agreement sets the terms of employment (pay and/or conditions) for a group of employees, and is usually registered with a Federal or State industrial tribunal or authority.

stages in the employment process, ranging from selection for interviews to the hiring decision conditional on being interviewed, to the level of wages actually offered. In principle, the level of discrimination in the pre-interview stage – which is what we estimate in our field experiment described below – could be negatively or positively correlated with discrimination in hiring decisions and wage offers.

Can we learn more about employers' 'tastes for discrimination' by examining reports of Australians' attitudes to these minority groups? One way to address this is to use surveys asking Australians if immigration from particular regions should be reduced. According to a telephone survey of randomly selected representative voting-age Australians conducted in the first quarter of 2007, around 12 per cent of Australians thought immigration from Europe should be reduced, 23 per cent thought immigration from Asia should be reduced, and 38 per cent thought immigration from the Middle East should be reduced (Issues Deliberation Australia, 2007). Surveys on attitudes to intermarriage find similar results (Dunn, 2003; Forrest and Dunn, 2007). These findings certainly seem to suggest that, for whatever reason, there is prejudice in Australia against particular ethnic groups. This could manifest itself in taste-based discrimination by employers, workers or customers. Next, we consider whether or not there is discrimination in hiring, as measured by the initial stage of the process – callback for an interview.

The correspondence discrimination experiment

The basic notion underlying correspondence discrimination studies is that an estimate of the extent of hiring discrimination can be determined by conducting an experiment in which fictional CVs, carrying ethnically identifiable names, are sent to employers. By comparing the callback rates for different ethnic groups, the researcher can estimate the degree of ethnic discrimination in a particular context.

According to a comprehensive review of the literature (Riach and Rich 2002), correspondence discrimination studies were initially conducted by British sociologists in 1969 (Jowell and Prescott-Clarke 1970). Since then, researchers have applied the technique to Australia, Canada, France, the Netherlands, Sweden and the United States. In audit studies, researchers have also trained pairs of actors to show up for job interviews, apply for rental housing and negotiate to purchase used cars (for a recent survey, see Pager (2007)). Using written CVs, the correspondence discrimination technique has been used to measure discrimination on the basis of gender, age, obesity, having a criminal record, facial attractiveness and sexual orientation. As noted above, in-person audit studies have been criticised on several bases, including the possibility that the actors may not in fact appear identical to employers.[12] In response to these criticisms, correspondence studies replace fictitious personal candidates with fictitious online or paper applications, thereby reducing potential heterogeneity in unobservables. This is the approach we follow in this chapter. However, correspondence studies are still vulnerable to the critique of Heckman and Siegelman (1993), who show that if the distribution of unobservable productivity-relevant attributes of the various groups differs, the correspondence studies may produce over or underestimation of discrimination.[13]

During the six months from April 2007 to October 2007, we applied for over 4,000 jobs using a major online job-finding website. We applied for jobs in Australia's three largest cities – Sydney, Melbourne and Brisbane. For each job category, we created four fake CV templates, obtained from a broad internet search for similar CVs and tailored to the particular job. Applicants' names appeared in large type at the top of the CV, and were randomised across CV types. Note that we have a total of five ethnic groups. To ensure that the four applicants at each firm were from four different ethnic groups, we randomised and then 'balanced'; that is, if a firm's random draw included two people from the same ethnic group, we did another random draw. We continued to make random draws until each firm had four applicants from different ethnic groups.

Such a large sample size provides sufficient statistical power to look not only at differences across five ethnic groups (Anglo-Saxon, Indigenous, Chinese, Italian and Middle Eastern), but also to see whether such effects differed by

12 Heckman (1998) and Heckman and Siegelman (1993) present a number of additional critiques of the methodology used in correspondence and audit studies. Since these primarily deal with studies that use actors, we do not address them here, but one response may be found in Pager (2007).

13 Neumark (2010) shows that, if correspondence studies explicitly include variations in applicant quality, an unbiased estimate of discrimination can be uncovered. Neumark (2010) applied his technique to the correspondence study of Bertrand and Mullainathan (2004), and showed that their measured discrimination was actually an *under*estimate. Our experiment was designed and undertaken before Neumark's paper was written, and we were unable to follow his approach since employers in our experiment did not respond to differences in applicant quality in a systematic fashion across job types (for example higher-educated applicants received more callbacks in some job types, and fewer callbacks in others).

gender, city and job type. For example, we still have around 280 individuals per cell when looking at differences by ethnicity and city. However, our results are fragile once we go to three-level tabulations (for example, ethnicity by job type by gender), so we do not show such results in our tabulations. Booth and Leigh (2010) focus specifically on issues of gender.

In selecting appropriate occupations for this study, we focused on jobs that did not require any post-school qualifications, and for which the application process was relatively straightforward (to ensure that we could complete a sufficient number of applications to have good statistical power).

Conjectures

While our primary goal is to establish the extent of discrimination and how it varies across ethnic minorities in Australia, we also wished to test a number of related conjectures. These are as follows.

First, we aim to test the conjecture that employers differentially discriminate in response to perceived customer preferences. To assess this, we deliberately select occupations for our analysis that involve face-to-face contact and those that do not. The four occupations we select are: waitstaff, data entry, customer service and sales. Data entry involves no customer contact, and therefore, customer discriminatory preferences should not play a role in the employer's callback decision. In contrast, waitstaff jobs entail a high degree of interpersonal contact. Hence, for these jobs, we would expect ethnic applicants to receive lower callback rates if customer discriminatory preferences matter.

Examples of the types of jobs falling within these occupational categories are as follows. Waitstaff jobs included positions at bistros, cafes, bars, restaurants and hotels. Data entry positions – also known as document processing officers or technical records officers – included jobs working for an airline, a radio station, a bank and a charity. Customer service jobs were a mix of telephone support and face-to-face positions (it was often difficult to distinguish these from the information available) and included staffing the front desk at a bowling alley, answering customer support calls at a private health insurance company, and staffing the front desk at a parking garage. Sales positions were almost entirely involved in-person sales, and included jobs at a tiling store, a supermarket, an electrical goods store and a pizzeria.

Table 9.2 gives average wages and the share of the female component in these occupations, based on data from the Australian Bureau of Statistics' Employee Earnings and Hours survey, conducted in August 2006. The four jobs, more feminised than the non-managerial workforce as a whole, also have a slightly above-average share of employees from non-English-speaking backgrounds. Across the four jobs, workers are paid about three-quarters of average wages.

Table 9.2: Characteristics of the jobs

	Wage ($)	Female share (%)	NESB share (%)
Waitstaff	18.90	80	17
Data entry	19.10	85	15
Customer service	21.60	68	17
Sales	18.50	69	16
All FT non-managerial	26.00	46	15

Notes: NESB = non-English speaking background, denotes respondents who were born in a non-English-speaking country; FT = full-time; Since we only have access to the 2-digit occupation code, we classify the four occupations using ISCO-88 codes 51, 41, 42 and 52, respectively.

Sources: ABS Employee Earnings and Hours Survey, 2006; HILDA, pooling waves 1–6.

The second conjecture that we wished to test was whether or not employers in different Australian cities differentially discriminate against ethnic minority applicants. We therefore applied for jobs in Australia's three largest cities: Sydney, Melbourne and Brisbane. These cities differ in terms of their ethnic composition (with Sydney being the most ethnically diverse of the three), their immigration history and in the prevailing rate of unemployment at the time of our study (with Brisbane having the tightest labour market).

Our third conjecture is whether or not racial-majority employers discriminate against minority groups. We explore this in two ways, which will be explained in greater detail towards the end of this section. The first involves matching on the characteristics of the postcode in which the employer is located. The second exploits the fact that, for many jobs, we know the name of the contact person listed on the advertisement, the person who responded to one or more of our applicants, and sometimes both.

Collecting the data

For each job category, we created four fictional CV templates that we used to apply for jobs. These were obtained from a broad internet search for similar CVs and tailored by us to the particular job. The CV template was augmented with the addition of an address (we selected four street-suburb combinations in middle-income neighbourhoods, and randomised the street number between 1 and 20). Two sample CVs are depicted in Figures A9.1 and A9.2.

The ethnicity of the applicant was denoted by an ethnically distinguishable name, which appeared in large print at the top of the CV. For each ethnic group, we identified five female first names, five male first names and five last names, which were combined randomly to create the job applicant's name. Ideally, we would have obtained access to a large database of Australians, containing names and self-identified ethnicity. However, we were unable to locate a suitable public database, and sample surveys such as the HILDA Survey (or Indigenous databases such as those held by the Australian Institute of Aboriginal and Torres Strait Islander Studies) turned down our requests to tabulate lists of common names. We therefore chose our Anglo-Saxon, Italian, Chinese, and Middle Eastern names by consulting the website,[14] and our Indigenous names by consulting the indexes of various books listing Indigenous artists.[15] The full list of names used in this study is provided in Table A9.1.

The job-finding website that we used had an online application process. For each advertised position, we submitted four applications, ensuring, as described previously, that each of the four applications was from a different ethnic group.[16] Each application included a short covering letter, plus a fake CV. For each sex cell, we set up an email address plus a separate phone line with an answering machine. (All answering machines had a message left by a person with a regular Australian accent. We did this because applicants

14 www.behindthename.com.

15 Since our CVs suggest that the job applicants are aged in their twenties, it is unlikely that employers would have thought that female applicants with non-Anglo names were actually Anglo respondents who had taken on a non-Anglo last name by marriage.

16 A referee pointed out that our results hold when there is an Anglo-Saxon applicant with similar merits applying for the same position. If there was not an applicant with an Anglo-Saxon name, the callback rates for the ethnic minorities would probably have been higher. We would also point out that if there had been more than one Anglo-Saxon applicant with similar merits applying for the same position the callback rate could well have been lower.

were supposed to differ only with regard to their ethnicity, and we wanted to guard against the possibility that a prospective interviewer would simply hang up if they heard a foreign-sounding voice.) Employers could invite the applicant back for an interview by either sending an email or making a telephone call.

The results

Table 9.3 sets out the callback rates from the experiment. For Anglo-Saxon-sounding names, the mean callback rate was 35 per cent.[17] However, names connoting the four minority groups received a lower callback rate, with Indigenous applicants obtaining an interview 26 per cent of the time, Chinese 21 per cent of the time, Italian 32 per cent of the time and Middle Eastern 22 per cent of the time. For Indigenous, Chinese and Middle Eastern applicants, the difference is highly statistically significant at the 1 per cent level, but the Anglo vs. Italian difference is only statistically significant at the 10 per cent level (see last column of Table 9.3, where the *P*-value on the difference is 0.940).[18]

The middle column of Table 9.3 expresses the difference as a ratio. This is useful because it provides an intuitive metric for the level of discrimination in terms of the number of additional job applications that a minority applicant must submit to get the same number of callbacks as an Anglo applicant. These ratios indicate that, in order to get as many interviews as an Anglo applicant, an Indigenous person must submit 35 per cent more applications, a Chinese person must submit 68 per cent more applications, an Italian person must submit 12 per cent more applications, and a Middle Eastern person must submit 64 per cent more applications.

17 We also tested for differences between Catholic and Protestant names, but found no mean difference between the two groups. Because Catholic respondents were identified both by name and by having a Catholic school on their CV, we were concerned that they might not make an appropriate control group for the purpose of focusing on ethnicity. We therefore dropped Catholic CVs from the sample for the current analysis.

18 Although all applicants attended school in Australia, and we are able to hold constant their education and experience, it is possible that stereotypes about productivity still remain. However, as noted below, we find little evidence that second-generation immigrants have inferior English-speaking skills.

Table 9.3: Callback rates by soundingness of name and applicant gender

	Callback rate (%)	Ratio (Anglo-Saxon / minority rate)	Difference (Anglo-Saxon − minority rate)	*P*-value on difference
Male and female applicants				
Anglo-Saxon (*N*=837)	35	NA	NA	NA
Indigenous (*N*=848)	26	1.35	0.09	0.0000
Chinese (*N*=845)	21	1.68	0.14	0.0000
Italian (*N*=835)	32	1.12	0.04	0.0940
Middle Eastern (*N*=845)	22	1.64	0.14	0.0000
Female applicants				
Anglo-Saxon (*N*=422)	38	NA	NA	NA
Indigenous (*N*=442)	31	1.23	0.07	0.0311
Chinese (*N*=374)	21	1.82	0.01	0.0000
Italian (*N*=410)	37	1.03	0.01	0.7858
Middle Eastern (*N*=434)	25	1.52	0.13	0.0001
Male applicants				
Anglo-Saxon (*N*=403)	33	NA	NA	NA
Indigenous (*N*=426)	22	1.51	0.11	0.0003
Chinese (*N*=403)	22	1.54	0.12	0.0002
Italian (*N*=461)	28	1.21	0.06	0.0686
Middle Eastern (*N*=435)	19	1.76	0.14	0.0000
Does ethnic discrimination differ by applicant gender?	$\chi^2(4)=6.68$ *P*-value = 0.15			

Notes: To test whether ethnic discrimination differs significantly by applicant gender, we run the probit regression: $\text{Interview}(0, 1)=\alpha+\beta I^{Female}+\gamma I^{Ethnicity}+\lambda(I^{Female}\times I^{Ethnicity})+\varepsilon$; The dependent variable is a dummy for receiving an interview, while I^{Female} and $I^{Ethnicity}$ are, respectively, indicators for being female and being in each of the four minority ethnic categories. The chi-squared test above is a test for the joint significance of the four λ coefficients.

The female applicant results indicate that female Italian applicants are not discriminated against (relative to female Anglo applicants), but otherwise, the minority groups all have significantly lower callback rates (see the *P*-values in the last column). Notice that the difference between callback rates for Indigenous and Anglo females is statistically significant at the 3 per cent level, while for Chinese and Middle Eastern females relative to Anglo females, it is statistically significant at the 1 per cent level. Male applicant results show that, relative to Anglo applicants of the same sex, discrimination is generally worse for minority men than for minority women (the exception being those with Chinese-sounding names), and for all groups except Italian, the difference is statistically significant at the 1 per cent level.[19] However, when we formally test whether ethnic discrimination differs by gender, we cannot reject the hypothesis that the level of discrimination is the same for men and women of the same ethnic group. In Booth and Leigh (2010), we explore gender differences in more detail and find that, overall, female candidates are more likely to receive a callback than male candidates (the differences are largest for waitstaff and data entry occupations).

One way to benchmark our results is to compare the number of additional applications that a minority candidate must submit in order to expect the same number of interviews. Another is to think about the kind of labour market that minority applicants face.[20] In effect, we can ask the question: what would the prevailing unemployment rate have to be for an Anglo person to face the same job-finding task as a member of a minority group?

To answer this, we exploit the fact that the unemployment rate differs across time and across the three cities in our experiment. Using only Anglo-Saxon respondents, we run a simple probit regression of whether a given respondent gets an interview on the prevailing unemployment rate in that month and city. The coefficient from this regression is –0.065 (standard error 0.033), suggesting that a 1-point increase in the unemployment rate reduces the probability of an Anglo-Saxon applicant getting an interview by 6.5 per cent. On average, the prevailing unemployment rate during our analysis was 4.3 per cent.

However, the analysis in the previous paragraph, taken together with the results in Table 9.3, suggests the following. First, Indigenous applicants faced the same difficulties in obtaining an interview as Anglo applicants when the unemployment rate was 5.6 per cent. Second, Chinese applicants faced the same difficulties in obtaining an interview as Anglo applicants when the unemployment rate was 6.4 per cent. Third, Italian applicants faced the same difficulties in obtaining an interview as

19 We are inclined not to make much of the larger effect for Chinese women, since many non-Chinese would probably have difficulty distinguishing between male and female Chinese first names.

20 Another approach would be to benchmark the magnitude of our effects against the benefit of more education. However, returns to education did not differ systematically within jobs. We return to this issue below.

Anglo applicants when the unemployment rate was 4.8 per cent. Fourth, Middle Eastern applicants faced the same difficulties in obtaining an interview as Anglo applicants when the unemployment rate was 6.4 per cent.

In summary, we have found clear evidence of discrimination in selection for interviews for entry-level jobs in Australia. Of course, the audit discrimination technique only observes the first stage of the employment process – selection for an interview – and hence we cannot comment on the second stage of receiving a job offer. Nonetheless, our results provide clear evidence of ethnic discrimination at the callback stage. This contrasts with the pooled cross-sectional estimates are summarised in Table 9.1, based on survey data and combine the various stages of the employment process. Thus, employment in that table involves selection for callback and selection for an employment offer at the interview stage. But this regression approach may not provide an accurate answer, as we noted in the Introduction. If an individual's ethnicity is correlated with some unobserved productive trait, differences in economic outcomes are likely to reflect more than just discrimination. In contrast to those regression results based on survey evidence, our field experiment is a randomised experiment. As such, it is better able to establish causality, and it provides strong evidence for the existence of discrimination at the callback stage. Next, we attempt to tease out more information about the reasons for such discrimination and to test the conjectures outlined in the previous section.

Is there evidence of customer discrimination?

We constructed our experiment so that some of the jobs for which we applied required no customer contact, and therefore, customer discriminatory preferences should play no role in the employer's callback decision. In contrast, others entail a high degree of interpersonal contact. A test for whether or not customer preferences might matter involves testing if the degree of ethnic discrimination differs across the four job types in the survey. These are waitstaff, data entry, customer service and sales. If customer discrimination is important, then one should expect to see substantially more discrimination in jobs that involve the highest degree of interpersonal contact (waitstaff) than those involving no customer contact (data entry).

Table 9.4: Callback rates by soundingness of name and job type

	Callback rate (%)	Ratio (Anglo-Saxon / minority rate)	Difference (Anglo-Saxon – minority rate)	P-value on difference
Waitstaff				
Anglo-Saxon (*N*=223)	50	NA	NA	NA
Indigenous (*N*=215)	29	1.70	0.20	0.0000
Chinese (*N*=200)	25	1.99	0.25	0.0000
Italian (*N*=211)	39	1.27	0.10	0.0288
Middle Eastern (*N*=214)	22	2.27	0.28	0.0000
Data entry				
Anglo-Saxon (*N*=222)	34	NA	NA	NA
Indigenous (*N*=209)	21	1.60	0.13	0.0031
Chinese (*N*=199)	19	1.82	0.15	0.0004
Italian (*N*=213)	29	1.18	0.05	0.2472
Middle Eastern (*N*=207)	20	1.71	0.14	0.0011
Customer service				
Anglo-Saxon (*N*=196)	26	NA	NA	NA
Indigenous (*N*=215)	28	0.91	-0.02	0.5836
Chinese (*N*=215)	23	1.12	0.03	0.5196
Italian (*N*=201)	32	0.79	-0.07	0.1337
Middle Eastern (*N*=220)	25	1.02	0.01	0.9048
Sales				
Anglo-Saxon (*N*=196)	31	NA	NA	NA
Indigenous (*N*=209)	27	1.16	0.04	0.3369
Chinese (*N*=231)	18	1.71	0.13	0.0018
Italian (*N*=210)	26	1.19	0.05	0.2717
Middle Eastern (*N*=204)	20	1.59	0.12	0.0081
Does ethnic discrimination differ between waitstaff and data entry?	$\chi^2(4) = 3.55$ *P*-value = 0.47			

Notes: To test whether ethnic discrimination differs significantly by job, we run the probit regression: Interview(0, 1)=$\alpha+\beta I^{Waitstaff}+\gamma I^{Ethnicity}+\lambda(I^{Waitstaff}\times I^{Ethnicity})+\varepsilon$; The dependent variable is a dummy for receiving an interview, while $I^{Waitstaff}$ and $I^{Ethnicity}$ are, respectively, indicators for applying for a waitstaff job and being in each of the four minority ethnic categories. The chi-squared test above is a test for the joint significance of the four λ coefficients. We run this test with waitstaff and data entry positions only.

These results are presented in Table 9.4. Across the four jobs, we observe the greatest amount of discrimination against minority applicants seeking waitstaff jobs. A Chinese and Middle Eastern person seeking a job as a waiting staff member must submit twice as many applications in order to get as many interviews as an Anglo-Saxon applicant. However, there is only slightly less discrimination in data entry jobs, and a formal test cannot reject that the degree of discrimination is the same in both occupations. This suggests that relatively little of the observed discrimination can be attributed solely to customer-based discrimination.

Curiously, the one job in which the level of discrimination appears to be lower is customer service, in which there is no statistically significant discrimination against any of the minority ethnic groups. This is also the one occupation in which those with more education were significantly more likely to receive an interview (a pattern that did not hold in other occupations, as we discuss below). This suggests that there could potentially be less discrimination in higher-skilled occupations than in the lower-skilled jobs analysed here.

Are there differences in discrimination across cities?

Our second conjecture was that employers in the major Australian cities differentially discriminate against ethnic minority applicants. The three largest cities – Sydney, Melbourne and Brisbane – differ in terms of their immigration history and ethnic composition. For example, Melbourne has the largest proportion of immigrant Italians and Sydney of Chinese and Middle Eastern immigrants. The cities also differed slightly in their unemployment rates at the time of our study (with Brisbane having the tightest labour market). To what extent do levels of discrimination differ across the three cities in our experiment?

Table 9.5: Callback rates by soundingness of name and city

	Callback rate (%)	Ratio (Anglo-Saxon / minority rate)	Difference (Anglo-Saxon – minority rate)	*P*-value on difference
Brisbane				
Anglo-Saxon (*N*=269)	42	NA	NA	NA
Indigenous (*N*=281)	30	1.41	0.12	0.0030
Chinese (*N*=283)	27	1.57	0.15	0.0002
Italian (*N*=286)	33	1.28	0.09	0.0261
Middle Eastern (*N*=280)	28	1.51	0.14	0.0005
Melbourne				
Anglo-Saxon (*N*=282)	27	NA	NA	NA
Indigenous *N*=272)	18	1.48	0.09	0.0154
Chinese (*N*=271)	17	1.61	0.10	0.0039
Italian (*N*=282)	29	0.93	-0.02	0.5722
Middle Eastern (*N*=284)	16	1.64	0.10	0.0026
Sydney				
Anglo-Saxon (*N*=286)	38	NA	NA	NA
Indigenous (*N*=295)	31	1.25	0.08	0.0537
Chinese (*N*=284)	20	1.92	0.18	0.0000
Italian (*N*=267)	34	1.14	0.05	0.2450
Middle Eastern (*N*=281)	21	1.80	0.17	0.0000
Does ethnic discrimination differ by city?	Sydney vs Melbourne $\chi^2(4)=4.59$ *P*-value = 0.33	Sydney vs Brisbane $\chi^2(4)=4.47$ *P*-value = 0.35	Brisbane vs Melbourne $\chi^2(4)=5.00$ *P*-value = 0.29	-

Notes: To test whether ethnic discrimination differs significantly by applicant gender, we run the probit regression: Interview(0, 1) = $\alpha+\beta I^{City}+\gamma I^{Ethnicity}+\lambda(I^{City}\times I^{Ethnicity})+\varepsilon$; The dependent variable is a dummy for receiving an interview, while I^{City} and $I^{Ethnicity}$ are, respectively, indicators for being in a particular city and being in each of the four minority ethnic categories. The chi-squared test above is a test for the joint significance of the four λ coefficients. We run this test three times, for each of the three city-pair combinations.

In Table 9.5, we present results tabulated separately for Brisbane, Melbourne and Sydney. In general, the patterns are quite similar. In each of the cities, discrimination is highest against Chinese and Middle Eastern applicants, followed by Indigenous applicants, followed by Italian applicants. However, the point estimates are suggestive of non-trivial differences. For example, if they are to get as many interviews as an applicant with an Anglo name, Chinese applicants must put in 57 per cent more applications in Brisbane, but 92 per cent more applications in Sydney. In addition, there is a statistically significant degree of discrimination against Italians in Brisbane, but no evidence of discrimination against Italians in Melbourne.[21] To the extent that such differences exist, they could be due to the tightness of the labour market, the ethnic mix of the city or differences in social norms. However, when we formally test the hypothesis that discrimination is equal across the three cities, we are unable to reject it for any of the three city-pair combinations. (Focusing on individual ethnicities, the only significant difference is the degree of discrimination against Italians in Brisbane and Melbourne.)

Does discrimination vary with employer characteristics?

Our third conjecture was that ethnic-majority employers discriminate against minority groups. To test this, we investigate whether the level of discrimination varies systematically with employer characteristics. We explore this in two ways. First, we match on the characteristics of the postcode in which the employer is located, using data from the 2006 census. This has the great advantage of precision, and we might expect that employers who are located in areas with a high minority composition might have chosen to locate there, or might themselves be non-Anglo, or might instead have had greater exposure to other minorities. While we cannot distinguish between these various conjectures, we nonetheless think it is worth investigating this avenue to see if we can establish any links between employer location and ethnic discrimination.

21 Perhaps this is not surprising given that Melbourne has the largest concentration of Italians.

Table 9.6: Applicant ethnicity and employer neighbourhood characteristics

	[1] Overseas-born share	[2] Born in same country	[3] Same ancestry
Indigenous applicant	-0.167*** (0.046)	-0.090*** (0.027)	-0.090*** (0.026)
Chinese applicant	-0.153*** (0.048)	-0.127*** (0.028)	-0.130*** (0.028)
Italian applicant	-0.098* (0.052)	-0.068** (0.028)	-0.075** (0.035)
Middle Eastern applicant	-0.205*** (0.042)	-0.127*** (0.024)	-0.127*** (0.025)
Indigenous applicant × Overseas-born share	0.201 (0.140)	–	–
Chinese applicant × Overseas-born share	0.04 (0.142)	–	–
Italian applicant × Overseas-born share	0.137 (0.137)	–	–
Middle Eastern applicant × Overseas-born share	0.239* (0.140)	–	–
Overseas-born share	0.005 (0.100)	–	–
Indigenous applicant × Indigenous share	–	-1.578 (1.475)	-14.919 (14.715)
Chinese applicant × Chinese share	–	-0.326 (0.379)	-0.165 (0.270)
Italian applicant × Italian share	–	2.283 (2.041)	1.079 (1.098)
Middle Eastern applicant × Middle Eastern share	–	-1.626 (1.717)	-0.585 (0.762)
Indigenous share	–	0.328 (0.409)	1.11 (0.809)
Chinese share	–	0.650*** (0.189)	0.441*** (0.136)
Italian share	–	-1.879 (1.203)	-0.759 (0.628)
Middle Eastern share	–	-0.219 (0.532)	-0.211 (0.253)
Observations	2,701	2,701	2,701
Pseudo R^2	0.07	0.07	0.07

Notes: Marginal effects from a probit model. Standard errors in brackets. *, **, and *** denote statistical significance at the 10%, 5% and 1% levels respectively. All estimates include indicator variables for job type, city, and CV template. Share variables are the share born in a given country in column [2], and the share with a given ancestry in column [3].

The results of this exercise are shown in Table 9.6, where the sample is the 2,701 applicants for whom we know the postcode of the employer, and the dependent variable is the callback probability. In column [1], we interact the applicant's ethnicity with a measure of the share of respondents born overseas in the postcode. The interaction coefficients are generally positive, suggesting that discrimination is lower when there are more migrants in a neighbourhood. This interaction is significant (at the 10 per cent level) for Middle Eastern applicants. However, the magnitude of the effect is quite small, suggesting that discrimination against Middle Eastern applicants is only wiped out when four-fifths of the postcode is overseas-born.

In column [2], we interact the applicant's ethnicity with the share of people in the employer's postcode that were born in that country. In column [3], we interact the applicant's ethnicity with the share of people in the employer's postcode that have that ancestry. Although one main effect is significant (employers located in neighbourhoods with more Chinese residents have higher callback rates), the interaction effects are insignificant (we do not observe any systematic relationship between applicants' ethnicity and the share of their ethnic group in the employer's neighbourhood).

We next exploit the fact that for many jobs, we know the name of the contact person listed on the advertisement, the person who responded to one or more of our applicants, and sometimes both. Software known as OnoMap, developed by researchers at University College, London, was used to impute the ethnicity of these individuals, providing a proxy measure of the ethnicity of the person who made the hiring decision. OnoMap assigns ethnicity based on first names and last names, exploiting large databases in which individuals' true names and ethnicities are known. For more details of the coding algorithm, see Mateos, Webber and Longley (2007) and Mateos (2007).

Table 9.7: Applicant ethnicity and employer ethnicity

	[1] Contact non-Anglo	[2] Responder non-Anglo	[3] Contact or responder non-Anglo	[4] Contact same ethnicity	[5] Responder same ethnicity
Indigenous applicant	-0.111*** (0.025)	-0.132*** (0.036)	-0.111*** (0.025)	-0.106*** (0.024)	-0.126*** (0.033)
Chinese applicant	-0.178*** (0.023)	-0.236*** (0.034)	-0.169*** (0.024)	-0.169*** (0.021)	-0.225*** (0.031)
Italian applicant	-0.065** (0.027)	-0.054 (0.038)	-0.055** (0.027)	-0.063** (0.026)	-0.059* (0.035)
Middle Eastern applicant	-0.145*** (0.024)	-0.231*** (0.034)	-0.160*** (0.024)	-0.146*** (0.022)	-0.218*** (0.031)
Indigenous applicant × Non-Anglo employer	0.044 (0.084)	0.033 (0.087)	0.085 (0.074)	–	–
Chinese applicant × Non-Anglo employer	0.048 (0.087)	0.024 (0.085)	0.065 (0.073)	–	–
Italian applicant × Non-Anglo employer	0.081 (0.088)	-0.003 (0.086)	0.077 (0.074)	–	–
Middle Eastern applicant × Non-Anglo employer	-0.019 (0.078)	0.068 (0.085)	0.079 (0.073)	–	–
Non-Anglo employer	-0.001 (0.053)	0.021 (0.060)	0.016 (0.048)	–	–
Chinese applicant × Chinese employer	–	–	–	0.14 (0.102)	0.055 (0.101)
Italian applicant × Italian employer	–	–	–	-0.178** (0.086)	-0.244* (0.131)
Middle Eastern applicant × Middle Eastern employer	–	–	–	-0.125 (0.141)	-0.078 (0.219)
Chinese employer	–	–	–	0.157 (0.101)	0.209*** (0.077)
Italian employer	–	–	–	0.02 (0.039)	-0.001 (0.043)
Middle Eastern employer	–	–	–	0.041 (0.090)	0.021 (0.099)
Observations	2,335	2,319	3,313	2,335	2,319
Pseudo R^2	0.07	0.09	0.06	0.07	0.09

Notes: Marginal effects from a probit model; Standard errors in brackets; *, **, and *** denote statistical significance at the 10%, 5% and 1% levels respectively; All estimates include indicator variables for job type, city, and CV template. Employer ethnicity is imputed using the name of the contact in the job advertisement in columns [1] and [4], the name of the person who responded to candidates in columns [2] and [5], and either of those people in column [3] (if either is non-Anglo, the employer is coded as non-Anglo).

The results of this exercise are shown in Table 9.7, in the form of probit regressions where the dependent variable is the callback rate. In the first three columns, we simply classify contact people and responding people as Anglo (that is with names in the OnoMap Celtic or English categories), or non-Anglo (that is with names in the following OnoMap groups: African, East Asian and Pacific, European, Greek, Hispanic, International, Jewish and Armenian, Muslim, Sikh or south Asian). In columns [4]–[6], we classify employer names as being the same or different from the applicant's name (Italian applicants are matched to OnoMap's European and Greek groups, Chinese applicants are matched to OnoMap's East Asian and Pacific and South Asian groups, and Middle Eastern applicants are matched to OnoMap's Muslim group).[22]

We observe positive main effects for Chinese employers, who appear to have a higher callback rate. However, the only interaction effect we observe is for Italian employers, who appear to be significantly less likely to call back job candidates with Italian names. This is a surprising pattern, which suggests that a group with a relatively long history in Australia is actually less inclined to assist members of the same group.

How do our results compare with similar correspondence studies from other countries?

A survey by Riach and Rich (2002), supplemented with a literature review, returned 18 comparable correspondence studies (including ours), covering 34 minority ethnic groups. The results are set out in full in Table A9.2 and graphed in Figure 9.2. Of course, there are problems in making such comparisons, not least the different minorities tested, the different histories of immigration in each country, the economic state of the countries and the like. Nonetheless, this is a parsimonious way of making some comparisons. The first comparison is with the earlier Australian discrimination estimates from the correspondence study of Riach and Rich (1991), who ran an experiment in Melbourne between 1984 and 1988.

22 Matching more narrowly – for example matching Italian applicants to OnoMap's Italian names, and Chinese applicants to OnoMap's Chinese names – makes little difference to the results.

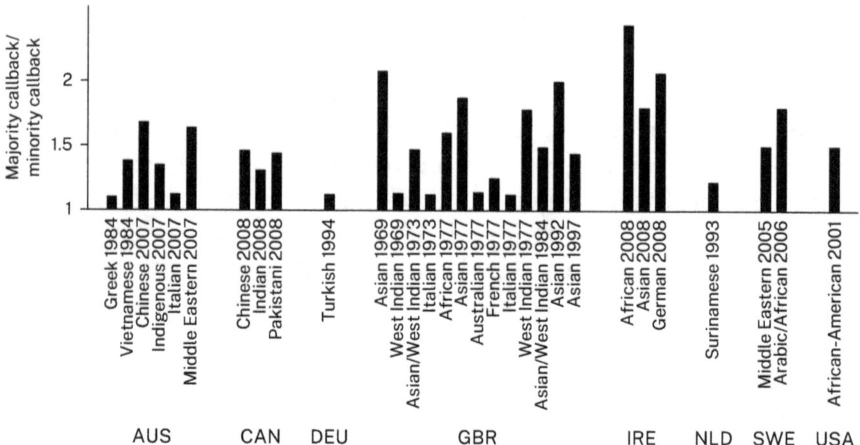

Figure 9.2. Comparing our results with prior correspondence studies

Note: Chart omits Bovenkerk et al. (1979), who found a ratio of 3.47 for Antillian job applicants in France in 1976.

In that study, the two minority groups were Greeks and Vietnamese. Although our study does not analyse either of those two groups, it is possible that discrimination involves regional stereotyping. To the extent that this is true, it is notable that we observe little change in the level of discrimination against migrants from southern Europe (comparing Greeks in 1986 with Italians in 2007), but a substantial increase in discrimination against migrants from South East Asia (comparing Vietnamese in 1986 with Chinese in 2007).[23]

Figure 9.2 also provides an international benchmark for our results, comparing only correspondence studies (ignoring studies that used actors to make contact in-person or via telephone).[24] For example, the level of callback discrimination against Indigenous Australians in 2007 was lower than the level of discrimination against African Americans in the United States in 2001.[25] The level of discrimination against Chinese Australians in 2007 is higher than the discrimination against Asians in the UK in 1997 and against Chinese in Canada in 2008, but lower than against Asians

23 However, if we restrict the 2007 sample to Melbourne applicants only, there is no apparent discrimination against southern Europeans applying for jobs in Australia in 2007.

24 So far as we are aware, ours is the most comprehensive survey to date of the available correspondence studies.

25 In their correspondence study, Bertrand and Mullainathan (2004) found that the ratio of white callbacks to black callbacks was 1.5. This is a lower level of discrimination than the estimate from the in-person audit studies conducted by Pager (2003) (a callback ratio of 2.43, focusing only on those without criminal convictions), and Pager et al. (2009) (a callback ratio of 2.04).

in Ireland in 2008. The level of discrimination against Middle Eastern Australians in 2007 appears similar to the level of discrimination against Arabic and Middle Easterners in Sweden in 2005–2007. And the level of discrimination against Italian Australians in 2007 is similar to the level of discrimination against Australians in the UK in 1977–1978.

Discussion and conclusion

The most common approach to estimating discrimination is through the use of surveys. However, such an approach may potentially provide biased estimates of the true extent of discrimination. For example, if earnings surveys do not contain good measures of productive characteristics such as school quality, and these characteristics are systematically correlated with both ethnicity and earnings, then their omission may bias estimates of labour market discrimination. Similarly, in the case of attitudinal surveys, there is a risk that survey respondents may proffer the socially acceptable answer rather than their actual belief.

To address these concerns, we conducted a large-scale correspondence discrimination experiment. This involved sending fake CVs to employers to obtain an experimental measure of the relationship between job callbacks and the ethnic soundingness of the applicant's name. We find clear evidence of discrimination, with Chinese and Middle Easterners both having to submit at least 50 per cent more applications in order to receive the same number of callbacks as Anglo candidates. Indigenous applicants also suffer a statistically significant level of discrimination, though the effects are smaller (for example, Indigenous applicants in Australia appear to fare a little better than African Americans in the US job market). We observe virtually no discrimination against Italian applicants. To the extent that we can compare our results with earlier evidence for Australia, our results do not suggest that ethnic discrimination fell from 1986 to 2007.

Naturally, the use of field experiments to measure discrimination has its own limitations. For example, the way in which ethnicity is denoted may not necessarily be representative of the general population. In our experiment, we use names that were chosen on the basis that we judged them to be representative of the various ethnic groups. This allows us to conduct an experiment in which we only vary the names, but it has the limitation that our results will not necessarily generalise to individuals of the same ethnicity, but with an Anglicised name. Another limitation is that our experiment provides a precise estimate on the callback stage, but we are unable to speak of discrimination at the interview stage, nor on the job. Indeed, a drawback of the correspondence approach relative to the audit approach is that the pure correspondence approach does not allow one to explore discrimination at different stages of the application procedure (progressing from application, to invitation for an interview, to job offer, as was done by Bovenkerk, Gras and Ramsoedh, 1995, for Moroccan versus Dutch male applicants for semiskilled jobs). Hence, our estimates are probably an underestimate of the extent of discrimination in the labour market. Moreover, as Pager et al. (2009, p. 793) note, the emphasis on jobs advertised through the online job site also probably understates the extent of discrimination, since firms wanting to discriminate may be more likely to use informal networks.

Yet in spite of these caveats, our findings are important, since our study is one of the first to compare multiple groups of immigrants in a country in which one in four individuals is born overseas. As noted at the start of section II, these groups range from earlier intakes of Italians to more recent intakes of Chinese and Middle Eastern individuals, as immigration policy in Australia has been progressively relaxed to admit immigrants from more diverse backgrounds. In a stark reminder of how far our country has yet to go, we have found clear evidence of discrimination against ethnic minorities – especially the more recently admitted groups – at the initial stage of the job-finding process. But what explains this prejudice? The higher rate of discrimination in the most customer-focused job (waitstaff) is consistent with some degree of customer-based discrimination. However, the fact that we observe discrimination in an occupation requiring no direct customer contact (data entry) suggests that customer discrimination is not the whole story. Other alternatives could include taste-based discrimination (on the part of co-workers or employers) or statistical discrimination. We have not been able to distinguish between these two broad hypotheses, in common with the vast majority of other studies investigating this issue with a variety of different methodologies. We suspect it is a bit of both: statistical discrimination in the face of uncertainty and the conservative tastes of the majority group revealed by attitudinal survey evidence.

In audit or correspondence studies, fictitious individuals who are identical in all respects apart from the one of interest apply for jobs. Audit studies have been criticised on numerous grounds, including whether or not the applicants from different groups actually appear identical to employers. In response to these criticisms, correspondence studies substitute fictitious online or paper applications for fictitious personal candidates, thereby reducing potential heterogeneity in unobservables. This was the approach followed in this chapter. However, correspondence studies are still vulnerable to the critique of Heckman and Siegelman (1993), who show that, if the distribution of unobservable productivity-relevant attributes of the various groups differs, the correspondence studies may produce over or underestimation of discrimination. This is an important argument that we have not been able to address in our study. Neumark (2010) shows that, if correspondence studies explicitly include variations in applicant quality, an unbiased estimate of discrimination can be uncovered. It is interesting to note that Neumark (2010) applied his technique to the correspondence study of Bertrand and Mullainathan (2004) and showed that their measured discrimination was actually an underestimate. Since our experiment did not reveal systematic returns to applicant quality, Neumark's procedure is not open to us. However, in future work, we hope to pursue this line of research.

Acknowledgements

This chapter was first published as Booth, A.L., Leigh, A., and Varganova, E. (2011). 'Does ethnic discrimination vary across minority groups? Evidence from a field experiment', *Oxford Bulletin of Economics and Statistics,* 74(4):547–573. doi.org/10.1111/j.1468-0084.2011.00664.x.

For valuable comments, we are grateful to two anonymous referees, Boyd Hunter, Gigi Foster, Steven Haider, and seminar participants at the 2010 World Conference of the EALE and the Society of Labor Economists, The Australian National University's Social and Political Theory Seminar, The Australian National University Centre for Aboriginal Economic Policy Research seminar, the Australasian Labour Econometrics Workshop, and Monash University. Iktimal Hage-Ali and Amy King put us in touch with Gabriella Hannah, who is quoted at the start of the chapter. Pablo Mateos kindly allowed us to use a beta version of his OnoMap software to impute ethnicity to the names of employers. Mathias Sinning provided invaluable programming assistance and Susanne Schmidt provided outstanding research assistance. The background section of this chapter uses unit record data from the HILDA Survey. The HILDA Project was initiated and is funded by the Australian Government Department of Families, Housing, Community Services and Indigenous Affairs (FaHCSIA) and is managed by the Melbourne Institute of Applied Economic and Social Research

(MIAESR). The findings and views reported in this chapter, however, are those of the authors and should not be attributed to either FaHCSIA or the MIAESR. We take very seriously the ethical issues surrounding this research. Our experiment received approval from The Australian National University's Human Research Ethics Committee. It involves some deception of participants – for a thoughtful discussion on the ethics of deception in such field experiments, see Riach and Rich (2004).

References

ABS (Australian Bureau of Statistics). (2009). *Employee Earnings and Hours.* Cat No. 6306.0, ABS, Canberra.

Arrow, K.J. (1998). 'What has economics to say about racial discrimination?', *The Journal of Economic Perspectives*, 12:91–100.

Becker, G.S. (1971). *The Economics of Discrimination.* Chicago: The University of Chicago Press.

Berman, G., and The Victorian Equal Opportunity & Human Rights Commission. (2008). *Harnessing Diversity: Addressing Racial and Religious Discrimination in Employment*, Victorian Equal Opportunity & Human Rights Commission, Melbourne.

Bertrand, M., and Mullainathan, S. (2004). 'Are Emily and Greg more employable than Lakisha and Jamal? A field experiment on labor market discrimination', *American Economic Review*, 94(4):991–1013. doi.org/10.1257/0002828042002561.

Booth, A.L., and Leigh, A. (2010). 'Do employers discriminate by gender? A field experiment in female-dominated occupations', *Economics Letters*, 107(2):236–238. doi.org/10.1016/j.econlet.2010.01.034.

Bovenkerk, F., Kilborne, B., Raveau, F., and Smith, D. (1979). 'Comparative aspects of research on discrimination against non-white citizens in Great Britain, France and the Netherlands'. In Berting J., Geyer F. and Jurkovich R. (eds), *Problems in International Comparative Research in the Social Sciences*, Oxford: Pergamon Press, pp. 105–122.

Bovenkerk, F., Gras, M., and Ramsoedh, D. (1995). 'Discrimination against migrant workers and ethnic minorities in access to employment in the Netherlands', International Migration Paper No. 4, ILO, Geneva.

Brown, C., and Gay, P. (1985). *Racial Discrimination 17 Years After the Act*. London: Policy Studies Institute.

Bursell, M. (2007). 'What's in a name? A field experiment test for the existence of ethnic discrimination in the hiring process', Working Paper No. 2007:7, The Stockholm University Linnaeus Center for Integration Studies, Stockholm.

Carlsson, M., and Rooth, D.-O. (2007). 'Evidence of ethnic discrimination in the Swedish labour market using experimental data', *Labour Economics*, 14(4):716–729. doi.org/10.1016/j.labeco.2007.05.001.

Cobb-Clark, D.A. (2003). 'Public policy and the labour market adjustment of new immigrants to Australia', *Journal of Population Economics*, 16:655–681. doi.org/10.1007/s00148-003-0153-2.

Dunn, K. (2003). 'Racism in Australia: Findings of a survey on racist attitudes and experiences of racism', National Europe Centre Paper No. 77, The University of New South Wales, Sydney.

Eagly, A.H., and Kite, M.E. (1987). 'Are stereotypes of nationalities applied to both women and men?' *Journal of Personality and Social Psychology*, 53(3):451–462. doi.org/10.1037/0022-3514.53.3.451.

Esmail, A., and Everington, S. (1993). 'Racial discrimination against doctors from ethnic minorities', *British Medical Journal*, 306(6879):691–692. doi.org/10.1136/bmj.306.6885.691.

Esmail, A., and Everington, S. (1997). 'Asian doctors are still being discriminated against', *British Medical Journal*, 314:1619. doi.org/10.1136/bmj.314.7097.1619.

Firth, M. (1981). 'Racial discrimination in the British labour market', *ILR Review*, 34:265–272. doi.org/10.1136/bmj.306.6879.691.

Forrest, J., and Dunn, K. (2007). *Strangers in Our Midst? Intolerance and Discrimination Toward Minority Cultural Groups in Victoria*. Report to VicHealth.

Goldberg, A., Mourinho, D., and Kulke, U. (1995). *Labour Market Discrimination Against Foreign Workers in Germany*. International Migration Papers 7, ILO, Geneva. Available at: www.ilo.org/sites/default/files/wcmsp5/groups/public/%40ed_protect/%40protrav/%40migrant/documents/publication/wcms_201039.pdf.

Hatton, T.J. (2005). 'Explaining trends in UK immigration', *Journal of Population Economics*, 18:719–740. doi.org/10.1007/s00148-005-0015-1.

Heckman, J.J. (1998). 'Detecting discrimination', *Journal of Economic Perspectives*, 12(2):101–116. doi.org/10.1257/jep.12.2.101.

Heckman, J., and Siegelman, P. (1993). 'The Urban Institute audit studies: Their methods and findings'. In Fix, M., and Struyk, R.J. (eds), *Clear and Convincing Evidence: Measurement of Discrimination in America*, Washington, DC: Urban Institute Press, pp. 187–258.

Hubbuck, J., and Carter, S. (1980). *Half a Chance? A Report on Job Discrimination against Young Blacks in Nottingham.* Commission for Racial Equality, London.

Issues Deliberation Australia. (2007). 'The voice of Australians: A national random sample survey of the Australian population'. In *Australia Deliberates: Muslims and Non-Muslims in Australia.*

Jowell, R., and Prescott-Clarke, P. (1970). 'Racial discrimination and white-collar workers in Britain', *Race*, 11(4):397–417. doi.org/10.1177/030639687001100401.

Kabir, N., and Evans, E. (2002). 'Muslims and the Australian labour market, 1980–2001', *Immigrants & Minorities*, 21(3):70–95. doi.org/10.1080/02619288.2002.9975047.

Leigh, A. (2007). 'Does raising the minimum wage help the poor?' *Economic Record*, 83(263):432–445. doi.org/10.1111/j.1475-4932.2007.00432.x.

Mahuteau, S., and Junankar, P.N. (2008). 'Do migrants get good jobs in Australia? The role of ethnic networks in job search'. In Junankar P.N., *Economics of Immigration: The Impact of Immigration on the Australian Economy*, London: Palgrave Macmillan.

Mateos, P., Webber, R., and Longley, P. (2007). 'The cultural, ethnic and linguistic classification of populations and neighbourhoods using personal names', CASA Working Paper No. 116, Centre for Advanced Spatial Analysis, University College London, London.

Mateos, P. (2007). 'A review of name-based ethnicity classification methods and their potential in population studies', *Population Space and Place*, 13(4):243–263. doi.org/10.1002/psp.427.

McGinnity, F., Nelson, J., Lunn, P., and Quinn, E. (2009). *Discrimination in Recruitment: Evidence from a Field Experiment.* Dublin: The Equality Authority and The Economic and Social Research Institute.

McIntosh, N., and Smith, D. (1974). 'The extent of racial discrimination,' Political and Economic Planning Broadsheet No. 547, London.

Neumark, D. (2010). 'Detecting discrimination in audit and correspondence studies', NBER Working Paper No. 16448, NBER, Cambridge.

Oreopoulos, P. (2009). 'Why do skilled immigrants struggle in the labor market? A field experiment with six thousand resumes', NBER Working Paper No. 15036, Cambridge.

Pager, D. (2003). 'The mark of a criminal record', *American Journal of Sociology*, 108(5):937–975. doi.org/10.1086/374403.

Pager, D. (2007). 'The use of field experiments for studies of employment discrimination: Contributions, critiques, and directions for the future', *The ANNALS of the American Academy of Political and Social Science*, 609(1): 104–133. doi.org/10.1177/0002716206297542.

Pager, D., Western, B., and Bonikowski, B. (2009). 'Discrimination in a low-wage labor market: A Field Experiment', *American Sociological Review*, 74(5):777–779. doi.org/10.1177/000312240907400512.

Poynting, S., and Noble, G. (2004). *Living with Racism: The Experience and Reporting by Arab and Muslim Australians of Discrimination, Abuse and Violence Since 11 September 2001*. Report to The Human Rights and Equal Opportunity Commission, University of Western Sydney, Sydney.

Riach, P.A., and Rich, J. (1991). 'Testing for racial discrimination in the labour market', *Cambridge Journal of Economics*, 15(3):239–256. doi.org/10.1093/oxfordjournals.cje.a035168.

Riach, P., and Rich, J. (2002). 'Field experiments of discrimination in the market place', *The Economic Journal*, 112(483):F480–F518. doi.org/10.1111/1468-0297.00080.

Riach, P.A., and Rich, J. (2004). 'Deceptive field experiments of discrimination: Are they ethical?' *Kyklos*, 57(3):457–470. doi.org/10.1111/j.1467-6435.2004.00238.x.

Walker, I. (2001). 'The changing nature of racism: from old to new?' In Augoustinos M. and Reynolds K. (eds), *Understanding Prejudice, Racism and Social Conflict*, London: Sage, pp. 24–42.

Appendix

Table A9.1: Ethnically distinct names

Anglo first names	Female: Jennifer, Lisa, Kimberly, Sarah, Amy Male: Martin, Andrew, Phillip, Adam, Brian
Anglo last names	Abbott, Adams, Johnson, Mitchell, Robinson
Middle Eastern first names	Female: Fatima, Lala, Nadine, Anan, Hiyam Male: Ahmed, Hassan, Bilal, Mahmoud, Rafik
Middle Eastern last names	Hariri, Baghdadi, Chikhani, Kassir, Gemayel
Indigenous first names	Female: Betty, Winnie, Daisy, Dorothy, Peggy Male: Bobby, Jimmy, Tommy, Wally, Ronnie
Indigenous last names	Japanangka, Tjungarrayi, Djukukul, Tipungwuti, Puruntatameri
Chinese first names	Female: Ping, Ming, Xiu, Ya, Nuying Male: Tai, Hong, Yin, Peng, Hu
Chinese last names	Chen, Lin, Huang, Lee, Chang
Italian first names	Female: Maria, Anna, Rosa, Angela, Giovanna Male: Giuseppe, Giovanni, Antonio, Mario, Luigi
Italian last names	Rosso, Ferrari, Bianchi, Romano, Galeotti

Table A9.2: Comparison with other correspondence discrimination studies

Study	Country	Year(s) of test	Minority	Ratio (majority callbacks/minority callbacks)
Riach and Rich (1991)	Australia	1984–88	Vietnamese Greek	1.38 1.10
Booth et al. (this study)	Australia	2007	Indigenous Chinese Italian Middle Eastern	1.35 1.68 1.12 1.64
Oreopoulos (2009)	Canada	2008	Indian Chinese Pakistani	1.31 1.46 1.44
Bovenkerk et al. (1979)	France	1976–77	Antillian	3.47
Goldberg, Mourinho and Kulke (1995)	Germany	1994	Turkish	1.12
McGinnity et al. (2009)	Ireland	2008	African Asian German	2.44 1.80 2.07

Study	Country	Year(s) of test	Minority	Ratio (majority callbacks/minority callbacks)
Bovenkerk et al. (1995)	Netherlands	1993–94	Surinamese	1.22
Carlsson and Rooth (2007)	Sweden	2005–06	Middle Eastern	1.50
Bursell (2007)	Sweden	2006–07	Arabic/African	1.80
Jowell and Prescott-Clarke (1970)	UK	1969	Asian West Indian	2.08 1.13
McIntosh and Smith (1974)	UK	1973	Asian/West Indian Italian	1.47 1.12
Firth (1981)	UK	1977–78	Asian West Indian Australian French African	1.95 1.76 1.14 1.25 1.60
Hubbuck and Carter (1980)	UK	1977–79	Asian West Indian Italian	1.80 1.81 1.12
Brown and Gay (1985)	UK	1984–85	Asian/West Indian	1.49
Esmail and Everington (1993)	UK	1992	Asian	2.00
Esmail and Everington (1997)	UK	1997	Asian	1.44
Bertrand and Mullainathan (2004)	US	2001–02	African-American	1.50

Notes: All studies dated before 2000 (except Goldberg et al. 1995) are summarised in Riach and Rich (2002). Note that Jowell and Prescott-Clarke (1970) changed not only the names but also the qualifications. For Bovenkerk et al. (1995), we take the average of the estimate for Surinamese males (1.27) and females (1.17). Estimates from Oreopoulos (2009) are based on respondents with Canadian qualifications and experience. Note that we summarise only estimates from correspondence studies, and not those in which actors contacted employers in-person or by telephone.

Matthew O'Brien

Personal Detail:

15 Boundary Rd
Mortdale, Sydney
Tel: 91149283
E-mail: obrienluck@gmail.com

Personal Profile:

World class customer service agent with excellent communication & interpersonal skills. Consistently achieve quality, service and financial metrics. Committed to team success-able to multitask, and meet deadlines. Flexible and detail oriented with a commitment to understanding procedures. Demonstrate integrity & compliance-confidentiality in handling correspondence & customer files and code of ethics.

Skills:

- Accurate and rapid typing.
- Proficient in Microsoft Office/Word & the Internet.
- Knowledge of Excel, Access, Lotus Notes, IDT, IP Agent and other software applications.
- Word processing skills
- Performing administrative duties for Senior Management Personnel.
- Banking, processing procedures, product and services

Work Experience:

2005–2007
Service Specialist
Medibank Private, Sydney

2001 to 2005
Customer Service Representative
Optus, Sydney

1997 to 2001
Administrative Assistant
National Bank, Sydney

Highlights of Qualifications:

- Inbound call center, customer service and banking experience.
- Work effectively in a changing environment refocusing efforts with a positive attitude.
- Not afraid to think outside the box.
- Ensure customer care goals are achieved efficiently and effectively.
- Provide excellent customer service to both clients and providers quickly and accurately.
- Communicate unpleasant or negative information in a tactful manner.
- Establish and maintain control of inbound calls using a well-organised structure.
- Resolve complex or basic inbound calls using sound business judgment.
- Promoting the company's products and services as a benefit to the client.
- Provide ongoing and comprehensive communication.

Education:

Certificate in Paralegal Studies
Completed Year 12
Diploma of Business Administration

Reference:

Available on request

Figure A9.1: Sample CV

Dorothy Japanangka

6 Cavendish St
Stanmore, Sydney
Tel: 91149463
E-Mail: japanangka.f@gmail.com

Experience:

10/2004–03/2007
Food Prep Chef
University Union Court
Prepared food items for chef to use in recipes being served the following day. Helped in other areas of the kitchen and in dining area as needed.

7/2003–10/2004
Hungry Jacks, Sydney
Prepared buns and burger meat, chicken etc for use in burgers during business hours. Also washed dishes and assisted in garbage disposal.

8/2001–11/2002
Domino's Pizza, Sydney
Preparation of pizza toppings, pizzas and salad ingredients at various stages. Took telephone orders. General cleaning of the store. I was promoted to a management position which involved assisting with all operational tasks, scheduling, inventory, training of new employees, book keeping and cash handling.

Skills:

Food Preparation and Serving Related First-Line Supervisors/Managers of Food Preparation and Serving Workers.

Education:

Finished Year 12
Strathfield South College

Bachelor of Arts
University of Technology, Sydney

References:

Please let me know if you need references.

Figure A9.2: Sample CV

Section III: Gendered behavioural responses: Evidence from experiments

10

Gender differences in risk behaviour: Does nurture matter?

Alison L Booth and Patrick Nolen

It is well known that women are underrepresented in high-paying jobs and in high-level occupations. Recent work in experimental economics has examined to what degree this under-representation may be due to innate differences between men and women. For example, gender differences in risk aversion, feedback preferences or fondness for competition may help to explain some of the observed gender disparities. If the majority of remuneration in high-paying jobs is tied to bonuses based on a company's performance, then, if men are less risk-averse than women, women may choose not to take high-paying jobs because of the uncertainty. Differences in risk attitudes may even affect individual choices about seeking performance feedback or entering a competitive environment.

Understanding the extent to which risk attitudes are innate or shaped by environment is important for policy. If risk attitudes are innate, the under-representation of women in certain areas may be solved only by changing the way in which remuneration is rewarded. However, if risk attitudes are primarily shaped by the environment, changing the educational or training context could help to address under-representation. Thus, the policy prescription for dealing with the under-representation of women in high-paying jobs will depend upon whether the reason for the absence is innate to an individual's gender.

Why women and men might have different preferences or risk attitudes has been discussed, but not tested by economists. Broadly speaking, these differences may be due to either nurture, nature or some combination of the two. For example, boys are pushed to take risks when participating in competitive sports, whereas girls are often encouraged to remain cautious. Thus, the riskier choices made by men could be due to the nurturing received from parents or peers. Likewise, the disinclination of women to take risks could be the result of parental or peer pressure not to do so.

With the exception of Gneezy et al. (2009) and Gneezy and Rustichini (2004), the experimental literature on competitive behaviour has been conducted with college-age men and women attending co-educational universities. Yet, the education literature shows that the academic achievement of girls and boys responds differentially to co-education, with boys typically performing better and girls worse than in single-sex environments (Kessler et al. 1985; Brutsaert 1999). Moreover, psychologists argue that the gendered aspect of individuals' behaviour is brought into play by the gender of others with whom they interact (Maccoby, 1998, and references therein). In this chapter, we sample a different subject pool from that normally used in the literature to investigate the role that environmental factors, which we label 'nurturing', might play in shaping risk preferences.[1] We use students in the UK from years 10 and 11 who are attending either single-sex or co-educational schools. We will examine the effect on risk attitudes of two types of environmental influences – randomly assigned experimental peer groups and the educational environment. Finally, we will compare the results of our experiment with survey information – stated attitudes to risk obtained from a post-experiment questionnaire – to examine if reported and observed levels of risk aversion differ.

An important paper by Gneezy et al. (2009) explores the role that culture plays in determining gender differences in competitive behaviour. Gneezy et al. (2009) investigate two distinct societies – the patriarchal Maasai tribe of Tanzania and the matrilineal Khasi tribe in India. Although they find that, in the patriarchal society, women are less competitive than men – which is consistent with experimental data from Western cultures – in the matrilineal society, women are more competitive than men. Indeed,

1 In a companion paper, Booth and Nolen (2012), we investigate how competitive behaviour (including the choice between piece rates and tournaments) is affected by single-sex schooling.

the Khasi women were found to be as competitive as the Maasai men.[2] The authors interpret this as evidence that culture has an influence.[3] We also use a controlled experiment to see if there are gender differences in the behaviour of subjects from two distinct environments or 'cultures'. But our environments – publicly funded single-sex and co-educational schools – are closer to one another than those in Gneezy et al. (2009), and it seems unlikely that there is much evolutionary distance between subjects from our two separate environments.[4] Any observed gender differences in behaviour across these two distinct milieus are unlikely to be due to nature but more likely to the nurturing received from parents, teachers, peers or to some combination of these three.

Women are observed to be, on average, more risk-averse than men, according to the studies summarised in Eckel and Grossman (2002).[5] This could be through inherited attributes or nurture. The available empirical evidence suggests that parental attributes shape these risk attitudes. For instance, Dohmen et al. (2012) find, using the German Socioeconomic Panel (GSOEP), that individuals with highly educated parents are significantly more likely to choose risky outcomes. In this chapter, we examine whether, in addition to characteristics such as parental background, environment also plays a role in shaping risk preferences.

To examine whether the environment affects individuals' risk preferences, we study the choices made by students when they are randomly assigned to two different environments: same-sex or mixed-gender peer groups. Group effects have been explored in previous work by Gneezy et al. (2003), Niederle and Yestrumskas (2008) and Datta Gupta et al. (2005) but those studies all used students from co-educational environments, focused on competitive tasks and did not investigate risk attitudes. Besides looking at the effect of a peer group randomly created in the laboratory, we also examine how students from different educational environments – single-sex and co-educational schools – may have different risk preferences.

2 The experimental task was to toss a tennis ball into a bucket that was placed three metres away. A successful shot meant that the tennis ball entered the bucket and stayed there.

3 Interestingly, the authors find no evidence that, on average, there are gender differences in risk attitudes within either society.

4 We use subjects from two adjacent counties in south-east England, Essex and Suffolk. One would be hard pressed to argue that Essex girls and boys evolved differently from Suffolk girls and boys, popular jokes about 'Essex man' notwithstanding.

5 However, some experimental studies find the reverse. For example, Schubert et al. (1999), using as subjects undergraduates from the University of Zurich, show that the context makes a difference. Although women do not generally make less risky financial choices than men, they are less likely to engage in an abstract gamble.

One of the strengths of our experiment is that we are able to look at an environment created in the laboratory – the experimental peer group – and one that is from the field – educational background. Although the experimental peer group is randomly assigned, students were not randomly assigned to school types. Therefore, to examine the effect of nurture from our second environment, we will have to deal with issues of selection. Our experiment was carefully constructed to deal with these. First, we sampled from two different counties – one with grammar schools and another without.[6] Second, we designed the experiment so we could obtain good measures of cognitive ability in the early stages of the experiment. Third, we developed a post-experiment questionnaire to gather information on where students lived and their family background. The data from the questionnaire facilitated the construction of a plausible instrument for single-sex school attendance. Fourth, we asked our participating co-educational schools to provide students only from the higher ability academic stream so that they would be more comparable with the grammar school students.[7]

Our final goal is to use the controlled experiment to see if commonly asked survey questions about risk yield the same conclusions about gender and risk aversion as those based on an experiment. During the experiment, our subjects chose to make risky choices with real money at stake. At the end of the experiment, they answered questions about their risk attitudes as well as responded to a hypothetical lottery question.[8] We are therefore able to compare actual behaviour with stated attitudes. This allows us to investigate (i) if girls and boys behave differently when there is actual money at stake; (ii) if girls and boys differ significantly in their stated attitudes to risk;[9] (iii) if there are significant gender differences in the distance between actual choices made under uncertainty and stated behaviour under uncertainty; and (iv) if the general risk question is sufficient to describe actual risk-taking behaviour. In so doing, we explore the degree to which observed gender differences in choices under uncertainty and stated risk attitudes

6 Grammar schools in the UK are selective state-funded schools for secondary school students.

7 To compare students of roughly the same ability, we recruited students from the top part of the distribution in the two co-educational schools in Essex; only students in the top academic streams from those schools were asked to participate. Students from Suffolk do not have the option to take the 11+ exam and therefore, higher ability students are unlikely to be selected out of Suffolk schools in the same way as in Essex. Nonetheless, we only recruited students from the top academic streams in Suffolk as well.

8 They were also asked questions about their family background, to be discussed later. These formed controls in the regression analyses.

9 For instance, boys might state that they are more risk-loving as a form of bragging.

vary across subjects who have been exposed to single-sex or co-educational schooling. Furthermore, we are able to provide a comparison of results from a controlled experiment to commonly asked survey questions.

Hypotheses

Women and men may differ in their propensity to choose a risky outcome because of innate preferences or because the existence of gender stereotypes – well documented by Akerlof and Kranton (2000) – encourages girls and boys to modify their innate preferences. Our prior is that single-sex environments are likely to modify students' risk-taking preferences in ways that are economically important.

To test this, we designed a controlled experiment in which subjects were given an opportunity to choose a risky outcome – a real-stakes gamble with a higher expected monetary value than the alternative outcome with a certain payoff – and in which the sensitivity of observed risk choices to environmental factors could be explored. Suppose there are preference differences between men and women. Then, using the data generated by our experiment to estimate the probability of choosing the real-stakes gamble, we should find that the female dummy variable is statistically significant. Furthermore, if any gender difference is due primarily to nature, the inclusion of variables that proxy the students' 'socialisation' should not greatly affect the size or significance of the estimated coefficient to the female dummy variable. However, if proxies for 'socialisation' are found to be statistically significant, this would provide some evidence that nurturing plays a role.

Our hypotheses can be summarised as follows.

Conjecture 1. Women are more risk-averse than men

As summarised in Eckel and Grossman (2002), most experimental studies have found that women are more risk-averse than men. A sizeable number of the studies used elementary and high-school-aged children from co-ed schools (Harbaugh et al. 2002). Since our subject pool varies from this standard young adult sample, in that it involves students from both single-sex and co-ed schools, we will first examine whether or not there are gender differences in risk aversion. We expect to find that women in our sample are, on average, more risk-averse than men.

Conjecture 2. Girls in same-gender experimental groups are less risk-averse than girls in mixed-gender experimental groups

Psychologists have shown that the framing of tasks and cultural stereotypes does affect the performance of individuals (see inter alia Steele et al. 2002). Thus, a girl assigned to a mixed-gender experimental group may feel that her gender identity is threatened when she is confronted with boys. This might lead her to affirm her femininity by conforming to perceived male expectations of girls' behaviour, and consequently making less risky choices if she perceives risk avoidance as a feminine trait. Should the same girl be assigned instead to an all-girl group, such reactions would not be triggered.

To test Conjecture 2, we randomly assign students to the same or mixed-gender groups in the experiment. This allows us to examine whether the gender composition of a group affects the risk preferences of girls. Since subjects are randomly assigned to groups, unobservables should not be driving the effects.

Conjecture 3. Girls from single-sex schools are less risk-averse than girls from co-ed schools

Studies show that there may be more pressure for girls to maintain their gender identity in schools where boys are present than for boys when girls are present (Maccoby 1990; Brutsaert 1999). In a co-educational environment, girls are more explicitly confronted with adolescent subculture (such as personal attractiveness to members of the opposite sex) than they are in a single-sex environment (Coleman 1961). This may lead them to conform to boys' expectations of how girls should behave to avoid social rejection (American Association of University Women 1992). If risk avoidance is viewed as being a part of female gender identity while risk-seeking is a part of male gender identity, then being in a co-educational school environment might lead girls to make safer choices than boys.

How might this actually work? It is helpful to extend the identity approach of Akerlof and Kranton (2000) to this context. Adolescent girls in a co-ed environment could be subject to more conflict in their gender identity, since they have to compete with boys academically, while at the same time, they may feel pressured to develop their femininity to be attractive to boys.

Moreover, there may be an externality at work, since girls are competing with other girls to be popular with boys. This externality may reinforce their need to adhere to their female gender identity.

If this is true, we would expect girls in co-ed schools to be less likely than girls in single-sex schools to take risks. One might also expect co-ed schoolboys to be more likely to take risks than single-sex schoolboys, although the education literature suggests that there is greater pressure for girls to maintain their gender identity in schools where boys are present than for boys when girls are present (Maccoby 1990, 1998).[10]

Given that subjects are not randomly assigned to a school, we will control for factors that could potentially be correlated with attendance, as will be explained later. Suppose we find that, conditional on observable factors, girls from single-sex schools choose to enter the tournament more than girls from co-ed schools. This would provide more support for the case that nurture plays a role in determining risk preferences than if the controls explained all the difference in the choice whether or not to take a real-stakes gamble.

Conjecture 4. Girls in same-gender environments (all-girl experimental groups or single-sex schools) are no less risk-averse than boys

The psychological and educational literature cited before suggests that girls, rather than boys, are likely to respond to the same-gender environments. The question is: how much will girls change? Given that we hypothesise that girls will be less risk-averse because of same-gender environments, we conjecture that girls' risk attitudes in single- sex environments will be the same as their male counterparts. If this is the case, it would suggest that the gender differences in observed risk attitudes are due to the environment and are not innate.

10 There is also evidence that in co-ed classrooms, boys get more attention and dominate activities (Sadker et al. 1991; Brutsaert 1999).

Conjecture 5. Gender differences in risk aversion are sensitive to the way the preferences are elicited

To test this, we compare the results from the choice of whether or not to engage in a real-stakes gamble with responses obtained from two post-experiment survey questions. The first survey question is on general risk attitudes, whereas the second asks how much the respondent would invest in a risky asset using hypothetical lottery winnings.[11] Moreover, abstract real-stakes gambles might generate different gender gaps in risky choices than context-specific hypothetical gambles (Schubert et al. 1999).

In particular, we examine how much, if at all, the answers about general risk attitudes or the hypothetical lottery explain observed choices made in the real-stakes experimental gamble. This allows us to examine how close stated risk attitudes are to observed behaviour and to see if girls and boys differ on any 'gap' that may exist. For example, suppose that boys state that they are more risk-seeking than they are in actuality, perhaps because being risk-loving is associated with a notion of 'hegemonic masculinity' governing male gender identity (Kessler et al. 1985). If so, then boys might overstate their willingness to take risks when responding to a gender-attitudes survey question – after all, no real outcome depends on it – but be more likely to express their true risk aversion when confronted with a real-stakes gamble. In contrast, if being risk-loving is not part of female identity, there should be less distance in outcomes for girls.

Experimental design

Our experiment was designed to test the Conjectures listed above. To examine the role of nurturing, we recruited students from co-educational and single-sex schools to be subjects. We also designed an 'exit' survey to elicit information about family background characteristics. At no stage were the schools we selected, or the subjects who volunteered, told why they were chosen. Our subject pool is relatively large for a controlled, laboratory-type experiment. We wished to have a large number of subjects from a variety of educational backgrounds to be able to investigate the Conjectures outlined before.

11 Both questions will be given in full later in the chapter.

Next, we first discuss the educational environment from which our subjects were drawn, and then the experiment itself.

Subjects and educational environment

In September 2007, students from eight publicly funded schools in the counties of Essex and Suffolk in the UK were bused to the Colchester campus of the University of Essex to participate in the experiment. Four of the schools were single-sex.[12] The students were from years 10 or 11, and their average age was just under 15 years. On arrival, students from each school were randomly assigned to 65 groups of four. Groups were of three types: all-girls, all-boys or mixed. Mixed groups had at least one student of each gender, and the modal group comprised two boys and two girls. The composition of each group – the appropriate mix of single-sex schools, co-educational schools and gender – was determined beforehand. Thus, only the assignment of the 260 girls and boys from a particular school to a group was random. The school mix was two co-educational schools from Suffolk (103 students), two co-educational schools from Essex (45 students), two all-girl schools from Essex (66 students) and two all-boys schools from Essex (46 students).

In the county of Suffolk, there are no single-sex publicly funded schools. In the county of Essex, the old 'grammar' schools remain, owing to a quirk of political history.[13] These grammar schools are single-sex and, like the co-educational schools, are publicly funded. It is highly unlikely that students themselves actively choose to go to single-sex schools. Instead, Essex primary school teachers, with parental consent, choose the more able Essex children

12 A pilot was conducted several months earlier, in June at the end of the previous school year. The point of the pilot was to determine the appropriate level of difficulty and duration of the actual experiment. The pilot used a different subject pool to that used in the real experiment. It comprised students from two schools (one single-sex in Essex and one co-educational in Suffolk) who had recently completed year 11. The actual experiment conducted some months later, at the start of the new school year, used, as subjects, students who had just started years 10 or 11.

13 In the UK, schools are controlled by local area authorities but frequently 'directed' by central government. Following the 1944 Education Act, grammar schools became part of the central government's tripartite system of grammar, secondary modern and technical schools (the latter never got off the ground). By the mid-1960s, the central Labour government put pressure on local authorities to establish 'comprehensive' schools in their place. Across England and Wales, grammar schools survived in some areas (typically those with long-standing Conservative boroughs) but were abolished in most others. In some counties, the grammar schools left the state system altogether and became independent schools; these are not part of our study. However, in parts of Essex, single-sex grammar schools survive as publicly funded entities, whereas in Suffolk, they no longer exist.

to sit for the Essex-wide exam for entry into grammar schools.[14] Parents must be resident in Essex for their children to be eligible to sit the entrance examination (the 11+). However, residential mobility across regions is very low in Britain (Boheim and Taylor 2002). To attend a grammar school, a student must apply and then attain above a certain score, which varies from year to year. Therefore, students at the single-sex schools are not a random subset of the students in Essex, since they are selected based on measurable ability at age 11.

One of the strengths of our experiment is that, although it does not solve the selection problem into single-sex and co-educational schools, it was carefully constructed to mitigate selection issues. First, we designed the experiment so we could obtain good measures of cognitive ability in the early stages of the experiment. We then use them as controls in the main part of the experiment. Second, we developed a post-experiment questionnaire to gather information on where students lived and their family background. This facilitates the construction of plausible instruments for school choice. Third, we asked our participating co-educational schools, from both Essex and Suffolk, to provide students only from the higher ability academic stream so that they would be more comparable to the grammar school students, as noted in footnote 7.

The experiment took place in a very large and spacious auditorium, with 1,000 seats arranged in tiers.[15] Students in the same group were seated in the same row with an empty seat between each person. There was also an empty row in front of and behind each group. Although subjects were told which other students were in the same group, they were sitting far enough apart for their work to be private information. If two students from the same school were assigned to a group, they were forced to sit as far apart as possible; for example, in a group of four, two other students would sit between the students from the same school. There was one supervisor, a graduate student, assigned to supervise every five groups. Once the experiment began, students were told not to talk. Each supervisor enforced this rule and also answered individual questions.

14 If a student achieves a high enough score on the exam, they can attend one of the 12 schools in the Consortium of Selective Schools in Essex (CSSE). The vast majority of these are single-sex. The four single-sex schools in our experiment are part of the CSSE.

15 Students were very clear about who was in their group and – while nothing was explicitly stated – they could see if their group was all-girls, all-boys, or mixed. Other studies, such as Gneezy and Rustichini (2004), also look at the effects of single-sex environments by making the reference group obvious while not quarantining the students.

Experiment

Five rounds were conducted during the experiment. In Appendix A, we give full details of all rounds and describe payments and incentives, which varied from round to round.[16] In this chapter, we focus on the results from the round involving the real-stakes gamble or fiver lottery. After the experiment ended, students filled out a post-experimental questionnaire that had questions on risk attitudes, family background, and that also included a hypothetical investment decision using the proceeds from winning a lottery.[17]

A description of the real-stakes gamble (called the 'fiver' lottery) and the two main survey questions are discussed below.

'Fiver' Lottery. Each student chooses Option 1 or Option 2. Option 1 is to get £5 for certain. Option 2 is to flip a coin and get £11 if the coin comes up heads or get £2 if the coin comes up tails.

Survey Question: General Risk. Each student was asked: 'How do you see yourself: Are you generally a person who is fully prepared to take risks or do you try to avoid taking risks?' The students then ranked themselves on an 11-point scale from 0 to 10, with 0 being labelled 'risk-averse' and 10 as 'fully prepared to take risks'. This was the same general risk question asked in the 2004 wave of the GSOEP.

Survey Question: Hypothetical Lottery. Each student was asked to consider what they would do in the following situation:

> imagine that you have won £100,000 in the lottery. Almost immediately after you collect the winnings, you receive the following financial offer from a reputable bank, the conditions of which are as follows: (i) there is a chance to double your money within two years; (ii) it is equally possible that you could lose half the amount invested; (iii) you have the opportunity to invest the full amount, part of the amount or reject the offer. What share of your lottery winnings would you be prepared to invest in this financially risky yet lucrative investment?

16 Payment was randomised in the same manner as in Datta Gupta et al. (2005) and Niederle and Vesterlund (2007). As students are paid for a round that is randomly selected at the end of the experiment, each individual should maximise their payoff in each round to maximise the payment overall. Moreover, as only one round was selected for payment, students did not have the opportunity to hedge across tasks.

17 Results from the first few rounds, designed to elicit differences in competitive behaviour under piece rates and tournaments, are reported in Booth and Nolen (2012).

The subject then ticked a box indicating if they would invest £100,000, £80,000, £60,000, £40,000, £20,000 or Nothing (reject the offer). The same version of this hypothetical investment question was asked in the 2004 wave of the GSOEP.

The payments (both the show-up fee of £5 plus any payment from performance in the randomly selected round) were in cash and were hand-delivered in sealed envelopes (clearly labelled with each student's name) to the schools a few days after the experiment. The average payment was £7. In addition, immediately after completing the Exit Questionnaire, each student was given a bag containing a soft drink, a packet of crisps and a bar of chocolate.

Descriptive statistics

We will be examining risk preferences by experimental peer group and schooling type. Since the experimental peer group was randomly assigned, we expect that observables should not differ by group type: same or mixed gender. However, since school type was not randomly assigned, we will control for ability, learning and any other background attribute that could drive the schooling result. Table 10.1 shows girls' and boys' summary statistics by experimental peer group and school type.

Panels (a) and (c) of Table 10.1 compare the means of same-gender experimental groups (all-girls or all-boys) with the mixed-gender groups, for girls and boys, respectively. There are no statistical differences – except for age for girls and the number of siblings for boys – suggesting that the randomisation was implemented successfully. Therefore, when examining risk preferences in the following section, we control for age and number of siblings in some specifications. Note also that there is no statistically significant difference in means for risk choice (the Fiver Lottery) for either girls or boys. However, Panel (a) shows that the difference for girls is 0.12, and this is significant at the 11 per cent level.

Table 10.1: Descriptive statistics by gender, experimental peer group and school background

Variables	Girls						Boys					
	Experimental group			Schooling			Experimental group			Schooling		
	Mixed	All-girls	Difference	Co-education	Single-sex	Difference	Mixed	All-boys	Difference	Co-education	Single-sex	Difference
Chose 'Fiver' lottery	0.61	0.73	0.12	2.16	2.62	0.46***	0.85	0.8	−0.05	2.88	3.13	0.25
Round 1 score	2.38	2.32	−0.06	0.54	0.86	0.32***	2.90	3.16	0.26	0.88	0.78	−0.10
Round 2 score	3.92	3.93	0.01	3.78	4.14	0.36	4.90	4.97	0.07	4.71	5.17	0.46
Number of siblings	0.84	1.04	0.2	0.88	1.05	0.17	0.60	0.98	0.38**	0.85	0.61	−0.24
Number of female siblings	0.70	0.71	0.01	0.80	0.57	−0.23*	0.77	0.77	0.00	0.87	0.68	−0.19
Age	14.73	14 98	0.25***	14.80	14.95	0.15	14.71	14.56	−0.15	14.81	14.48	−0.33**
Mother went to uni (=1)	0.28	0.26	−0.02	0.13	0.49	0.36***	0.34	0.20	−0.14	0.15	0.43	0.28***
Father went to uni (=1)	0.28	0.31	0.03	0.16	0.52	0.36***	0.44	0.34	−0.10	0.27	0.54	0.27***
Co-ed school travel time (min)	7.92	6.89	−1.03	6.21	8.06	1.85*	7.15	6.5	−0.65	7.16	6.8	−0.36
Single-sex school travel time (min)	18.80	17.47	−1.33	23.09	15.32	−7.77***	15.05	17	1.95	21.95	12.96	−8.99***
Average risk score (scale = 0–10)	6.73	6.54	−0.19	6.40	6.95	0.55*	6.85	6.71	−0.14	6.90	6.69	−0.21
Hypothetical lottery investment (£1,000)	3.24	3.47	0.23	2.76	4.24	1.48	3.26	4.22	0.96	3.73	3.48	−0.25

Notes: * Significant at a 10% level; ** significant at a 5% level; *** significant at a 1% level.

Now consider panels (b) and (d) of Table 10.1, which compare the means of students at single-sex and co-ed schools for girls and boys, respectively. Inspection reveals a number of observable differences. For instance, both girls and boys at single-sex schools are more likely to have parents who went to university. Girls at single-sex schools are less risk-averse than their co-ed counterparts (they are more likely to choose the 'fiver' lottery and to report a greater willingness to take risks). It is interesting that this is not the case for boys. Boys at single-sex schools are likely to be older than boys at co-ed schools, and girls at single-sex schools have fewer siblings than girls at co-ed schools. When examining the effect of the schooling environment, we will control for these observed differences in some specifications.

Experimental results

In this section, we discuss whether or not the results from the fiver lottery support our first conjectures. We then use a series of robustness checks to see, first, if the evidence stands up to the use of different control groups and, second, if the results alter when we instrument for single-sex schooling.

'Fiver' lottery

The expected monetary value of the fiver lottery discussed before is £6.50, which is greater than the alternative choice – a certain outcome of £5. Assuming a constant relative risk aversion utility function of the type $u(x) = x^{1-\sigma}/(1-\sigma)$, where σ is the degree of relative risk aversion, we calculate that the value of making an individual just indifferent between choosing the lottery and a certain outcome is approximately 0.8. Individuals with $\sigma \geq 0.8$ will choose a certain outcome, whereas those with $\sigma < 0.8$ will choose the lottery.[18]

To examine if there are any gender differences in the choice of whether or not to enter the fiver lottery, we construct an indicator variable that takes the value one if the individual chooses to enter the fiver lottery and zero otherwise. This becomes our dependent variable in a probit model of the probability of choosing the lottery. Table 10.2 shows the marginal effects of those probit regressions.

18 This was calculated from $pu(x)+(1-p)u(y)=u(z)$, where $p=0.5$, $x=11$, $y=2$ and $z=5$. We use the specific CRRA functional form for $u()$ given in the text. Our imposed value of σ is higher than that at which German adults switch from a safe to an uncertain outcome, found by Dohmen et al. (2010). See also Holt and Laury (2002).

Table 10.2: Dependent variable (=1) if student chose Option 2 in 'fiver' lottery

Coefficient	[1]	[2]	[3]	[4]	[5]	[6]	[7]
Female (=1)	-0.16*** (0.05)	-0.36*** (0.07)	-0.37*** (0.07)	-0.34*** (0.11)	-0.39*** (0.09)	-0.43*** (0.08)	-0.46*** (0.09)
Single-sex (=1)	–	-0.13 (0.10)	-0.13 (0.10)	-0.06 (0.18)	-0.21** (0.10)	-0.10 (0.08)	-0.11 (0.10
Female × single-sex	–	0.33*** (0.06)	0.33*** (0.06)	0.30** (0.12)	0.38*** (0.07)	0.42*** (0.10)	0.51*** (0.14)
All-girls group	–	0.12* (0.06)	0.12* (0.06)	0.14** (0.06)	0.11* (0.06)	0.13* (0.07)	0.13* (0.07)
All-boys group	–	-0.05 (0.10)	-0.04 (0.10)	-0.05 (0.11)	-0.00 (0.10)	-0.04 (0.08)	-0.04 (0.08)
Maze score R^1	–	–	-0.01 (0.03)	–	–	–	–
Maze score R^2–R^1	–	–	0.02 (0.02)	–	–	–	–
Marginal effect for female single-sex (female × single-sex = 1)	–	-0.07 (0.05)	-0.06 (0.05)	-0.03 (0.06)	-0.10 (0.07)	–	–
Controls	No	No	No	Yes	No	No	No
Controls × female	No	No	No	Yes	No	No	No
Controls × single-sex	No	No	No	Yes	No	No	No
Controls × female × single-sex	No	No	No	Yes	No	No	No
Model	Probit	Probit	Probit	Probit	Probit	LPM	IV LMP
Constant	–	–	–	–	–	0.90*** (0.05)	0.90*** (0.06)
Observations	260	260	260	260	260	260	260
R^2	–	–	–	–	–	0.131	0.107
F-stat for IV variables	–	–	–	–	–	–	118.9

Notes: *** $p<0.01$; ** $p<0.05$; * $p<0.1$; Columns [1]–[4] and [6]–[7] use entire sample. Column [5] uses only students from single-sex schools, students who took 11+ examination, and students from Suffolk. Controls: mother went to university (=1); father went to university (=1); number brothers; sisters; student aged 14 (=1). Robust SEs in parentheses.

Column [1] of Table 10.2 shows that, on average, girls choose to enter the lottery 16 percentage points less than boys. The sign and significance of this coefficient are consistent with other work looking at gender and risk aversion, and suggest that, in our sample, female students are also more risk-averse than male students. This provides evidence for Conjecture 1. Next, we want to investigate if the gender differences alter when environmental factors reflecting nurture are incorporated into the estimation.

The specification in column [2] adds controls for school type and experimental group composition. In this specification, the gender gap becomes even more pronounced – girls in co-ed schools choose to enter the lottery 36 percentage points less than boys from co-educational schools. Furthermore, we have evidence that nurture has an effect on risk preferences. First, the coefficient for being in an all-girls group is statistically significant and positive: girls randomly assigned to all-girl groups are more likely to choose to enter the 'fiver' lottery. Because our estimates show that girls assigned to single-sex peer groups are less risk-averse than those who are assigned to mixed-gender groups, evidence is provided in support of Conjecture 2.[19] Of note is that the same-gender peer group is only affecting girls; the all-boys coefficient is insignificant. Second, the single-sex school coefficient is statistically insignificant, but the coefficient of single-sex schooling interacted with female is significant and positive. Therefore, school background only affects the risk preferences for girls at this level of risk aversion and has no effect on boys. The risk preferences of boys are not affected by either environmental variable, whereas the risk preferences of girls are significantly affected by both environmental factors. This provides strong evidence for conjecture three.

We now check the robustness of the results in support of Conjectures 2 and 3. We do this by looking at the effect of cognitive skills, by using different sub-samples and by saturating our regression with all observable differences that were found in Table 10.1.

19 The all-girls coefficient is robust to different types of analysis. For instance, if regressions are run on subsamples comprising only students from co-ed schools, or only students from single-sex schools, the all-girl coefficient is still significant. Thus, there is a positive effect of being in an all-girls group for each type of student. Furthermore, if dummy variables for mixed-gender groups with three or two boys are used as controls, the significance of the all-girls coefficient does not go away.

Sensitivity analysis

Why should cognitive skills affect individuals' economic preferences?[20] Differences in perception of risky options due to cognitive ability may systematically affect individuals' choices, as argued by Burks et al. (2009). The more complex the option is, the larger the noise. If people with high cognitive skills perceive a complex option more precisely than people with low cognitive skills, they will be more likely to choose riskier options. How do our estimates alter when we add in these measures of cognitive ability? When controlling for ability and performance in the previous rounds, as in column [3] of Table 10.2, the all-girls coefficient does not change or become insignificant. Likewise, there is little change to the coefficient for single-sex education or for single-sex education interacted with being female.[21]

To examine if observable differences between the samples are driving our results, we saturate our preferred specification. Column [4] of Table 10.2 includes all controls whose means differed across subgroups in Table 10.1, and their interactions with female, single- sex, and the female, single-sex interaction. After controlling for observables and their interactions with schooling background, we find that the coefficients only change slightly. In fact, the randomly assigned variable, all-girls group, becomes more significant, but the single-sex female interaction changes slightly. This, again, supports Conjecture 2. However, given the slight change in the female, single-sex interaction, we next investigate more closely the evidence in favour of Conjecture 3.

To test the robustness of the female, single-sex coefficient, we first estimate the model on a different subgroup, and second, we use an instrumental variable. Initially, we discuss the results from the estimation on different subgroups.

Earlier, we noted that a student's attendance at a single-sex school is likely to be influenced by their ability as well as by the choices of their parents or teachers.[22] Therefore, students from single-sex schools may not be a random

20 Dohmen et al. (2010), using a random sample of around 1,000 German adults, found that lower cognitive ability is associated with greater risk aversion and more pronounced impatience. A similar result was found in by Burks et al. (2009), with a sample of 1,000 trainee truckers in the US.

21 To see if the impact of performance in the first two rounds differed by gender, we also experimented with interacting maze score from R^1 and maze score R^2–R^1 with gender and this did not change our estimates of interest. As mentioned earlier, since the round that was paid was randomly chosen, we would not expect effort to change across rounds.

22 As noted earlier, Essex primary school teachers and parents choose which children sit for the Essex-wide exam for entry into grammar schools. Parents must be resident in Essex for their children to be eligible to sit the entrance examination (the 11+).

subset of the students from Essex. However, it should be remembered that we asked only top students from co-educational schools to participate in the experiment. As a sensitivity analysis, we compare single-sex students to a different comparison group: students from Suffolk, plus students in Essex who took the 11+ exam. Column [5] of Table 10.2 is estimated on a subsample comprising students from Suffolk, students who took the 11+ examination and students from single-sex schools. Students in Suffolk have to attend their closest school, so they are likely to be a more representative sample. Furthermore, if 'parental pushiness' is an issue, then those students who took the 11+ examination should look more like the single-sex students. Using this subsample, we see that the gender gap actually becomes slightly larger: girls are 39 percentage points less likely to enter the lottery. However, the coefficient for single-sex schooling is also negative and significant. This suggests that boys in co-ed schools are more likely to take risks and perhaps 'show off' for the girls (that stereotype threat could be causing the gender gap in risk aversion to be larger). This evidence would fit with the discussion of Conjecture 2. Girls in all-girl groups are again more likely to enter the lottery than girls in co-ed groups, also providing evidence for Conjecture 2. Notice also that the interaction of single-sex schooling and female, although remaining significantly negative, becomes slightly larger in absolute terms.

Now, we turn to our final robustness check. To control for the fact that students at single-sex schools are a non-random subset of the student population, we instrument for single-sex school attendance using the difference in travel time between the closest co-ed and single-sex school. First, we present the regression results of the linear probability model (LPM) in column [6] of Table 10.2, whereas the results for the IV are in column [7] of Table 10.2. We used the six-digit residential postcode for each student to calculate the distances to the nearest single-sex school and to the nearest co-ed school.[23] We next calculated a variable equal to the minimum time needed to travel to the closest single-sex school minus the minimum time to travel to the closest co-educational school. We break this variable into two instruments: difference in minutes of travel time if the difference in travel time is less than the average, and difference in minutes of travel time if the difference in travel time is more than the average. We then instrumented

23 To calculate this, we used the postcode of each school and the postcode in which a student resides. We then entered the student's postcode in the 'start' category in MapQuest (www.mapquest.co.uk/mq/directions/mapbydirection.do) and the school's postcode in the 'ending address'. Mapquest then gave us a 'total estimated time' for driving from one location to the other. It is this value that we used. Thus, the 'average time' is based on the speed limit of roads and the road's classification (i.e. as a motorway or route).

for attendance at a single-sex school using a two-step process. First, we estimated the probability of a student attending a single-sex school, where the explanatory variables were an Essex dummy (taking the value one if the student resides in Essex and zero otherwise) and an interaction of Essex-resident with the two travelling-time variables. We then estimated the regression reported in column [7], which is an LPM, where we use predicted single-sex school attendance in place of the original single-sex school dummy.[24] Since the equation uses predicted values, we bootstrapped the standard errors for attending a single-sex school.[25] Even here, we find that the female, single-sex schooling interaction and all-girls group variable are statistically significant; indeed, the coefficient to the interaction of female with single-sex schooling is even larger.

Given these robustness checks, we therefore conclude that there is strong evidence for Conjecture 3 – that the schooling environment can affect risk preferences.

Conjecture 4 was that girls in single-sex environments (all-girls groups or single-sex schools) would be just as likely to enter the lottery as boys. In each column [2]–[5] in Table 10.2, we presented the marginal effect for a girl in a single-sex school compared to a boy in a co-ed school. In each case, the estimated effect is insignificant. However, if one were to take the point estimates seriously, then the single-sex schooling environment has reduced the gender gap by over 70 per cent in all cases. The all-girls group coefficient is not as large as the female, single-sex interaction, and, therefore, there is still a significant gap when groups are controlled for. Thus, we have mixed evidence for Conjecture 4.

Given these robustness checks and the continued significance of the all-girls group variable and the single-sex, female interaction, there seems to be strong evidence for Conjectures 2 and 3, that girls in same-gender groups enter the lottery more than girls in mixed-gender groups and that single-sex girls enter the lottery more than co-ed girls. There is also evidence for part of Conjecture 4, that girls in single-sex environments take the risky option as much as boys. The marginal effects for single-sex girls compared with co-ed boys is negative in all columns of Table 10.2, but they are insignificant,

24 The first-stage results for the IV regression are included as Table A10.1. The F-statistic for the instruments is 118.9 and is listed at the bottom of column [7] in Table 10.2. Note that we do not enter travel time linearly because the data showed a non-linear trend.

25 We randomly drew 1,000 different samples from our experimental data to calculate the bootstrap results.

suggesting that single-sex girls choose the risky option as much as boys. However, the size of the coefficient on the all-girls group dummy variable is not large enough to cancel out the negative coefficient on the female dummy variable. Therefore, girls in same-gender groups are not entering the lottery as much as co-ed boys. Since girls in some same-gender environments are not choosing the risky option as much as boys, we cannot fully support this hypothesis. The length of time a girl has been exposed to the same-gender environment – three years on average for girls at single-sex schools and only 30 minutes for girls in single-sex groups – may explain the difference in the size of the effect. However, the support for Conjectures 2, 3 and part of 4 provides strong evidence that nurture is affecting the risk attitudes of girls and also that the magnitude of this effect is large; completely cancelling out the gender gap in some cases. We next examine whether this finding can also be revealed using commonly asked survey questions about risk.

Survey versus experimental results

The experimental setting provided evidence that nurturing affects a girl's behaviour under uncertainty. We now examine whether survey questions could have been used to obtain those results and if the answers to commonly used survey questions provide any predictive power in explaining how a subject behaves in an experimental setting. To see if a student's answer to the general risk question provided any insight into whether the student would enter the fiver lottery, we reran that probit regression with an additional control for general risk attitude. The marginal effects are reported in column [2] of Table 10.3. The results show that choosing the fiver lottery is positively correlated with how prepared a student is to take risks. But inclusion of risk attitudes does not take away the explanatory power of the single-sex, female interaction or of the all-girls group coefficient.[26] Furthermore, the interaction of responses to the general risk question with being female is statistically insignificant. If student responses to the general risk attitudes question pick up their unobserved propensity to overstate their risk-loving, then the insignificance of this interaction implies that neither sex overstates more than the other.

26 This result is robust to entering a dummy variable for each option in the general risk scale, or for entering a squared term for the general risk question.

Table 10.3: Examining the experimental and survey results

Variables	Dependent variable							
	(=1) If a student chose Option 2 in 'Fiver' round			Readiness to take risk (0–10)		Hypothetical lottery outcome		
	[1]	[2]	[3]	[4]	[5]	[6]	[7]	[8]
Female (=1)	-0.36*** (0.07)	-0.51*** (0.13)	-0.33*** (0.08)	-0.23 (0.21)	-0.44 (0.37)	-0.79 (0.58)	-0.92 (0.75)	-0.29 (0.23)
Single-sex (=1)	-0.13 (0.10)	-0.12 (0.10)	-0.13 (0.10)	-0.09 (0.22)	-0.21 (0.40)	-0.34 (0.56)	-0.31 (0.71)	-0.11 (0.22)
Female × single-sex	0.33*** (0.06)	0.32*** (0.06)	0.28*** (0.06)	0.37 (0.27)	0.75 (0.50)	1.83** (0.71)	2.25** (0.89)	0.70*** (0.27)
All-girls (=1)	0.12* (0.06)	0.13** (0.06)	0.12** (0.05)	-0.09 (0.16)	-0.18 (0.29)	0.25 (0.43)	0.29 (0.55)	0.09 (0.16)
All-boys (=1)	-0.05 (0.10)	-0.06 (0.11)	-0.04 (0.10)	-0.07 (0.23)	-0.12 (0.42)	1.00 (0.61)	1.24* (0.75)	0.38* (0.23)
Readiness to take risk (0–10)	-	0.04* (0.02)	-	-	-	-	-	-
Female × readiness to take risk	-	0.04 (0.03)	-	-	-	-	-	-
Invest £20,000 (=1)	-	-	-0.07 (0.14)	-	-	-	-	-
Invest £40,000 (=1)	-	-	0.06 (0.11)	-	-	-	-	-
Invest £60,000 (=1)	-	-	0.04 (0.12)	-	-	-	-	-
Invest £80,000 (=1)	-	-	0.34*** (0.04)	-	-	-	-	-
Invest £100,000 (=1)	-	-	-0.14 (0.28)	-	-	-	-	-
Female × invest £20,000 (=1)	-	-	0.05 (0.13)	-	-	-	-	-
Female × invest £40,000 (=1)	-	-	-0.13 (0.18)	-	-	-	-	-
Female × invest £60,000 (=1)	-	-	0.16** (0.08)	-	-	-	-	-
Female × invest £80,000 (=1)	-	-	-0.88*** (0.02)	-	-	-	-	-

Variables	Dependent variable							
	(=1) If a student chose Option 2 in 'Fiver' round			Readiness to take risk (0–10)		Hypothetical lottery outcome		
	[1]	[2]	[3]	[4]	[5]	[6]	[7]	[8]
Female × invest £100,000 (=1)	–	–	0.13 (0.12)	–	–	–	–	–
Model type	Probit	Probit	Probit	Ordered probit	OLS	OLS	Tobit	Ordered probit
Constant	–	–	–	–	6.94*** (0.27)	3.41*** (0.45)	2.87*** (0.59)	–
Observations	260	255	259	255	255	259	259	259
R^2	–	–	–	–	0.019	0.058	–	–

Notes: Cutoffs for the ordered probit regression in column [4] are: −2.79, −2.55, −1.65, −1.27, −0.75, −0.46, 0.32, 0.86, and 1.52. Cutoffs for the ordered probit regression in column [8] are: −0.72, −0.05, 0.64, 1.22, 1.9. All cutoffs from both ordered probit regressions are significant at the 1% level, except for −0.05, which is insignificant. Robust standard errors in parenthesis; *** $p<0.01$; ** $p<0.05$; * $p<0.1$.

Likewise, when we use the student's answer to the hypothetical lottery – column [3] of Table 10.3 – the explanatory power of the single-sex female interaction and being in an all-girls group coefficient remains statistically significant even though some of the coefficients to the survey response are also statistically significant. However, there is little difference in how boys and girls responded to the survey question, as the hypothetical amount interacted with being female has little explanatory value. This again suggests that the survey questions are being answered in a similar way by both boys and girls.

Since the general risk question and the answer to the hypothetical lottery are typically positively correlated with choosing to enter the fiver lottery, we now examine if the answers to the two survey questions could have been used as dependent variables instead of the real-stakes experimental outcome.[27] Column [4] of Table 10.3 uses the responses to the general risk question as the dependent variable. In this case, the regression model used is ordered

27 A priori, we would expect different responses to the risk attitudes and the hypothetical lottery questions. The hypothetical lottery question is not as straightforward as the simple risk attitudes questions because it involves not only a time dimension (the outcome will not be realised until two years hence) and uncertain returns but also a choice of investment amounts. Risk aversion and impatience are thus conflated in responses to this question, as discussed in Booth and Katic (2011). The fact that it is more complex may also raise narrow bracketing issues, whereby 'a decision maker who faces multiple decisions tends to choose an option … without full regard to the other decisions and circumstances that she faces' (Rabin and Weizsacker 2009, 1508).

probit. Notice that all of the variables of interest are now statistically insignificant. There is no gender effect (the female dummy is not significant); there is no school-level nurturing (the single-sex and female interaction is insignificant), and there is no effect of the experimental peer group. Even if OLS is used – as done in column [5] of Table 10.3 – or a binary variable is created from the general risk attitudes question – using any cut point ranging from 3 to 8 – the survey question does not yield the same results as the real-stakes experimental lottery.

Columns [6]–[8] of Table 10.3 use the responses to the hypothetical risky financial investment as the dependent variable. As noted earlier, this not only represents a risky investment decision, as distinct from the abstract gamble for real stakes represented by the fiver lottery, but it also involves hypothetical amounts. Column [6] reports the results from OLS estimation, allowing a straightforward interpretation of the results. Notice that the female dummy has a statistically insignificant effect but that the interaction of female with single-sex schooling is statistically significant at the 5 per cent level. These estimates suggest that, ceteris paribus, girls from single-sex schools are willing to invest more than boys from co-ed schools. In other words, they invest nearly one and a half units more (where each unit involves an increase in the money the individual would invest in the lottery of around £20,000). They also invest significantly more than co-ed girls.

As a comparison, in column [7], we report results from a tobit model (used because a student can choose to put none of her hypothetical lottery winnings in the risky investment). Again, only the single-sex school and female interaction is significant at the 5 per cent level. The magnitude is larger than in the column of OLS estimates. Finally, column [8] reports results from an ordered probit model and again, only the single-sex and female result is significant (5 per cent level). This suggests that, while the hypothetical lottery investment does not provide the same evidence about relative risk aversion as the real-stakes experimental lottery, the interaction of females with single-sex schooling remains positive and statistically significant across the three estimation methods.

In summary, using the survey question as the dependent variable would suggest that, while there is no gender difference in risk aversion, women attending single-sex schools are not only as likely as men to enter the real-stakes gamble, but they also invest more in the hypothetical risky investment than do co-ed women and all men.

Given the results in Table 10.3, it seems that there is mixed evidence for Conjecture 5. Although the commonly used general risk attitude question is positively correlated with actual risky choices made under uncertainty, the determinants of these general risk attitudes differ quite markedly from the determinants of actual risky choices under uncertainty. This suggests that relying only on general risk attitudes might lead researchers to make misleading inferences about gender differences in choice under uncertainty. In contrast, the determinants of the amounts invested from the hypothetical lottery had some similarities to the determinants of actual risky choices under uncertainty. Estimating the determinants of amounts invested from the hypothetical lottery yielded the insight that girls attending single-sex schools invest more in the risky outcome than boys. The real-stakes experimental lottery showed that girls from single- sex schools were as likely as boys to enter the lottery, which is not inconsistent with the hypothetical lottery results. This example illustrates the complementary roles of experimental and survey data and suggests that gender differences in risk aversion differ across contexts.

Conclusion

Women and men may differ in their propensity to choose a risky outcome because of innate preferences or because pressure to conform to gender stereotypes encourages girls and boys to modify their innate preferences. Single-sex environments are likely to modify students' risk-taking preferences in economically important ways. To test this, we designed a controlled experiment in which subjects were given an opportunity to choose a risky outcome – a real-stakes gamble with a higher expected monetary value than the alternative outcome with a certain payoff – and in which the sensitivity of observed risk choices to environmental factors could be explored. The results of our real-stakes gamble show that gender differences in preferences for risk-taking are indeed sensitive to whether the girl attends a single-sex or co-ed school. Girls from single-sex schools are as likely to choose the real-stakes gamble as boys from either co-ed or single-sex schools, and more likely than co-ed girls. That girls in co-educational institutions have a lower preference for risk is interesting, since this is the norm for children in schools in many countries, including the UK.

Moreover, we found that gender differences in preferences for risk-taking are sensitive to the gender mix of the experimental group, even when these groups are placed within a larger co-educational milieu. In particular, we found that girls are more likely to choose risky outcomes when assigned to all-girl groups. This finding is relevant to the policy debate on whether or not single-sex classes within co-ed schools could be a useful way forward.

We also found that gender differences in risk aversion are sensitive to the method of eliciting preferences. While the commonly used general risk attitude question is positively correlated with actual risky choices made under uncertainty, the determinants of these general risk attitudes differ quite markedly from the determinants of actual risky choices under uncertainty. This suggests that to rely only on survey-based general risk attitudes might lead researchers to make misleading inferences about gender differences in choice under uncertainty. In contrast, the determinants of the amounts invested from the hypothetical lottery had some similarities to the determinants of actual real-stakes gambles under uncertainty.

To summarise our main results, on average, girls from single-sex schools are found in our experiment to be as likely as boys to choose the real-stakes lottery. This suggests that observed gender differences in behaviour under uncertainty found in previous studies might reflect social learning rather than inherent gender traits, a finding that would be hard, if not impossible, to show using survey-based evidence alone. We hope that future work will further explore these issues in situations where there has been random assignment of students to single-sex education, a policy that some jurisdictions are currently contemplating introducing.

Finally, we note that our experiment does not allow us to tease out why these behavioural responses were observed for girls in all-female environments. In an interesting recent paper, Lavy and Schlosser (2011) found that an increase in the proportion of girls improves boys' and girls' cognitive outcomes in mixed-gender classes. They attributed this to lower levels of classroom disruption and violence, improved inter-student and student–teacher relationships and reduced teachers' fatigue. However, this mechanism does not address the single-sex school effects that we have found in our analysis. Conjectures as to why girls in single-sex schools have different risk preferences from their co-ed counterparts, as we have found, might include the following. Adolescent females, even those endowed with an intrinsic propensity to make riskier choices, may be discouraged from doing so because they are inhibited by culturally driven norms and beliefs about the appropriate mode of female behaviour – avoiding risk. But once they are placed in an all-female environment, this inhibition is reduced. No longer reminded of their own gender identity and society's norms, they find it easier to make riskier choices than women who are placed in a co-ed class. We hope in future research to further investigate these hypotheses.

Acknowledgements

This chapter was first published as Booth, A.L., and Nolen, P. (2012). 'Gender differences in risk behaviour: Does nurture matter?', *The Economic Journal*, 122(558):F56–F78. doi.org/10.1111/j.1468-0297.2011.02480.x.

For helpful suggestions, we thank the editor, two anonymous referees, various seminar participants, and Uwe Sunde and Nora Szech. We also thank the students who participated in the experiment and their teachers who facilitated this. Financial support was received from the Australian Research Council, the British Academy, the Department of Economics at the University of Essex and the Nuffield Foundation. We take very seriously the ethical issues surrounding this research. This experiment received approval from the Ethics Committee of the University of Essex.

References

Akerlof, G., and Kranton, R. (2000). 'Economics and identity', *Quarterly Journal of Economics*, 115:715–753. doi.org/10.1162/003355300554881.

American Association of University Women. (1992). *How Schools Shortchange Girls*. Washington, DC: American Association of University Women.

Boheim, R., and Taylor, M. (2002). 'Tied down or room to move? Investigating the relationship between housing tenure, employment status and residential mobility in Britain', *Scottish Journal of Political Economy*, 49(4):369–392. doi.org/10.1111/1467-9485.00237.

Booth, A., and Nolen, P. (2012). 'Choosing to compete: How different are girls and boys?', *Journal of Economic Behavior & Organization*, 81(2):542–555. doi.org/10.1016/j.jebo.2011.07.018.

Booth, A., and Katic, P. (2011). 'Cognitive skills and risk preferences'. Mimeo, The Australian National University.

Brutsaert, H. (1999). 'Coeducation and gender identity formation: A comparative analysis of secondary schools in Belgium', *British Journal of Sociology of Education*, 20(3):343–353. doi.org/10.1080/01425699995308.

Burks, S., Carpenter, J., Goette, L., and Rustichini, A. (2009). 'Cognitive skills affect economic preferences, strategic behavior, and job attachment', *Proceedings of the National Academy of Sciences of the USA*, 106(19):7745–7750. doi.org/10.1073/pnas.0812360106.

Coleman, J. (1961). *The Adolescent Society*. New York: Free Press.

Datta Gupta, N., Poulsen, A., and Villeval, M.-C. (2005). 'Male and female competitive behavior: Experimental evidence'. IZA Working Paper No. 1833. Available at: docs.iza.org/dp1833.pdf.

Dohmen, T., Falk, A., Huffman, D., Schupp, J., Sunde, U., and Wagner, G. (2011). 'Individual risk attitudes: Measurement, determinants, and behavioral consequences', *Journal of the European Economic Association*, 9(3):522–50. doi.org/10.1111/j.1542-4774.2011.01015.x.

Dohmen, T., Falk, A., Huffman, D., and Sunde, U. (2010). 'Are risk aversion and impatience related to cognitive ability?', *American Economic Review*, 100(3): 1238–1260. doi.org/10.1257/aer.100.3.1238.

Dohmen, T., Falk, A., Huffman, D., and Sunde, U. (2012). 'The intergenerational transmission of risk and trust attitudes', *The Review of Economic Studies*, 79(2):645–677, doi.org/10.1093/restud/rdr027.

Eckel, C., and Grossman, P. (2002). *Differences in the Economic Decisions of Men and Women: Experimental Evidence*, Amsterdam: Elsevier.

Gneezy, U., Leonard, K., and List, J. (2009). 'Gender differences in competition: Evidence from a matrilineal and a patriarchal society', *Econometrica*, 77(5):1637–1364. doi.org/10.3982/ECTA6690.

Gneezy, U., Niederle, M., and Rustichini, A. (2003). 'Performance in competitive environments: Gender differences', *The Quarterly Journal of Economics*, 118(3): 1049–1074. doi.org/10.1162/00335530360698496.

Gneezy, U., and Rustichini, A. (2004). 'Gender and competition at a young age', *American Economic Review Papers*, 94(2):377–381. doi.org/10.1257/00028280 41301821.

Harbaugh, W., Krause, K., and Vesterlund, L. (2002). 'Risk attitudes of children and adults: Choices over small and large probability gains and losses', *Experimental Economics*, 5(1):53–84. doi.org/10.1023/A:1016316725855.

Holt, C., and Laury, S. (2002). 'Risk aversion and incentive effects', *American Economic Review*, 92(5):1644–1655. doi.org/10.1257/000282802762024700.

Kessler, S., Ashenden, D., Connell, R., and Dowsett, G. (1985). 'Gender relations in secondary schooling', *Sociology of Education*, 58(1):34–48. doi.org/10.2307/2112539.

Lavy, V., and Schlosser, A. (2011). 'Mechanisms and impacts of gender peer effects at school', *American Economic Journal: Applied Economics*, 3(2):1–33. doi.org/10.1257/app.3.2.1.

Lawrence, P. (2006). 'Men, women, and ghosts in science', *PLoS Biology*, 4(1):13–15. doi.org/10.1371/journal.pbio.0040019.

Maccoby, E. (1990). 'Gender and relationships: a developmental account', *American Psychologist*, 45(4):513–20. doi.org/10.1037/0003-066X.45.4.513.

Maccoby, E. (1998). *The Two Sexes: Growing up Apart, Coming Together*, Cambridge: Harvard University Press.

Niederle, M., and Vesterlund, L. (2007). 'Do women shy away from competition? Do men compete too much?', *The Quarterly Journal of Economics*, 122(3):1067–1101. doi.org/10.1162/qjec.122.3.1067.

Niederle, M., and Yestrumskas, A. (2008). 'Gender differences in seeking challenges: The role of institutions'. NBER Working Paper No. 13922. Available at: www.nber.org/papers/w13922.

Rabin, M., and Weizsäcker, G. (2009). 'Narrow bracketing and dominated choices', *American Economic Review*, 99(4):1508–1543. doi.org/10.1257/aer.99.4.1508.

Sadker, M., Sadker, D., and Klein, S. (1991). 'The issue of gender in elementary and secondary education', *Review of Research in Education*, 17:269–334.

Schubert, R., Brown, M., Gysler, M., and Brachinger, H. (1999). 'Financial decision-making: Are women really more risk-averse?', *American Economic Review*, 89(2):381–385. doi.org/10.1257/aer.89.2.381.

Steele, C., Spencer, S., and Aronson, J. (2002). 'Contending with group image: The psychology of stereotype and social identity threat', *Advances in Experimental Social Psychology*, 34:379–440. doi.org/10.1016/S0065-2601(02)80009-0.

Appendix A: The experiment

In the experiment, students were escorted into a large auditorium. One individual read aloud the instructions to everyone participating. All the graduate supervisors hired to supervise groups were given a copy of the instructions, were involved in the pilot that had taken place and had gone through comprehensive training. These supervisors answered questions if they were raised.

Below is the text of the slides that were shown to the students when they arrived at the auditorium:

Slide 1

Welcome to the University of Essex!

Today you are going to be taking part in an economics experiment.
Treat this as if it were an exam situation:

- No talking to your neighbours.
- Raise your hand if you have any questions.

There will be no deception in this experiment.

Slide 2

The experiment today will involve completing three rounds of mazes.
Rules for completing a maze:

- Get from the flag on the left-hand side to the flag on the right-hand side.
- Do not cross any lines!
- Do not go outside of the box.

We will now go through an example!!

Comment: At this point students were shown one practice maze and were walked through how to solve it, illustrating the three points raised above.

Slide 3

The supervisors in your row will be handing you maze packets throughout the session. At all times you need to put your seat letter and number on the packet and your name. Please make sure you know your row letter and seat number.

Your seat is also on your badge. It is the middle grouping. For example, if your badge was 1-A3-F your seat number should be A3. Make sure this is correct now.

Mazes: You should do the mazes in order.

If you cannot solve a maze, put an X through it and go onto the next maze.

If you do not put an X through it, none of the following mazes will be marked.

Note: If you do not have the correct seat number on your maze packets, you may be paid incorrectly.

Slide 4

We are going to be doing six rounds of mazes.

Before each round of mazes we will explain how you will be paid for that round. After all six rounds of mazes are finished, we will choose one round to 'implement'.

That means you will get paid for your performance in that round.

The round for which you will be paid will be chosen randomly from this cup.

You will also receive GBP 5 for showing up today.

Since you do not know for which round you will be getting paid, you should do your best in each round and treat each round separately.

Slide 5

You will get 5 minutes to solve up to 15 mazes. Please solve as many mazes as you can.

Do not begin until I say go!

For this round, you will get £0.50 for each maze you solve correctly.

Example: If you solve eight mazes correctly, you will earn £4.

Please make sure you have put your name and seat on the maze packet now. Are there any questions?

OK –??? GO!
OK –??? STOP
No Talking!

Slide 6

Now you will get £2 for each maze you solve correctly, IF you solve the most mazes correctly in your group.

Your group consists of you and the three other people sitting in your 'row' who have the same first number on their badge.

Example: If your badge number is 1-B2-M then your group consists of you and the three other students with the badges 1-**-* in your row.

If you are in group 1 and you solve eight mazes correctly, then:

- IF everyone else in your group solved fewer than eight mazes correctly, you will get £16.
- IF someone in your group solved nine mazes correctly, you would get £0.

Note: Ties will be broken randomly. Thus, IF two people in your group solve eight mazes correctly, we flip a coin to see who gets the £16.

Are there any questions?

Slide 7

You will get 5 minutes to solve up to 15 mazes.

Please solve as many mazes as you can.

Please make sure you have put your name and seat on the maze packet now. Do not begin until I say go!

OK –??? GO!
OK –??? STOP
No Talking!

Slide 8

In this round you choose between two options.

Option 1: Get £0.50 per maze you solve correctly.

Option 2: Get £2 per maze you solve correctly IF you solve more mazes correctly than the other three people in your group did LAST round.

Example: Say you solve eight mazes correctly this round.

If you choose Option 1, you get £4.

If you chose Option 2:

- You get £16 IF the other three people in your group solved fewer than eight mazes correctly in Round 2.
- You get £0 IF one other person solved nine mazes correctly in Round 2.

Note: Ties will be broken randomly. Thus, IF one person in your group solved eight mazes correctly in Round 2, we flip a coin to see if you get the £16.

Are there any questions?

Slide 9

A supervisor will now come by and give you a card for you to circle Option 1 or Option 2.

Option 1: Get £0.50 per maze you solve correctly.

Option 2: Get £2 per maze you solve correctly IF you solve more mazes correctly than the other three people in your group did LAST round.

Circle your choice, fold the paper and give it back to the supervisor. You need to write your seat number on the piece of paper.

Do not tell anyone your choice!

You will get 5 minutes to solve up to 15 mazes. Please solve as many mazes as you can

Do not begin until I say go!

Please make sure you have put your name and seat on the maze packet now. Do not begin until I say go!

OK –??? GO!
OK –??? STOP
No Talking!

Slide 10

In this round, you will not have to do any mazes.

Everyone will be given £5 to play with. Think of the £5 as already being your own money.

You now face a choice:
Option 1: Keep your £5.
Option 2: Gamble with your £5.

IF you choose Option 2, you will flip a coin at the end of this round:

- IF the coin comes up heads, you will get £11.
- IF the coin comes up tails, you will get £2.

A supervisor will now hand you a piece of paper. Choose Option 1 or Option 2 and then fold the paper.

Please put your seat number on the option card. Do not tell anyone your choice!

Everyone will now stand up when the supervisor comes to you and flip a coin. Your supervisor will record the flip.

Slide 11

Thank you for completing the mazes!

Your last set of mazes will now be collected – please stay seated. I will now pull the number from the hat. AND!?

You will be handed a survey – read the questions very carefully and make sure you respond to ALL the questions, including the ones at the very end. After everyone is done completing the survey, a supervisor will hand you some refreshments.

Make sure you put your seat on the survey!

Then, after 10–15 minutes, your supervisor will give you an envelope with your money and ask you to sign a piece of paper. Then you will go to your bus.

Please keep your winnings confidential. THANKS!

Comment: Due to the time it took to fill all the envelopes with money, subjects ended up receiving the money two days later, as the students needed to get back to their schools to be picked up by their parents.

Table A10.1: Dependent variable (=1) if student attends single-sex school

Variable	[1]
Essex (=1)	0.84*** (0.05)
Essex × less than average travel time to single-sex school (min)	-0.03*** (0.01)
Essex × more than average travel time to single-sex school (min)	-0.02*** (0.00)
Female (=1)	0.00 (0.07)
All-girls group (=1)	0.00 (0.06)
All-boys group (=1)	0.09 (0.07)
Constant	0.02 (0.04)
Observations	260
R^2	0.476

Note: ** *p*<0.01; ** *p*<0.05; * *p*<0.1; Robust standard errors in parentheses.

11

Do single-sex classes affect academic achievement? An experiment in a co-educational university

Alison L Booth, Lina Cardona Sosa and Patrick Nolen

Introduction

More women than men attend university, yet women are under-represented in technical fields like mathematics, the physical sciences and engineering (National Academy of Sciences, 2006). They are also under-represented in economics, the discipline on which we focus in this chapter.

Some universities and academics have tried to reduce gender gaps in economics by targeting females who study these subjects. For example, Harvard Business School has implemented policies such as special training for women aimed at decreasing gender disparities that develop after women begin their studies, and the American Economic Association has introduced a mentoring and network program for female economists. While both approaches have been shown to increase female performance and retention in their areas, policymakers have not adopted programs of this type at a national level. More recently, a new initiative to increase the number of women in economics has been launched by Harvard University:

The Undergraduate Women in Economics Challenge.[1] In this chapter, we report an additional approach to those that have been put forward thus far: the use of single-sex classes within a co-educational environment as a potential means of improving female outcomes. Thus, we contribute an important piece of evidence to inform this initiative and to the broader issue of gender in the classroom.

Single-sex education can be provided at either the school level (in which case all classes within the school are single-sex) or at the class level (in which case certain classes within a school are single-sex but the overall school environment is co-educational). The treatment discussed in our chapter is of the latter type – some single-sex classes within a co-ed university. However, most of the studies within the literature on single-sex education fall into the former type – single-sex classes within a single-sex school, and the vast majority of these are directed at primary and secondary education.

US policymakers have, over the past decade or so, allowed the expansion of single-sex education into primary and secondary schools, with the idea that the effects on females will carry on into later life. According to the National Association for Single Sex Public Education, in 2002, there were only about a dozen US public schools offering single-sex classes. In 2010, there were 540, of which 91 were all-girl or all-boy schools (in other words, schools in which all classes were single-sex).[2] This expansion in single-sex education, however, has occurred despite the lack of much conclusive evidence showing the benefits of single-sex education, be it in classes or schools. Indeed, a 2005 US Department of Education systematic review found 'minimal' evidence supporting single-sex education; Smithers and Robinson (2006) argue that observed benefits of single-sex education are due to student selection into schools; Halpern et al. (2011) state 'there is no well-designed research showing that single-sex education improves students' academic performance' and argue that 'there is evidence that sex segregation increases gender stereotyping and legitimizes institutional sexism.'

1 For more information, see UWE webpage: scholar.harvard.edu/goldin/UWE.

2 This represents a small proportion (<1 per cent) of the nearly 100,000 public schools in the US at that time (see nces.ed.gov/fastfacts/display.asp?id=84). In the private sector there are proportionately 10 times more fully single-gendered schools (10 per cent according to Morrison (2014) or almost 10 per cent using weighted averages presented in Long and Conger (2013)). That the proportion is higher in the private sector – and is growing (Morrison, 2014) – might be viewed as indicating a demand for single-sex schools. In the UK, of independent private schools, 27 per cent are single-sex (see ISC (2014)).

However, despite the criticisms of single-sex education, there are a number of potential psychological reasons for expecting a positive effect for young women in single-sex classes. For example, females in all-female classes may feel more confident and gain higher levels of self-efficacy (Gist and Mitchell, 1992); they may experience a reduction in stereotype threat (as discussed in Spencer et al., 1999; Steele, 1997; or Steele et al., 2002) or a reduction in psychological threat (as discussed in Cohen et al., 2006).

Recently, there have been some important new studies aiming to estimate the effect of single-sex education on various educational and economic outcomes. These typically rely on comparing students attending different types of primary or secondary schools, or, within a school, comparing students who already knew they were likely or unlikely to attend single-sex classes. For instance, Park et al. (2012) compared students in co-ed high schools that are primarily publicly funded with students in gender-segregated schools that are primarily privately funded. Eisenkopf et al. (2015) examined students who chose to attend a school where 85 per cent of the population was female, meaning it is very likely that many students would be in single-sex classes. Booth and Nolen (2012a, 2012b) looked at publicly funded selective single-sex schools that they compared with the academic stream of publicly funded co-educational schools. In these studies, the ex ante choice of a primarily female school may bias the results, as argued by Jackson (2012), who shows that females who benefit from single-sex education are those with a preference to attend single-sex schools. It was for this reason that we chose in the present study to assign students randomly to single-sex and co-ed classes in a field experiment, and to follow them over time.

While, as noted, there are few studies estimating the effects of single-sex education – be it in classes or in schools – there is a related literature showing that the proportion of females in a classroom or local environment has an effect on the educational and economic outcomes of students at primary and secondary levels. For example, Lavy and Schlosser (2011) found that, as the proportion of females in a classroom increased, the cognitive outcomes of both males and females improved. Other studies look either directly or indirectly at the subsequent choices of technical majors for students in secondary schools and find that these choices are affected by the proportion of females in a classroom.[3] That is not the focus of our present chapter; instead, we investigate the educational outcomes of university students who have already chosen a course of study.

In view of this literature and the policy importance of the topic, we designed a field experiment to examine the effects of single-sex classes on the performance of first-year university students in a highly ranked and publicly funded economics department. There are several novel features of our approach. First, we randomly assigned students to a single-sex environment, and hence selection was not an issue. As noted above, few other studies have estimated the effects of single-sex schooling with random assignment. Specifically, we randomly assigned first-year economics students into all-female, all-male, or co-educational classes, and we then examined the effect on first-year scores and pass rates, and on scores in subsequent years of the degree program.

The second novel feature of our approach is that we implemented this random assignment to single-sex classes in the economics faculty of a co-educational university — the University of Essex.[4] This is in contrast to earlier studies that have primarily focused on the effects of fully sex-segregated primary and secondary schools. Our results are therefore of particular relevance to the many co-educational colleges and universities interested in reducing existing gender inequalities in higher education.

The remainder of the chapter is set out as follows. The following sections lay out the experimental design, context, and subjects involved, as well as report descriptive information about the data and the predetermined variables. We then present and discuss the main results, present the behavioural changes and discuss the overall findings.

3 For example, Schneeweis and Zweimüller (2012) showed that a female studying in a class with a higher proportion of females is more likely to choose to study in a technical school later on. Annelli and Giovanni (2013) found that a woman in a high-school class with a larger share of female peers will have a higher wage; this is primarily because the higher proportion of same-sex peers increases the likelihood a woman will choose majors associated with high earning jobs such as economics, business, medicine or engineering.

4 While the important study of Oosterbeek and van Ewijk (2014) looks at varying the proportion female in university students' co-educational study groups, they did not consider fully sex-segregated groups, which are the focus of our interest.

Experiment design

Below, we discuss the educational environment, the randomisation, and the student evaluation.

Subjects and educational environment

The students in our experiment arrived at the University of Essex in October 2010, and they all took a year-long Introductory Economics course, either EC111 or EC100. EC111 is primarily for economics students, while EC100 is primarily for students in the business school. The Introductory Economics course was one of the four required year-long courses that students had to take in their first year. Introductory courses run over 20 weeks and have the same structure: each week, a senior professor from the economics department gives a two-hour lecture and a graduate teaching assistant (TA) gives a one-hour class. The lecture takes place in a large auditorium, while the one-hour class is taught by a TA in a small classroom that can hold at least 30 students.

We emphasised, when training the TAs, that they were not to discuss with students any of the details – or objectives – of the experiment. In classes, the TAs discuss problem sets with students; these problem sets relate directly to the material taught in that week's Introduction to Economics lectures, and are designed by the professor in charge of that course. The professor also tells the TAs what material should be covered in each class.[5]

During their first year of study, students received 240 hours of instruction, 60 hours per course. The focus of our experiment was the one hour of class time per week taught by TAs in the Introductory Economics course and its impact on educational outcomes. That amounts to 20 hours of instruction, or 8.3 per cent of the total instruction received by a student in the first year.

5 The problem sets are the same across all classes in EC100 and in EC111 (though they differ between EC100 and EC111).

Random assignment to classes

We begin this section by providing a brief background to the institutional framework behind UK undergraduate admissions, before describing in detail the University of Essex admissions and how the randomisation of students to classes was achieved.

All students (both home and international) wishing to study for an undergraduate degree in the UK must apply by recording their interest – well in advance of the start of the academic year – with the Universities and Colleges Admissions Service. This is a UK-based central organisation whose main role is processing applications for entry into UK universities. At the same time, secondary school students are also required to rank up to five preferred universities. This is done before the final secondary school exams.

Students who apply to Essex University are given a university-specific registration number as soon as their application is complete. Students subsequently confirm whether Essex is their top choice or a backup. Registration numbers for students who do not pick Essex as a top choice are then reused for other applicants.

Since each applying student can – and usually does – list up to five schools, there is little certainty that a student who has listed Essex University as one of their preferred places to study will actually end up there. Indeed, fewer than 80 per cent of students who initially register an interest in Essex end up attending (because of the one in five aspects). Therefore, many of the earlier Essex registration numbers are often reassigned as students get conditional offers elsewhere. Given the substantial reuse and reordering of registration numbers, there is considerable randomness associated with their final arrangement. Some low numbers will belong to early applicants, while others will be late applicants who did not get into the university of their choice.

We now describe how students were allocated to classes. Before incoming first-year students arrived on campus, the timetabling-office randomly assigned them to a single-gender or co-educational class for the Introductory Economics course. The randomisation was conducted based on the number of classes, the unique identifying registration number given to each student as described above, and gender.

Students were ordered by registration number and then assigned to classes one by one until all classes in a course were filled. For example, in EC111 (where there were three all-female classes, four all-male, and 10 co-ed), the student with the lowest registration number was assigned to the first single-sex class (either all-female or all-male, depending on the student's gender), the student with the second-lowest registration number was then assigned to the next appropriate single-sex class, and so on until there was one student in each of the three all-female classes or in each of the four all-male classes. Then the next student, with the gender where the respective single-sex classes were filled, was placed into the first co-ed class. Once all single-sex classes had one student, the next students with the lowest registration numbers were placed in the remaining co-ed classes until all classes had one student. The process then started again and continued until each class had two students, then three students, and so on. The procedure continued until all students were assigned to a class. Thus, lower registration numbers are equally likely in single-sex and co-ed classes.[6]

As in other years, our cohort was, roughly, 35 per cent female and 65 per cent male. We assigned these students to a total of 37 classes: of these, 20 were in EC100 and 17 classes in EC111. Of the 20 classes in EC100, four were all-female, seven were all-male, and nine were co-ed. Of the 17 classes in EC111, three were all female, four were all male, and 10 were co-ed. That means – at the class level – we have seven all-female classes, 11 all-male classes, and 19 co-ed classes.[7] We chose to create this number of all-male and all-female classes because it kept the gender distribution in co-ed classes at roughly what it would have been without the experiment; that is, in the 19 co-ed classes, each class was, on average, 30 per cent female and 70 per cent male.

Once assigned to a class, students were not allowed to change their class and attendance at the assigned class was enforced.[8] The procedures regarding class assignments and attendance are the same used each year. There was no change in the way students were assigned to classes in any of the other

6 Please note that this method is akin to a matched pair design and is similar to the method used in Miguel and Kremer (2004, p165), though, there, schools were listed alphabetically, and every third school was treated.

7 Given that treatment was at the class level, we cluster standard errors at the class level and also look at class-level regressions in the results section.

8 The university is required to take attendance so that it can provide evidence that international students who are in the UK on student visas are actually attending classes. Indeed, the visa requirements for most international students include the provision that they must attend lectures and classes.

year-long courses, and courses were scheduled by timetabling so that there was no conflict between class times and any lectures. Furthermore, the assignment to classes in other courses was independent of the Introductory Economics class assignment. At no stage were the students told the purpose of the class assignment, nor did we have any enquiries. All students enrolled in the course are supposed to attend the classes and do the compulsory exercises. Lectures and classes began immediately after student arrival on campus. During the first course meeting, students took an IQ test, filled out a demographic questionnaire, and participated in a risk and competition experiment. The IQ test was a modified 20-minute version of Raven's Matrices appropriate for university-aged students and different languages. Our sample consisted of 570 first-year students.

Student grades

It is important to understand the grading details, as these affect students' incentives to exert effort during the year. The grade for Introductory Economics is based on assignments, tests and an end-of-year written examination. The academic year comprises three terms. At the end of the first term, students are given a take-home assignment that they are required to do on their own. They are also given a one-hour test in a lecture hall while being supervised. At the end of the second term, students again do a take-home assignment and take a one-hour test. Each term, the assignments and tests are marked by the class teacher, who can see the name of the student.[9] Generally, no curve is forced on the assignment or test marks; the course professor gives a detailed outline of what marks should be awarded based on potential answers. However, the professor responsible for the course does look at marks to make sure there are no discrepancies across TAs. During the summer term (the third and final term for the academic year), students are not presented with any new material but are invited to several revision lectures and – towards the middle of this term – take a mandatory two-hour exam. As is the standard procedure in the UK, that exam is double-blindly marked by two members of the economics department, and neither marker knows the name or gender of the student. Furthermore, an external

9 As shown in Lavy (2008) when teachers are aware of the gender of the student prejudices can occur in marking that could lead to gender differences in test scores that are not there when objective measures are used.

examiner – a senior professor from another UK university – reviews the exams afterwards to ensure they are of a particular standard and that the marks are appropriate. No curve is forced on final exam marks.[10]

A student's overall grade in the course is based on a 'max-rule'. The scores from assignments and tests are averaged. If the average is above the exam mark, the student's final mark will be based on 50 per cent of the coursework (assignments and tests) mark plus 50 per cent of the exam mark. If the coursework average is below the exam score, then the student's final mark will be the exam mark. Students know this rule from the beginning – it is explained to them during the first lecture – and all courses in the economics department are graded in the same manner.[11] Given that coursework may not count towards the final score, a number of students choose not to do it. However, all students must take the exam.

Degrees in the UK are classified into one of four categories: a first-class degree, which is the best degree classification; an upper second (also referred to as a 2.1), which is the second-best classification; a lower second degree (also referred to as a 2.2), which is the third-best classification; or a third-class degree, which is the lowest classification. At Essex University (and at many other British universities), the degree classification is based on the scores students get in their second and third years only. In order to continue into the second year of study, all a student has to do is 'pass' all courses in the first year, that is, get a score of 40 per cent or higher in all four courses. Thus, when looking at the effect of single-sex classes in the first year, we will focus not only on scores but also on the margin that will matter the most for students, whether or not they passed their course.

If a student does not pass the first year (where passing is defined as getting 40 per cent or more in all courses), the student nearly always has to take the entire year again (unless there are extenuating circumstances such as illness). A non-trivial number of students fail their first year (nearly 20 per cent in our sample).

10 One potential outcome measure might be the double-blind exam scores, as at first blush these appear to be completely 'clean' measures of achievement. However, students' efforts in studying for the exam would be influenced by what they already know about their homework grades. Students with better homework grades might work harder for the exams because they have learned they have a talent for that subject, or they might slack off for the same reason. Therefore it is important to focus on all components of the students' grades and their overall score.

11 Note that the max-rule is applied by the economics department automatically, and students do not themselves make any choice about its application ex post. However, they might choose to do no coursework; indeed at least 15 per cent of our sample did not do all the coursework.

Allocation of TAs

Lectures for the courses were given on Monday and Tuesday. Then classes were taught from after the last lecture on Tuesday until Friday, so that the material from the lecture that week was discussed in the classes that week. Classes were only held for part of the day on Wednesday because the afternoon was reserved for sports matches and club meetings. Therefore, the majority of classes were on Thursday and Friday. TAs were PhD students who were assigned to classes by the director of graduate studies. Each TA usually taught three classes, and the director aimed to assign that person classes all on the same day. Therefore, once the TAs were assigned, we made sure that each TA taught both co-ed and single-sex classes. That means that, roughly, there were the same number of single-sex classes and co-ed classes on each day. We tried to balance classes between morning and afternoon sessions, but with only 37 classes, that was not always possible. However, the regression results show that the time of day and day of the week of classes did not predict the treatment status of a class (either single-sex or co-ed), and therefore, it suggests that our assignment mechanism worked.

Descriptive statistics

In this section, we report descriptive statistics for the predetermined characteristics, followed by density figures showing differences between the treatment and control groups across men and women combined, as well as disaggregated by gender. We report these densities across several measures of academic performance in Introductory Economics. We use the sample of all students taking the Introductory Economics course.

Since class type was randomly assigned, we expect that predetermined characteristics should not differ by class type. Summary statistics and differences in means between individuals attending single-sex and co-ed classes are reported in Table 11.1. Panel A shows the 19 variables at the individual level, while Panel B reports those variables at the class level. At the bottom of each panel we present the relevant *p*-values for the joint test of whether the predetermined variables predict assignment to single-sex classes at either the individual or class level. Under the table, we report the number of cases for each panel, plus some further information, including how *p*-values were calculated.

Table 11.1: Descriptive statistics at individual and class level

	Women				Men			
	Co-ed	All-female	Difference	S.E. of difference	Co-ed	All-female	Difference	S.E. of difference
Panel A – Variables (individual level)								
IQ raw score	11.92	11.45	−0.47	[0.480]	12.13	11.45	−0.68	[0.435]
Student attended a single-sex high school (=1)	0.31	0.26	−0.05	[0.072]	0.25	0.29	0.03	[0.052]
Age	18.85	18.52	−0.33***	[0.065]	18.69	18.66	−0.03	[0.049]
Native language English (=1)	0.23	0.34	0.12	[0.074]	0.42	0.43	0.01	[0.056]
White (=1)	0.52	0.55	0.03	[0.076]	0.61	0.50	−0.11**	[0.056]
Black (=1)	0.27	0.19	−0.08	[0.063]	0.16	0.27	0.12**	[0.046]
Student is eldest child (=1)	0.53	0.60	0.07	[0.071]	0.45	0.43	−0.02	[0.052]
Number of siblings	1.30	1.43	0.13	[0.194]	1.65	1.47	−0.18	[0.164]
Number of sisters	0.66	0.94	0.28*	[0.166]	0.91	0.86	−0.05	[0.121]
Mother has university degree (=1)	0.49	0.38	−0.11	[0.075]	0.44	0.39	−0.05	[0.056]
Mother stayed at home (=1)	0.13	0.17	0.04	[0.056]	0.24	0.25	0.00	[0.050]
Father has university degree (=1)	0.61	0.49	−0.12	[0.076]	0.51	0.52	0.01	[0.056]
Born in UK (=1)	0.22	0.32	0.10	[0.064]	0.42	0.39	−0.03	[0.051]
Born in EU (=1)	0.42	0.37	−0.05	[0.070]	0.24	0.24	0.00	[0.045]
Big Five: Agreeableness	12.70	12.51	−0.19	[0.370]	12.61	12.66	0.05	[0.279]
Big Five: Conscientiousness	13.26	13.61	0.35	[0.464]	13.77	13.45	−0.32	[0.319]
Big Five: Extraversion	14.10	13.40	−0.70	[0.437]	13.47	13.28	−0.19	[0.302]

	Women				Men			
	Co-ed	All-female	Difference	S.E. of difference	Co-ed	All-female	Difference	S.E. of difference
Big Five: Neuroticism	12.80	12.84	0.03	[0.449]	11.44	11.61	0.18	[0.292]
Big Five: Openness	14.72	13.70	−1.02	[0.619]	14.71	14.31	−0.40	[0.403]
p-value of joint test whether variables predict assignment to all-female class for girls = 0.34								
p-value of joint test whether variables predict assignment to all-male class for boys = 0.20								
Panel B – Variables (class level)								
TA is female (=1)	0.42	0.29	−0.14	[0.214]	0.42	0.18	−0.24	[0.169]
Class before 2 pm (=1)	0.58	0.43	−0.15	[0.226]	0.58	0.64	0.06	[0.194]
Class at end of week (=1)	0.74	0.86	0.12	[0.204]	0.74	0.46	−0.28	[0.175]
Class size at end of year	16.00	18.00	2.00	[1.507]	16.00	16.14	0.14	[1.263]
p-value of joint test whether class level variables predict if a class is all-female = 0.22								
p-value of joint test whether class level variables predict if a class is all-male = 0.30								

Notes: *** $p<0.01$; ** $p<0.05$; * $p<0.1$; There are 570 students in the sample of which 202 are female, 123 are in all-female classes, and 173 are in all-male classes. There are 37 classes of which seven are all-female, and 11 are all-male. Class at end of week = 1 if a class was held on a Thursday or Friday. Dummies were used for missing values in the individual-level regressions for the p-values.

Our particular interest in Table 11.1 is in checking the balance of predetermined characteristics across co-ed and single-sex classes. As with all randomisations, some differences are likely to occur. Perusal of the table reveals that the only variables whose difference across class-types is statistically significant are age and number of sisters for women, and for men, ethnicity. From Panel B, it can be seen that there are no statistically significant differences in the four class-level variables across class type for either gender. At neither the individual nor the class level can the variables jointly explain assignment to a single-sex class for males or females.

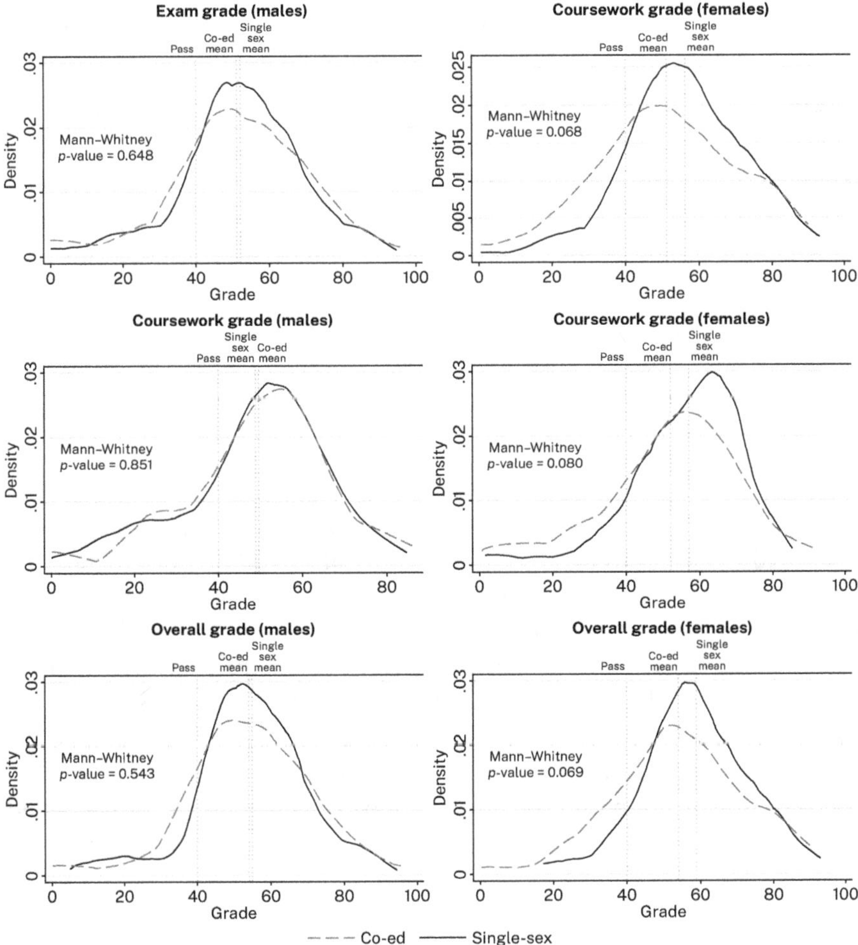

Figure 11.1: Grade distributions

Our main results can be seen descriptively in Figure 11.1, which displays treatment and control group densities for exam grades, coursework grades, and overall grades (which can include for any individual either only the exam mark, or a 50:50 mix of exam and coursework, depending on which is higher). The solid line is for men and women in single-sex classes, while the dashed line is for men and women in co-ed classes. The horizontal axis ranges from a possible score of 0 per cent to a maximum of 100 per cent (never awarded in this type of course). The vertical dashed line at 40 per cent shows the pass mark, while the second vertical dashed line gives the co-ed mean grade. (Note that in the male figures the co-ed mean is for men in a co-ed class, while in the female figures the co-ed mean is for women in a co-ed class.)

First, consider the distributions of scores on the exam, which was mandatory and double-blindly graded. For women in all-female classes, the distribution lies to the right of the more dispersed distribution for women in co-ed classes, and the distributions are significantly different (Mann–Whitney p-value = 0.068). This is not the case for men. Notice, for men in all-male classes, the distribution has a slightly lower variance than for men in co-ed classes, though they are not significantly different (Mann–Whitney p-value = 0.648). Next, we turn to coursework grades, given in the middle of Figure 11.1. For men, there is little difference in the distributions of coursework grades for the treatment and control groups. This contrasts with the situation for women: here, the distribution for women in the treatment group is more right-skewed than it is for the control group.

Finally, we consider the overall end-of-year grades for men and women presented at the bottom of Figure 11.1. Again, we find that there is no significant difference in the distributions for men in co-ed and single-sex classes (Mann–Whitney p-value = 0.543), while the distribution for women in all-female classes is significantly different from that for women in co-ed classes (Mann–Whitney p-value = 0.069). Furthermore, we see that, for women in co-ed classes in particular, the distribution is fatter in the left tail than it is for women in single-sex classes. Thus, inspection of Figure 11.1 reveals that women in the control group (co-ed) are more likely to be found performing poorly than are both women in single-sex classes and all men.[12]

12 While the means were the same for students in co-ed and single-sex classes in Table 11.1, one might worry that they differed at different parts of the distribution and that this could have led to the effects seen in Figure 11.1. To examine this we check the balance across the entire distribution of predicted outcomes in Figure A11.1 and for IQ in particular in Figure A11.2 in the Appendix. There was no significant difference in the distributions of the predicted outcome or the distribution of IQ scores between co-ed and single-sex classes for men or women.

The distributions for women in Figure 11.1 suggest that there may have been a heterogeneous impact of the treatment for women: it appears that females at the lower part of the distribution benefited more from being assigned to an all-female class. To examine if there were differential effects, we follow Barrera-Osorio et al. (2011) and look at predicted versus actual outcomes for students in co-ed and single-sex classes. To predict outcomes, we used the 19 individual variables in Table 11.1 and regressed the exam score on those variables for students in co-ed classes. We did this separately for males and females. Using the estimated equation, we then predicted the exam score for each student and plotted the actual exam score against the predicted score the student achieved. Figure 11.2 shows local polynomial plots of actual versus predicted outcomes. In the graphs, if the predicted and actual scores were the same, they would line up on the 45-degree line.

For males, the predicted and actual scores line up fairly well for men in co-ed or all-male classes between the grades 38 and 61 (over 60 per cent of our sample has grades that fall in this range). Note, crucially, though, that the relationship between predicted and actual exam scores for men in all-male classes does not appear to differ from the relationship between predicted and actual exam scores for men in co-ed classes. This is not the case for females.

In the top right panel of Figure 11.2, we plot the predicted and actual exam scores for women in co-ed and all-female classes. For women in all-female classes who are predicted to score below 50, the actual scores are much higher than the predicted scores. However, for women in all-female classes predicted to score 50 or above, the predicted and actual scores line up in roughly the same fashion as they do for the co-ed classes. This suggests that women who might be expected to perform below average on the exam are benefiting from being in an all-female class.

Similarly, for women in all-female classes, the actual coursework scores are above predicted scores for women expected to be in the lower part of the distribution. This suggests that women who might have been in the bottom half of the coursework distribution are more likely to benefit from the treatment, while there is no effect (differential or otherwise) for men.

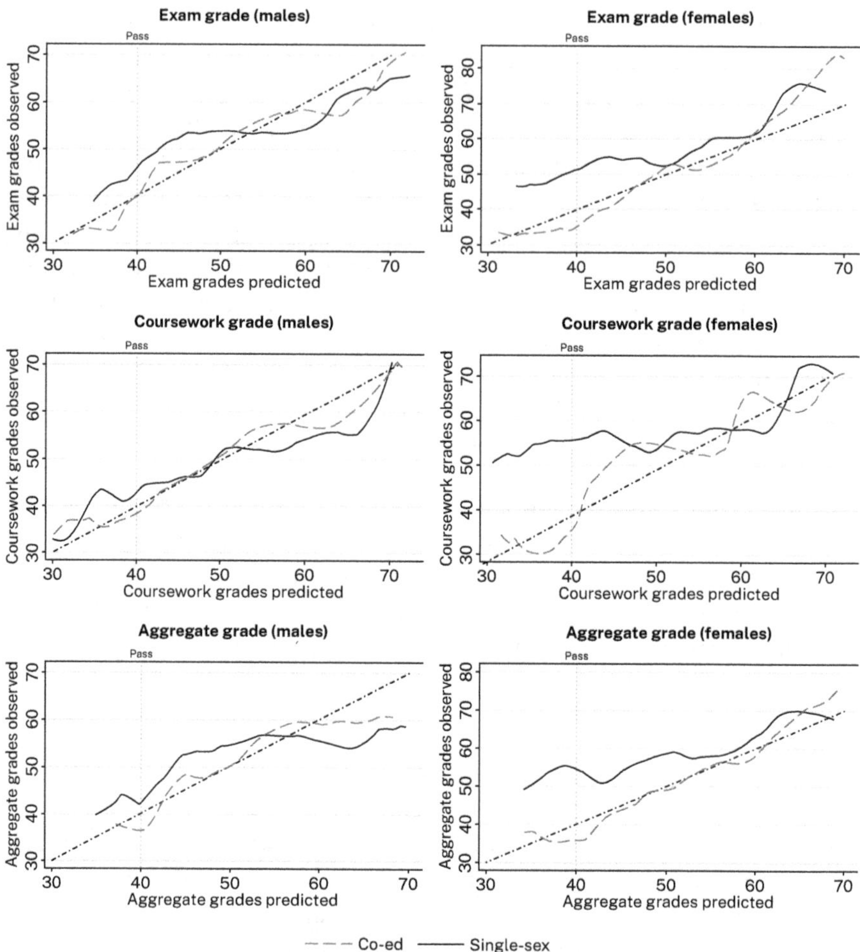

Figure 11.2: Results from local polynomial regressions, bandwidth = 4.18

Finally, we look at the aggregate grades (which can be either only the exam mark or 50:50 coursework and exam), shown at the bottom of Figure 11.2. Here we see some evidence that men may be benefiting from all-male classes at the lower part of the predicted distribution. For women, there is again the clear pattern that we have seen throughout: women at the lower part of the predicted distribution have much higher actual scores than what is predicted if they are assigned to all-female classes. In particular, women who might not have passed Introduction to Economics are benefiting more from the treatment.

Main regression results

Our goal here is to see whether or not the treatment – being in a single-sex class – increases the academic performance of students relative to the control of being in a co-educational class. We look at the impact of the treatment on a number of continuous dependent variables measuring first-year academic performance. However, recall that the marks a student receives in the first year do not affect the type of degree they earn upon graduating. Moreover, a student needs only to get 40 per cent or higher in all first year courses in order to continue her studies. For these reasons, we also report, below, estimates of the effect of single-sex classes on pass rates alone. Indeed, given the heterogeneous effect of the treatment for women suggested by Figure 11.2, we might expect that the effects on the pass rate may be larger than for the mean of the distribution. Finally, we report estimates of the treatment on longer-run outcomes – those in the second and third years, where obtaining scores above the pass mark actually matters for the student's final degree qualification.

Introductory economics scores

Regressions estimating the impact of the treatment on each of our three dependent variables (exam, coursework, aggregate grade) are reported in Table 11.2. All scores examined in Table 11.2 were normalised by the co-ed distribution for that outcome, so the estimated coefficients are expressed in terms of standard deviations. These values are reported at the bottom of each column. The notes at the bottom of Table 11.2 give further details. Standard errors, clustered at the class level, are shown in square brackets. For the OLS regressions, *p*-values for the variables of interest were also calculated using the Cameron et al. (2008) wild bootstrap method since there are only 37 clusters.

The first three columns of Table 11.2 present OLS results for the aggregate score. Column [1] reports estimates from a specification with just two explanatory variables – a single-sex treatment variable taking the value one if the individual is in an all-female or an all-male class, and zero otherwise, and another dummy variable taking the value one for females and zero otherwise. The coefficient of the single-sex treatment dummy is 0.140, and it is statistically significant at the 10 per cent level; aggregate scores were higher, on average, in the single-sex classes than the co-ed classes.

Table 11.2: Effects on Introductory Economics scores

Variables	Aggregate score			Exam score		Coursework score		Did all coursework (=1)	
	[1]	[2]	[3]	[4]	[5]	[6]	[7]	[8]	[9]
Single-sex class (=1)	0.140* [0.073] (0.074)	–	–	–	–	–	–	–	–
All-female (=1)	–	0.252* [0.146] (0.079)	0.243* [0.137] (0.088)	0.246* [0.142] (0.096)	0.258* [0.135] (0.064)	0.252* [0.135] (0.078)	0.108 [0.136] (0.534)	0.093* [0.036]	0.078* [0.032]
All-male (=1)	–	0.080 [0.084] (0.374)	0.041 [0.091] (0.664)	0.081 [0.091] (0.402)	0.015 [0.098] (0.892)	-0.068 [0.089] (0.480)	-0.061 [0.082] (0.538)	0.013 [0.036]	0.013 [0.028]
Female (=1)	0.143* [0.082]	0.046 [0.143]	-0.009 [0.152]	0.016 [0.147]	-0.046 [0.157]	0.133 [0.109]	0.090 [0.108]	0.045 [0.053]	0.034 [0.043]
All observables	No	No	Yes	No	Yes	No	Yes	No	Yes
Estimation method	OLS	OLS	OLS	OLS	OLS	OLS	OLS	Probit	Probit
Co-ed mean	53.70 [17.68]	53.70 [17.68]	53.70 [17.68]	51.36 [19.19]	51.36 [19.19]	50.19 [17.77]	50.19 [17.77]	0.84 [0.37]	0.84 [0.37]
Observations	570	570	570	570	570	570	570	570	570
R^2	0.019	0.021	0.117	0.022	0.106	0.044	0.192	–	–

Notes: *** p<0.01; ** p<0.05; * p<0.1; The mean and standard deviation for students in co-ed classes are presented for outcomes because the dependent variables were normalised by that distribution for the aggregate, exam and coursework scores. Therefore, the coefficients for regressions with those dependent variables are in terms of standard deviations of the distribution of scores for students in co-ed classes. For probit regressions, marginal effects are shown. Standard errors are clustered at the class level and shown in brackets. For the variables of interest, p-values for the coefficients are calculated via the Cameron et al. (2008) wild bootstrap method as well and shown in parentheses (reps = 1000); this could not be used for the probit regressions. Columns [10] and [11] use only the sample of students who turned in all coursework to be graded. Each regression also controls for whether a student is in EC111, but for brevity, it is not shown. The 'all observables' refers to the set of individual and class level controls listed in Table 11.1: IQ raw score; student went to a single-sex high school (=1); age; native language English (=1); white (=1);

student is eldest child (=1); number of siblings; number of sisters; Mother has University Degree (=1); Mother stayed at home (=1); Father has University Degree (=1); Born in EU (=1); The Big Five; TA female (=1); Class before 2 pm (=1); Class at End of Week (=1); and Class size (and its square both interacted with EC111 since there were different caps on class size for the two courses). Dummy variables were used for any missing values.

Column [2] reports estimates from a specification that differs from column [1] in that we now disaggregate the single-sex-class variable into separate all-female and all-male dummies. The estimated coefficients show that the impact of the treatment on aggregate scores is working through the all-female-class type, where the coefficient is 0.252 and is statistically significant at the 10 per cent level. This is interpreted as follows: being assigned to an all-female class leads to a 0.252 standard deviation increase in aggregate score.[13] The all-male coefficient is 0.08 and is not statistically significant. Analogously, the female coefficient has also diminished in magnitude and lost statistical significance (in comparison to the estimate in column [1]).

Column [3] is an expanded specification that we ran to explore the robustness of the treatment-variable estimates. It includes the full set of explanatory variables – all the individual and class-level variables listed in Table 11.1. The estimated coefficient on the all-female treatment variable changes little across the specifications in columns [2] and [3]. The all-male and female coefficients remain statistically insignificant, estimated in column [3], just as they were in column [2] – our preferred specification.

Columns [4] and [5] of Table 11.2 present the OLS results for exam score. The specification in column [4] is the analogue to column [2], while column [5] is the analogue to column [3]. Across both specifications, the all-female coefficients are of similar magnitude and statistically significant at the 10 per cent level. The all-male and all-female coefficients remain very imprecisely estimated across these specifications too. Being in an all-female class has a positive and significant effect for females.

Next, in columns [6] and [7], we report estimates of similar specifications for coursework score. The estimated all-female coefficient in column [6] is roughly the same in the analogous specifications in columns [2] and [4]. However, in column [7] – which includes all predetermined variables – the estimated coefficient for all-female is no longer significant, and the point estimate has decreased by more than half. Since the gender and identity

13 That represents an 8.3 per cent increase in the overall score for females in an all-female class. Also, as shown in Table A11.2, there was no significant difference in the all-female effect for students in EC100 and EC111 and if we control for GTA fixed effects the results are the same.

of the student are known by the TA marking the coursework, and the student may choose not to turn in the assignments, the grade given by TAs could be influenced by this knowledge and behaviour. Furthermore, not all students take the coursework seriously, as indicated by the fact that many do not complete the set of four pieces of coursework. These could be possible reasons for the lack of robustness of the all-female estimate on coursework. To explore some reasons, we next look at the probability of doing all coursework and the average score if one did all coursework.

In column [8], we see that women assigned to an all-female class are more likely to do all the coursework assignments. When all predetermined variables are added in column [9], the all-female coefficient stays significant and positive and is only slightly smaller in magnitude: women in all-female classes are, roughly, 8 percentage points, or 10 per cent, more likely to do all coursework. Since we do not have a robust effect on the coursework score, all we can say is that, for women, the treatment is associated with a greater probability of doing all the coursework.[14]

To summarise, Table 11.2 shows that students in single-sex classes did better than their counterparts assigned to co-ed classes; the result is driven by women assigned to all-female classes. Females in all-female classes did a quarter of a standard deviation better in their end-of-the-year grade than females in co-ed classes. This effect is primarily driven by the 0.246 standard deviation increase in the exam scores for women in all-female classes, as there is no robust effect on coursework scores. Being assigned to an all-female class did cause females to do more of the coursework assignments, though; they were 10 per cent more likely to have done all assignments.

First-year pass rates

As already noted, a student needs to get 40 per cent or higher in first year courses in order to continue their studies. For this reason, and given the heterogeneous results suggested by the descriptive analysis above, we also estimate the single-sex-class effect on pass rates in Introductory Economics, since this is the margin that matters for continuation. Our main dependent variable of interest is whether or not a student passed the Introductory Economics course. These results are shown in Table 11.3.

14 In the last two columns of Table A11.2 we look at the effect on coursework scores for students that did all the coursework. This is a selected sample and we find no effect being assigned to a single-sex class.

Table 11.3: Effects on passing the course and year

Variables	Passed course (=1)		% of students passed		Scored 70 and above (=1)		Passed year (=1)	
	[1]	[2]	[3]	[4]	[5]	[6]	[7]	[8]
All-female (=1)	0.067** [0.031]	0.060** [0.025]	0.063** [0.027]	0.067** [0.030]	0.014 [0.067]	0.035 [0.056]	0.082** [0.038]	0.069* [0.036]
All-male (=1)	0.034 [0.029]	0.036 [0.025]	0.050 [0.031]	0.084** [0.035]	−0.015 [0.042]	−0.014 [0.043]	0.015 [0.030]	0.010 [0.033]
Female (=1)	−0.019 [0.040]	−0.041 [0.045]	–	–	0.056 [0.054]	0.038 [0.058]	−0.000 [0.051]	−0.011 [0.054]
Individual-level controls	No	Yes	No	No	No	Yes	No	Yes
Class-level controls	No	Yes	No	Yes	No	Yes	No	No
Estimation method	Probit	Probit	OLS	OLS	Probit	Probit	Probit	Probit
Co-ed mean	0.87 [0.34]	0.87 [0.34]	0.86 [0.09]	0.86 [0.09]	0.19 [0.40]	0.19 [0.40]	0.81 [0.39]	0.81 [0.39]
Observations	570	570	37	37	570	570	570	570
R^2	–	–	0.116	0.274	–	–	–	–

Notes: *** $p<0.01$; ** $p<0.05$; * $p<0.1$; The mean and standard deviation for students in co-ed classes are presented where stated. For probit regressions, marginal effects are shown. Standard errors are clustered at the class level and shown in brackets. Regressions in columns [1]–[6] also control for whether a student is in EC111, but, for brevity, it is not shown. 'Individual-level controls' refer to the set of individual controls listed in Table 11.1: IQ raw score; student went to a single-sex high school (=1); age; native language English (=1); white (=1); student is eldest child (=1); number of siblings; number of sisters; Mother has university degree (=1); Mother stayed at home (=1); Father has university degree (=1); Born in EU (=1); The Big Five. 'Class-level controls' refer to the set of class level controls listed in Table 11.1: TA female (=1); Class before 2 pm (=1); Class at end of week (=1); and Class size (and its square both interacted with EC111 since there were different caps on class size for the two courses). Dummy variables were used for any missing values.

Columns [1]–[4] provide strong evidence of a positive effect of single-sex classes for females; females assigned to all-female classes are more likely to pass the Introductory Economics course than females assigned to co-ed classes. Column [1] shows that women in all-female classes are 6.7 percentage points more likely to pass their Introductory Economics course than those assigned to co-ed classes. For all students in co-ed classes in the introductory courses, the percentage passing was 87 per cent, so the increase of 6.7 percentage points represents a 7.7 per cent increase in the pass rate for females. That is a large effect, given that no additional resources were needed. When we add, in column [2], predetermined individual-level and class-level controls from Table 11.1, the point estimate changes little.

Since our field experiment takes place at the class level, we also report class-level regressions in columns [3] and [4] of the percentage of students in a class passing. Here the number of observations is 37. Column [3] reports the parsimonious specification while column [4] adds predetermined class-level controls. Column [3] shows that the pass rate for all-female classes was 6.3 percentage points higher than for co-ed classes. When the class-level variables are included, there is only a small increase in the magnitude of this coefficient. Indeed, the point estimates are very similar across these four columns, showing that women in all-female classes are between 6.0 and 6.7 percentage points more likely to pass Introductory Economics than their counterparts assigned to co-ed classes. The similarity in the magnitude of the estimated effect of being in an all-female class across all four specifications shows we have a robust estimate of the effect of being in a single-sex class for females.

The pass mark of 40 per cent is at the lower end of the distribution. Figure 11.2 suggested that this was where assignment to an all-female class had the biggest effect. Nonetheless, we wished to further explore, using regression techniques, what was happening towards the top of the mark distribution. We therefore estimated the effect of class type on the probability of obtaining a first-class mark in Introductory Economics. (In the UK, a first-class mark is 70 per cent and over, and in our sample, 110 students, or 19 per cent, achieved this.) These results are displayed in columns [5] and [6] of Table 11.3. Both specifications support what was suggested in Figure 11.2, namely that single-sex classes did not affect the top of the distribution.

Finally, we investigated if the treatment in Introductory Economics had a spillover effect on our subjects' first year performance overall, proxied by its effects on passing the entire year. These estimates are reported in columns [7] and [8] of Table 11.3. Both specifications show that women in an all-female class for Introductory Economics had a significantly greater probability of passing the entire year, relative to women in co-ed classes. No similar effect was found for men in all-male classes.[15] A student must pass all their courses in the first year to progress into the second year, and being assigned to an all-female class increases a woman's chance of passing her Introductory Economics class.[16] Hence, perhaps unsurprisingly, a female assigned to an all-female class is more likely to pass the entire year and be allowed to progress into the second year. This is important because it means a student is not allocating effort towards the Introduction to Economics and away from other courses.

Overall, the results in Tables 11.2 and 11.3 provide a compelling picture of the effect of single-sex classes on first year outcomes. Females in all-female classes for Introductory Economics are more likely to pass their first year course than females in co-ed classes; the effect of being in an all-female class is much stronger at the lower end of the distribution, and the effects are present even in the double-blind marked exams that are reviewed by external examiners. Thus, there is strong evidence that women studying Introductory Economics in a co-educational university can benefit from being in an all-female class. But are these short-run effects that last only for one year, or do they have a longer-run effect? To this issue we now turn.

15 Columns [1]–[3] have a positive insignificant point estimate for the all-male coefficient, but in column [4] it is significant. The change in significance is driven by an increase in the point estimate, not by an increase in precision. Therefore, we could lack the power to identify a small, positive effect of single-sex education for males (Park et al. (2012) shows a positive effect at the secondary school level). Figure 11.2 shows that low-skilled males may benefit (but that high-skilled males might be harmed). Therefore, with only one significant estimate in Table 11.3 and mixed suggestions in Figure 11.2, we cannot say we have conclusive evidence that single-sex classes are beneficial for males.

16 Introduction to Economics is the core course for Economics students and one of the two core courses for Business students. All other courses in the first year (for example, Methods of Economic Analysis) – which are all required and prescribed by the departments – build on the material in EC100 and EC111. Therefore, Introduction to Economics is the main gateway course, and if a student cannot pass it, then it is unlikely she will pass the other courses. This is one reason that the point estimate on all-females in column [7] is potentially larger than for the Introduction to Economics course itself; the material learned helps students in other classes. However, with all controls (our preferred specification), as shown in column [8], the point estimate for passing the year is the same as for Introduction to Economics itself.

Longer-run academic effects

We begin with a descriptive, graphical analysis of students' academic performance after the first year. Figure 11.3 displays the distributions of the students' final grades on graduation. The final degree grade is determined by a weighting of 40 per cent of the second-year average and 60 per cent of the third-year average grade. The distributions, shown separately for men and women, are disaggregated by treatment and control groups. The grades for the overall degree form the basis for the degree classification that each student receives at graduation.

The distributions for women in single-sex classes are less left-skewed than for their counterparts in co-ed classes. This is in contrast to the male distributions.[17] Recall that these distributions are only for students who actually continued in the university; therefore, the results are to be interpreted with caution since the treatment also had an effect on the probability of a female continuing with her studies. As this selection is likely negative, the results suggest that the effects of treatment carry over throughout the second and third years.

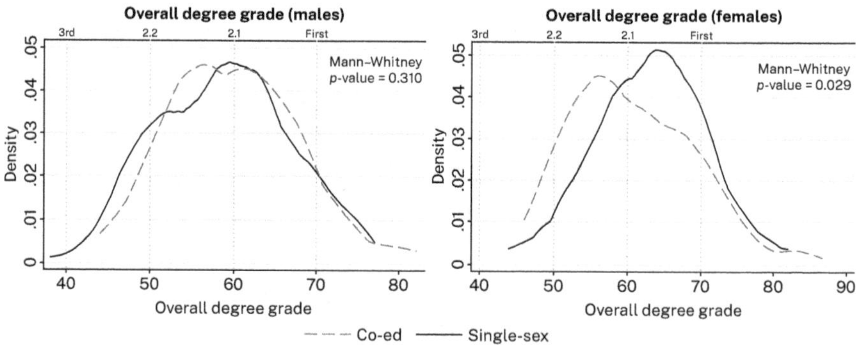

Figure 11.3: Distribution of final degree grade by gender

17 Figure A11.3 shows the average grade distributions for students in the second and third year of university. In the second year, females assigned to all-female classes in their first year Introductory Economics classes (and who are now only in co-ed classes and lectures) were doing better than those who were assigned to co-ed classes. The difference in the distributions is significant (Mann–Whitney *p*-value = 0.003). This is not the case for males. In the third year, the distribution for females assigned to all-female classes still lies clearly to the right of that for females assigned to co-ed classes, although the statistical significance is reduced to the 10 per cent level (Mann–Whitney *p*-value = 0.101).

Figure 11.3 appears to show that the treatment is having an effect on the overall degree score. However, the results in the figure cannot be interpreted as causal because the sample is changing from year to year: only 505 of the 570 students are left in the second year, and only 487 are still enrolled and earn a grade in the third year; and the treatment had an effect on the probability of a female continuing. However, the bias introduced in the sample selection is very likely working against us in finding an effect. This is because women assigned to all-female classes who now continue in their studies are the marginal ones who scored lower in the first year.[18] To examine the causal effect of our treatment on later outcomes, though, we will look at degree receipt.

We have information on whether a student earned a degree and, if they did, the classification of their degree. An advantage of looking at the degree classification of students is that we can use all observations that were originally treated; that is, we have complete outcome data for all randomised subjects. Thus, we can get at the causal effect of being assigned to a single-sex class on one's degree outcome. In the UK, degree class is the most important higher educational outcome, with degrees classified into one of the following categories: a first class degree (with an overall average of 70 per cent+); an upper second (60–69 per cent); a lower second (50–59 per cent); or a third (40–49 per cent). Scores below 40 per cent are a failure. 'Good' degrees are regarded as those that are upper second and above. With such a degree, students can carry on to postgraduate work and get a good job.[19]

The degree outcomes for our 2010 cohort of economics students are illustrated in Figure 11.4, which presents differences in degree classification for single-sex and co-ed classes. Once more, the raw data suggest that single-sex classes have benefitted women, who are more likely to get a good degree than their co-ed counterparts. Moreover, they are less likely to get no degree.

18 Table A11.1 shows regression results that further explore the differences in the distributions shown in Figure 11.3.

19 In the UK the primary hurdle to getting a graduate job is earning a degree classified as an upper second or first (see Feng and Graetz (2017) or Smith et al. (2000)). A 'good degree' also means that a student will earn much more over her lifetime in the labor force. Getting a lower second degree means a student can continue studies in some MSc programs or enter some graduate positions but her options will be limited.

Table 11.4: Effect on degree classification

Variables	First-class degree (=1)		First or 2.1 degree (=1)		Third-class degree or fail (=1)		Fail (=1)	
	[1]	[2]	[3]	[4]	[5]	[6]	[7]	[8]
All-female (=1)	0.051 [0.042]	0.084** [0.042]	0.299*** [0.072]	0.280*** [0.073]	−0.141*** [0.034]	−0.119*** [0.034]	−0.125*** [0.023]	−0.104*** [0.021]
All-male (=1)	0.001 [0.040]	−0.002 [0.039]	0.018 [0.052]	0.009 [0.046]	−0.001 [0.036]	0.023 [0.031]	−0.034 [0.031]	−0.019 [0.028]
Female (=1)	0.084* [0.048]	0.065 [0.044]	−0.003 [0.079]	0.011 [0.085]	−0.022 [0.046]	−0.010 [0.045]	−0.018 [0.041]	−0.014 [0.039]
Individual-level controls	No	Yes	No	Yes	No	Yes	No	Yes
Co-ed mean	0.13 [0.34]	0.13 [0.34]	0.46 [0.50]	0.46 [0.50]	0.23 [0.42]	0.23 [0.42]	0.18 [0.39]	0.18 [0.39]
Observations	566	566	566	566	566	566	566	566

Notes: *** $p<0.01$; ** $p<0.05$; * $p<0.1$; Marginal Effects are reported. The mean and standard deviation for males in co-ed classes are presented for outcomes. Standard errors are clustered at the class level and shown in brackets. The 'individual-level controls' refers to the set of individual controls listed in Table 11.1: IQ raw score; student went to a single-sex high school (=1); age; native language English (=1); white (=1); student is eldest child (=1); number of siblings; number of sisters; Mother has university degree (=1); Mother stayed at home (=1); Father has university degree (=1); Born in EU (=1); The Big Five. Dummy variables were used for any missing values.

Table 11.5: Potential channels and behavioural changes

Variables	TA score		Did all coursework (=1)	Proportion of classes attended	Passed course (=1)	Passed course (=1)
	[1]	[2]	[3]	[4]	[5]	[6]
All-female (=1)	0.184 [0.631]	−0.480 [0.480]	0.093** [0.036]	0.243** [0.115] (0.044)	0.028 [0.031]	–
All-male (=1)	0.120 [0.404]	−0.148 [0.483]	0.013 [0.036]	0.050 [0.137] (0.666)	0.033* [0.020]	–
Female (=1)	–	–	0.045 [0.053]	0.159 [0.119]	−0.043 [0.042]	−0.055 [0.054]
Did all coursework (=1)	–	–	–	–	0.345*** [0.051]	0.362*** [0.021]
Proportion of classes attended	–	–	–	–	0.137*** [0.051]	0.032 [0.021]
TA fixed effects	No	Yes	No	No	No	No
Estimation method	OLS	OLS	Probit	OLS	Probit	Probit
Co-ed mean	4.22 [0.29]	4.22 [0.29]	0.84 [0.37]	0.59 [0.24]	0.87 [0.34]	0.87 [0.34]
Observations	37	37	570	570	570	274
R^2	0.074	0.602	–	0.025	–	–

Notes: *** $p<0.01$; ** $p<0.05$; * $p<0.1$. The mean and standard deviation for students in co-ed classes are presented, where stated. TA scores and the proportion of classes attended were normalised by the respective distribution. Therefore, the coefficients for the regressions in columns [1], [2], and [5] are in terms of standard deviations of the distribution for students in co-ed classes. For probit regressions, marginal effects are shown. Standard errors are clustered at the class level and shown in brackets. In column [5], variables of interest p-values for the coefficients are calculated via the Cameron et al. (2008) wild bootstrap method as well and shown in parentheses (reps = 1000). Column [6] only uses students from co-ed classes. All regressions control for whether a student is in EC111, but, for brevity, it is not shown.

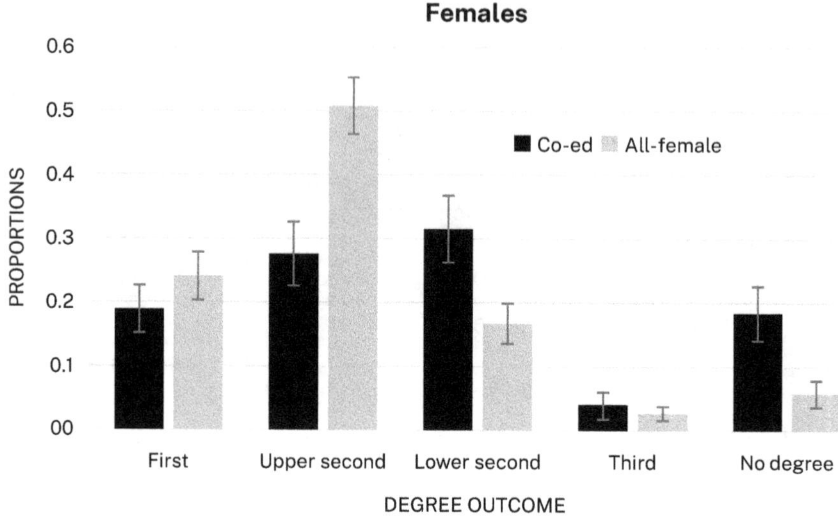

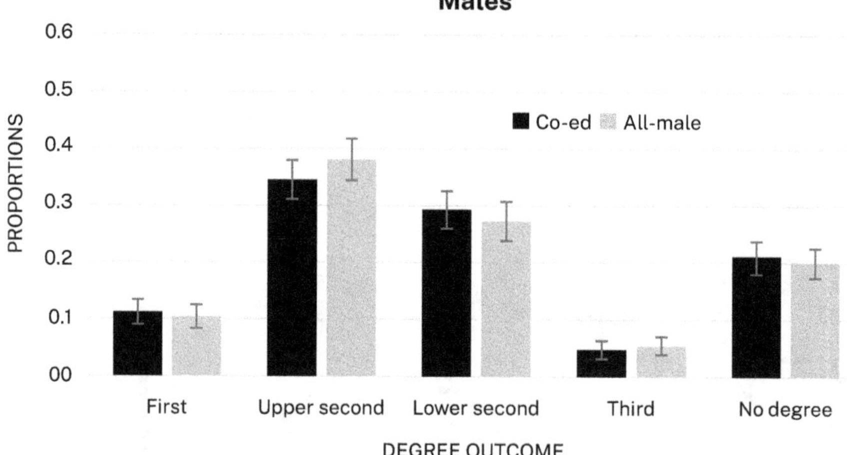

Figure 11.4: Degree classification

In Table 11.4, we estimate the causal effect of being assigned to a single- sex class in one's first year on one's degree outcome.[20] Table 11.4 presents the results from regressing gender and class type on the degree classification variables; the standard errors are once more clustered at the class level.[21]

In columns [1] and [2], we report estimates of the probability of obtaining a first class degree. In columns [3] and [4], we report estimates of the probability of obtaining either a first class or an upper-second class degree; here, the dependent variable takes the value one for a first-class or upper-second class degree, and zero otherwise. We see that women in all-female classes were significantly more likely to be awarded a 'good degree' (classified as either a first or second class, first division) than their counterparts in the co-ed classes. These estimates confirm the findings from the unconditional distributions of Figure 11.4. For men, the all-male class effect is statistically insignificant.

The estimated effect of being assigned to an all-female class in first year is a 28 percentage point increase in the likelihood of getting a 'good degree.' That is a 61 per cent increase for females. This means that the intervention had a very large impact on the employability of females graduating from Essex.

Finally, columns [5] and [6] of Table 11.4 give marginal effects from the estimation of the probability of obtaining a third-class degree or a fail, while the probability of failing is shown in column [6]. In both probit models, women in all-female classes are significantly less likely to be in that degree classification than their counterparts in the current classes. Indeed, being in an all-female class means a woman is 10.4 percentage points less likely to fail out of university; that is, a 57 per cent decrease in the likelihood that she does not get a degree.

In summary, we find that the effects of assignment to an all-female class carried on well into final degree grades and final degree classification. Women assigned to all-female classes are more likely to get 'good degrees' and are less likely to fail out of university. Since access to postgraduate study and to good jobs in the UK is affected by degree class, the effects are likely to be even longer-run than simply affecting degree classification.

20 We have 566 observations for our degree receipt analysis. We lose four students who had extenuating circumstances and were allowed additional time to study towards their degrees. Those students, therefore, cannot be classified into achieving a specific degree classification or no degree because they are technically still enrolled at the university or could choose to re-enrol after the 'extenuating circumstances' have been resolved. We did run the regressions where we allocated the four students to having each type of degree and our results did not change.

21 We also estimated class-level regressions where the dependent variable was the proportion in class who got the particular degree classification and found the same results as those reported in this chapter.

Behavioural changes and potential channels

In this section, we explore the mechanisms that might be driving the effects of single-sex classes on females. In particular, we focus on whether the treatment was associated with potentially grade-enhancing changes in student behaviour – such as attending classes or doing all the assignments – and we also examine if the TAs might have taught women assigned to all-female classes differently.

Columns [1] and [2] in Table 11.5 examine whether there is evidence that TAs might have changed their teaching style in single-sex classes. At the end of the academic year, before students take their exams or know their overall grades, students rate their TAs on a scale from 1 to 5. A score of 5 means a student strongly agrees that 'Overall the classes were taught well' and a score of 1 means a student strongly disagrees with the statement. Column [1] shows that TAs teaching all-female classes did not get a higher score than TAs who taught co-ed or all-male classes.[22] However, since no TA only taught single-sex classes, we can include TA fixed effects to see if a TA was given a higher score when teaching a single-sex class rather than a co-ed class. This is done in column [2]; TAs did not receive any higher score when they taught a single-sex class (either all-female or all-male).[23]

Recall that students in the first year are given the opportunity to do coursework assignments, which can help their grade through the 'max-rule' as described earlier. In column [3], we replicate the results from column [8] of Table 11.2 and show that females assigned to an all-female class are 9.3 percentage points more likely to do all the coursework (an 11 per cent increase). Besides coursework, though, attendance in the classes taught by TAs could help a student learn the material better and be better prepared for the exam. As we see in column [4], being in an all-female class increases attendance by 0.243 standard deviations of the co-ed mean attendance. Thus, an obvious question is: could the single-sex effect for females be explained by the choice to do more optional coursework and the increase in attendance?

22 The scores are normalised by the co-ed class mean shown at the bottom of the columns. Thus, as before, the coefficients are in terms of standard errors of that distribution

23 One may question if the TA score is correlated with the quality of instruction. We explored this and found that students in classes where TAs received higher scores were more likely to pass the course and that the all-female coefficient stays the same.

To see how the changed behaviour of a student is associated with passing, we include both doing all coursework and attendance in column [5].[24] The all-female coefficient is just about half of what it is in our preferred specification from Table 11.3. This means, even given the biases associated with controlling for attendance and doing all the coursework (both of which were positively affected by the treatment), only half the effect of the all-female coefficient can be explained away. Finally, we use only the co-ed population in column [6] and estimate the effect of doing all coursework and attending classes on the likelihood of passing. Using these estimates, we also find that the behavioural changes can explain only about half of the estimated effect of being assigned to an all-female class.[25] This suggests that female student effort may be an important mechanism driving the effect of all-female classes, but that a pure effort explanation must go beyond simply turning in homework and showing up for class.[26]

Conclusion

This chapter reports the results of a field experiment designed to examine the effects of single-sex classes on the performance of first-year university students in a highly ranked and publicly funded economics department. The novel features of our design are twofold. First, we randomly assigned students to a single-sex or a co-ed class environment, and hence selection is not an issue. Second, we implemented this random assignment to single-sex classes in the economics faculty of a co-educational university.

24 Table 11.5 focuses on the pass rate. Table A11.3 looks at how doing all coursework and attending classes also affects exam scores and degree classifications. As with the pass rates, the effect of intermediate outcomes on aggregate and exam scores in the first year can only explain, at most, half of the all-female effect. With regard to degree classification, the intermediate outcomes can explain none of the effect of the all-female impact.

25 Column [6] shows doing all coursework is associated with a 0.362 increase in the pass rate and that increasing attendance by one standard deviation is associated with a 0.032 increase in the pass rate. Being assigned to an all-female class increased the likelihood of doing all coursework by 0.093 and of attending classes by 0.243 standard deviations. That suggests the behavioural changes account for $0.362 \times 0.093 + 0.032 \times 0.243 = 0.04$, which is <60 per cent of the effect of our preferred specification in Table 11.3.

26 Also, the coefficient on all-male is significant now (at the 10 per cent level). In this case it is due to the fact that the estimate has become more precise. Given that being in an all-male class has no effect on doing all coursework or attendance, then controlling for those two aspects is equivalent to saturating the regression and could give us more power to estimate the effect of single-sex education on males. However, this is the only case where the all-male point estimate was similar to other specifications (as in columns [6] and [7]) and became significant when we controlled for more observable factors.

We examined whether single-sex classes within a co-educational environment have an effect on female test scores, pass rates, and continuing to study at university, as well as longer-run outcomes such as degree class. We found that females assigned to all-female classes score a quarter of a standard deviation higher in their Introductory Economics class and are 7.3 per cent more likely to pass the course. Furthermore, the benefits to females of single-sex classes appear to carry over past the first year and lead to a 57 per cent decrease in the likelihood that a female does not graduate with a degree in economics and a 61 per cent increase in the likelihood that she graduates with a 'good degree.'

These results all occurred with no additional expenditure on the part of the university. Typically, programs that increase female pass rates or improve student performance are much more costly. For example, a study on the Achievement Awards demonstration in Israel by Angrist and Lavy (2009) found that females were more likely to earn a high school matriculation certificate if offered $1,500 for completion, but that men were not any more likely to earn the qualification. While comparing the costs and benefits of programs based on different outcome variables is not easy, a program like ours that causes a female to be 7.7 per cent more likely to pass a course, score a standard deviation better overall in classes, and leads to a 57 per cent decrease in the likelihood she doesn't graduate with an economics-based degree at no additional cost is rather extraordinary.

Our study focuses on only a few aspects of single-sex classes – their effects on first-year pass rates, grades across years and degree class. While these outcomes are likely to influence wages and job prospects for students, other factors that we are not examining – such as socialisation – could also play a role in labour market outcomes.[27] Therefore, while we find large positive effects of single-sex first year classes for females studying economics, we wish to emphasise that more research is needed. For instance, it is not clear if more than one hour of single-sex education in a co-educational institution is going to be more beneficial or if fully gender-segregated education would produce better results.[28]

27 Booth et al. (2014), using a different experimental subsample, report how risk attitudes evolved across the first eight weeks of the Introductory Economics course, and showed how women in single-sex classes modified their risk preferences over time.

28 Our results are not directly comparable with those of Oosterbeek and van Ewijk (2014), who conducted a randomised experiment for first year undergraduate students of economics and business at Amsterdam University. Their treatment was the share of females in the classroom (which they manipulated to be between 0.14 and 0.51). They do not find any effect of proportion female on individuals' outcomes. In contrast, we have a female class-ratio of either 1 or 0. When the ratio is 1 (single-sex class) we observe a positive effect on females.

We also emphasise that our analysis conditions on women who selected to study economics at a top-rated university department, and it is possible that selectivity of subject area and/or institution might be a bigger margin driving gender gaps than the one we have explored. Nonetheless, the margin that we are examining in our chapter shows that persistence is still important even among students at a selective university, and this is of considerable policy relevance. For example, Arcidiacono et al. (2016) show, using data for minorities in STEM fields at the University of California campuses, that minorities entering STEM programs have lower persistence rates despite the fact that they would have graduated had they attended different schools.

The research on schools summarised by Halpern et al. (2011) suggests that having all instruction done in a single-sex environment has no positive effect or could be harmful. In contrast, we have shown that single-sex classes within a broader co-educational environment benefit females in a subject area where women are in the minority. However, will there be benefits for women studying in subject areas where females are in the majority? Will the benefits of single-sex classes be even greater when women are even more of a minority? Will men benefit from single-sex classes if they are in the minority? Clearly, more research is necessary to establish if there is an optimal amount of education in single-sex classes that is beneficial for students, and in what other contexts females or males might benefit.

Since we do not yet fully understand the mechanism driving our findings, there is a worry that expansion of our treatment could lead to unintended consequences, as found in a quite different context by the intervention reported in Carrell and West (2010). For instance, while students did not notice the few single-sex classes in this study, if the experiment were expanded and all classes in Introductory Economics were single-sex, they would surely notice this expanded policy. Nevertheless, any extension of our treatment should further explore the underlying mechanisms, and we hope that further studies will replicate and expand on our research in order to shed more light on this important issue.

Acknowledgements

This chapter was first published as Booth, A.L., Cardona Sosa, L., and Nolen, P. (2018). 'Do single-sex classes affect academic achievement? An experiment in a co-educational university', *Journal of Public Economics*, 168:109–26. doi.org/10.1016/j.jpubeco.2018.08.016.

The experiment reported in the paper was conducted at the University of Essex, whose Ethics Committee provided approval. An earlier version of this chapter appeared as an IZA Discussion Paper No 7207. We thank the anonymous referees for their comments on an earlier draft, and we are particularly grateful to the editor for his many helpful suggestions.

For helpful comments on an earlier version of this chapter, we thank the editor Jonah Rockoff, two anonymous referees, and seminar participants at the economics departments of the Paris School of Economics, The Australian National University, Glasgow University, the University of Reading, Heidelberg University, and the University of Essex.

References

Angrist, J., and Lavy, V. (2009). 'The effects of high stakes high school achievement awards: Evidence from a randomized trial', *American Economic Review*, 99(4): 301–331. doi.org/10.1257/aer.99.4.1384.

Annelli, M., and Giovanni, P. (2013). 'The long-run effects of high-school class gender composition', NBER Working Paper No. 18744.

Arcidiacono, P., Aucejo, E.M., and Hotz, V.J. (2016). 'University difference in the graduation of minorities in STEM fields: Evidence from California', *American Economic Review*, 106(3):525–562. doi.org/10.1257/aer.20130626.

Barrera-Osorio, F., Bertrand, M., Linden, L.L., and Perez-Calle, F. (2011). 'Improving the design of conditional transfer programs: Evidence from a randomized education experiment in Colombia', *American Economic Journal: Applied Economics*, 3(2):167–195. doi.org/10.1257/app.3.2.167.

Booth, A.L., and Nolen, P.J. (2012a). 'Choosing to compete: How different are girls and boys?', *Journal of Economic Behavior& Organization*, 81(2):542–555. doi.org/10.1016/j.jebo.2011.07.018.

Booth, A.L., and Nolen, P.J. (2012b). 'Gender differences in risk behaviour: Does nurture matter?', *The Economic Journal*, 122(558):F56–F78. doi.org/10.1111/j.1468-0297.2011.02480.x.

Booth, A.L., Cardona Sosa, L., and Nolen, P.J. (2014). 'Gender differences in risk aversion: Do single-sex environments affect their development?', *Journal of Economic Behavior & Organization*, 99:126–154. doi.org/10.1016/j.jebo.2013.12.017.

Cameron, C., Gelbach, J., and Miller, D. (2008). 'Bootstrap-based improvements for inference with clustered errors', *The Review of Economics and Statistics*, 90(3):414–427. doi.org/10.1162/rest.90.3.414.

Carrell, S., and West, J. (2010). 'Does professor quality matter? Evidence from random assignment of students to professors', *Journal of Political Economy*, 118(3):409–432. doi.org/10.1086/653808.

Cohen, G., Garcia, J., Apfel, N., and Master, A. (2006). 'Reducing the racial achievement gap: A social-psychological intervention', *Science*, 313(5791):1307–1310. doi.org/10.1126/science.1128317.

Eisenkopf, G., Hessami, Z., Fischbacher, U., and Ursprung, H. (2015). 'Academic performance and single-sex schooling: Evidence from a natural experiment in Switzerland', *Journal of Economic Behavior & Organization*, 115:123–143. doi.org/10.1016/j.jebo.2014.08.004.

Feng, A., and Graetz, G. (2017). 'A question of degree: The effects of degree class on labor market outcomes', *Economics of Education Review*, 61:140–161. doi.org/10.1016/j.econedurev.2017.07.003.

Gist, M.E., and Mitchell, T.R. (1992). 'Self-efficacy: A theoretical analysis of Its determinants and malleability', *The Academy of Management Review*, 17(2):183–211. doi.org/10.2307/258770.

Halpern, D., Eliot, L., Bigler, R., Fabes, R., Hanish, L., Hyde, J., Liben, L., and Martin, C. (2011). 'The pseudoscience of single-sex schooling', *Science*, 333(6050):1706–1707. doi.org/10.1126/science.1205031.

Independent Schools Council (ISC). (2014). *ISC 2014 Census Report*. London: Independent Schools Council.

Jackson, C.K. (2012). 'Single-sex schools, student achievement, and course selection: Evidence from rule-based student assignments in Trinidad and Tobago', *Journal of Public Economics*, 96(1–2):173–187. doi.org/10.1016/j.jpubeco.2011.09.002.

Lavy, V. (2008). 'Do gender stereotypes reduce girls' or boys' human capital outcomes? Evidence from a natural experiment', *Journal of Public Economics*, 92(10–11):2083–2105. doi.org/10.1016/j.jpubeco.2008.02.009.

Lavy, V., and Schlosser, A. (2011). 'Mechanisms and impacts of gender peer effects at school', *American Economic Journal: Applied Economics*, 3(2):1–33. doi.org/10.1257/app.3.2.1.

Long, M.C., and Conger, D. (2013). 'Gender sorting across K-12 schools in the United States', *American Journal of Education*, 119(3):349–372. doi.org/10.1086/669853.

Miguel, T., and Kremer, M. (2004). 'Worms: Identifying impacts on education and health in the presence of treatment externalities', *Econometrica*, 72(1):159–217. doi.org/10.1111/j.1468-0262.2004.00481.x.

Morrison, N. (30 April, 2014). 'Single-sex education belongs in the 21st century'. *Forbes*. Available at: www.forbes.com/sites/nickmorrison/2014/04/30/single-sex-education-belongs-in-the-21st-century/#1c41fcd030bd.

National Academy of Sciences. (2006). *Beyond Bias and Barriers: Fulfilling the Potential of Women in Academic Science and Engineering*. Washington, DC: National Academies Press.

Oosterbeek, H., and van Ewijk, R. (2014). 'Gender peer effects in university: Evidence from a randomized experiment', *Economics of Education Review*, 38:51–63. doi.org/10.1016/j.econedurev.2013.11.002.

Park, H., Behrman, J., and Choi, J. (2012). 'Causal effects of single-sex schools on college entrance exams and college attendance: Random assignment in Seoul high schools', *Demography*, 50(2):447–469. doi.org/10.1007/s13524-012-0157-1.

Schneeweis, N., and Zweimüller, M. (2012). 'Girls, girls, girls: Gender composition and female school choice', *Economics of Education Review*, 31(4):482–500. doi.org/10.1016/j.econedurev.2011.11.002.

Smith, J., McKnight, A., and Naylor, R. (2000). 'Graduate employability: Policy and performance in higher education in the UK', *The Economic Journal*, 110(464):F382–F411. doi.org/10.1111/1468-0297.00546.

Smithers, A., and Robinson, P. (2006). *The Paradox of Single-Sex and Co-Educational Schooling*. Buckingham: Carmichael Press.

Spencer, S.J., Steele, C.M., and Quinn, D.M. (1999). 'Stereotype threat and women's math performance', *Journal of Experimental Social Psychology*, 35(1):4–28. doi.org/10.1006/jesp.1998.1373.

Steele, C.M. (1997). 'A threat in the air: how stereotypes shape intellectual identity and performance', *American Psychologist*, 52(6):613–629. doi.org/10.1037/0003-066X.52.6.613.

Steele, C., Spencer, S., and Aronson, J. (2002). 'Contending with group image: The psychology of stereotype and social identity threat', *Advances in Experimental Social Psychology*, 34:379–440. doi.org/10.1016/S0065-2601(02)80009-0.

Appendix

Table A11.1: Effect on average scores in the second and third years, along with the overall degree average

Variables	Second-year average		Third-year average		Overall degree average	
	[1]	[2]	[3]	[4]	[5]	[6]
All-female (=1)	0.410** [0.173] (0.018)	0.401** [0.159] (0.026)	0.201 [0.158] (0.220)	0.189 [0.154] (0.250)	0.290* [0.169] (0.098)	0.286 [0.162] (0.090)
All-male (=1)	-0.084 [0.124] (0.048)	-0.096 [0.116] (0.406)	-0.104 [0.136] (0.480)	-0.081 [0.124] (0.560)	-0.140 [0.137] (0.316)	-0.100 [0.130] (0.468)
Female (=1)	-0.058 [0.149]	-0.071 [0.143]	0.243 [0.147]	0.258* [0.141]	0.111 [0.156]	0.140 [0.156]
Individual-level controls	No	Yes	No	Yes	No	Yes
Co-ed mean	58.41 [9.27]	58.41 [9.27]	61.07 [8.03]	61.07 [8.03]	60.29 [7.95]	60.29 [7.95]
Observations	505	505	487	487	487	487
R^2	0.031	0.128	0.045	0.129	0.041	0.141

Notes: *** $p<0.01$; ** $p<0.05$; * $p<0.1$; The mean and standard deviation for students in co-ed classes are presented for outcomes because the dependent variables were normalised by that distribution. Therefore, the coefficients for regressions are in terms of standard deviations of the distribution of scores for students in co-ed classes. Standard errors are clustered at the class level and shown in brackets. For the variables of interest, *p*-values for the coefficients are calculated via the Cameron et al. (2008) wild bootstrap method as well and shown in parentheses (reps = 1000). Average scores are only calculated for students who passed the previous year; otherwise, the student is withdrawn from the university. Therefore, the sample is decreasing from year to year. The 'individual-level controls' refers to the set of individual controls listed in Table 11.1: IQ raw score; student went to a single-sex high school (=1); age; native language English (=1); white (=1); student is eldest child (=1); number of siblings; number of sisters; Mother has university degree (=1); Mother stayed at home (=1); Father has university degree (=1); Born in EU (=1); The Big Five. Dummy variables were used for any missing values.

Table A11.2: Effects on Introductory Economics scores

Variables	Aggregate score		Exam score		Coursework score	
	[1]	[2]	[3]	[4]	[5]	[6]
All-female (=1)	0.277** [0.132]	0.282* [0.160]	0.308** [0.129]	0.288* [0.158]	0.113 [0.118]	0.031 [0.126]
All-female * EC111	−0.124 [0.192]	–	−0.181 [0.203]	–	–	–
All-male (=1)	0.045 [0.093]	0.048 [0.083]	0.021 [0.101]	0.027 [0.079]	−0.106 [0.102]	−0.078 [0.077]
Female (=1)	−0.007 [0.152]	−0.024 [0.163]	−0.044 [0.157]	−0.072 [0.168]	0.057 [0.095]	0.020 [0.104]
All observables	Yes	Yes	Yes	Yes	No	Yes
TA fixed effects	No	Yes	No	Yes	No	No
Co-ed mean	53.70 [17.68]	53.70 [17.68]	51.36 [19.19]	49.38 17.26	55.50 [12.83]	55.50 [12.83]
Observations	570	570	570	570	495	495
R^2	0.118	0.134	0.107	0.127	0.029	0.164

Notes: *** *p*<0.01; ** *p*<0.05; * *p*<0.1; The mean and standard deviation for students in co-ed classes are presented for outcomes because the dependent variables were normalised by that distribution for the aggregate, exam, and coursework scores. Therefore, the coefficients for regressions with those dependent variables are in terms of standard deviations of the distribution of scores for students in co-ed classes. The 'all observables' refers to the set of individual and class level controls listed in Table 11.1: IQ raw score; student went to a single-sex high school (=1); age; native language English (=1); white (=1); student is eldest child (=1); number of siblings; number of sisters; Mother has University Degree (=1); Mother stayed at home (=1); Father has University Degree (=1); Born in EU (=1); The Big Five; TA female (=1); Class before 2 pm (=1); Class at End of Week (=1); and Class size (and its square both interacted with EC111 since there were different caps on class size for the two courses). When TA fixed effects are included, though, the TA female (=1) control is not included. Dummy variables were used for any missing values.

Table A11.3: Behavioural changes and other outcomes

Variables	Aggregate score	Exam score	First degree	First or 2.1 degree	3rd degree or fail	No degree
	[1]	[2]	[3]	[4]	[5]	[6]
All-female (=1)	0.113 [0.129]	0.120 [0.126]	0.035 [0.038]	0.282*** [0.065]	−0.104*** [0.035]	−0.086*** [0.023]
All-male (=1)	0.048 [0.080]	0.052 [0.084]	0.003 [0.035]	0.042 [0.041]	−0.008 [0.031]	−0.039 [0.028]
Female (=1)	−0.054 [0.131]	−0.075 [0.131]	0.072 [0.044]	−0.011 [0.082]	−0.015 [0.040]	−0.008 [0.041]
Did all coursework	1.004*** [0.132]	0.858*** [0.137]	0.062 [0.053]	0.285*** [0.071]	−0.276*** [0.070]	−0.245*** [0.073]
Proportion of classes attended	0.260*** [0.034]	0.253*** [0.033]	0.050*** [0.016]	0.094*** [0.021]	−0.067*** [0.016]	−0.057*** [0.013]
Observations	570	570	566	566	566	566
R^2	0.291	0.240	–	–	–	–

Notes: *** *p*<0.01; ** *p*<0.05; * *p*<0.1; In columns [1] and [2], scores are normalised so the coefficients are in terms of standard deviations of the distribution of scores for students in co-ed classes. For the probit regressions in columns [3]–[6], marginal effects are shown. Standard errors are clustered at the class level and shown in brackets. Each regression also controls for whether a student is in EC111, but for brevity, it is not shown.

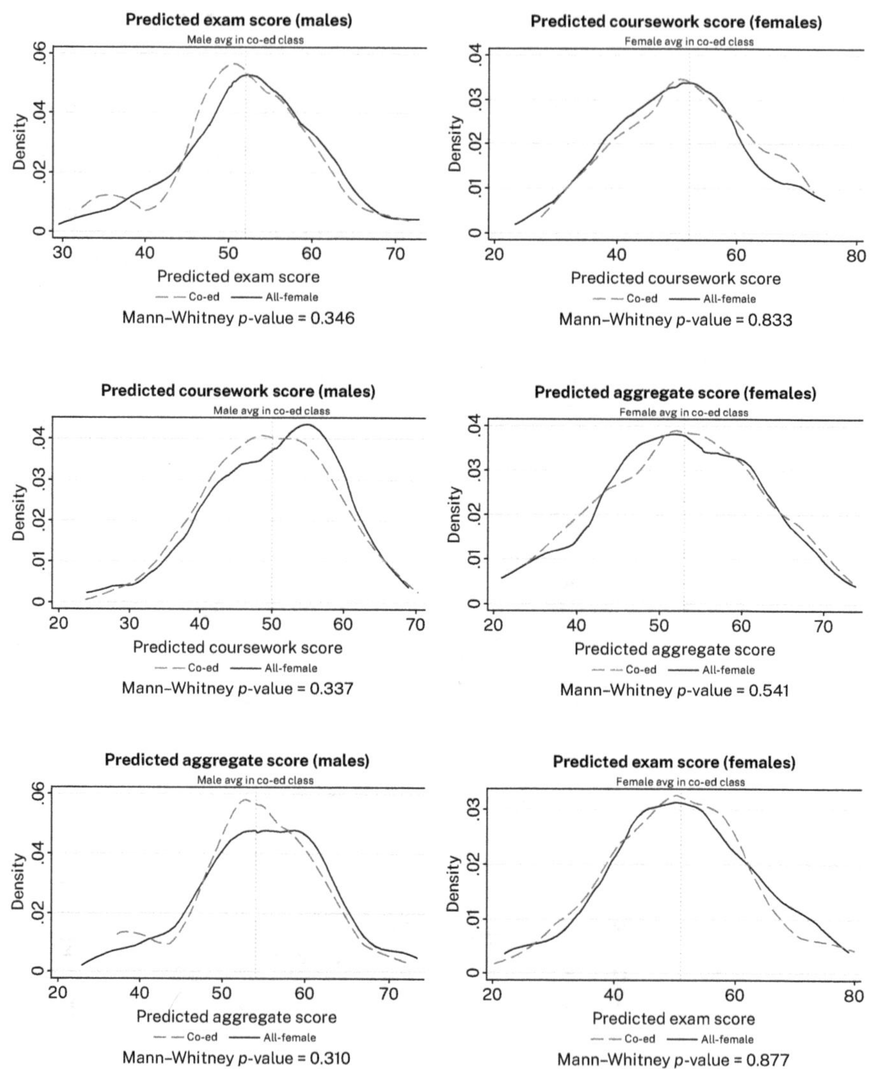

Figure A11.1: Predicted distributions for key outcomes

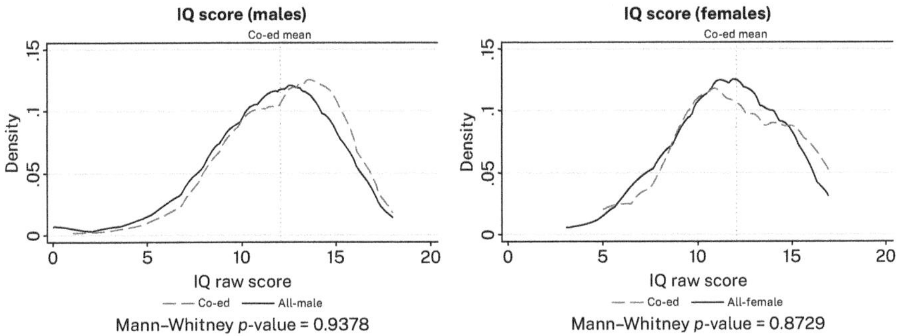

Figure A11.2: Distribution of raw IQ scores by treatment

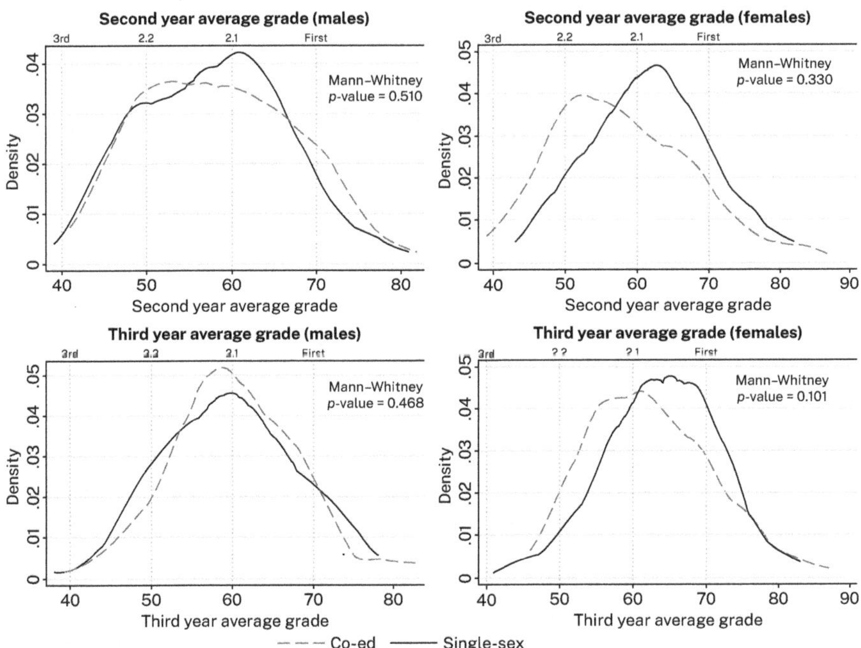

Figure A11.3: Average grades

12

Gender differences in willingness to compete: The role of culture and institutions

Alison L Booth, Elliott Fan, Xin Meng and Dandan Zhang

Gender gaps in labour market outcomes can be observed in most societies, regardless of their stage of development. Recent studies have linked such phenomena with gender behavioural differences in the willingness to compete (Gneezy et al. 2003; Gneezy and Rustichini 2004; Niederle and Vesterlund 2007). The question then arises as to what determines male and female differences in competitive inclination. Economists have not reached a consensus over this issue. Many studies have believed that this is due mainly to nature: women and men are built differently. For example, there is some evidence that the menstrual cycle and hormone level affects competition inclination (Buser 2012). Moreover, in some societies, the gender gap in competition inclination is found to exist as early as the age of three years and to persist for many years to come (Sutter and Gltzle-Rutzler 2015).

Recently, though, further studies have provided evidence indicating that nurture affects individuals' competitive inclination. Gneezy et al. (2009) examine the issue of whether the gender gap in competitiveness is due to nature or nurture by comparing gender gaps in competitiveness between a patriarchal society and a matrilineal society. They find that, while women in the patriarchal society are less competitively inclined than men, their counterparts in the matrilineal society are more competitive than men. Their study indicates that culture matters and that it is possible to nurture women to be more competitive. Booth and Nolen (2012) compare gender gaps in competitive behaviour between girls and boys aged 14 and 15 from single-sex and co-educational environments, and find robust differences between the competitive choices of girls from single-sex and co-educational schools. Moreover, girls from single-sex schools behave more like boys when randomly assigned to mixed-sex experimental groups. Their results suggest that observed gender differences in other studies might reflect social learning rather than inherent gender traits.

'Culture' is a collective term that encompasses ideas, values, identities, customs, social norms and social behaviour. Culture is said to be formed in the long term and persists for generations (Akerlof and Kranton 2000; Hofstede and Hofstede 2005; Guiso et al. 2006; Alesina et al. 2013). Yet studies have found that institutions, social interactions and indoctrination can affect social norms, social preferences, beliefs and behaviour (Manski 2000; Alesina and Fuchs-Schundeln 2007; Tabellini 2010; Voigtlander and Voth 2015; Lippmann et al. 2016). Thus, some aspects of 'culture' can be formed or changed in a relatively short period. If this is the case and if this part of 'culture' matters in nurturing women's competitive behaviour, then policy intervention may contribute to the further narrowing of gender gaps in labour market outcomes.

This chapter aims to test whether or not the gender gap in competitive inclination can be altered in a relatively short period by changing social norms induced by institutional changes. Our regions of interest are Mainland China and Taiwan, both of which descend from the same Confucian traditions, but whose experiences from 1949 onwards dramatically diverged. The subjects of our experiment are different birth cohorts of men and women who were exposed to different regimes during their crucial developmental age, and we investigate gender differences in their competitive choices.

From 1949 onwards, Mainland China experienced a series of dramatic changes in its social and economic institutions. During the first 30 years (1949–77), the ruling Communist Party – guided by Marxist ideology – implemented a centrally planned economy. Like most communist regimes, within a short period, Mainland China denounced old Chinese culture and established new social norms. Among them, gender equality was promoted to replace the traditional Confucian view that women are subordinate to men and that women should be 'obedient, quiet, self-effacing, ignorant, and devoting herself only to the service of the family'. During those years, especially during the Cultural Revolution (1966–76), women's position in society was strongly promoted while Confucian ideology was vilified. A widely known political slogan in Mainland China promoting women's status in society was 'women hold up half of the sky'. In addition to encouraging women to participate in the labour market, propaganda was spread that a society should not tolerate people who can work but choose not to; those who did so were regarded as 'social parasites' (Meng 2000; Yao and You 2016). As a result of such promotion and indoctrination, women's labour force participation rate in Mainland China was at a similar level as their male counterparts (Croll 1983), and the gender earnings gap was small (Meng and Kidd 1997).

Market-oriented economic reforms began in 1978, and these helped China achieve unprecedented economic growth. At the same time, the Marxist ideology was gradually replaced by an acceptance of individualistic and free-market ideology. During this period, many old Chinese traditions managed to creep back, and socialist norms have largely been forgotten. Consequently, available data show that urban women's labour force participation rate dropped from 78 per cent in 1988 to 57 per cent in 2004. In the meantime, the gender earnings gap continued to widen (Zhang et al. 2008).

Such dramatic changes in institutions and social norms are highly likely to affect individuals who, during the crucial developmental age, were exposed to one of the two regimes (Alesina and Fuchs-Schundeln 2007). In particular, with regard to the gender gap in competitive inclination, we expect that women who grew up during the communist regime would be more confident about themselves, and hence have a stronger competitive inclination conditional on their level of competence, while women who grew up mainly during the post-reform regime may be less inclined to compete. At the same time, there might be a countering force. As the economy progresses and education levels increase, the growing dominance of market factors may promote individually based preferences and increase awareness of gender equality (Cai et al. 2012; Xu and Hamamura 2014), and hence, increase women's competitive inclinations.

To examine whether or not the 30 years of communist indoctrination have changed women's behaviour, we conducted controlled laboratory experiments with birth cohorts of Mainland Chinese subjects who spent their crucial developmental age under different regimes. To control for the potential counterforce – induced over time by more education and market domination and induced gender equality awareness – we conducted the same laboratory experiments with Taiwanese subjects born in the same years. Taiwan is a region that was subject to the same Confucian traditions and that also went through significant economic growth. However, it has not been subject to the ideological transformation experienced by Mainland China. Using the results from the Taiwan experiments to gauge the general effect of economic growth, we find that the Mainland women who were subject to the communist regime during the crucial developmental age were more inclined to compete than their male counterparts. In contrast, for our other two cohorts – one that was partially subject to the communist regime and partially subject to the new regime, and the other that was fully subject to the new regime – we observe either the opposite pattern or else no gender difference. We also find that, controlling for competence level, Mainland women are on average more competitive than their counterparts in Taiwan for every birth cohort, a finding that perhaps relates to the role model effect from their indoctrinated parents (Fernandez et al. 2004).

Are our findings truly due to the influence of communist ideology? In the exit surveys, we asked participants to report, from a list of personal attributes, those that their parents and schools encouraged them to develop when they were young. A significant proportion of the older cohorts of Mainland participants chose from these attributes 'gender equality' and 'being unselfish', whereas no cohort differences were found among the Taiwanese participants. We also explored responses to two questions asking respondents whether they support or disagree with the statements that the government should implement policy to reduce income inequality and that governments should intervene in the economy as little as possible. Our oldest Mainland cohort is more likely to agree with the former statement and to disagree with the latter one. For the Taiwanese participants, no cohort difference is found.

Our design ruled out the possibility that women's lack of competitive inclination is due mainly to innate ability. The fact that, within the same large cultural background, different cohorts of women exhibit a sharp difference in competitive inclination suggests that institutions and culture interact to affect individuals' behaviour. If culture is a selective outcome, previous studies using long-lasting cultural differences, such as matrilineal versus patrilineal societies (Gneezy et al. 2009; Zhang 2015), may not be able to clearly identify the nurture effect due to the potential that societies could have selected into different cultures. In our setting, however, the effect of nurture via relatively short-term indoctrination is clearly demonstrated.

Our research also adds to an increasing number of studies confirming that induced change in social norms does indeed affect individual preferences and behaviour. We will briefly consider two interesting examples that are complementary to our own. The first is by Liu et al. (2014), who investigated how Confucianism affects economic preferences of subjects in Mainland China and Taiwan by priming their subjects – university students – with Confucianism within the context of their experiment. Their finding that Chinese and Taiwanese subjects responded differently to this priming is interpreted as the result of different histories and experiences. The preferences they investigate include risk attitudes, loss aversion, time preference and trust for both boys and girls, but they do not consider gender differences in subjects' willingness to compete, which is the major behaviour focus of our chapter. A second related study is that of Zhang (2015), who compares the competitive behaviour of experimental subjects from three ethnic groups (the Han, the Yi and the Mosuo (a polygamous and matrilineal group)) at a high school in south-west Mainland China in 2009. None of these subjects lived through the communist regime, which is the institutional change investigated in this chapter. The last two ethnicities, who are minorities in China, were held to be exempt from the communist reforms relative to their Han counterparts. The author finds no evidence of a gender gap in competitive inclination among these young Han Chinese, but a large gap for the Yi. The Mosuo girls were as competitively inclined as the Han Chinese.

Like these studies, we investigate the impact of different life experiences on behavioural outcomes. But in contrast to these studies, we directly recruit adult subjects who spent their formative years during the communist regime, as well as those who grew up just after the economic reform, in order to identify the impact of a relatively short-term communist indoctrination on behavioural differences. In so doing, we follow the psychological and economic literature indicating that behavioural traits are mainly developed during individuals' formative years (Kohlberg and Mayer 1972; Heckman 2007; Klimstra 2013). Moreover, we recruited as subjects individuals from the same ethnicity, in order to abstract from the issues that Zhang (2015) investigates.

The remainder of this chapter is structured as follows. We provide background information on socioeconomic changes that occurred in Mainland China and Taiwan in the past 70 years and how they affected gender roles in the two societies differently. We then introduce the experimental design, our sample and summary statistics. Finally, we present the main results and examine whether the observed difference in gender gap in competitive inclination is indeed due to the communist propaganda.

Background

Women's position in Mainland Chinese society changed dramatically over the course of the last seven decades. Traditionally, Chinese culture had a very strong gender bias. The Confucian view of women is that they are subordinates of men, they are weak and are born to serve others (Croll 1995). A virtuous woman should be 'obedient, quiet, self-effacing, ignorant, and devoting herself only to the service of the family' (Tseng 1992). In the period prior to the Second World War, women had limited freedom in society. They had to obey their fathers and brothers before marriage, their marriages were arranged, and after marriage, they belonged to their husbands' family and had to obey their husband and mother-in-law's domination. In the event that they were widowed, they were required to obey their sons (Hinton 1966; Croll 1983; Ma 1995; Zhang 2015). The end of the Second World War saw the Communist Party (CCP) seize control from their predecessor – the Kuomintang (National Party) – in Mainland China, while the latter formed the government in Taiwan.

Since 1949, Mainland China has been ruled by the CCP, which adopted communist ideology and aimed to change Chinese society according to this ideology. Gender equality was at the top of the agenda for social transformation, perhaps following the role model of the Communist Party in the then-Soviet Union (Little 2011). The state undertook a series of legal reforms to establish the equality of women in marriage and family, in education and election rights, and in land rights and the right to participate in the labour market (Niida 1964; Croll 1995). They organised women to redefine and to promote their economic, social and political interests (Croll 1983; Mow et al. 2004). The New Marriage Law was introduced in 1950. This upheld the principles of free marriage, monogamy, equal rights for men and women, the protection of the natural rights of women, and opposed the patriarchal marriage practices centred on the interests of husbands and males (Niida 1964; Yao and You 2016). All these new ideas were in direct contradiction to the social norm of Confucianism that had dominated China for thousands of years. To change views and social norms in a short period, the CCP used mass media propaganda to popularise the new ideas. These included positive and negative campaigns. On the positive side, slogans such as 'women can hold up half the sky', 'men and women are equal', 'working is glorious' and 'make your own marriage decision' appeared on propaganda posters, newspapers and government documents. On the negative side, it was widely believed that a society would not tolerate individuals who were able but chose not to work. Those choosing not to work would be regarded as 'social parasites' (Meng 2000). At the same time, Confucianism was denounced, especially during the Cultural Revolution period (Lu 2004).

Figure 12.1 plots the density of the key words of 'women hold up half the sky' and 'gender equality' that appeared in *People's Daily*, the official CCP newspaper, over the past 67 years (the density is calculated using the number of times these key words appeared in articles published in *People's Daily* each year divided by the total number of articles that appeared in the paper in that year). The figure shows that there were three peak periods: 1950–5; 1970–6; and 1995. The first peak occurred during the early days of the introduction of the New Marriage Law. The second was during the Cultural Revolution period, while the third was 1995, which was the year the UN Fourth Women's Conference was held in Beijing. Of the three peaks, the Cultural Revolution period is the most intensive one.

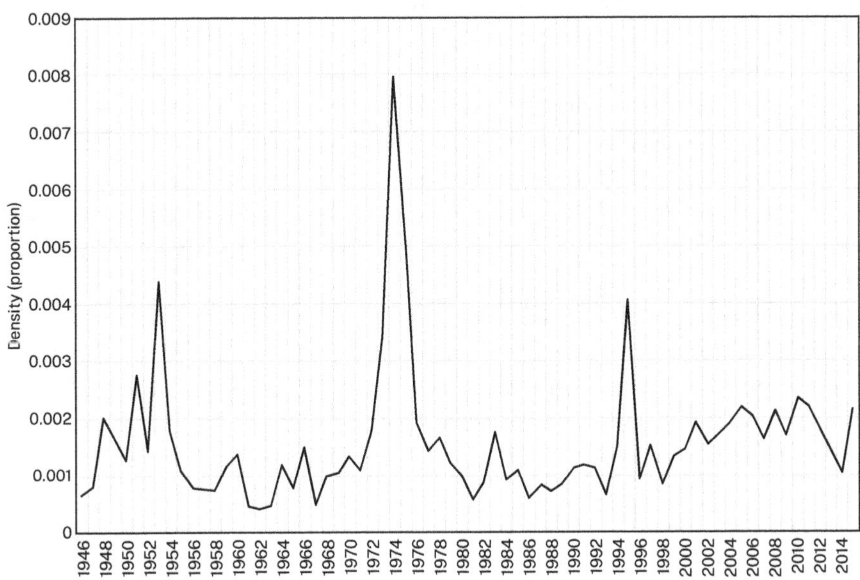

Figure 12.1: Density of the phrases 'half the sky' and 'gender equality' in *People's Daily*

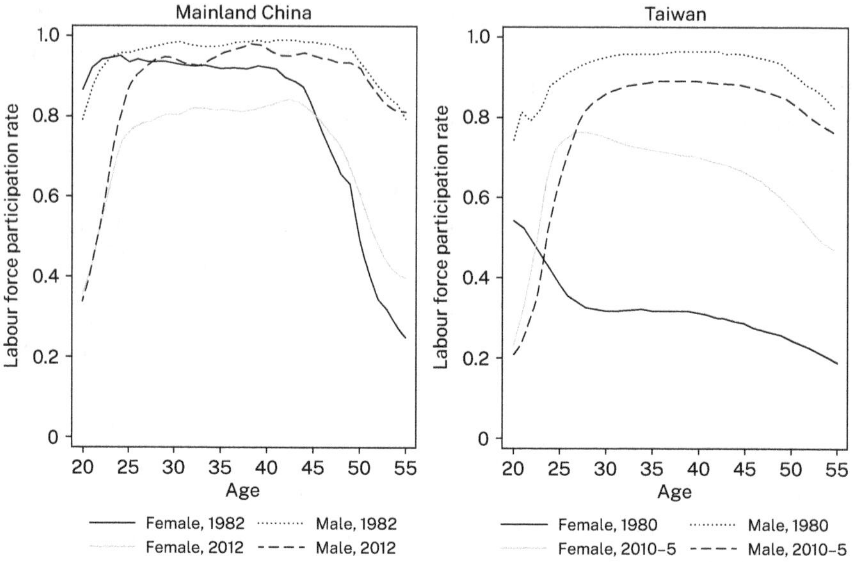

Figure 12.2: Labour force participation for Mainland China and Taiwan

Taiwan's population is mostly Han Chinese who were born on the Mainland or have ancestors who were Han Chinese from the Mainland. Taiwan shares the same language and has a similar initial culture to that of Mainland China. One of the most important parts of this initial culture is Confucian values, beliefs and ethics, which have been passed down in Taiwan from parents to children and from teachers to students (Liu et al. 2014). Unlike the Mainland, Taiwan did not experience a revolutionary ideological change after the Second World War, and traditional cultural values remain dominant. Nevertheless, as the economy developed and educational levels improved, society became more aware of gender equality issues, and the extreme Confucian values regarding women's position in society gradually evolved into a more modern view. As such, women's labour force participation rate has been increasing, and as a result of women's financial independence, women are challenging traditional gender roles both within families and in workplaces. Figure 12.2 presents the male and female labour force participation rates by age and gender for the years of the early 1980s and early 2010s for non-agriculture workers in Mainland

China and Taiwan.[1] The figures show that the labour force participation rate of Mainland women was very high in the earlier days, but over the past 30 years, it has dropped significantly, especially for prime-aged women. Thus, as the Chinese economy grew, women's labour force participation rate reduced. The opposite is true in Taiwan.

Although Taiwanese women are, on average, less likely to participate in the labour market, as the Taiwanese economy grew over the past 30 years, primary-age women's participation rate has been increasing. The different trends described in these figures are largely due to the institutional and cultural changes described in this section. If we assume that economic growth should have a general trend of increasing women's labour force participation, the fact that in Mainland China, women's labour force participation is reducing as the economy grows suggests that a strong counterforce exists. We argue that, to a large extent, this counter force is related to the institutional changes described above.

Experimental design and the data

We investigated whether or not individuals exposed to different regimes and social norms about women's position in a society vary in their willingness to compete. To do this, we needed to identify birth cohorts that were exposed to different regimes. Based on Figure 12.1, in Mainland China, the period with the most intensive propaganda on gender equality was that of the Cultural Revolution. We therefore chose, as our treatment group, individuals born in 1958 (aged 8–17 during the Cultural Revolution) and whose schooling years thus overlapped with the Cultural Revolution. They were not too old to have lost their cognitive ability at the time of the experiment (aged 57 in 2015), but were old enough to have spent their crucial development age during the Cultural Revolution. We have two comparison cohorts: (i) individuals born in the year the Cultural Revolution began (1966), and who spent three of their early primary school years during the Cultural

1 For Mainland China, we use the 1982 Population Census data for the early period and the China Family Panel Survey (CFPS) for the most recent period. We use only the urban population to generate this figure. The 1982 census is the first year we have data available for Mainland China. For the year near our experiment, we are unable to access unit record data from the 2010 Population Census. As an alternative, we used the representative CFPS data, which is close to our experiment year. For Taiwan, we use the 1980 census data. Also, due to the unavailability of the 2010 census data we use, instead, 2010–5 data from the Taiwan Family Income and Expenditure surveys, conducted by Directorate-General of Budget, Accounting and Statistics Executive Yuan.

Revolution and the remainder of their schooling years in the economic reform era (1977 onwards); and (ii) individuals born in 1977 who spent their entire lives in the economic reform era.

We aimed at sampling around 100 individuals in each birth cohort from Beijing, the capital city of Mainland China, equally divided along the gender line. A similar number of Taiwanese subjects was recruited from Taipei, the capital city of Taiwan, and among the same cohorts, in the same gender divide.

To ensure that our subjects were roughly representative of the population at large, we obtained the gender-education-employment distribution within each birth cohort from a combination of the National Bureau of Statistics Urban Household Survey data 2009 and the 1 per cent 2010 Population Census data for the Beijing sample. For Taipei, we used the Manpower Survey 2010–2015.[2] These distributions are then used as our sampling quota to recruit subjects. The recruitment was carried out by survey companies in Beijing and Taipei through internet or telephone contacts from the survey companies' own subject pools. We also used social media (Facebook in Taipei and WeChat in Beijing) ourselves to supplement the survey companies' recruitment efforts. In Taipei, we further advertised in communities through neighbourhood magistrates, elected officials at the bottom administration divisions around Taipei city. The advertisement texts in Mandarin are consistent between the two cities.[3] The original sample quota by cohort-gender-education-employment cells and the final sample distribution among these cells for Beijing and Taipei are available online (Booth et al. 2018, Appendix Table A.4). They show that, by and large, our final samples are consistent with the original quota.[4]

Experiments

We conducted a series of experiments with our sample subjects, including the following games: competition, trust, risk and loss aversion. These are widely used in the experimental literature investigating economic preferences. Below, we discuss our experimental procedures and then describe in detail

2 The reason we used different data sets for Beijing or the same survey data from multiple years for Taipei is to enlarge the sample sizes.

3 See Booth et al., 2018, Appendix B for the translated English text.

4 All our Taipei subjects report their ethnicity as Han Chinese except for three individuals who did not respond to this question. For Beijing, all subjects but nine individuals are Han Chinese. Six stated they were Manchuria, which is not an ethnically diverse area.

the two games reported in this chapter: the competition and the risk game. The precise form of these games is available online (Booth et al. 2018, Appendix C).

Our sample subjects were invited to come to one of several identical lecture rooms in either Peking University or National Taiwan University. The experiments were conducted in large lecture rooms, in which participants were seated separately with enough space in between to ensure no interference from one another. Participants were given a show-up fee of CN¥75 in Beijing, which is equivalent to around US$12, and in Taipei, it was NT$510 or approximately US$16.[5] Participants were told that they had been selected to participate in an experiment and that, during the experiment, they would have the opportunity to earn some money and the exact amount they could earn would depend on their own decisions and their luck. All participants were given the option of not participating, both before and during the experimental sessions, but no one opted out. At the end of the experiment, one of the tasks was randomly chosen for payment.

The experiments in Beijing were conducted between 24 April and 23 May 2015, while in Taipei they lasted from 25 July to 5 September 2015. To ensure consistency in the running of the experiments, Xin Meng (one of the co-authors of the study) and James Zhang (our research assistant (RA) from The Australian National University) trained RAs in both Peking University and National Taiwan University. Moreover, both Xin Meng and James Zhang were present during the experiments in both places, although the actual sessions were mainly conducted by two of the authors of this chapter (Fan and Zhang for Taipei and Beijing, respectively) together with a team of 15 to 20 trained student RAs from the National Taiwan University and Peking University. The experiments were all conducted in Mandarin, using pen and paper to avoid the potential problem that our older cohort might not be computer-literate. Each participant received hard copies of the instructions for each game immediately before the beginning of each game, and these instructions were then also read out loud to the group as a whole. There were opportunities to ask questions, and test questions were included in the answering sheets for each game to enable us to ascertain

5 The difference in payments between the two cities is due to the fact that the average earnings of Taipei is 1.5 times of that the average earnings in Beijing. Due to our budget constraint, we paid Taipei participants 1.33 times of their Beijing counterparts.

whether participants understood the instructions.[6] Participants marked their answer to each test question and their decision for each game on a paper form (the answering sheet), which was distributed to the participants after reading the instructions to them for each game. Below, we discuss the competition game and risk game procedures, with details provided online (Booth et al. 2018, Appendix C).

The design of the competition game loosely follows that of Niederle and Vesterlund (2007).[7] More specifically, three rounds of the game were conducted. The task in each round consisted of finishing, in five minutes, as many additions of sets of five two-digit numbers. In the first round, individuals were paid based on a piece rate: each correct answer was compensated by CN¥12 in Beijing and NT$78 in Taipei. Round 2 was a compulsory tournament in which each subject was randomly assigned an anonymous partner. Those completing the most correct answers were awarded, in Beijing and Taipei, CN¥24 and NT$156 for each correct answer, respectively; whereas those who lost in the tournament received nothing. In the third round, subjects were asked to make a choice: either to be paid by piece rate or tournament. The piece-rate payment was the same as for Round 1, while that for the tournament was the same for Round 2. However, for this third round, the results of those who chose to compete were compared with the scores of their partners in Round 2.[8]

All sessions followed the same order of the three rounds described above. An advantage in conducting three rounds of the competition game is that we can use the results from the first two rounds (the mandatory piece rate and the tournament) to control for individuals' competence as well as their ability to sustain pressure (difference in performances between the first two rounds).

The risk game follows Gneezy and Potters (1997) and involves a series of lottery choices. Subjects need to choose, for each of the 11 choices, between receiving an amount with certainty (CN¥101 in Beijing and NT$662 in Taipei, which was approximately US$15 and US$20, respectively) or

6 Most respondents answered the test questions correctly. Thirty observations from the Beijing sample and 14 observations from the Taipei sample failed to answer the test questions for rounds 1 and 2 of the competition game correctly. We experimented with including dummies for these observations in or excluding them from our regression analysis later in the chapter.

7 Niederle and Vesterlund (2007) provided feedback to the subjects at the end of the each round of the competition game regarding their own performance. We did not do so in our setting.

8 This is to ensure subjects' choice on whether to compete is not due to issues not relating to competition inclination, such as not wanting to impose negative externalities on others or strategic response to beliefs about other participants' choices.

a lottery with a 50 per cent chance of receiving a larger amount and a 50 per cent chance of receiving nothing. The lottery-winning amount increases gradually from CN¥135 or NT$889 in the first choice to CN¥475 or NT$2109 in the 11th choice. Risk-loving subjects would choose the lottery over certainty even when the potential gain is small, while risk-averse individuals would only choose the lottery over certainty when the potential gain from so doing becomes sufficiently large. The particular choice used for the payoff for this game depends on a random draw of a ping-pong ball from a box with 11 numbered balls (from 1 to 11) by one of the participants at the end of the risk game. Once the choice was determined, another participant was randomly selected to toss a coin, which determined the outcome for those who had chosen a lottery.[9]

Exit survey

After completion of the games, all participants were asked to fill out an exit survey questionnaire. In addition to the general demographic details, labour market outcomes and personality traits of the individuals and their family members, we also asked a series of questions designed to elicit information about the environment in which individuals were brought up. These included questions about the attributes encouraged by parents and by schools during that period. The attributes included being independent, hard-working, responsible, imaginative, tolerant and respectful of others, trusting other people, giving and looking after those less fortunate; gender equality; thrift and saving money; determination and perseverance; religious faith; unselfishness and competitiveness. In addition, a set of opinion questions regarding preferences for government intervention was included in the survey.

We also administered a simplified five-minute Raven's Matrices Test to gauge participants' intellectual ability. The test is a widely accepted indicator of higher-order general mental ability that does not rely on cultural context or prior experience. Originally designed to provide information about subjects' ability using a non-verbal setting uncontaminated by linguistic background, its results have been shown to be consistent across cultures and over time (Raven 2000).

9 However, as we played three games and the competition game with three different rounds in each session, only one of the five game/round was used for the actual payoff. Which particular game/round was used for the final payoff in each session was determined randomly by drawing balls with number 1 to 5 from a box.

Summary statistics

Table 12.1 reports the summary statistics of the subjects' characteristics by region, gender and cohort. Our sample is not entirely balanced across cohorts and genders. In particular, the number of observations for the 1958 male cohort in Beijing is small relative to the other cohort cells in Beijing or Taipei (see the top panel of Table 12.1).

Table 12.1: Summary statistics

	Beijing		Taipei	
	Females	**Males**	**Females**	**Males**
Number of observations				
1958	57	41	66	65
1966	57	60	62	56
1977	61	58	56	54
Years of schooling				
1958	11.94	12.42	10.91	12.20
1966	12.68	12.59	12.74	12.89
1977	14.41	14.09	14.80	14.04
Raven scores				
1958	4.27	5.16	6.29	6.25
1966	5.47	5.90	6.94	7.30
1977	6.75	7.55	7.69	8.02
Mother's years of schooling				
1958	6.64	6.23	4.55	4.15
1966	7.544	8.02	4.9	5.82
1977	10.38	10.41	8.53	8.69
Number of siblings				
1958	2.98	2.49	4.31	3.41
1966	1.84	1.73	3.14	2.91
1977	0.63	0.71	2.53	1.70
Marital status				
Married	88.00	91.82	62.50	68.57
De facto	2.29	0.63	0.54	1.14
Single	2.86	2.52	24.46	25.14
Divorced	5.71	5.03	7.61	5.14
Widowed	1.14	0.00	4.89	0.00

Source: Authors' calculation from the data.

In terms of years of schooling, the gender differences across the cohorts are similar in Beijing and Taipei. While there is a visible female disadvantage for the 1958 cohort, it disappears for the later cohorts. Years of schooling are calculated based on the highest level of education reported by individual subjects and the normal number of years of education for each level in Mainland China and Taiwan to obtain a comparable measure across the two cities. However, during the Cultural Revolution, most Mainland urban schools were closed for between three and seven years.[10] Many birth cohorts whose education was interrupted during that period were given certificates for the level of education they were supposed to have completed, despite the fact that they did not receive that education. After the period of school closure, although schools were reopened and children at schools were educated, the quality of education during the Cultural Revolution was very questionable (Deng and Treiman 1997; Meng and Gregory 2002). Within our sample, the Beijing cohort born in 1958 had their education interrupted for a total of six years during the Cultural Revolution. The 1966 birth cohort was also affected for three years in their early primary school education due to the lower quality of education in those years. The relevance of these interruptions will be highlighted later when we discuss subjects' performance in competition games.

We also report summary statistics for mothers' education, number of siblings and marital status variables. All the variables exhibit large differences among the cohorts from Beijing and Taipei. On average, Beijing cohorts have higher values for 'mother's education' for all cohorts. Taipei cohorts have significantly more siblings than their Beijing counterparts, while the Beijing cohorts are more likely to be married than single relative to their Taipei counterparts. These may all be related to policy and social norm differences.

Table 12.2 presents the summary statistics of the competition game. The first panel shows the proportion of people choosing to compete in the third round in each cohort-gender cell for Beijing and Taipei separately. The last two columns in this panel report gender gaps in competitive inclination and t-ratios for the differences. The results indicate that, for the Beijing subjects, the 1958 women are statistically significantly more likely to choose to compete than their male counterparts, while women in the 1966 cohort

10 All levels of schools were closed in urban areas in Mainland China between 1966 and 1969. Then, primary and junior high schools were reopened in 1968–9 academic year. However, senior high schools did not reopen for recruitment until 1972, while the merit-based university entrance did not resume until after the Cultural Revolution in 1977 (Deng and Treiman, 1997; Meng and Gregory, 2002).

are less likely to choose to compete. No statistically significant difference is observed for the 1977 cohort. For our Taipei sample, however, no gender difference in competition inclination is observed for any cohort.

Table 12.2: Summary statistics for the competition game

	Probability of choosing to compete in Round 3					
	Females		Males		Females – Males	
	Observations	Mean	Observations	Mean	Observations	Mean
Beijing						
1958	57	0.26	41	0.12	0.14*	1.72
1966	57	0.26	60	0.45	-0.19**	2.13
1977	61	0.44	58	0.47	-0.02	0.25
Taipei						
1958	66	0.42	65	0.51	-0.08	0.95
1966	62	0.45	56	0.54	-0.08	0.91
1977	56	0.59	54	0.57	0.02	0.16

	Beijing			Taipei		
	Females	Males	Difference	Females	Males	Difference
Number of correct answers in Round 1						
1958	7.30	5.20	2.103***	11.44	11.74	-0.299
1966	9.53	9.45	0.076	12.37	11.45	0.925
1977	11.46	9.95	1.511**	12.02	11.35	0.666
Number of correct answers in Round 2						
1958	8.19	6.98	1.217**	13.08	13.06	0.014
1966	11.11	10.37	0.739	13.45	13.25	0.202
1977	12.80	11.69	11.14	13.07	12.69	0.386

Notes: *** $p<0.01$; ** $p<0.05$; * $p<0.1$.

Source: Authors' calculation from the data.

The middle panel of Table 12.2 reports the average number of correct answers achieved in the first round (piece rate) of the competition game by each cohort-gender cell. The last two columns of the panel show the gender difference in performance for Beijing and Taipei separately. The bottom panel shows the same data for the second round (compulsory tournament) of the competition game.

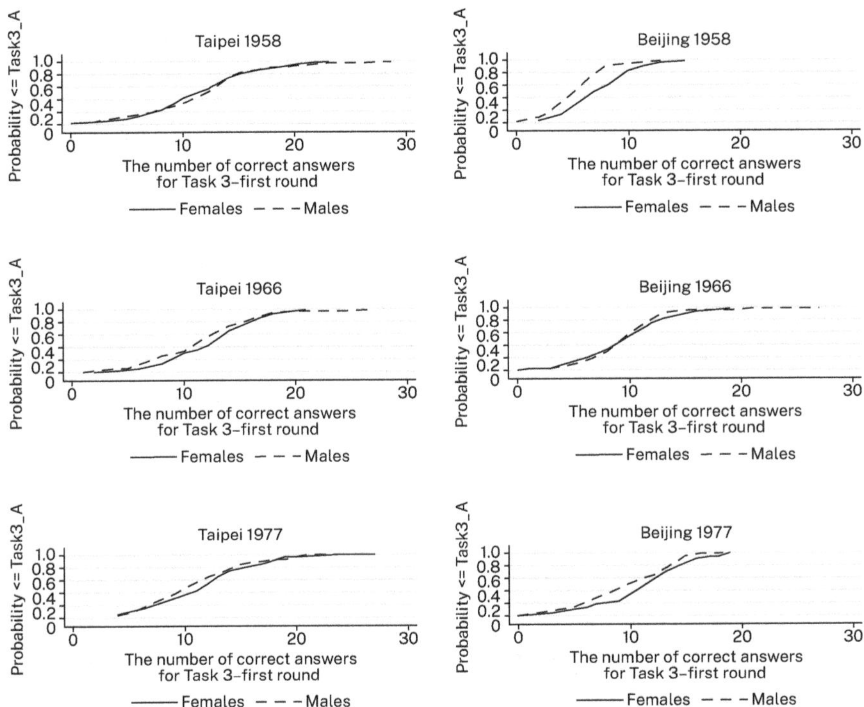

Figure 12.3: Cumulative density function: number of correct answers Round 1

Figures 12.3 and 12.4 present the cumulative density functions for these two rounds by each gender, cohort and region as well. These data confirm that, on average, the Beijing cohorts performed badly relative to their Taipei counterparts, especially the 1958 cohort, whose education interruption during the Cultural Revolution is clearly revealed from these performance results. Table 12.2 shows that males and females in the 1958 Beijing cohort completed, respectively, 5.2 and 7.3 correct answers in the first round and 7.0 and 8.2 in the second round. Their completed correct answers in the first round are only 44 per cent and 64 per cent of the correct answers completed by their Taipei counterparts, respectively. While the 1966 Beijing male and female cohorts are doing better than their 1958 counterparts, they still only completed 82 per cent and 77 per cent of the correct answers supplied by their Taipei counterparts. The results from the bottom two panels of Table 12.2, as well as from the cumulative density plots, indicate that the simple differences in competitive inclination without controlling for differences in performance in the number of correct answers may not be comparable across cohorts and across Beijing and Taipei. We control for differences in performance in our preferred specifications in the following section.

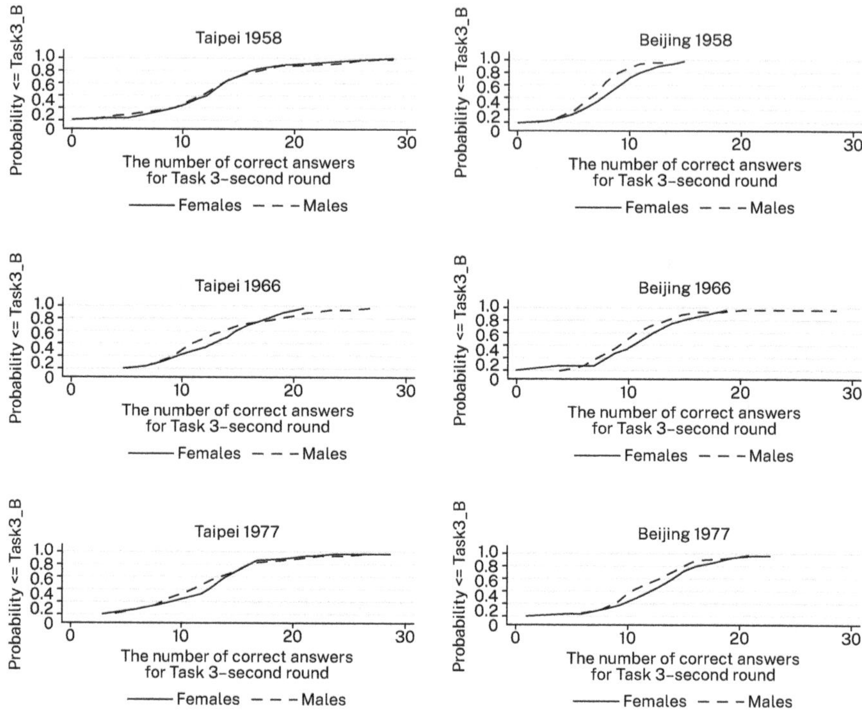

Figure 12.4: Cumulative density function: number of correct answers Round 2

Gender gap in willingness to compete

Niederle and Vesterlund (2007) discussed in detail the factors that may affect gender differences in competitive inclination in addition to preference for competition. In particular, they discussed gender differences in over-confidence, risk aversion and feedback aversion. In addition, men and women may differ in performance under pressure. To examine whether gender difference in competitive inclination varies across different birth cohorts, we estimate the following regression:

(1) $Comp_{ij} = \alpha + \beta_j Coh_{ij} + \kappa Male_{ij} + \rho_j Coh_{ij} \times Male_{ij} + \theta W_{ij} + \gamma X_{ij} + \varepsilon_{ij}$,

where the subscripts i and j indicate the individual and the birth cohort, respectively (j = 1966 or 1977); $Comp_{ij}$ = 1 if the subject chooses the tournament in the third round and 0 if the subject chooses piece rate. Coh_{ij} is a birth cohort dummy variable indicating the cohort born in 1966 and 1977; $Male_{ij}$ is the male indicator. $Coh_{ij} \times Male_{ij}$ are two interaction terms between the dummy variable for birth cohort 1966 and that for 1977, and the male dummy variables. Variables measuring ability and game characteristics performance are included in the vector W_{ij}. These variables are risk aversion, over-confidence, IQ, performance, an individual's ability to perform under pressure, the gender composition of the session and the number of participants in each session.[11] Individual characteristics are incorporated into the vector X_{ij}, including years of schooling, the individual's mother's years of schooling and the number of siblings they have. ε_{ij} denotes the random error term. Thus, the coefficient κ measures the gender difference in competitive inclination for the 1958 cohort, while $\kappa+\rho_{1966}$ and $\kappa+\rho_{1977}$ measure the gender differences in competitive inclination for the 1966 and 1977 cohorts, respectively.

We initially estimate (1) for Beijing and Taipei separately with three different model specifications:

1. the simple model without controlling for W_{ij} and X_{ij};
2. the simple model plus W_{ij}; and
3. adding the additional control variables of X_{ij}.

Table 12.3: Estimated results for equation (1)

	Beijing			Taipei		
	[1]	[2]	[3]	[4]	[5]	[6]
Dummy for males	-0.141* [0.078]	-0.149* [0.087]	-0.159* [0.087]	0.083 [0.088]	0.040 [0.081]	0.037 [0.085]
Dummy for 1966	0.000 [0.083]	-0.092 [0.088]	-0.119 [0.093]	0.027 [0.088]	-0.042 [0.082]	-0.049 [0.085]
Dummy for 1977	0.179** [0.087]	-0.003 [0.088]	-0.057 [0.103]	0.165* [0.090]	0.046 [0.088]	0.010 [0.093]
Male* 1966	0.328*** [0.117]	0.295** [0.121]	0.299** [0.124]	0.001 [0.127]	0.026 [0.116]	0.014 [0.119]
Male* 1977	0.164 [0.121]	0.201* [0.118]	0.212* [0.120]	-0.099 [0.129]	-0.047 [0.118]	-0.058 [0.117]
Dummy for Round 1 = Round 2	-	0.191** [0.078]	0.200** [0.080]	-	0.017 [0.072]	0.016 [0.072]
Dummy for Round 1<2	-	0.040 [0.066]	0.045 [0.067]	-	0.138** [0.064]	0.146** [0.065]

11 The 'risk aversion' variable is obtained from the risk game; 'over-confidence' is measured by the difference in self-assessed potential performance in the competition game and their actual performance; 'performance' and 'IQ' are measured by the number of correct answers in the second round and the simple Raven's test score; 'sustainability to pressure' is measured by a set of dummy variable indicating difference in performance under the piece rate and the tournament payment methods.

	Beijing			Taipei		
	[1]	[2]	[3]	[4]	[5]	[6]
Dummy for Round 2 = Round 3	–	0.026 [0.071]	0.022 [0.071]	–	0.000 [0.070]	0.000 [0.070]
Dummy for Round 2<3	–	–0.054 [0.060]	–0.055 [0.060]	–	–0.013 [0.055]	–0.023 [0.056]
Risk aversion (switching point)	–	–0.001 [0.001]	–0.001 [0.001]	–	–0.002*** [0.001]	–0.002*** [0.001]
No. correct answers in Round 2	–	0.035*** [0.009]	0.035*** [0.009]	–	0.042*** [0.006]	0.043*** [0.007]
Raven test score	–	0.019 [0.012]	0.017 [0.012]	–	0.042*** [0.012]	0.041*** [0.012]
Over-confidence	–	0.037 [0.026]	0.032 [0.026]	–	0.030 [0.024]	0.033 [0.024]
Dummy for single-sex sessions	–	–0.046 [0.057]	–0.047 [0.058]	–	0.120** [0.050]	0.105** [0.051]
No. participants in the session	–	-0.005 [0.004]	-0.005 [0.004]	–	0.008 [0.005]	0.008 [0.005]
Years of schooling	–	–	0.007 [0.010]	–	–	-0.010 [0.007]
Mother's years of schooling	–	–	0.000 [0.006]	–	–	0.011* [0.007]
No. of siblings	–	–	–0.018 [0.020]	–	–	-0.013 [0.017]
Observations	334	332	330	359	356	345
R^2	0.065	0.150	0.151	0.015	0.223	0.231
Test for gender difference (male – female) by cohort						
Cohort 1958	–0.141*	–0149*	–0.159*	0.083	0.040	0.037
SE	[0.078]	[0.087]	[0.087]	[0.088]	[0.081]	[0.085]
Cohort 1966	0.187**	0.146	0.140	0.084	0.066	0.051
P-values ($\kappa+\rho_{66}=0$)	(0.034)	(0.106)	(0.130)	(0.365)	(0.470)	(0.581)
Cohort 1977	0.023	0.052	0.053	–0.016	–0.007	–0.021
P-values ($\kappa+\rho_{77}=0$)	(0.804)	(0.565)	(0.554)	(0.873)	(0.936)	(0.815)

Notes: *** $p<0.01$; ** $p<0.05$; * $p<0.1$; Robust standard errors in squared brackets; those in the parentheses are p-values from the joint significant tests.

Source: Authors' own estimations.

Table 12.3 reports the full regression results together with the gender gap in competitive choice for each cohort. The results at the bottom panel of Table 12.3 labelled 'gender difference by cohort' indicate that there is a negative gender gap for the Beijing 1958 cohort. On average, without controlling for anything (column [1]), the Beijing 1958 males are 14 per cent less likely to choose to compete than their female counterparts. For the same cohort in the Taipei sample (column [4]), however, males are around 8.3 per cent more likely to compete than their female counterparts, though the coefficient is not precisely estimated.

Columns [2] and [5] report the estimates from model 2, in which we control for other factors potentially contributing to the willingness to compete. These include individuals' competence in performing correct additions, risk aversion, over-confidence, potential ability to sustain pressure and gender composition and the size of the game session. From columns [2] and [5], we see that the 1958 female cohort in Beijing is 14.9 per cent more competitively inclined, an increase from 14.1 per cent in model 1, while for the Taipei cohort, the male advantage is more than halved. For the Beijing sample, the only other factors affecting whether individuals choose to compete are their adding-up ability (number of correct answers in Round 2) and their ability to sustain pressure (difference in number of correct answers in rounds 1 and 2). However, for the Taipei sample, we see that risk aversion, the Raven's test score, as well as whether the session attended is a single-sex session also play an important role. In columns [3] and [6], we control for further individual characteristics. Again, the female advantage for the Beijing 1958 cohort increased further to 15.9 per cent, while for the same cohort in Taipei, the male advantage reduced to 3.7 per cent. We now compare the competitive inclination of the 1958 Beijing women with their younger counterparts. The results from model 1 (column [1]) suggest that the 1966 women are equally competitive as the 1958 cohort, while the 1977 cohort is more competitive than their 1958 counterparts. However, once we control for model 2 (column [2]) for the competence level and other potential reasons for choosing to compete, the coefficients for both the 1966 and 1977 cohorts become negative but statistically insignificant. This suggests that women across cohorts are equally competitive. Further controlling for personal characteristics (column [3]), the size of the negative coefficients increases, but none are precisely estimated. Nevertheless, the coefficient for the 1966 relative to the 1958 cohort is reasonably large (-0.12). The situation is similar for the Taipei women.

We next estimate the following pooled regression for Beijing and Taipei, shown in (2). This allows us to compare not only the gender gap in competitive inclination across cohorts within each region but also that between Beijing women and their Taipei counterparts:

$$(2)\ Comp_{ij} = \alpha + \beta_j Coh_{ij} + \kappa Male_{ij} + \rho_j Coh_{ij} \times Male_{ij} + \theta W_{ij} + \gamma X_{ij} + \pi B_{ij} + \beta^b Coh_{ij} \times B_{ij} + \kappa^b Male_{ij} \times B_{ij} + Coh_{ij} \times Male_{ij} \times B_{ij} + \theta^b W_{ij} \times B_{ij} + \gamma^b X_{ij} \times B_{ij} + \varepsilon_{ij},$$

where B is an indicator for the Beijing sample and the superscript ^{b} denotes the coefficient for the Beijing sample.

Booth et al. (2018, Appendix A, Table A.1) indicate how to interpret the coefficients from (2). The selected results from estimation of (2) are reported in Table A12.2, and the implied differences in competitive inclination, both across cohorts within a region and across regions, are reported in Table 12.4.

The results here confirm those obtained from Table 12.3, namely that women in the 1958 Beijing cohort are more competitively inclined than their male counterparts, whereas controlling for all variables (model 3 in Table 12.4), none of the other cohorts in either Beijing or Taipei exhibits a significant gender difference.

Table 12.4: Gender gap in competitive inclination across cohorts and regions

Pooled sample estimation	Model 1		Model 2		Model 3	
	Taipei	Beijing	Taipei	Beijing	Taipei	Beijing
1958 male vs. female	0.083 [0.088]	−0.142* (0.075)	0.039 [0.081]	−0.151* (0.082)	0.037 [0.085]	−0.159* (0.069)
1966 male vs. female	0.084 (0.364)	0.186** (0.031)	0.064 (0.477)	0.148* (0.096)	0.051 (0.577)	0.139 (0.123)
1977 male vs. female	−0.016 (0.873)	0.022 (0.804)	−0.008 (0.929)	0.051 (0.568)	−0.019 (0.815)	0.053 (0.552)
1966 female vs. 1958 female	0.027 [0.088]	0.000 (0.272)	−0.042 [0.082]	−0.095 (0.272)	−0.049 [0.085]	−0.119 (0.194)
1977 female vs. 1958 female	0.165* [0.090]	0.179** (0.040)	0.045 [0.088]	−0.004 (0.965)	0.010 [0.093]	−0.057 (0.582)
BJ 1958 female vs. TP 1958 female	−0.161* [0.085]	–	0.786*** [0.286]	–	0.643* [0.338]	–
BJ 1966 female vs. TP 1966 female	−0.188** (0.030)	–	0.733** (0.013)	–	0.573* (0.093)	–
BJ 1977 female vs. TP 1977 female	−0.142 (0.112)	–	0.737** (0.016)	–	0.576 (0.106)	–

Note: *** p<0.01; ** p<0.05; * p<0.1; BJ = Beijing; TP = Taipei; Robust standard errors in squared brackets; those in the parentheses are p-values from the joint significant tests.

Do these results indicate that the observed gender gap for the Beijing 1958 cohort is mainly due to the male 1958 group being less competitive than the women? We examine this issue in several steps. First, we examine whether women in the Beijing 1958 cohort are more or less competitively inclined than their younger counterparts. The second panel of Table 12.4 reports these results. It shows that the 1958 women in Beijing are no less, if not more, competitively inclined than the 1966 and 1977 cohort women in Beijing. In particular, relative to the 1966 women in Beijing, they are almost 12 per cent more likely to choose to compete, although this is not precisely estimated.

Second, we compare women in Beijing with their respective cohort women in Taipei. These results are exhibited in the third panel. We show that women in the Beijing 1958, 1966 and 1967 cohorts are all more competitively inclined than their respective counterparts in Taipei. The differences in their competitive inclination are large. For the 1977 cohort, however, the difference is precisely estimated only in model 2.

Third, using results from model 3, we also test whether women in the Beijing 1958 cohort are more competitively inclined than the Taipei 1958 males and both genders in the Taipei 1966 and 1977 cohorts. The test results confirm that they are indeed more competitively inclined than these other groups.

We now investigate if the pattern observed in our laboratory setting is consistent with real-world outcomes. An important gender equality measure should be labour force participation. However, the official retirement age for Mainland China is 50–55 for women and 60 for men, while in Taiwan it is 60 for women and 65 for men. The 1958 cohort was aged 57 at the time the experiments were conducted, and at that time, our Mainland female cohort had reached retirement age, while the Mainland male cohort and both genders in Taiwan had not. Thus, it is hard to compare labour force participation rates across cohorts and regions. Therefore, we instead use individuals' take-home income from workplaces (including wages, bonuses, subsidies or retirement income) and income from both workplaces and government (mainly for retirement income). Table 12.5 reports these average monthly incomes by cohort and gender as well as male/female income ratios. The data revealed in Table 12.5 (bottom row of top panel) suggest that, on average, Beijing women bring home 37 per cent less income than their male counterparts if we only count income they obtained from workplaces and work-related pensions (the top panel, third column). If we also take into account pensions and other transfers from the government, the ratio reduces to 25 per cent. In Taipei, however, the take-home income gap between males and females is around 61 per cent in both cases.

Table 12.5: Gender income gap

	Beijing			Taipei		
	Males	**Females**	**Male/female**	**Males**	**Females**	**Male/female**
All income from workplaces (including retirement income)						
1958	3,729	3,755	0.99	7,615	3,888	1.95
1966	6,210	4,170	1.48	11,035	6,378	1.73
1977	7,518	5,242	1.43	9,237	7,128	1.29
Total	6,047	4,408	1.37	9,228	5,746	1.60
Income from workplaces and government						
1958	4,529	5,036	0.90	7,735	4,277	1.81
1966	6,324	4,462	1.41	11,036	6,428	1.72
1977	7,518	5,567	1.35	9,308	7,177	1.30
Total	6,296	5,034	1.25	9,295	5,914	1.57

	Relative to person of opposite sex with same age/education, your income is					
	Beijing			**Taipei**		
	More	**Less**	**Same**	**More**	**Less**	**Same**
Males						
1958	26.83	14.63	58.54	31.15	29.51	30.34
1966	25.00	20.00	55.00	32.14	35.71	32.14
1977	27.59	15.52	56.90	31.48	27.78	40.74
Females						
1958	33.33	8.77	57.89	38.71	22.58	38.71
1966	33.33	10.53	56.14	59.02	11.48	29.51
1977	37.70	9.84	52.46	50.91	14.55	34.55

Source: Authors' calculation from exit survey data.

When we compare the gender income gap by cohort, we find that, except for the 1958 Beijing cohort, the gender wage gaps $[(Wage_m / Wage_f) - 1]$ for all the cohorts in both Beijing and Taipei are positive. For the Beijing 1958 cohort, women bring home, on average, more income than their male counterparts. If we only count incomes from workplaces, the difference is a mere 1 per cent. If we consider pensions from the government as well, the difference increases to 10 per cent.

In the survey, we also ask individuals whether they think their own income is more, less, or about the same as an individual at the same age, same education level, but opposite gender. We report the proportion of each cohort/gender group's opinion for both Taipei and Beijing in the third panel of Table 12.5. In general, more than 50 per cent of individuals in both genders and all cohorts in Beijing reported that their income is the same as their opposite-gender counterparts. The ratio is slightly higher for older than younger cohorts. The proportion in each Taipei cohort choosing equal payment is substantially lower. Surprisingly, a large proportion of women in the Taipei cohorts believe they earn more than their male counterparts.

We conducted a few sensitivity tests for the robustness of our estimated results reported in Table 12.3. First, as discussed earlier (footnote 4), the results from the pre-experiment test on whether the subjects understood the game show that there are a few individuals in both the Beijing and Taipei samples who appear not to have understood the game very well. Our main results included these people, and here we test including a dummy variable to indicate them or excluding them from the estimation. The results are reported in Panel (a) of Table 12.6. As can be seen from Table 12.6, either adding a dummy variable or excluding these people from the estimation does not change our results.

Second, we also examine whether the estimated gender difference in willingness to compete across cohorts is capturing differences in work experience rather than exposure to different institutional regimes. If those who work more become more confident, which in turn increases one's competitiveness, the older cohort would also exhibit a higher level of willingness to compete, though it cannot explain the difference in the gender gap across cohorts. We nevertheless test the possibility of work experience being the driving force by generating individuals' work experience variable based on their reported work history. This variable is then added to our regression of (2), and the results are reported in columns [1] and [2] in Panel (b) of Table 12.6. The results show that, in both the Beijing and Taipei samples, adding this variable does not change our main results on gender gaps in willingness to compete across different cohorts.

Table 12.6: Sensitivity tests

Panel (a)	**Test for incl. or excl. of obs. who misunderstood the game**					
	Beijing			**Taipei**		
	Total sample no control [1]	**Total sample incl. dummy [2]**	**Excl. mist sample [3]**	**Total sample no control [1]**	**Total sample incl. dummy [2]**	**Excl. mist sample [3]**
Dummy for males	−0.159* [0.087]	−0.160* [0.087]	−0.155* [0.094]	0.037 [0.085]	0.035 [0.086]	0.031 [0.087]
Dummy for 1966	−0.119 [0.093]	−0.117 [0.093]	−0.110 [0.100]	−0.049 [0.085]	−0.050 [0.085]	−0.091 [0.088]
Dummy for 1977	−0.057 [0.103]	−0.056 [0.103]	−0.048 [0.112]	0.010 [0.093]	0.009 [0.094]	0.013 [0.095]
Male* 1966	0.299** [0.124]	0.302** [0.123]	0.282** [0.134]	0.014 [0.119]	0.015 [0.119]	0.051 [0.122]
Male* 1977	0.212* [0.120]	0.212* [0.119]	0.181 [0.126]	−0.058 [0.117]	−0.056 [0.118]	−0.065 [0.119]
Dummy for mistake	–	−0.077 [0.085]	–	−0.026 [0.133]	–	–
Observations	330	330	300	354	354	340
R^2	0.15	0.15	0.16	0.23	0.23	0.24

Pannel (b)	Beijing sample			
	Control for work experience		Intergeneration test	
	Beijing [1]	Taipei [2]	Mother [3]	Father (4)
Dummy for males	−0.158* [0.088]	0.061 [0.086]	−0.155* [0.088]	−0.155* [0.087]
Dummy for 1966	−0.121 [0.100]	−0.049 [0.084]	−0.111 [0.094]	−0.108 [0.094]
Dummy for 1977	−0.064 [0.138]	−0.021 [0.096]	−0.002 [0.126]	0.006 [0.125]
Male* 1966	0.298** [0.124]	−0.011 [0.120]	0.300** [0.124]	0.298** [0.124]
Male* 1977	0.212* [0.120]	−0.085 [0.119]	0.208* [0.120]	0.208* [0.120
No. years worked	0.000 [0.005]	−0.004 [0.003]	–	–
Years mum under Mao regime	–	–	−0.005 [0.007]	–
Years dad under Mao regime	–	–	–	−0.006 [0.007]
Observations	330	354	330	330
R^2	0.15	0.24	0.15	0.15

Notes: *** $p<0.01$; ** $p<0.05$; * $p<0.1$. Other control variables included here are the same as those in Table 12.3; robust standard errors in squared brackets.

Finally, we also investigate whether there is an intergenerational impact of indoctrination using a variable measuring the number of years parents spent when they were young in the communist era. In other words, we use the number of years between 1949 and 1978 during which parents were aged 7–20 years of age. The results for the Beijing sample for mother and father separately are reported in columns [3] and [4] in Panel (b) of Table 12.6. These results indicate little intergenerational behavioural impact and that, controlling for intergenerational effects, our main results still hold. However, due to the high collinearity between the birth cohort dummies and the parental communist experience, 94 per cent of the 1977 cohort had parents who had such experience as opposed to 2 per cent for the 1958 cohort and 20 per cent for the 1966 cohort. It is therefore possible that the small gender gap in willingness to compete for the 1977 Beijing cohort as compared to their 1966 cohort counterparts may be partially due to the intergenerational impact.

Mechanisms

Alesina and Fuchs-Schundeln (2007) discussed the endogenous role political regimes play in forming people's tastes for public social policies. They provide strong evidence that there is a feedback effect from the regime on people's attitudes. In our experiment, the finding that women in the 1958 Beijing cohort are more willing to compete may well be related to this feedback effect. In this section, we further explore the mechanisms through which women growing up under different regimes form different preferences. To examine if there is a long-lasting communist indoctrination effect, we follow Alesina and Fuchs-Schundeln (2007) and check what other evidence there is in our data that indicates attitudes towards government intervention in social and economic affairs differ across cohorts and regions. In our exit survey, we asked subjects if they believe that the government should play a role in reducing income inequality in general and if they support the view that the less intervention from the government in the economy, the better. The answers are given on a scale of 1 to 5, with 1 being strongly disagree and 5 being strongly agree. Using these data as the dependent variables, we estimate using OLS a modified version of (2) without the game controls and add log individual income into the vector X_{ij}. The selected results are reported in the first two columns of Table 12.7, where we report three panels: the top panel reports the selected estimated coefficients from the regressions of modified (2), the middle panel reports the implied differences across cohorts and regions based on the top panel coefficients and the bottom panel reports differences between Beijing women/men and Taipei women/men based on results from the regressions that look only at aggregated differences and disregard cohort variations.

Table 12.7: Results from subjective questions

	Preference		Mother's teaching			School's teaching		
	Reduce inequality [1]	Less intervention [2]	Gender equality [3]	Competition [4]	Unselfishness [5]	Gender equality [6]	Competition [7]	Unselfishness [8]
Beijing	1.767*** [0.624]	-1.565* [0.837]	0.735*** [0.276]	0.064 [0.299]	0.882*** [0.288]	0.816** [0.335]	0.602* [0.322]	0.917*** [0.311]
Dummy for 1966 × Beijing	−0.332 [0.223]	−0.245 [0.250]	−0.028 [0.131]	−0.091 [0.122]	−0.212 [0.132]	−0.227* [0.129]	0.136 [0.132]	−0.160 [0.127]
Dummy for 1977 × Beijing	0.142 [0.241]	−0.256 [0.307]	0.217 [0.146]	0.061 [0.131]	0.063 [0.143]	0.011 [0.140]	0.293** [0.147]	0.022 [0.135]
Dummy for male × Beijing	−0.130 [0.208]	−0.224 [0.281]	−0.053 [0.137]	−0.075 [0.125]	−0.163 [0.132]	−0.203 [0.131]	0.089 [0.137]	0.032 [0.126]
Dummy for 1966 × male × Beijing	0.490 [0.303]	0.305 [0.373]	0.112 [0.187]	0.089 [0.173]	0.340* [0.186]	0.263 [0.185]	−0.154 [0.188]	0.143 [0.178]
Dummy for 1977 × male × Beijing	−0.298 [0.314]	0.511 [0.397]	−0.081 [0.187]	−0.061 [0.167]	0.107 [0.184]	−0.160 [0.184]	−0.256 [0.189]	−0.347** [0.173]
Dummy for 1966	0.155 [0.134]	0.385** [0.157]	−0.084 [0.086]	0.070 [0.077]	0.215* [0.086]	0.099 [0.089]	−0.058 [0.088]	0.042 [0.082]
Dummy for 1977	0.003 [0.165]	0.164 [0.176]	−0.044 [0.097]	−0.012 [0.079]	−0.007 [0.091]	−0.105 [0.094]	−0.112 [0.097]	−0.089 [0.082]
Dummy for males	0.332** [0.142]	0.667*** [0.188]	0.025 [0.086]	0.049 [0.074]	0.035 [0.081]	0.105 [0.086]	−0.050 [0.087]	−0.062 [0.071]
Dummy for 1966 × male	−0.329 [0.203]	-0.712*** [0.248]	0.051 [0.122]	−0.093 [0.109]	-0.231* [0.120]	−0.158 [0.124]	0.142 [0.124]	−0.008 [0.108]
Dummy for 1977 × male	−0.023 [0.214]	−0.564** [0.259]	0.048 [0.126]	−0.071 [0.105]	0.093 [0.121]	0.208* [0.125]	0.135 [0.126]	0.218** [0.107]
Observations	687	687	685	685	685	686	686	686
R^2	0.041	0.054	0.058	0.031	0.054	0.073	0.048	0.119

	Preference		Mother's teaching			School's teaching		
	Reduce inequality [1]	Less intervention [2]	Gender equality [3]	Competition [4]	Unselfishness [5]	Gender equality [6]	Competition [7]	Unselfishness [8]
Derived from regression by cohort								
BJ 1958 male vs. female	0.202	0.443**	-0.028	-0.026	-0.128	-0.098	0.039	-0.030
BJ 1966 male vs. female	0.363**	0.036	0.135	-0.030	-0.019	0.007	0.027	0.105
BJ 1977 male vs. female	-0.119	0.390*	-0.061	-0.158*	0.072	-0.050	-0.082	-0.159*
BJ 1966 female vs. 1958 female	-0.177	0.140	-0.112	-0.021	0.003	-0.128	0.078	-0.118
BJ 1977 female vs. 1958 female	0.145	-0.092	-0.173	0.049	0.056	-0.094	0.181*	-0.067
BJ 1958 female vs. TP 1958 female	1.767***	-1.565*	0.735***	0.064	0.882***	0.816**	0.602*	0.917***
BJ 1966 female vs. TP 1966 female	1.435**	-1.810**	0.707**	-0.027	0.670**	0.589*	0.738**	0.757**
BJ 1977 female vs. TP 1977 female	1.909***	-1.821**	0.955***	0.125	0.945***	0.827**	0.896***	0.939***
Derived from aggregate regression								
BJ female vs. TP female	1.685***	-1.699**	0.735***	0.053	0.781***	0.752**	0.691**	0.894***
BJ male vs. TP male	1.610*	-1.676**	0.690**	-0.021	0.784***	0.590*	0.643**	0.862***

Notes: Robust standard errors in squared brackets; *** $p<0.01$; ** $p<0.05$; * $p<0.1$. The middle panel is calculated based on the coefficients from the top panel of Table 12. while the regression coefficients used to calculate the bottom panel results are not shown here. Most of the significant levels in the middle and bottom panels are based on the *p*-value from joint significant tests, except for the rows labelled 'BJ 1958 female versus TP 1958 female' and 'BJ female versus TP female', which are directly obtained from the coefficients for Beijing dummy variable in each regression and the significance level is based on t-statistics. 'BJ' and 'TP' are abbreviations for Beijing and Taipei, respectively.

The results for the state-intervention preference variables suggest that, in general, the Mainland Chinese female cohorts, relative to the Taiwanese female cohorts, are much more likely to support the view that the government should try to reduce income inequality and much less likely to think that the less government intervention in the economy, the better. On a scale of 1 to 5 points, the three female cohorts are 1.4 to 1.9 points more likely to support the government reducing inequality and 1.6 to 1.8 points less likely to think that less government intervention in the economy the better. These are very large differences, between 28 per cent to 38 per cent of the total scores. These results are largely consistent across the three female cohorts.

If we examine the bottom panel, which treats male and female subjects in Beijing and Taipei as single groups, we see that this conclusion applies to males as well. Thus, after 40 years of market-oriented economic reform, the society is still largely geared towards equality and government intervention. This finding is in line with that of Alesina and Fuchs-Schundeln (2007) – that communist propaganda has a long-lasting effect. In addition, our results indicate that individuals who grew up subject to a heavy dose of indoctrination, and individuals who largely grew up with a new ideology, all seem to prefer more state intervention in social and economic affairs. This latter finding differs slightly from that of Alesina and Fuchs-Schundeln (2007), which revealed that in East Germany, those born after 1975 have a much weaker preference for government intervention relative to their older counterparts. This difference between their results and ours may relate to two broad sets of factors. First, after German reunification, Communism was discredited, and there was a large migration from East to West Germany. Second, in Mainland China, the Communist Party is still the ruling party, even though the economy largely operates under market economic rules. Interestingly, according to our results, only the behaviour of the cohort that grew up during the communist regime is in line with the communist indoctrination, while the behaviour has changed for cohorts growing up in the economic reform era. Yet the attitudinal differences across cohorts seem to be limited. This may be related to the lack of continuation in propaganda on gender issues, which affects gender willingness to compete, as we will discuss below,[12] whereas the government's role in the economy persisted in the reform era.

12 See the discussion below on parental and school teaching on gender equality. There we observe that in Beijing, relative to the 1966 and 1977 cohorts, there is a higher probability that the 1958 cohort was taught gender equality by mothers and schools.

Is the difference in gender willingness to compete and in the preference for government intervention for social and economic issues really a reflection of indoctrination? There is a small literature that discusses intergenerational transmission of cultural norms (Bisin and Verdier 2000; Tabellini 2010; Nunn and Wantchekon 2011).[13] In the post-experiment survey, we follow their ideas and ask respondents to pick, from a list of qualities or attributes, those that their parents and school encouraged when they were young. We report here the results from our examination of three attributes that are related to the competitive inclination and preference for inequality in general:

- encourage to believe that men and women are equal;
- encourage to be competitive; and
- encourage to be unselfish.

We generate two dummy variables for each of these qualities: whether the mother or school encouraged individuals to have these qualities (yes = 1, 0 otherwise). The modified version of (2) is estimated using a linear probability model (LPM) for ease of interpretation of the coefficients. The results for mothers' encouragement and schools' encouragement are reported in columns [3]–[8] of Table 12.7. The three panels separately report the regression coefficients; the implied differences across gender, cohorts and region; and the aggregated differences between Beijing and Taipei for females and males. The results on gender equality (both from mothers' and schools' teaching) show that there is no consistent gender difference within each Beijing cohort. Relative to the 1958 Beijing females, those who were born later are consistently less likely to have either their mother or school encourage them to believe in gender equality. Although the size of the differences is large (9 per cent to 13 per cent), none of the differences are precisely estimated. Relative to Taipei women, however, Beijing women in all three cohorts are more likely to have their parents or school encourage them to have the view of gender equality. The difference in probability ranges from 70 per cent to 74 per cent for mothers' encouragement and 59 per cent to 82 per cent for schools' encouragement. This is not only the case for females; the bottom panel shows that Beijing males were equally more likely to have their mothers and schools encourage them to adopt the view of gender equality than their Taipei counterparts.

13 The basic idea of the Tabellini model is that individuals inherit parental norms and make decisions accordingly.

Regarding being competitive, Mainland parents do not seem to have prepared their children any more than their Taiwan counterparts. However, schools in Beijing did, but this seems to be more so for the later cohorts than for the 1958 cohort. Mainland parents and schools are more likely to teach their children to be unselfish than their Taiwan counterparts – further evidence of the communist indoctrination. This is true for all female and male cohorts. It is also true that the probability is higher for the 1958 Beijing cohort than that for the later Beijing cohort, but the differences are not statistically significant.

How did propaganda affect individuals' behaviour and preferences 40 years after the change of the regime? Psychologists have long been discussing how social norms about sex roles may affect children's personality characteristics and behavioural competencies to prepare them to fulfil the societal expectations so that they can perform those roles (Horner 1972; Fitzgerald and Betz 1983).

Our post-experiment survey implemented the 'Big Five inventory', which consists of 44 questions designed to elicit individuals' personality traits. The psychological literature has identified the overlap between extroversion and competitiveness (Hogan 1986; Digman 1990; Chen et al. 2011). Recent empirical studies on online game players also identified that individuals who have higher scores on openness, extroversion, and conscientiousness are more likely to be players (Teng 2008). We examine across gender-cohort-region differences in the 'Big Five' personality by estimating (2) without controlling for W_{ij} and X_{ij}.[14] The implied difference in personality traits derived from the estimated results is reported in Table 12.8.

We find that females in all Beijing cohorts are more extroverted than their male counterparts, though only the 1977 cohort exhibits a statistically significant difference. More importantly, all three cohorts of Beijing women are statistically significantly more extroverted than their Taipei counterparts. The aggregated estimation (the bottom panel of Table 12.8) also confirms that Beijing females are more extroverted than Taipei males and females, and they are more extroverted than Beijing males. However, it does not seem to be the case that there are significant cohort differences in extroversion. If anything, the 1958 cohort seems to be slightly less extroverted than their younger counterparts, but the differences are not statistically significant.

14 The reason we include no personal control is because most of the controls are endogenous.

Table 12.8: Derived differences in personality traits by gender, cohort and region

	Extroversion	Openness	Agreeableness	Neuroticism	Conscientiousness
Derived from regression by cohort					
BJ 1958 male vs female	−0.122	−0.230**	−0.244**	−0.015	−0.138
BJ 1966 male vs female	−0.016	−0.025	−0.005	−0.110	0.160*
BJ 1977 male vs female	−0.205**	−0.172*	−0.262**	0.027	−0.182*
BJ 1966 female vs 1958 female	0.014	−0.025	−0.138	0.028	−0.113
BJ 1977 female vs 1958 female	0.136	0.167*	0.109	−0.054	0.137
BJ 1958 female vs TP 1958 female	0.238***	0.325***	0.026	−0.093	−0.001
BJ 1966 female vs TP 1966 female	0.348***	0.189**	−0.073	−0.216***	−0.101
BJ 1977 female vs TP 1977 female	0.235**	0.217**	0.219***	−0.318***	0.121
Derived from aggregate regression					
BJ female vs TP female	0.279***	0.252***	0.058	−0.208***	0.010
BJ male vs TP male	0.045	−0.087	−0.040	−0.039	−0.106*
BJ females vs TP males	0.153***	0.043	0.126**	−0.005	−0.061
BJ male vs BJ female	−0.108*	−0.130**	−0.166***	−0.034	−0.045

Notes: BJ = Beijing; TP = Taipei.

Source: Derived from authors' estimation of regressions reported in Booth et al. (2018).

With regard to openness, for the 1958 and 1977 birth cohorts, we observed statistically significant gender differences within the Beijing sample. Women are more open than men. Beijing women are also more open than Taipei women in every cohort, and the size of the difference is the largest for the 1958 cohort. Further, at the aggregated level, Beijing women have higher openness scores than their Beijing male, Taipei male and Taipei female counterparts. Once again, we fail to detect across-cohort variations among Beijing females, which may help to shed light on why the 1958 Beijing women are more competitive.

For agreeableness, neuroticism and conscientiousness, we find similar but less statistically significant patterns. The Beijing women seem to be more agreeable, less neurotic and more conscientious than Beijing males, Taipei females and Taipei males. These results provide some weak evidence that perhaps indoctrination at a young age could affect an individual's personality and subsequently affect individuals' behaviour. To this end, more research is needed.

Conclusions

In the laboratory experiment reported in this chapter, we explored how evolving cultural norms in Mainland China changed individuals' preferences. From 1949 onwards, China experienced dramatic changes in its socioeconomic institutions that started with communist central planning and the deliberate establishment of new social norms, including the promotion of gender equality in place of the Confucian view of female 'inferiority'. Market-oriented reforms, begun in 1978, have helped China achieve unprecedented economic growth, and at the same time, Marxist ideology was gradually replaced by the acceptance of individualistic free-market ideology. During this reform period, although the Communist Party remained firmly in place, many old traditions crept back, and social norms gradually changed again.

The subjects of our experiment were different birth cohorts of men and women who were exposed to one of the two regimes outlined above during their crucial developmental age, and we investigated gender differences in their competitive choices. To summarise, our conjecture was that the cohort exposed to the most extreme gender equality propaganda would not only behave differently from other cohorts in Mainland China, but also from Taiwan – their counterparts in a society with similar ethnic and Confucian roots but with a divergent history and economic growth path from 1949.

In particular, we investigated gender differences in competitive choices for three different birth cohorts in Beijing, using their counterparts in Taipei (who were subject to the same original Confucian traditions) to control for the general time trend.

Our main results confirm:

- females in Beijing are significantly more likely to choose to compete than females from Taipei;
- Beijing females from the 1958 birth cohort are more competitive than their male counterparts, as well as more competitive than later Beijing birth cohorts;
- for Taipei, there are no statistically significant differences across cohort or gender in willingness to compete.

In summary, our findings confirm that exposure to different institutions and social norms during the crucial developmental age changes individuals' behaviour. By recruiting subjects who spent their entire formative years during the communist regime and those who spent their entire formative years just after the communist regime, we show that exposure to the strong gender equality message for a relatively short period can change women's willingness to compete. To the extent that today's world is embarking on a journey to defy the old gender order, this finding may have important policy implications. Our findings also provide further evidence that gender differences in economic preferences are not innately determined.

Acknowledgements

This chapter was previously published as Booth, A., Fan, E., Meng, X., and Zhang, D. (2018). 'Gender differences in willingness to compete: The role of culture and institutions', *The Economic Journal*, 129(618):734–764. doi.org/10.1111/ecoj.12583.

We thank James Jilu Zhang for excellent research assistance. We thank Anpeng Li, who provided data extracted from *People's Daily* for Figure 12.1. Funding from the Australian Research Council, the College of Business and Economics at ANU and National Taiwan University is gratefully acknowledged. Ethics approval for the experiment was obtained from the Ethics Committee of The Australian National University and that of National Taiwan University. Thanks also to Bob Gregory, Sen Xue and seminar participants at The Australian National University, Deakin University, University of Western Australia and at the meetings of the European Association of Labour Economics in Ghent.

References

Akerlof, G., and Kranton, R. (2000). 'Economics and identity', *The Quarterly Journal of Economics*, 115(3):715–753. doi.org/10.1162/003355300555201.

Alesina, A., and Fuchs-Schundeln, N. (2007). 'Good-bye Lenin (or not?): The effect of communism on people's preferences', *American Economic Review*, 97(4):1507–1528. doi.org/10.1257/aer.97.4.1507.

Alesina, A., Giuliano, P., and Nunn, N. (2013). 'On the origins of gender roles: Women and the plough', *The Quarterly Journal of Economics*, 128(2):469–530. doi.org/10.1093/qje/qjt005.

Bisin, A., and Verdier, T. (2000). '"Beyond the melting pot": Cultural transmission, marriage, and the evolution of ethnic and religious traits', *The Quarterly Journal of Economics*, 115(3):955–988. doi.org/10.1162/003355300554953.

Booth, A.L., and Nolen, P.J. (2012). 'Choosing to compete: How different are girls and boys?', *Journal of Economic Behavior & Organization*, 81(2):542–555. doi.org/10.1016/j.jebo.2011.07.018.

Booth, A., Fan, E., Meng, X., and Zhang, D. (2018). 'Gender differences in willingness to compete: The role of culture and institutions', *The Economic Journal*, 129(618):734–764. doi.org/10.1111/ecoj.12583.

Buser, T. (2012). 'The impact of the menstrual cycle and hormonal contraceptives on competitiveness', *Journal of Economic Behavior & Organization*, 83(1):1–10. doi.org/10.1016/j.jebo.2011.06.006.

Cai, H., Kwan, V., and Sedikides, C. (2012). 'A sociocultural approach to narcissism: The case of modern China', *European Journal of Personality*, 26(5):529–535. doi.org/10.1002/per.852.

Chen, X.P., Xie, X., and Chang, S. (2011). 'Cooperative and competitive orientation among Chinese people: Scale development and validation', *Management and Organization Review*, 7(2):353–379. doi.org/10.1111/j.1740-8784.2011.00215.x.

Croll, E. (1983). *Chinese Women since Mao*. London: Zed Books.

Croll, E. (1995). *Changing Identities of Chinese Women: Rhetoric, Experience, and Self-Perception in Twentieth-Century China*. Hong Kong: Hong Kong University Press; London: Zed Books.

Deng, Z., and Treiman, D.J. (1997). 'The impact of the Cultural Revolution on trends in educational attainment in the People's Republic of China', *American Journal of Sociology*, 103(2):391–428. doi.org/10.1086/231212.

Digman, J.M. (1990). 'Personality structure: Emergence of the five-factor model', *Annual Review of Psychology*, 41:417–440. doi.org/10.1146/annurev.ps.41.020190.002221.

Fernandez, R., Fogli, A., and Olivetti, C. (2004). 'Mothers and sons: Preference formation and female labor force dynamics', *The Quarterly Journal of Economics*, 119(4):1249–1299. doi.org/10.1162/0033553042476224.

Fitzgerald, L., and Betz, N. (1983). 'Issues in the vocational psychology of women'. In W.B. Walsh and S.H. Osipow (eds), *Handbook of Vocational Psychology*, vol. 1, pp. 83–159. Hillsdale: Erlbaum.

Gneezy, U., and Potters, J. (1997). 'An experiment on risk taking and evaluation periods', *The Quarterly Journal of Economics*, 112(2):631–645. doi.org/10.1162/003355397555217.

Gneezy, U., and Rustichini, A. (2004). 'Gender and competition at a young age', *American Economic Review*, 94(2):377–381. doi.org/10.1257/0002828041301821.

Gneezy, U., Niederle, M., and Rustichini, A. (2003). 'Performance in competitive environments: Gender differences', *The Quarterly Journal of Economics*, 118(3):1049–1074. doi.org/10.1162/00335530360698496.

Gneezy, U., Leonard, K.L., and List, J.A. (2009). 'Gender differences in competition: Evidence from a matrilineal and a patriarchal society', *Econometrica*, 77(5):1637–1664. doi.org/10.3982/ECTA6690.

Guiso, L., Sapienza, P., and Zingales, L. (2006). 'Does culture affect economic outcomes?', *Journal of Economic Perspectives*, 20(2):23–48. doi.org/10.1257/jep.20.2.23.

Heckman, J. (2007). 'The economics, technology, and neuroscience of human capability formation', *Proceedings of the National Academy of Sciences*, 104(33): 13250–13255. doi.org/10.1073/pnas.0701362104.

Hinton, W. (1966). *Fanshen: A Documentary of Revolution in a Chinese Village*. New York: Vintage Books.

Hofstede, G., and Hofstede, G.J. (2005). *Cultures and Organizations: Software of the Mind*, 2nd edn. New York: McGraw-Hill.

Hogan, R. (1986). *Hogan Personality Inventory*. Minneapolis: National Computer Systems.

Horner, M. (1972). 'Toward an understanding of achievement-related conflicts in women', *Journal of Social Issues*, 28(2):157–175. doi.org/10.1111/j.1540-4560.1972.tb00023.x.

Klimstra, T. (2013). 'Adolescent personality development and identity formation', *Child Development Perspectives*, 7(2):80–84. doi.org/10.1111/cdep.12017.

Kohlberg, L., and Mayer, R. (1972). 'Development as the aim of education', *Harvard Educational Review*, 42(4):449–496. doi.org/10.17763/haer.42.4.kj6q8743r3j00j60.

Lippmann, Q., Georgieff, A., and Senik, C. (2016). 'Undoing gender with institutions: Lessons from the German division and reunification', Working Paper, Paris School of Economics.

Little, D. (2011). 'Marxism, communism, and women', [blog post]. Dearborn: University of Michigan.

Liu, E.M., Meng, J., and Wang, J.T. (2014). 'Confucianism and preferences: Evidence from lab experiments in Taiwan and China', *Journal of Economic Behavior & Organization*, 104:106–122. doi.org/10.1016/j.jebo.2013.09.008.

Lu, X. (2004). *Rhetoric of the Chinese Cultural Revolution: The Impact on Chinese Thought, Culture, and Communication*. Columbia: University of South Carolina Press.

Ma, L. (1995). *The Culture of Yi Women*. Chengdu: Sichuan Minzu Chubanshe.

Manski, C.F. (2000). 'Economic analysis of social interactions', *Journal of Economic Perspectives*, 14(3):115–136. doi.org/10.1257/jep.14.3.115.

Meng, X. (2000). 'Institutions and culture: Women's economic position in mainland China and Taiwan'. Department of Economics, Research School of Pacific and Asian Studies, The Australian National University.

Meng, X., and Gregory, R. (2002). 'The impact of interrupted education on subsequent educational attainment: A cost of the Chinese Cultural Revolution', *Economic Development and Cultural Change*, 50(4):935–959. doi.org/10.1086/342761.

Meng, X., and Kidd, M. (1997). 'Labour market reform and the changing structure of wage determination in China's state sector during the 1980s', *Journal of Comparative Economics*, 25(3):403–421. doi.org/10.1006/jcec.1997.1481.

Mow, S., Tao, J., and Zheng, B. (2004). *Holding Up Half the Sky: Chinese Women Past, Present, and Future*. New York: Feminist Press.

Niederle, M., and Vesterlund, L. (2007). 'Do women shy away from competition? Do men compete too much?', *The Quarterly Journal of Economics*, 122(3):1067–1101. doi.org/10.1162/qjec.122.3.1067.

Niida, N. (1964). 'Land reform and new marriage law in China', *The Developing Economies*, 2(1):3–15. doi.org/10.1111/j.1746-1049.1964.tb00667.x.

Nunn, N., and Wantchekon, L. (2011). 'The slave trade and the origins of mistrust in Africa', *American Economic Review*, 101(7):3221–3252. doi.org/10.1257/aer.101.7.3221.

Raven, J. (2000). 'The Raven's progressive matrices: Change and stability over culture and time', *Cognitive Psychology*, 41(1), pp. 1–48. doi.org/10.1006/cogp.1999.0735.

Sutter, M., and Glatzle-Rutzler, D. (2015). 'Gender differences in the willingness to compete emerge early in life and persist', *Management Science*, 61(10):2339–2354. doi.org/10.1287/mnsc.2014.1981.

Tabellini, G. (2010). 'Culture and institutions: Economic development in the regions of Europe', *Journal of the European Economic Association*, 8(4):677–716. doi.org/10.1111/j.1542-4774.2010.tb00537.x.

Teng, C.I. (2008). 'Personality differences between online game players and nonplayers in a student sample', *Cyberpsychology, Behavior, and Social Networking*, 11(2):232–234. doi.org/10.1089/cpb.2007.0064.

Tseng, P.S. (1992). 'The Chinese women: Past and present'. In Y.N. Li (ed.), *Chinese Women Through Chinese Eyes*, pp. 72–86. Armonk: An East Gate Book.

Voigtlander, N., and Voth, H.J. (2015). 'Nazi indoctrination and anti-semitic beliefs in Germany', *Proceedings of the National Academy of Sciences of the United States of America*, 112(26):7931–7936. doi.org/10.1073/pnas.1414822112.

Xu, Y., and Hamamura, T. (2014). 'Folk beliefs of cultural changes in China', *Frontiers in Psychology*, 5:1066. doi.org/10.3389/fpsyg.2014.01066.

Yao, Y., and You, W. (2016). 'Half sky over China: Women's political participation and sex imbalances: 1950–1990'. Unpublished manuscript, Peking University.

Zhang, Y.J. (2015). 'Culture, institutions, and the gender gap in competitive inclination: Evidence from the communist experiment in China'. MPRA Papers No. 47356, University Library of Munich.

Zhang, J., Han, J., Liu, P.W., and Zhao, Y. (2008). 'Trend in the gender earnings differential in urban China, 1988–2004', *ILR Review*, 61(2):224–243. doi.org/10.1177/001979390806100205.

13

Performance in mixed-sex and single-sex competitions: What we can learn from speedboat races in Japan

Alison L Booth and Eiji Yamamura

Introduction

A growing literature investigates whether gender gaps in economic outcomes might be due to differences in male and female attitudes to competition or to risk.[1] Some experimental studies have found that the competitive choices men and women make differ according to whether they compete against men or women in competitive environments (see Gneezy et al. 2003; Gneezy and Rustichini 2004; Niederle and Vesterlund 2011; and Booth and Nolen 2012). Moreover, the actual performance can vary, as in Gneezy et al. (2003), who used experimental data to show that women's performance in competitions differs depending on the gender of their competitors.

1 Studies investigating gender differences in performance in competitive environments include Gneezy et al. (2003), Niederle and Vesterlund (2007, 2011), Booth (2009), Dreber et al. (2011), Cárdenas et al. (2012), and Niederle (2014). Studies exploring gender differences in preference to enter a competition include Gneezy et al. (2009), Booth and Nolen (2012), Apicella and Dreber (2015), and Buser et al. (2017), while studies analysing attitudes towards risk include Booth et al. (2014), Dreber et al. (2014) and Khachatryan et al. (2015). Buser et al. (2014) explore how preference for competition across genders affects academic task choice. In a study that is closest to ours, Backus et al. (2016) find that the gender composition of chess tournaments affects the behaviour of men and women in ways that are detrimental to female performance.

In this chapter, we adopt a different but complementary approach to these experiments by analysing unique performance data from a real-world activity that is by its very nature competitive and where potential payoffs from winning are high. Women have been competing in this activity since the early 1950s under exactly the same conditions as men, and all participants are randomly allocated to either single-sex or mixed-sex groups for the competition. The activity is speedboat racing. In this occupation, women represent approximately 13 per cent of all racers, and they are treated as equals of men. The rules of the race are strictly monitored, and any breach of the rules results in disqualification. The potential payoffs are very high, but severe sanctions on disqualified racers mean they cannot participate, resulting in a fall in annual revenue. Consequently, racers have a strong incentive to follow the rules in order to win the race. But they also face trade-offs because, in order to win, they may have to engage in risky lane changing to improve their position.

Using data from these races, we explore how female and male performance and strategies in the mixed-sex races differ from the single-sex races. Our data are in panel form, where we have information for each racer's performance time and strategy across all the races in which they have competed. Thus, we have a total of over 15,000 women-race observations and over 127,000 men-race observations.

After controlling for unobservable individual-specific effects and other performance-relevant factors, we subsequently find the following: (i) The performance of female racers is slower in the mixed-sex races than in the all-female races, while men's time is faster in the mixed-sex races than in the all-male races. (ii) Men adopt a more confident or aggressive strategy to obtain advantageous positions in the mixed-sex races than in the men-only races, whereas women adopt a less aggressive strategy in the mixed-sex races than in the women-only races. (iii) There are no gender differences in disqualifications across the mixed-sex and the single-sex races.

The first finding above is of particular interest. It shows that female competitive performance, even for women who have chosen a competitive career and are very good at it, is enhanced by being in a single-sex environment rather than in a mixed-sex environment in which they are a minority. Our two other findings are also of great interest, since they follow from our investigation of the mechanisms through which our first finding operates.

The remainder of the chapter is set out as follows. We describe the institutional background of the Japanese Professional Motor Boat Race, and provide an overview of the data and a brief discussion of strategies. We then explain the estimation approach, present the estimation results and interpret the major findings, drawing out implications for future research.

Speedboat racing in Japan

Speedboat racing in Japan takes the form of tournaments that are tightly controlled by a central federation, the Japanese Speedboat Racing Association. Male and female racers receive exactly the same intensive training, and there is only one training school, the Yamato Boat School. Not only do women train with the men under the same conditions, but they also participate and compete with men in the races under the same conditions. Well before a race day, individuals are randomly assigned to mixed-sex or single-sex races.

To qualify as a professional speedboat racer, individuals between the ages of 15 and 29 years must train for one year and pass a final examination at Yamato Kyotei Gakko (Yamato Boat School).[2] Because of this wide age window, individuals who gain entry are from a variety of backgrounds, ranging from individuals who have completed only junior high school to individuals whose highest educational qualification is from a university. Moreover, some of the entrants have also had a subsequent career after completing their education. Thus, the time since graduation from the boat school is not just picking up age.

In this section, we describe the institution of speedboat racing in some detail, since an understanding of this is important for interpreting the data and estimates. Unless otherwise noted, our principal source of information is Himura (2015). In speedboat racing in Japan, there are about 1,600 racers, aged between 18 and 70 years,[3] of whom around 1,400 are men and 200 women. There are 24 speedboat racing stadiums throughout Japan, and boat races are randomly held about four days a week in each stadium. Racers

2 There were 1,435 applicants for the 2015 entrance exam to the Yamato Boat School. Of these, only 35 were admitted (27 men and 8 women) and 25 graduated. Training covers driving techniques and inspection and maintenance of the engine and boat.

3 The youngest racer is 16 years old. There is no compulsory retirement age. While students can enter the Yamato Kyotei Gakko (Yamato Boat School) from 15 years of age, it takes a year to graduate and become a racer, and hence the rule is that the age of the youngest racer is 16 years. However, this is the exceptional case. In the dataset used in this chapter, the youngest racer is 18 years old.

go to many different stadiums to compete. The racing circuit is a large artificial pond or sectioned-off body of water that is 600 metres in length. Competitors race around it three times, leading to a total race distance of 1,800 metres. In each racing meet, there are 12 races, and six racers compete in any given race. The prizes offered are considerable.

On race meeting day and before each race, each racer's name is announced. That individual then drives the boat (randomly allocated to him or her for that day) a distance of 150 metres along a straight section of the circuit. His or her performance time is immediately reported, and this provides a public measure of the racer's condition. A short exhibition time is held to indicate good condition, since the time depends not only on physical and mental factors (that may or may not vary across days) but also on the boat and its engine, randomly allocated to the racer for that day.[4]

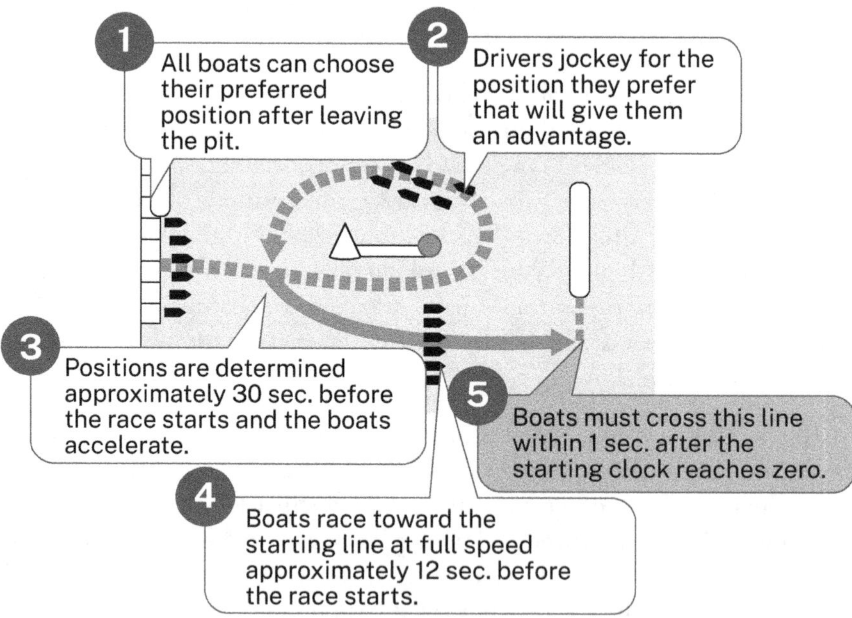

Figure 13.1: The premature start system

Source: Japan Boat Race Association (www.boatrace.jp).

4 Speedboat racing is financed from betting. The sport is run by local governments (the principal), that deputise tasks to the Japanese Motorboat Association (the agent). Local governments also own the boats, but the Japanese Motorboat Association is in charge of them. The boats used for racing at a particular stadium are always kept at that stadium.

Racers are obliged to inspect and mechanically maintain the boat and engine allocated to them and have no assistance in this task. They cannot reject either the boat or the engine that has been randomly assigned to them. Thus, racers are motivated to aim for a good exhibition time in order to understand the boat's condition and its match to their talents, and then to adopt a racing strategy dependent on that. Thus, racers use performance times in the exhibition run to obtain information not only about competitors but also about their own performance. This information is also used by bettors.

Speedboat racing uses the premature start system, in which boats must pass the starting line within 1 second after the starting clock reaches 0. 'Standby warm-up' refers to the period from the time racers receive the signal to leave the docks (pit) to the moment they cross the starting line. Racers' initial pits – and therefore lanes – are determined prior to the race by the committee of the association. However, racers can strategically change their lane during the initial period of turnaround, as illustrated in Figure 13.1 and may thus end up in a different position for the start of the race. Following in a position behind another boat is judged as a violation.

Racers and gender

Japanese speedboat racing is characterised by an openness to age and gender. Hence, a woman can compete with men and win if her performance time is the fastest of the racers in the mixed-sex race. For female racers, the difference between the women-only race and mixed-sex race is as follows: all five competitors are the same sex (female) in the women-only race, whereas in the mixed-sex race, almost all five competitors are the opposite sex. Consequently, we are able to examine how the gender of competitors influences women's performance. However, mixed-sex races are very different for men and women, since men always outnumber women in mixed races.

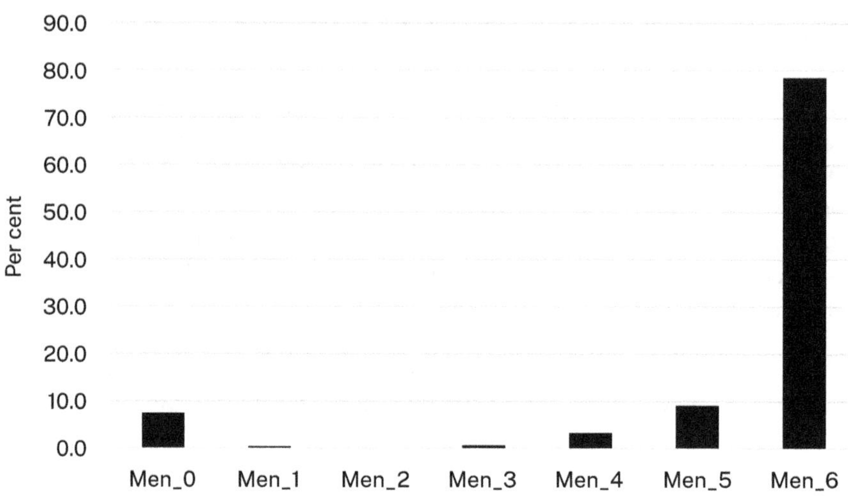

Figure 13.2: Composition of races according to number of male racers

Reflecting the gender ratio, there are only one or two women racers among six racers in most cases of mixed-sex races. Figure 13.2 breaks down races according to the number of men participating. In slightly fewer than 80 per cent of races, all six racers are men, while in 7 per cent of races, all six racers are women. The remainder – about 15 per cent – are mixed-sex races. Almost half of the mixed-sex races have only one woman competing with men racers. However, among different types of races, rules and conditions are equivalent.[5] Therefore, even in mixed-sex races, women racers are treated like men racers on an equal basis.[6] There is no difference in prize money between genders in the mixed-sex races or the all-male and all-female races.

Race grade, racer's grade, prizes and penalties

Race participants win prize money according to whether they finish first, second or third in each race. Moreover, all racers receive a fee for racing on race day, even if they are not placed. We define the order in which participants cross the finishing line as their place in that race. Races are also

5 An exception is minimum weight: men have to weigh more than 50 kg, and women have to be over 47.5 kg.

6 For all races, boats and motors are the same model and make and are used for only one year. However, individual performance may vary across boats and motors due to differences in deterioration and maintenance. To avoid unfairness across racers, allocation of machines is decided by drawing lots.

classified into five grades: super grade (SG), grade I (GI), grade II (GII), grade III (GIII), and 'usual' races. In the higher-grade races, the number of points that winners earn is greater (see Himura 2015). Any racer can participate in the 'usual' race, which is the bottom rank. In GIII races, racers under 30 years old with high winning rates are selected to participate. The criteria for being selected to participate in GII and GI races are stricter. In SG, racers are selected from top-ranked racers on the basis of prior performance. Within a year, the number of races is eight in the SG, around 40 in the GI, eight in the GII, around 50 in the GIII and almost every day for the 'usual' races.

Prize money for race winners is considerable: USD$300,000 (SG), $100,000 (GI), $40,000 (GII), $10,000 (GIII), and under $10,000 ('usual' racers). There are also other monetary prizes. In SG, for example, prize winnings are around $150,000 (second place), $50,000 (third), $20,000 (fourth), $10,000 (fifth), and under $10,000 (sixth).

The Japanese Motorboat Association selects race participants. Various status racers, from the top to the bottom levels, are evenly and randomly assigned to participate in the 'usual' races. As a result, the top-class racers participate not only in the high-grade races such as SG and GI but also in the 'usual' races.

As noted, a racer obtains points according to his or her order in the race. For example, in the bottom-grade race ('usual' race) and the next-to-bottom race (GIII), points accumulated in first, second, third, fourth, fifth, and sixth places are 10, 8, 6, 4, 2, and 1, respectively (Himura 2015). In the case of GI and GII (SG), 1 point (2 points) is added to each of the points listed above. But penalties are also possible. For instance, participants navigating poorly and breaking rules in the race or the turnaround period lose 7 points.

Individuals' aggregated points in a season are subsequently used to select participants in the top-grade (SG) race. Racers disqualified for interrupting other racers are automatically excluded from SG races. There is an extra element to point accumulation; each individual's points are aggregated for three years, and the total then determines racers' grades, known as A1, A2, B1, and B2. (We use this as a measure of ability.) Participants disqualified for interrupting others during a race lose 15 points. If they break the rules – for the actual race or in the turnaround period – they lose 2 points. Hence, racers have a considerable incentive not only to win the race but also to avoid rule-breaking and potentially losing their grade classification.

For the four grades of racer, average annual earnings associated with each grade are as follows: A1 (top) grade: $330,000; A2 grade: $190,000; B1 grade: $80,000; and B2 grade: $50,000. Higher-grade racers are allowed to participate in more races. Even on a day when there are no high-grade races, A1 racers can take part in the 'usual' race and so can earn something. Furthermore, higher-grade racers can also participate in higher-grade races with greater rewards. Percentages of women racers for A1, A2, B1, and B2 are about 11 per cent, 19 per cent, 46 per cent, and 23 per cent, respectively, while for men, they are around 21 per cent, 20 per cent, 43 per cent, and 14 per cent, respectively. Therefore, as a whole, the composition of ranks of racers for women is lower than men.

Racing in an inner lane confers an advantage. While racers are allowed to change lanes during the race, they are disqualified and face severe penalties if they interrupt other racers' runs. Thus, changing to an inner lane requires a highly skilled technique in order not to interrupt others. In the case of disqualification, apart from losing points, racers are penalised by being prohibited from racing for one month and banned from participating in GI and SG races for a year. Disqualification thus reduces aggregated points and lowers the chance of shifting to a higher grade, inevitably reducing annual revenue. All in all, top-class racers are skilled enough to change to a better lane while not interrupting other racers to avoid disqualification.

Strategies

In speedboat racing, contestants can choose a number of ways to boost their performance as well as adversely affect the performance of their immediate competitors. These activities involve costs, and contestants therefore face simple trade-offs when making decisions. By increasing effort and other performance-enhancing activities, a racer increases their probability of winning, but this extra effort is costly. The bigger the prize spread, the greater the expected gain from winning, and hence the more worthwhile it may be to boost one's own performance.

Strategies to improve own performance include not only effort in the actual race but also fine-tuning the engine of the randomly allocated boat and dieting before race day to be at an optimal weight. Strategies that adversely affect the performance of immediate competitors include seizing command of an inner lane as well as insulting or otherwise intimidating competitors (known in cricket as 'sledging'). While lane changing is easily observable, sledging is not. And yet it is a potent way to weaken opponents' concentration, causing them to underperform.

Psychological factors affect own performance and responses to the activities of other contestants. In our data, we have mixed-sex and single-sex races, so we can explore how the performance of men and women differs across these environments. The literature shows that women prefer not to compete against men (see Apicella and Dreber 2015; Cárdenas et al. 2012; Khachatryan et al. 2015). But in speedboat racing, women are sometimes compelled to go through their random allocation to boat race groups. This allocation is known several months before the actual races.

Racing a speedboat against others involves skill not only at manoeuvring the boat but also at jockeying for a desirable position, since the inner lanes confer an advantage. However, while lane changing can bring benefits, it can also bring costs, because the rules are strict and breaking them leads to serious penalties. Owing to male characteristics of 'over-confidence' or a greater tendency to take risk (found, for example, in Dreber et al. 2014; Almenberg and Dreber 2015), male speedboat racers may be more likely than women to adopt an aggressive strategy – or to be successful at it – for it is possible that women are less confident in mixed races, and as a result, aggressive male behaviour is more successful. Within our dataset, this is proxied by lane changing. Our prediction is that women racers follow a less aggressive or confident strategy than men and are less successful at lane changing. (Unfortunately, we do not have information on the number of attempted infractions relative to the number a person is actually charged with. Hence, we cannot test the hypothesis that even if women racers are found to be less aggressive, they are less likely to be penalised than men in the mixed-sex race.)

We now consider individual performance in the solo exhibition race. It is hard to separate out strategic and psychological factors within our data. However, both affect performance in the actual race, in which peer effects as well as own decisions play a part. In contrast, strategy plays a much smaller role in the exhibition run. This is because, in the exhibition run, participants run solo and do not compete directly with other race participants. Thus, jockeying for position is not relevant. But there are other ways in which competitors can sabotage performance in an exhibition run. Chowdhury and Gürtler (2015) extensively surveyed studies investigating sabotage in competitions. They report widespread evidence of sabotage, defined as an activity conducted to damage others and driven by material benefits for the saboteur. In the context of speedboat racing, it would be easy for a participant to take a subtly menacing attitude towards a competitor. One example might be glaring, which may so unnerve the recipient that his or her performance is affected, in both the exhibition run and the actual race. Such behaviour is likely to be very hard to observe by the race organisers. There is also a possibility that a subset of racers might collude to slow down another racer. Again, we have no data on this and simply mention it as a possibility.

Data and descriptive statistics

Our data are individual records for the period April 2014 to October 2015 from Boat Advisor, the database of Japanese speedboat racing.[7] Of the 24 boat race stadiums in Japan, only seven provide all racers' records, and we used these to construct a panel dataset for the number of racers and the races in which they participated. The seven stadiums cover a wide variety of locations and statuses.[8] In a racing meet, racers participate in two or three races. For the period studied, there are 202 female and 1,430 male racers. The average number of races in which each of these individuals participated was 250, resulting in 400,000 person-race observations. Our estimating subsample comprises all those races with complete information about racers' records, which yields approximately 140,000 person-race observations. This is a far larger sample than other datasets used to consider gender differences in preferences and behaviour that are obtained from experiments (Dreber et al. 2011, 2014; Cárdenas et al. 2014) and from survey data (Buser et al. 2014; Almenberg and Dreber 2015). Furthermore, as well as information about racer's performance measured by the race time, time in exhibition run, and whether a penalty was received, we have detailed information about the characteristics of the race: place and day of the week, the grade of the race,

7 While a racer's engine is randomly assigned by lot, the starting lane or dock position is assigned in a more complicated way. The committee aims to reduce disparity in racers' winning probabilities, and states publicly that lanes are assigned to equalise the condition of racers to run a close race. In this sense, the assignment of lanes has been done in a quasi-random way.

8 Our seven stadiums (at Suminoe, Marugame, Kiryu, Miyajima, Biwako, Karatsu and Amagasaki) are representative of the other stadiums. To check this, we compared average characteristics of our stadiums with the average for the rest with regard to each of the following: days of racing meets in a year, total number of visitors, average purchase per visitor, average revenue per day and days of meets for SG and GI races. There was no statistically significant difference between our seven and all the others.

gender composition of the race, and the condition of racers as captured, for examples, by their weight on the day of the race and their lane in the race. With regard to weight, although individuals are randomly allocated to single-sex and mixed-sex races, this occurs several months before the races in which they are to participate. Thus, racers might conceivably alter their weight in response to these allocations.

We use this rich dataset to explore gender differences in performance in competitive circumstances. The subsample of women-race observations is slightly over 15,000, whereas that for men is over 120,000. Figure 13.3 shows the relation between place in the race and race lane. As is well known, racers gain an advantage if they are given an inner lane (Himura 2015), and Figure 13.3 illustrates this.

Racers are classified, as already noted, into five grades: SG, GI, GII, GIII, and 'usual' races. To participate in the higher-grade races with greater prize money, racers are required to have performed well in races so far. Therefore, the higher the grade of race, the faster the participants should be.

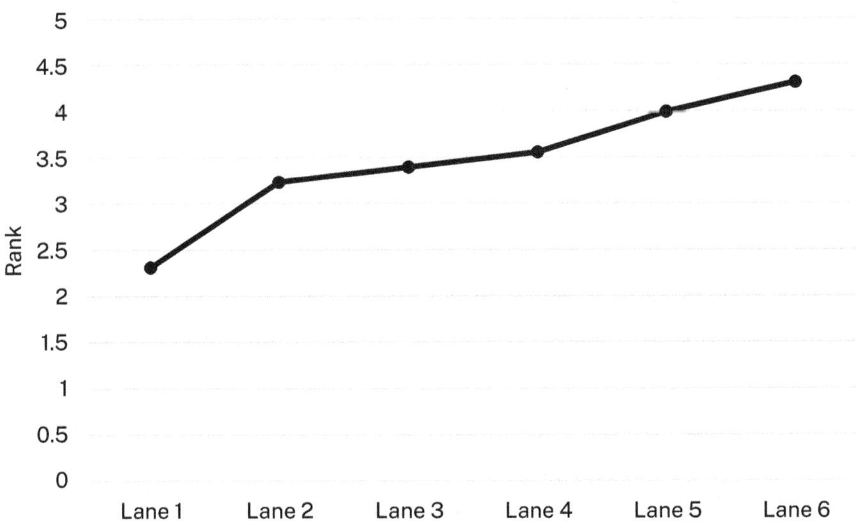

Figure 13.3: Mean of place in the race according to lanes

Table 13.1: Basic statistics and definition of variables used in estimation

	Women	Men	Difference
	[1]	[2]	[1] - [2]
Race time (seconds)	113.2	112.7	0.05***
Place in the race	3.68	3.43	0.25***
Exhibition time (seconds)	6.72	6.73	-0.01***
Weight (kg)	47.5	52.0	-4.5***
Number of lanes changed down towards the first lane	0.07	0.12	-0.05***
Number of lanes changed up towards the sixth lane	0.09	0.09	-0.005**
Poor navigation	0.0003	0.0004	-0.0002
Disqualification	0.0010	0.0012	-0.0002
Mixed-sex race	0.31	0.12	0.19***
Number of opposite-sex racers	1.25	0.15	1.10***
Number of higher-grade racers	1.77	1.53	0.24***
Number of lower-grade racers	1.36	1.47	-0.10***
Number of more experienced racers	2.54	2.36	0.17***
Number of less experienced racers	2.21	2.37	-0.15***
Number of heavyweight racers	1.51	4.45	-2.93***
Number of lightweight racers	0.14	3.54	-3.40***
Exhibition rank_1 (1st place)	0.182	0.165	0.017***
Exhibition rank_2	0.172	0.166	0.06*
Exhibition rank_3	0.167	0.166	0.001
Exhibition rank_4	0.166	0.167	-0.001***
Exhibition rank_5	0.161	0.167	-0.006***
Exhibition rank_6 (last place)	0.152	0.167	-0.015***
Race grade_1 (SG)	0.002	0.001	-0.008***
Race grade_2 (GI)	0.048	0.055	-0.007***
Race grade_3 (GII)	0.00	0.01	-0.01***
Race grade_4 (GIII)	0.342	0.047	0.295
Race grade_5 (Usual)	0.608	0.878	-0.270
Lane_1 (inner lane)	0.154	0.168	-0.014***
Lane_2	0.159	0.168	-0.009***
Lane_3	0.160	0.167	-0.007**
Lane_4	0.165	0.167	-0.002
Lane_5	0.175	0.166	0.009***

	Women	Men	Difference
	[1]	[2]	[1] - [2]
Lane_6 (outer lane)	0.186	0.166	0.020***
Number of racers	202	1,430	-
Observations	15,472	127,020	-

Notes: Statistically significant at *** 1%, ** 5%, and 1%; Number of competitors whose status is higher than the racer is used to capture other racers' skill and techniques. Number of competitors whose status is lower than the racer also included. In addition, we obtain the graduation period (from Yamato speedboat racers school, where boys and girls must graduate to get a racer licence). Time passed since graduation is considered to be the degree of experience. From this, we construct the number of competitors who have experience higher (or lower) than the racer and include it as a control. Heavyweight racers are defined as equivalent to or heavier than 48.2 kg, which is the 75th percentile for a male racer's weight. The number of heavyweight racers is the number of heavyweight racers participating in the race. Lightweight racers are defined as equivalent to or heavier than 50.2 kg, which is the 25 percentile for female racers' weight. The number of lightweight racers is the number of lightweight racers participating in the race. Poor navigation is defined as unfairly interfering with other racers, although not to a serious degree. If its degree is serious, the racer is disqualified. Racers attempt to avoid poor navigation and disqualifications, so their occurrence is very rare. Therefore, mean values of poor navigation and disqualifications are very low.

Table 13.1 presents means, disaggregated by gender, of the main variables used in our analysis. (There are also some additional dummy variables included in the estimation but not reported; these are presented in the table notes.) The means are calculated from person-race observations, and the number of these is reported in the bottom row of the table. Table 13.1 shows that average male race times are faster than those of women, and this difference is statistically significant. However, the difference in exhibition time between male and female racers is considerably smaller. This difference in race times may be due to male racers having better strategies in competitive circumstances, whereas in less competitive circumstances (exhibition run), men and women racers' abilities are almost equivalent.

The second row of Table 13.1 reports the race rank. Thus, for all race observations, the average was between third and fourth place, with the difference between genders being 0.25 and statistically significant. The weight differences between women and men (reported in the fourth row) are as expected: men are significantly heavier.

The fifth row of Table 13.1 shows that in the turnaround period before the formal start of the race, 5 per cent of female racers changed their initial lane down towards the first lane, as compared with 8 per cent of men, a statistically significant difference. This suggests that male racers have a more aggressive strategy than women racers. (This is consistent with existing studies, for example, Gneezy et al. 2009, and Apicella and Dreber 2015.) One might expect aggressive lane changing to increase the probability of being caught for poor navigation and being disqualified. However, dummies for poor navigation and disqualification show that only 0.04 of men are caught for poor navigation and 0.12 per cent are disqualified, percentages only slightly higher than the 0.03 per cent and 0.10 per cent, respectively, found for women, and the differences are not statistically significant. Thus, while male racers appear to be more aggressive in terms of lane changing, they are no more likely to be caught for risky navigation. The proportions of women and men in mixed-sex races are 31 per cent and 12 per cent, respectively. Across all races, women face an average of 1.25 opposite-sex racers, while men face only 0.15.

Since boat racing ability, as measured by race time and place in race, differs slightly across the sexes, we need to control for ability when estimating the determinants of race time and race place for the mixed-sex and single-sex races. We construct two variables using the information we have for racers' grades (A1, A2, B1, and B2): the number of higher-grade and the number of lower-grade racers an individual faces in a race. Women typically face 1.77 higher-grade and 1.36 lower-grade racers, while the comparable figures for men are 1.53 and 1.47, respectively. To calculate racers' experience, we obtained each racer's graduation date and used the time elapsed since then as our proxy for experience. We find that, averaging across races, women typically face 2.54 more experienced racers and 2.21 less experienced racers, while the comparable figures for men are 2.36 and 2.37, respectively.

There is a considerable difference in the gender composition of race grades. First, consider the gender proportions of participants in race grade 5 (the 'usual' races). Here we see that 60 per cent of woman-race observations are found in the lowest-grade race as compared with 88 per cent of men-race observations. However, in race grade 4, there are only 5 per cent of all male observations, which is lower than the 34 per cent for females. Aggregating race grade 4 and race grade 5 indicates that almost 95 per cent of male observations, as well as of female observations, are found here. There is little difference in the gender rates for race grades 1, 2, and 3, although it should be noted that race grade 3 is 0 for women, and so women racers did not participate in GII races at all. As noted previously, there are only eight races for GII in a year; thus, it is unsurprising that no women were observed here.

In Table 13.1, we also include means for randomly assigned starting lane (the lane or pit from which a participant starts at the very beginning of the race, before the turnaround period, as illustrated in Figure 13.1).

Table 13.1 shows differences in key variables between single-sex and mixed-sex races and also between women and men racers in each of these group types. For our purposes here, the most interesting comparison is female racer time between the single-sex and mixed-sex races: women run about 1.4 seconds faster in single-sex races than in mixed-sex races, a difference that is statistically significant at the 1 per cent level. For men, there is no statistically significant difference in race times between the single-sex and mixed-sex races. Accordingly, the raw data show that women racers' performance is influenced by the gender composition of the race, but this does not hold for men racers. With regard to the single-sex races, we find that the gender difference in race time is only 0.1 second – a tiny amount, although statistically significant. In the mixed-gender races, male racers' time is significantly faster by 1.6 seconds than women's. Therefore, the gender difference in the mixed-sex races is 16 times larger than in single-sex races.

While in this section we explored correlations in the raw data, we will next use fixed-effects regression techniques to control for other factors affecting our variables of interest. Before presenting these results, we outline our econometric model.

The econometric model

Our randomisation is key to enabling us to document our basic stylised fact: that the same woman performs relatively worse in terms of her race time in mixed-sex races as compared with single-sex races, while for the average male racer, the opposite is true. In our tables of regression, we report results for place in race and race time, a baseline model with the minimum number of controls. We estimate this separately for the subsamples of male and female racers, as well as for the pooled sample of men and women. We also report estimates from an expanded specification with additional controls in order to see if the direct effect of the mixed-sex variables alters once we control for the ability, experience and weight of competitors in each race. If male competitors are of higher ability or have more experience, the estimated coefficient to the treatment variables in the baseline model might be an overestimate of the actual true effect on females of being in a mixed-sex race. We also include in the expanded specification the weight of competitors, since heavier racers run more slowly. Later in the chapter, we will investigate whether women might reduce their effort in mixed races, and men might increase their effort by engaging in strategic behaviour with regard to the outcome variables of lane changing or weight.

Our expanded specification for various outcome measures is:

$$(1)\ R_{itk} = \alpha_0 + \alpha_1 M_{itk} + X'_{it}\beta + Y'_{it} C + \varepsilon_i + m_{tk} + \mu_{itk}$$

The dependent variable R denotes the performance of individual i on race day t at stadium k. These include place in race, the natural log of race time in seconds, lane changing, poor navigation, disqualification and exhibition time. In equation (1), the constant is denoted by α_0, while α_1 is the marginal effect of the independent variable of interest, M. (In some specifications, M will be the mixed-sex dummy, while in others, it will be the number of opposite-sex racers.) Other controls are captured by the row vector X_{it}.

As illustrated in Figure 13.3, the place in the race depends on the lane. Furthermore, on a race meeting day, there are 12 races in a stadium. Superior-graded racers tend to participate in the 10th to 12th among them, even if there are only 'usual' races in the day. In equation (1), these other factors are incorporated in the vector Y_{it}. C is the column vector of coefficients to be estimated. As explained in the previous section, we have data for seven racing stadiums and the races that occurred almost every day for around one and a half years. The conditions of races and racers vary by place and day because of the weather and the random allocation of the engine and the boat. To control for conditions, we include dummies for place and days of the race and their interactions, as represented in equation (1) by m_{tk}. Unobservable individual time-invariant characteristics are controlled for through fixed-effects estimation.

Results

Place in the race

Table 13.2 reports determinants of place in race, which range from first to sixth. Fixed-effects estimates of the parsimonious baseline model are presented in the first three columns of Table 13.2. We control for the randomly assigned starting lane as well as additional controls listed in the table notes. For all tables of estimates, we report in parentheses robust standard errors clustered on races. In brackets in each table, we provide means for the outcome variable for the relevant control group.

Table 13.2: Dependent variable: place in the race (fixed-effects estimates)

	Baseline			With control variables for ability		
	[1] All	[2] Women	[3] Men	[4] All	[5] Women	[6] Men
Mixed-sex dummy × women racer dummy	0.93*** (0.04)	–	–	0.74*** (0.04)	–	–
Mixed-sex dummy	-0.28*** (0.01)	–	–	-0.19*** (0.01)	–	–
Number of opposite-sex racers	–	0.19*** (0.01)	-0.23*** (0.01)	–	–	–
Number of higher-grade racers	–	–	–	0.18*** (0.004)	0.16*** (0.01)	0.18*** (0.004)
Number of lower-grade racers	–	–	–	-0.17*** (0.004)	-0.16*** (0.01)	-0.17*** (0.004)
Number of more experienced racers	–	–	–	0.06*** (0.01)	0.03 (0.03)	0.06*** (0.01)
Number of less experienced racers	–	–	–	0.06*** (0.01)	0.01 (0.03)	0.06*** (0.01)
Number of heavyweight racers	–	–	–	-0.03*** (0.002)	-0.06*** (0.01)	-0.03*** (0.002)
Number of lightweight racers	–	–	–	-0.02*** (0.005)	0.03*** (0.01)	0.01 (0.01)
Lane_1	[2.31]	[2.56]	[2.28]	[2.31]	[2.56]	[2.28]
Lane_2	0.81*** (0.01)	0.57*** (0.05)	0.84*** (0.02)	0.78*** (0.01)	0.54*** (0.05)	0.81*** (0.02)
Lane_3	0.92*** (0.02)	0.71*** (0.05)	0.95*** (0.02)	0.90*** (0.01)	0.68*** (0.05)	0.92*** (0.02)
Lane_4	1.05*** (0.02)	0.88*** (0.05)	1.07*** (0.02)	1.01*** (0.02)	0.83*** (0.05)	1.03*** (0.02)
Lane_5	1.38*** (0.02)	1.26*** (0.05)	1.40*** (0.02)	1.31*** (0.02)	1.16*** (0.05)	1.33*** (0.02)
Lane_6	1.63*** (0.02)	1.48*** (0.05)	1.64*** (0.02)	1.54*** (0.02)	1.36*** (0.05)	1.56*** (0.02)
Control group for mixed-sex dummy × women racer dummy	[3.44]	–	–	[3.44]	–	–
Control group for mixed-sex dummy	[3.46]	–	–	[3.46]	–	–

	Baseline			With control variables for ability		
	[1] All	[2] Women	[3] Men	[4] All	[5] Women	[6] Men
Control group for women racer dummy	[3.43]	–	–	[3.43]	–	–
Groups	1,632	202	1,430	1,632	202	1,430
Observations	139,929	15,210	124,719	139,929	15,210	124,719

Notes: Statistically significant at *** 1%. Robust standard errors clustered on races are shown in parentheses. Values within brackets are mean values of the base group (control group) for dummy variables. Dummies for race grade, location dummies and interaction dummies between locations and days are included but not reported. The number of interaction dummies between locations and days is 630.

Column [1] of Table 13.2, estimated for the sample of all men and women, shows that a woman places worse (that is, further from first place) when she is in an opposite-sex race, while a man places better (closer to first place) in mixed-sex races. For example, a woman randomly allocated to a mixed-sex race performs almost one place worse (the coefficient is 0.93) than if she were in a single-sex race, ceteris paribus. Men randomly assigned to mixed-sex races do significantly better than they do in single-sex races (the coefficient is –0.28). This implies that men racers' place in the race improves by 0.28 points on the 6-point scale when they run in mixed-sex races than in the single-sex races. Columns [2] and [3] of Table 13.2 are estimated on the subsamples of women and men, respectively, and the treatment variable is now the number of opposite-sex racers (rather than the simple dummy variable used in column [1]). For women, the estimated coefficient to the number of opposite-sex competitors is 0.19 and is precisely estimated, meaning that a woman's place is worsened by 0.19 on the 6-point scale with the number of opposite-sex competitors. In contrast, for men, we find that the estimated coefficient to the number of opposite-sex competitors is –0.23, implying that a man's place improves by 0.23 on the 6-point scale in the number of opposite-sex competitors. These effects are statistically significant at the 1 per cent level.

We now turn to another control variable of interest: the randomly assigned starting lane (from which a participant starts at the very beginning of the race, before the turnaround period). The innermost lane is the base in the regression tables. Estimated coefficients for dummy variables for the other lanes are statistically significant and positive. The magnitude of the coefficients is monotonically increasing across lanes; racers randomly allocated to outer lanes are less likely to win than those allocated to the inner lane.

Our randomisation is key to establishing a basic stylised fact: that the same woman performs relatively worse in terms of her place in race in mixed-sex races as compared with single-sex races, while for the average male racer, the opposite is true. Given this basic fact, can we say any more about how to interpret this finding? One candidate mechanism is that women who face higher-ability competitors choose to exert less effort, and this is why they do worse in mixed-sex races. To explore this potential mechanism, we include additional variables. Thus, in the last three columns of Table 13.2, we include proxies for relative ability and experience (the numbers of higher-grade and lower-grade racers that an individual competes against in a race, as well as the numbers of more experienced racers and less experienced racers).[9] In Table 13.4, we show the randomisation balance of our ability measures across mixed-sex and single-sex races.

We also include variables indicating the number of heavyweight racers and the number of lighter-weight racers an individual competes against. Lighter racers can race faster (less resistance in water) than a heavyweight one, and they can manoeuvre more quickly and have an advantage in invading an inner lane.[10] The greater the number of competitors who are lighter than a given racer, the less likely it is that that racer will win. Since women racers are lighter on average than men, the inclusion of this variable might reduce the estimated coefficient for gender.

Estimates reported in the last three columns of Table 13.2 show that even controlling for relative ability, experience and weight, women are more likely to place lower when racing against mixed-sex racers than they are when racing against all-female racers, while men place better (closer to first place) with mixed-sex competitors than they are with single-sex. The magnitude of the coefficients to the treatment variables differs slightly in this expanded specification, but it is still the case that women in mixed-

9 In this, we follow Yamane and Hayashi (2015), who observe peer effects among competitors in swimming races.

10 However, there are weight limits (51 kg for men, 47 kg for women). The difference in weight limit is the only advantage for women in the race. A racer whose weight is lower than the limit, is obliged to wear weights in his or her jacket.

sex races are slightly less likely to be poorly placed and men are slightly less likely to be well placed, as compared to the estimates with no ability controls. These effects remain statistically significant at the 1 per cent level.

We now turn to the estimated impact of the other controls. Table 13.2 shows that across all specifications in columns [3]–[6], more higher-grade (higher-ability) participants in a race reduce the likelihood of being well placed, while more lower-grade racers increase the likelihood of being well placed. This is as expected. Turning to experience, we see the estimated coefficients to these variables are positive for both more experienced and less experienced participants, but this effect is small and imprecisely estimated for women.

The estimated coefficient for the number of heavyweight racers is negative and statistically significant. The more heavyweight racers there are in a race, the more likely it is that a woman will place, a finding consistent with weight-reducing manoeuvrability and speed. The more lightweight racers there are in a race, the less likely a female is to place.

Our basic stylised fact from the baseline model was that the same woman performs relatively worse in terms of her place in race in mixed-sex races as compared with single-sex races, while for the average male racer, the opposite is true. Our expanded specification shows that this remains a stylised fact even after controlling for the ability, experience and weight of the other racers. But can we say any more about how to interpret this stylised fact? An additional candidate mechanism is that men might be more successful than women at changing lanes. Before investigating this, we first report the impact of the treatment variables on racers' recorded time in seconds.

Time in race in the baseline model

Race time and place in the race are both relevant information for bettors. Although place matters more to the individual since it translates directly into winning, a participant wants to travel faster in order to place. Table 13.3 reports fixed-effects estimates of the log of recorded race time in seconds, with the baseline and the expanded specifications including the same sets of controls as in Table 13.2.

Table 13.3: FE estimates of race time and place in race, with additional controls

Dependent variable: Log of time record in races (fixed-effects estimates)						
A	**Baseline**			**With control variables for ability**		
	[1] All	**[2] Women**	**[3] Men**	**[4] All**	**[5] Women**	**[6] Men**
Mixed-sex dummy × women racer dummy	0.009*** (0.001)	–	–	0.005*** (0.001)	–	–
Mixed-sex dummy	-0.002** (0.0004)	–	–	-0.0005 (0.0004)	–	–
Number of opposite-sex racers	–	0.002*** (0.0003)	-0.001** (0.0002)	–	0.001*** 0.0004)	-0.0006* (0.0004)
Control group for mixed-sex dummy × women racer dummy	[4.72]	–	–	–	–	–
Control group for mixed-sex dummy	[4.72]	–	–	–	–	–
Control group for women racer dummy	[4.72]	–	–	–	–	–
Groups	1,632	202	1,430	1,632	202	1,430
Observations	139,929	15,210	124,719	139,929	15,210	124,719

Dependent variable: Place in the race and log of time record in races (fixed-effects estimates): Examination of opposite-gender racers' influence on inner lane (advantageous) racers' performance				
B	**Place in the race**		**Log of time record in races**	
	[1] Women	**[2] Men**	**[3] Women**	**[4] Men**
Number of opposite-sex racers × inner lane dummy	0.04*** (0.01)	0.02 (0.02)	0.001*** (0.002)	0.0002 (0.0003)
Number of opposite-sex racers	0.18*** (0.01)	-0.18*** (0.02)	0.001*** (0.0004)	-0.001* (-0.0004)
Control group for inner lane dummy	[4.22]	[3.91]	[4.74]	[4.73]
Groups	202	1,430	202	1,430
Observations	15,210	124,664	15,210	124,664

Notes: Statistically significant at *** 1%, ** 5%, and 1%. Robust standard errors clustered on races are shown in value in parentheses. Values within brackets are mean values of base group (control group) for dummy variables. All control variables included in columns [4]–[6] of Table 13.2 are included but not reported. Inner lane dummy is 1 if the racer's lane is Lane_1, Lane_2 and Lane_3; otherwise, 0.

Column [1] of Table 13.3 shows that women run more slowly in the mixed-sex race, while men's time is faster. Columns [2] and [3] of Table 13.3A are estimated on the subsamples of women and men, respectively, and the treatment variable for each is now the number of opposite-sex racers. For women, we find that the estimated coefficient to the number of opposite-sex competitors is 0.002 and is precisely estimated, meaning that women's time is increasing with the number of opposite-sex competitors. In contrast, for men, we find that the estimated coefficient to the number of opposite-sex competitors is –0.001, implying that a man's time falls with the number of opposite-sex competitors. Note, though, that for men, the effect is less precisely estimated and it is statistically significant only at the 5 per cent level. Thus, we show once again that women's and men's performance in these competitions differs depending on the gender of their competitors.

Controlling for ability, experience, and the weight of competitors in columns [4] to [6] of Table 13.3A, we find that the magnitude of the treatment effect is reduced in column [4], where we use only dummy variables for whether the race is mixed-sex, though it is still very precisely estimated. In column [5] (women-only), a woman's time is increasing with the number of male competitors, while a man's time is reduced with the number of female competitors, ceteris paribus.

Lane changing

Are men more successful than women at lane changing, and might this help explain our stylised fact? We hypothesised that in mixed-sex races, women are less likely to change lanes either because they are less willing to engage in aggressive behaviour or because they are less confident in mixed settings. This would imply that not only are they less likely to squeeze their opponents out of their allocated lanes, but are also more likely themselves to be blocked from retaining an advantageous lane.

Racers randomly allocated to the inner lane enjoy that advantage only if they retain that position. Our initial examination of lane changing is shown in Table 13.3B, where we interact the number of opposite-sex racers with the inner lane dummy variable (taking the value 1 if the racer's lane is Lane_1, Lane_2, and Lane_3, otherwise 0). The first two columns present estimates of the determinants of place in race, and the last two columns display estimates of recorded race time in seconds. For women in an inner lane, their place in the race and their time worsen in the mixed-sex races. Moreover, if they are initially randomly allocated to the inner lane, their performance worsens even more (the combined effect is 0.19 + 0.03 + 0.22).

To investigate further gender differences in lane changing, we next estimate the determinants of the number of lanes changed down, in the turnaround period, towards the first lane (the inner lane), excluding observations of those who were initially randomly allocated to an inner lane. The estimated coefficients for the variables of interest are reported in columns [1]–[3] of Table 13.4. The dependent variable takes the value of 0 if racers do not change their lane and is positive if they do, with the value increasing with the number of lanes changed.

Table 13.4: Dependent variable: number of lanes changed down towards the first lane and towards the sixth lane

	Towards the first lane (excluding lane 1 racers)			Towards the sixth lane (excluding lane 6 racers)		
	[1] All	[2] Women	[3] Men	[4] All	[5] Women	[6] Men
Mixed-sex dummy × women racer dummy	-0.06*** (0.02)	–	–	–	0.18*** (0.02)	–
Mixed-sex dummy	0.04*** (0.01)	–	–	-0.03*** (0.008)	–	–
Number of opposite-sex racers	–	-0.02*** (0.005)	0.03*** (0.008)	–	0.04*** (0.007)	-0.03*** (0.006)
Number of higher-grade racers	-0.01*** (0.002)	-0.01*** (0.004)	-0.01*** (0.002)	0.02*** (0.002)	0.03*** (0.005)	0.02*** (0.002)
Number of lower-grade racers	0.03*** (0.002)	0.01** (0.004)	0.03*** (0.002)	-0.01*** (0.001)	0.01* (0.004)	-0.01*** (0.001)
Number of more experienced racers	-0.02*** (0.003)	-0.02** (0.007)	-0.02*** (0.003)	0.02*** (0.003)	0.02** (0.009)	0.02*** (0.003)
Number of less experienced racers	-0.001 (0.003)	0.002 (0.007)	-0.001 (0.003)	-0.0002 (0.003)	-0.01 (0.01)	0.003 (0.003)
Number of heavyweight racers	0.001 (0.002)	0.01*** (0.005)	0.001 (0.002)	-0.01*** (0.002)	-0.01 (0.01)	-0.01*** (0.002)
Number of lightweight racers	0.0003 (0.003)	-0.004 (0.004)	-0.004 (0.008)	-0.004 (0.004)	0.003 (0.005)	0.01 (0.01)
Control group for mixed-sex dummy × women racer dummy	[0.15]	–	–	[0.14]	–	–
Control group for mixed-sex dummy	[0.14]	–	–	[0.14]	–	–

	Towards the first lane (excluding lane 1 racers)			Towards the sixth lane (excluding lane 6 racers)		
	[1] All	[2] Women	[3] Men	[4] All	[5] Women	[6] Men
Control group for women racer dummy	[0.15]	–	–	[0.15]	–	–
Groups	1,632	202	1,430	1,632	202	1,430
Observations	116,531	12,854	103,677	116,558	12,383	104,175

Notes: Statistically significant at *** 1%. Robust standard errors clustered on races are shown in values in parentheses. Values within brackets are mean values of base group (control group) for dummy variables. Control variables included in Table 13.2 are included but not reported here; Guidance for dependent variable: in columns [1]-[3], the dependent variable is 0 if racers do not change their lane or change up the lane (towards 6) during the initial period of turnaround. The variable is a positive value if racers change down (towards 1). For instance, the variable is 5 (considered the most aggressive behaviour) if racers change from lane 6 to lane 1 during the period. The variable is 1 if racers change from lane 6 to lane 5. In this way, the variable is considered a proxy for the aggressiveness of the strategy, which ranges between 0 and 5. In columns [4]–[6], the dependent variable is 0 if racers do not change their lane or change down the lane (towards 1) during the initial period of turn turnaround. The variable is a positive value if racers change up (towards 6). Racers changed their lane towards 6 only if competitors behaved aggressively to intrude on their lane because racers do not have an incentive to change up. For instance, the variable is positive (considered as less aggressive to blocking competitors). The variable is 1 if racers change from lane 5 to lane 6. In this way, we make the variable a proxy for the degree of aggressiveness to block, which ranges between 0 and 5.

We also estimate the number of lanes changed down towards the sixth (outer) lane, excluding observations of those who were randomly allocated lane 6, with results reported in columns [4]–[6] of Table 13.4. Here, the dependent variable takes the value 1 if racers do not change their lane in the turnaround period and is positive if they do, with the value increasing in the number of lanes changed to a less advantageous position. This can therefore be thought of as a measure of inability to block more aggressive racers. For example, the dependent variable will take the value 1 if a racer has shifted one lane away from their allocated lane and into a less advantageous position.

We see from the first three columns that for men, the treatment variables (either the mixed-sex dummy or the number of opposite-sex racers) significantly increase the probability of shifting towards the most advantageous lane, whereas they reduce it for women. The last three columns of Table 13.4 show that for men, the treatment variables significantly reduce the probability of shifting towards the less advantageous lane, whereas they increase it for women. Taken together, these results suggest that women are less inclined to adopt strategically aggressive behaviour or are less successful at blocking it during the turnaround period when men take part in the race. In contrast, men are more inclined to follow and succeed at strategically aggressive behaviour during the turnaround period in the mixed-sex race. These results suggest that women in our dataset are less aggressive than men and less able to block aggressive competitors, and that this tendency is more pronounced when competing against men.

The determinants of rule-breaking

Table 13.5: Dependent variable: dummies for disqualification and for poor navigation (fixed-effects estimation)

	Disqualification			Poor navigation		
	[1] All	[2] Women	[3] Men	[4] All	[5] Women	[6] Men
Mixed-sex dummy × women racer dummy	-0.001 (0.002)	–	–	-0.001 (0.001)	–	–
Mixed-sex dummy	-0.0003 (0.0004)	–	–	0.0004 (0.0003)	–	–
Number of opposite-sex racers	–	-0.0003 (0.0004)	0.00002 (0.0005)	–	0.0001 (0.0002)	0.0005 (0.0004)
Control group for mixed-sex dummy × women racer dummy	[0.001]	–	–	[0.0004]	–	–
Control group for mixed-sex dummy	[0.001]	–	–	[0.0004]	–	–
Control group for women racer dummy	[0.001]	–	–	[0.0004]	–	–
Groups	1,633	202	1,431	1,633	202	1,431
Observations	142,492	15,472	127,020	142,492	15,472	127,020

Notes: Statistically significant at *** 1%. Robust standard errors clustered on races are shown in values in parentheses. Values within brackets are mean values of base group (control group) for dummy variables. All control variables included in columns [4]–[6] of Table 13.2 are included but not reported.

Next, we turn to the determinants of breaking rules. Columns [1]–[3] in Table 13.5 report fixed-effects estimates of disqualification, while columns [4]–[6] report the fixed-effects results for being penalised for poor navigation. The estimates show that neither of the treatment variables is statistically significant. Therefore, competing with opposite-sex racers does not have any effect on the likelihood of being caught for poor navigation or for being disqualified. In sum, the probability of losing points and grade by disqualification is the same regardless of gender, and this holds in spite of the fact that male racers are distinctly more active in lane changing. Since lane changing involves some risk of fouling, this suggests that males are able to develop aggressively strategic skills without being caught for rule-breaking. Clearly, there is a trade-off between the improved likelihood of winning if a racer changes lanes, on one hand, and the greater probability of being caught for fouling while changing lanes, on the other hand. It is possible that less risk-averse and more confident racers are able to perfect their lane-changing techniques without penalties or disqualification.

The gender differences we have observed are consistent with the experimental literature on gender differences in overconfidence and risk aversion (see Niederle and Vesterlund 2011; Eckel and Grossman 2008). If, on average, men exhibit these traits more than women, they may have become well-practised in lane changing without being penalised. In contrast, more risk-averse or less confident women may run safely to avoid the penalty and keep their grade and revenue.

Estimating the correlates of weight

Table 13.6: Dependent variable: log of weight on race day and log of recorded exhibition time (seconds) before races (fixed-effects estimation)

Dependent variable	**Log of weight on the race day**			
A	**[1] Women**	**[2] Women**	**[3] Men**	**[4] Men**
Mixed-sex dummy	-0.106* (0.061)	–	0.041*** (0.015)	–
Control group for mixed-sex dummy	[3.86]	–	[3.95]	–
Groups	202	202	1,431	1,431
Observations	15,472	15,472	127,020	127,020
Dependent variable	**Log of recorded exhibition time (seconds) before races**			
Mixed-sex dummy	0.095* (0.061)	–	0.025 (0.022)	–
Number of opposite-sex racers	–	0.020 (0.014)	–	0.036* (0.017)
Number of higher-grade racers	-0.008 (0.009)	-0.008 (0.009)	-0.012*** (0.003)	-0.012*** (0.003)

Dependent variable	Log of weight on the race day			
B	[1] Women	[2] Women	[3] Men	[4] Men
Number of lower-grade racers	0.011 (0.009)	0.012 (0.009)	0.010*** (0.003)	0.010*** (0.003)
Control group for mixed-sex dummy	[1.90]	–	[1.91]	–
Groups	202	202	1,431	1,431
Observations	15,472	15,472	127,020	127,020

Notes: * Statistically significant at 10%; *** Statistically significant at 1%. Robust standard errors clustered on races are shown in value in parentheses. In Panel (a), where the dependent variable is the log of weight, the set of control variables is equivalent to that in columns [1]–[3] of Table 13.2, but its results are not reported. In Panel (b), where the dependent variable is the log of exhibition time, the set of control variables is equivalent to that in columns [4]–[6] of Table 13.2, but its results are not reported. Estimated coefficients and standard errors are multiplied by 100 for ease of presentation and interpretation.

Table 13.6A reports fixed-effects estimates of the correlates of weight in kilograms as measured on race day. Since racers receive their schedule several months before an event, it is possible for them to adjust their weight in advance according to the types of races to which they have been randomly allocated in order to run faster. To the extent that individuals feel threatened by running against the opposite sex, they may exert extra effort by losing weight for the mixed-sex races. Our estimates in Panel A show that for women, measured weight is negatively associated with being in a mixed-sex race, and these coefficients are statistically significant at the 10 per cent level. In contrast, for men, measured weight is positively associated with being in a mixed-sex race, and these coefficients are statistically significant at the 1 per cent level. In our interpretation, a woman reduces her weight to prepare for competing with males. A male racer may fail to maintain a light weight because he does not take the female competitor seriously. But there are other factors that work to his advantage, including lane changing.

Performance in the exhibition run

While strategy likely plays a smaller role in the exhibition run than in the race, because participants run solo in the exhibition run, there are ways for competitors to potentially affect their own performance. For example, competitors with a preoccupied or distant demeanour immediately before the exhibition might give different impressions to men and women because of gender differences in perceptions of it. Of course, such behaviour is unobservable with our data, and we offer it only as a potential mechanism.

Panel B of Table 13.6 reports fixed-effects estimates of exhibition run times. Here we see that both the mixed-sex race dummy and the number of the opposite-sex racers are positive but imprecisely estimated. The positive coefficients suggest that racers exhibit more slowly before the mixed-sex race regardless of gender. However, the reason is likely to differ between men and women. Though we cannot test for this, we hypothesise here that male racers may not make a full effort in the mixed-sex races because they discount female competition, whereas a woman racer may not bring her ability into full play because of perceived pressure from male racers.

Coefficients of the number of higher-grade racers and the number of lower-grade racers show the negative and the positive signs, respectively. It is interesting that these signs differ from those in Table 13.2. What is more, they are significant for men but not for women. Men have greater incentives to run faster when competing with racers with better records. A woman's incentive, however, is influenced by her competitors' gender but not their skill and ability. All in all, Table 13.2 and Panel A of Table 13.6 suggest that the effect of a competitor's skill and ability depends on whether strategic interaction is absent (Panel A of Table 13.6) or present (Table 13.2).

Conclusion

Speedboat racing in Japan takes the form of tightly controlled tournaments for which women and men racers receive the same intensive training. Women racers participate and compete in races under the same conditions as men, and all individuals are randomly assigned to mixed-sex or single-sex groups for each race. In this chapter, we used a sample of over 140,000 observations of individual-level racing records obtained from the Japanese Speedboat Racing Association to examine how male-dominated circumstances affect women's and men's racing performance. We controlled for individual fixed effects plus a host of other factors affecting performance, including the competitor's ability within a race. Our estimates revealed that women are less likely to be placed in mixed-sex races than in all-women races, whereas men are more likely to be placed in mixed-sex races than in men-only races. We found the same results when we used the dependent variable time in a race. Moreover, in mixed-sex races, male racers tend to be more aggressive, as proxied by lane changing, in spite of the risk of being penalised if they contravene the rules, whereas women's strategies are less aggressive. We find no difference in disqualification rates between genders. We suggest that gender differences in risk attitudes and confidence may result in different responses to the competitive environment and that gender identity is also likely to play a role.

The first finding above is of particular interest. It shows that female competitive performance, even for women who have chosen a competitive career and are very good at it, is enhanced by being in a single-sex environment rather than in a mixed-sex environment in which they are a minority.

Our other findings are also of great interest, since they follow from our investigation of the mechanisms through which our first finding operates. In particular, we have argued that male racers are aggressive but not imprudent by taking into account competitors' conditions, as well as the risk of disqualification when jockeying for position.

The gender proportion in the mixed-sex speedboat races is skewed towards men. Women racers assigned by lot to a mixed-sex race will typically face five male competitors or, rather infrequently, four. We suggest that this gender imbalance may trigger awareness of gender identity for both men and women, and that this might go some way to explaining observed differences in behaviour across mixed-sex and single-sex groups.[11] For example, a man's gender identity may lead him to consider being defeated by women to be more dishonourable than by men, and he will try to avoid it.

Our findings may well have implications for other activities in which men and women compete with one another and where the gender balance is skewed in favour of men. One example is in the STEM disciplines, where being in a minority may well affect the performance of women in that situation.

Finally, we point out that sportspeople are likely to be particularly selected on willingness to compete and, to that extent, our effects of mixed-sex treatments may be relatively muted compared to other settings where selection is not as competitive. Alternatively, behaviour in repeated (daily) interactions may differ from that in a short race. We hope that future research will explore these issues further.

11 According to the gender-identity hypothesis, a society's prescriptions about appropriate modes of behaviour for each gender might result in individuals' experiencing a loss of identity should they deviate from the relevant code.

Acknowledgements

This chapter was first published as Booth, A., and Yamamura, E. (2018). 'Performance in mixed-sex and single-sex competitions: What we can learn from speedboat races in Japan', *The Review of Economics and Statistics*, 100(4):581–593. www.jstor.org/stable/26616223.

For their helpful comments, we thank the editor, Rohini Pande, and four anonymous referees, as well as Kyohei Yoneda, Yoshihide Ari, Takumi Nishi, Ryohei Hayashi, Shoko Yamane, Yoshiro Tsutsui, Fumio Ohtake, Tim Hatton, Aki Asano, participants at the 2016 Japanese Behavioural Economics Conference, and seminar participants at The Australian National University.

References

Almenberg, J., and Dreber, A. (2015). 'Gender, stock market participation and financial literacy', *Economics Letters*, 137:140–142. doi.org/10.1016/j.econlet.2015.10.009.

Apicella, C., and Dreber, A. (2015). 'Sex differences in competitiveness: Hunter-gatherer women and girls compete less in gender-neutral and male-centric tasks', *Adaptive Human Behavior and Physiology*, 1:247–269. doi.org/10.1007/s40750-014-0015-z.

Backus, P., Cubel, M., Guid, M., Sanchez-Pages, S., and López Manas, E. (2016). 'Gender, competition and performance: Evidence from real tournaments'. IEB Working Paper No. 27. doi.org/10.2139/ssrn.2858984.

Booth, A. (2009). 'Gender and competition', *Labour Economics*, 16(6):599–606. doi.org/10.1016/j.labeco.2009.08.002.

Booth, A., and Nolen, P. (2012). 'Choosing to compete: How different are girls and boys?'. *Journal of Economic Behavior & Organization*, 81(2):542–555. doi.org/10.1016/j.jebo.2011.07.018.

Booth, A., Cardona Sosa, L., and Nolen, P. (2014). 'Gender differences in risk aversion: Do single-sex environments affect their development?', *Journal of Economic Behavior & Organization*, 99:126–154. doi.org/10.1016/j.jebo.2013.12.017.

Buser, T., Dreber, A., and Möllerström, J. (2017). 'The impact of stress on tournament entry', *Experimental Economics*, 20(2):506–530. doi.org/10.1007/s10683-016-9496-x.

Buser, T., Niederle, M., and Oosterbeek, H. (2014). 'Gender, competitiveness, and career choices', *The Quarterly Journal of Economics*, 129(3):1409–1447. doi.org/10.1093/qje/qju009

Cárdenas, J.C., Dreber, A., von Essen, E., and Ranehill, E. (2012). 'Gender differences in competitiveness and risk taking: Comparing children in Colombia and Sweden', *Journal of Economic Behavior & Organization*, 83(1):11–23. doi.org/10.1016/j.jebo.2011.06.008.

Cárdenas, J.C., Dreber, A., von Essen, E., and Ranehill, E. (2014). 'Gender and cooperation in children: Experiments in Colombia and Sweden', *PLoS ONE*, 9(6):e90923. doi.org/10.1371/journal.pone.0090923.

Chowdhury, S.M., and Gürtler, O. (2015). 'Sabotage in contests: A survey', *Public Choice*, 164:135–155. doi.org/10.1007/s11127-015-0264-9.

Dreber, A., and Johannesson, M. (2008). 'Gender differences in deception', *Economics Letters*, 99(1):197–199. doi.org/10.1016/j.econlet.2007.06.027.

Dreber, A., von Essen, E., and Ranehill, E. (2011). 'Outrunning the gender gap – Boys and girls compete equally', *Experimental Economics*, 14(4):567–582. doi.org/10.1007/s10683-011-9282-8.

Dreber, A., von Essen, E., and Ranehill, E. (2014). 'Gender and competition in adolescence: Tasks matter', *Experimental Economics*, 17(1):154–172. doi.org/10.1007/s10683-013-9361-0.

Eckel, C., and Grossman, P. (2008). 'Men, women and risk aversion: Experimental evidence'. In C. R. Plott and V. L. Smith (eds), *Handbook of Experimental Economics Results*, pp. 1078–1086. Amsterdam: Elsevier.

Gneezy, U., Leonard, K., and List, J. (2009). 'Gender differences in competition: Evidence from a matrilineal and a patriarchal society', *Econometrica*, 77(5):1637–1664. doi.org/10.3982/ECTA6690.

Gneezy, U., Niederle, M., and Rustichini, A. (2003). 'Performance in competitive environments: Gender differences', *The Quarterly Journal of Economics*, 118(3):1049–1074. doi.org/10.1162/00335530360698496.

Gneezy, U., and Rustichini, A. (2004). 'Gender and competition at a young age', *American Economic Review*, 94(2):377–381. doi.org/10.1257/0002828041301821.

Himura, K. (2015). *Yokuwakaru Boat Race no Subete* [*Basic Knowledge about Boat Race*]. Tokyo: Sankei Books.

Khachatryan, K., Dreber, A., von Essen, E., and Ranehill, E. (2015). 'Gender and preferences at a young age: Evidence from Armenia', *Journal of Economic Behavior & Organization*, 118:318–332. doi.org/10.1016/j.jebo.2015.02.021.

Niederle, M. (2014). 'Gender'. NBER Working Paper No. 20788. doi.org/10.3386/w20788.

Niederle, M., and Vesterlund, L. (2007). 'Do women shy away from competition? Do men compete too much?', *The Quarterly Journal of Economics*, 122(3):1067–1101. doi.org/10.1162/qjec.122.3.1067.

Niederle, M., and Vesterlund, L. (2011). 'Gender and competition', *Annual Review of Economics*, 3:601–630. doi.org/10.1146/annurev-economics-111809-125122.

Yamane, S., and Hayashi, R. (2015). 'Peer effects among swimmers', *The Scandinavian Journal of Economics*, 117(4):1230–1255. doi.org/10.1111/sjoe.12124.

14

Gendered performance in competitions: Learning from a Korean quiz show

Alison L Booth and Jungmin Lee

Introduction

Despite substantial progress over the past few decades, we observe gender gaps in economic outcomes across almost all countries. Commonly cited reasons for these gender gaps are discrimination or claims that women are more sensitive than men to work–family conflicts and more inclined to make career sacrifices. However, obtaining promotion and pay raises often involves competition. If women dislike competition but men do not, fewer women will choose to enter a competitive environment, and there will be fewer women succeeding in competitions.[1] Understanding why women seem less inclined than men to compete may provide insights into why a gender gap still exists in the workplace and what type of policies might address this gap.

1 For example, using data from 17 countries, Koellinger et al. (2013) find that female under-representation in business ownership is due to their weaker confidence about entrepreneurial skills and higher fear of failure.

A growing experimental literature investigates whether or not gender gaps in economic outcomes might be due to inherent differences in male and female attitudes to competition, and a number of experimental studies do find that the competitive choices made by men and women differ.[2] In this chapter, we adopt a different but complementary approach to these experiments by analysing unique performance data from a real-world activity that is competitive by its very nature – the television quiz show for young people, Janghak. While several related studies have utilised US quiz show data to explore gender differences in competitive outcomes, our data represents a departure, since it comes from a show that differs from that basic format. Moreover, to date, no studies have explored these issues using data from South Korea. Yet the gender pay gap in Korea is the highest in the OECD, according to the 2017 OECD report, The Pursuit of Gender Equality.[3] Moreover, cultural factors have been found to have an important effect,[4] and South Korea is known as a Confucian country where people have son preferences.[5] It is therefore interesting to investigate if there are gender gaps in competitive performance among Korean children of high-school age, and to chart how these vary across different situations.

In our analysis, we compare the performance of high-ability adolescent girls and boys who participated in a series of publicly observed tournaments. These tournaments took place in the context of a long-running weekly South Korean television quiz show, entitled Janghak. Our aim is to gauge if there are gender differences in the behaviour of girls and boys of high-school age in this extremely competitive environment. We also wish to establish how contestants' behaviour alters as the game rules vary.

2 Studies investigating gender differences in performance in competitive environments include Gneezy et al. (2003), Niederle and Vesterlund (2007, 2011), Booth (2009), and Dreber et al. (2011). Research exploring gender differences in preference to enter a competition include Gneezy et al. (2009), Booth and Nolen (2012a, b), Apicella and Dreber (2015), Buser et al. (2017), Booth et al. (2019), while analyses of the determinants of risk attitudes include Booth et al. (2014), Dreber et al. (2014), and Khachatryan et al. (2015). Buser et al. (2014) explores how preference for competition across genders affects academic task choice.

3 Korea has the highest gender pay gap of any OECD country, and its women remain under-represented in public life. See also OECD (2017).

4 See, for example, Gneezy et al. (2009), Booth and Nolen (2012b) and Booth et al. (2019), who all establish that different cultures contribute to the competitiveness of males and females.

5 Son preferences have recently weakened but still exist, especially in terms of postnatal disparate treatments by parents (Lee, 2008; Choi and Hwang, 2020).

Different game rules are likely to be characterised by varying levels of stress, which earlier studies using different types of data have found affects males and females differently. As we shall argue later in the chapter, some of the game rules of the field data that we use are likely to be associated with considerable psychological pressure that may affect the performance of girls and boys differently.

We also examine how girls and boys behave differently as they advance to a higher round and get closer to winning the game when competitive pressure is escalated.[6] Jetter and Walker (2016) use data from the US television quiz show Jeopardy!, a quiz show that, while similar to ours in many respects, also has many different features. Utilising a sample of adult men and women, Jetter and Walker (2016) found that there are no gender differences in responding to questions and in accuracy in high-stakes situations. In a comparison of the behaviour of children, teenagers and college students from Jeopardy!, Jetter and Walker (2017) found no noticeable gender differences throughout all three subsamples.[7] Other studies that investigate two-stage competitions include Cai et al. (2019) and Iriberri and Rey-Biel (2019), and we adopt a two-stage approach similar to theirs in this chapter.

Our primary focus is on exploring how competitive performance differs with gender and, if there are gender differences, understanding the underlying mechanisms. Regarding the latter, our quiz show provides a quasi-experimental setting where competitive pressure on contestants varies exogenously across episodes as some of the game rules change. We focus on three major game features: fastest-finger buzzer, knockout and penalty.[8] By using different combinations of the three features, the game

6 For example, the exam performance of males and females is found to be affected differently by variations in future payoffs (see for example, Attali et al., 2011; Ors et al., 2013; Morin, 2015; Azmat et al., 2016). In addition, other studies in an exam context have found that penalties for a wrong answer affect women's performance more adversely than men's (see for example, Baldiga, 2014; Coffman and Klinowski, 2019). However, Funk and Perrone (2016) find the opposite in their field experiment.

7 Säve-Söderbergh and Lindquist (2017) used data from the Swedish children's version of Jeopardy! to focus on risk, which we are unable to do with our data. Comparing the wagering behaviour of children aged 10–11 with adults, they find gender gaps in risk-taking for adults but none for the girls and boys. Their children are younger than our contestants, whose mean age is just over 17 years.

8 Another interesting aspect to explore is the gender composition of contestants and its impact on performance. In this chapter, we do not find any significant effect, which is probably because our group of contestants is of a small size (five) and therefore there is not much variation in the gender composition. Booth and Yamamura (2018), utilising data from speedboat racing in Japan (a sport in which men and women racers are randomly assigned to single-sex or mixed-sex races), found that the same woman performs relatively worse in terms of her race time in mixed-sex races as compared with single-sex races, while for the average male racer, the opposite is true.

show changed its format for Round 1 five times during our sample period from February 2008 to December 2011. Such frequent institutional changes provide exogenous variation in competitive pressure, which we exploit to identify the causal effect of competitive pressure on performance and the gender difference.

To preview our main findings, we find there is an average gender gap in performance when we pool all Round 1 episodes of the quiz show game – girls perform worse than boys. The gender gap is large enough to make a significant difference in the probability of advancing to a higher round or ultimately winning the game. To explore underlying mechanisms that might explain this, we investigate how male and female performance varies under different rules of the game. We find that there are no gender gaps when stress is kept to a minimum – that is, in games without knockouts or penalties or in games without fastest-finger buzzers. However, in games with some of these features, there are significant gender gaps.[9]

In addition, we examine performance in Round 2 of the shows, where we find larger gender gaps. These are consistent with girls being increasingly hindered by psychological stress as the competition proceeds. Finally, we use question-by-question panel data to estimate performance in the games in which all players stay in for 25 questions. Here we find that girls are less likely to respond faster even when their winning probability is higher. We also find that their probability of answering correctly is lower. These results are consistent with girls' underconfidence (or boys' overconfidence) as well as with different behavioural responses to psychological pressure. It is interesting that we have found these gender gaps in game show performance in Korea, whereas they have not been found in the US (see Jetter and Walker 2016; Michael 2017). This may be because of different cultural values between the two countries, as highlighted in OECD (2017), or because of differences between the structure and rules of the two shows.

9 In the experimental literature, there are no clear results about gender and competition under stress. For example, Buser et al. (2017) find that women choose to compete more frequently when induced stress increases. On the other hand, in a lab experiment using male and female university students, Cahlikova et al. (2020) find that, for both men and women, the willingness to compete is not affected by induced stress. However, Shurchkov (2012) finds – in her lab experiment in which stress is induced by task stereotypes and time constraints – that gender gaps in performance under competition and preferences for competition are partly explained by the differential responses of men and women to these stresses.

The game show

Janghak Quiz and data collection

The Korean television game show Janghak Quiz is a weekly competition program where high-school students compete for a scholarship.[10] It is the oldest television game show in Korea, having been broadcast since 1973. Each episode hosts five contestants from five different high schools. The prize (scholarship) is substantial, amounting to about 1,000 or 2.000 USD for weekly winners, but they are advanced to monthly or annual competitions or can continue over weeks, in which cases the prize can increase up to 30,000 or 40,000 USD.

Any high school students who are interested in participating may apply. But to get into the game show, they have to take a qualifying test and pass the minimum standard.[11] Depending on the results from this test, they are then selected to participate. This means that contestants are selected rather than being a representative sample of all high-school students in Korea. Thus, we expect our participants to be more competitive than, and academically superior to, the bulk of the high-school population, since they have volunteered to play and are then selected by the game show organisers after passing the qualifying test.[12] However, since the preliminary test is a written test and the test questions are from the high-school curriculum, as are those in the main quiz show (as we will explain shortly), the organisers' selection of contestants is likely to be gender-neutral.

10 Janghak means 'scholarship' in Korean. See: EBS Learning (2013), available on YouTube: www.youtube.com/watch?v=Wytzq9ksXMQ, for an example of an episode. The video clip at the link shows the end of Round 1 where five contestants compete and the start of Round 2 where two are knocked out and three remaining ones continue to play.

11 Unfortunately, we do not have data on applicants who failed to pass the test. We do not have any information on the pass rate.

12 We have information on preliminary test scores for a subset of contestants (229, 25.4 per cent). In this limited sample, we find a gender gap; the average score for boys is 30 and that for girls is 27. The minimum score is 20, which is likely to be the cut-off score. Because of this initial gap, we presented the results after controlling for the qualifying-test score and the results for Round 2 conditional on Round 1 scores. Given the show's national reputation and entry competition among students, it is unlikely that the TV show producers selected worse-performing females. On the other hand, we cannot control for the variable for our analyses below by game formats because the observations with the information are from episode 655 to 703 where we have no variation in game formats associated with buzzer and knockout.

Related to the above point, it is important to note that girls account for only 36 per cent of all contestants in our sample. There are two possible explanations. First, girls might be academically worse than boys, so fewer girls could pass the test to get on the game show.[13] However, this is unlikely since Korean girls have above-average scores in PISA, and younger women have higher levels of educational attainment than their male peers (OECD 2017). A more plausible explanation is that girls are less likely to select into the game show than boys. They might dislike being exposed to people on TV. Another reason might be that girls do not like to enter competitive environments. In the latter case, girls' under-representation in the game show is already indicative of a gender gap in competitiveness, which is consistent with previous studies' finding that women do not prefer to enter a competition as much as men do (Niederle and Vesterlund 2007, 2011; Gneezy et al. 2009; Booth and Nolen 2012a, b; Apicella and Dreber 2015; Buser et al. 2017; Booth et al. 2019).

Studio audience size is small, mainly consisting of friends and family members. However, the show is televised nationwide by a public broadcaster, so contestants know that they will be watched by the anonymous many. The fact may create a feeling of social pressure for some contestants, especially when they perform badly, in addition to competitive pressure among contestants themselves.

Contestants are seated or stand in a row on a stage in front of the audience. The show host begins the show and explains the game rules briefly, and contestants introduce themselves. They usually say their name and school and make their resolution for the game, like 'I can win' or 'I will make my school be proud of me.' During the show, the host sometimes talks to contestants in an informal way for the purpose of relaxing them. We do not find any observable differences between boys and girls in their self-introduction or dialogue with the host.

All questions are prerecorded and read by a voice actor. Questions cover various subjects in the standard high-school curriculum, such as history, literature, natural science, music and arts. One thing to note here is that there is no question requiring mathematical problem-solving. For example,

13 This does not necessarily mean that boys are on average better than girls. According to the 'greater male variability hypothesis,' males display greater variability in traits such as cognitive ability than females do. In other words, human males are more likely than females to have very high or very low intelligence. There is considerable controversy around this (see, for example, Irwing and Richard, 2005; Lindberg et al., 2010).

there might be a question about the mathematician who first came up with the idea of integration, but there is no question about integration itself. This is important because our results would be biased if the quiz show were biased towards a specific gender.[14] Also, it is worth noting that we do not find any differences in the difficulty or contents of questions across episodes. This is because the game show is for educational purposes (as the broadcasting company is public, similar to PBS in the US) and the questions are based on the official school curriculum that is highly regulated in Korea.

For our econometric analysis, we constructed individual-level data giving basic information about contestants, such as sex, high school and grade, as well as their round-by-round score and rank. These data were collected by a research assistant who watched all the shows recorded from February 2008 to December 2011 (episodes 577 to 777). We excluded special episodes from the sample because they have different game formats. For example, we excluded one special show where students and their teachers were paired and competed as a team. In the end, for our empirical analysis, we focus on 180 shows with 900 contestants (= 180 × 5).

Changes in game rules and contestant assignment

Game formats and rules are a little complicated and changed several times during the sample period, and we are thus able to exploit these variations as they likely invoke different levels of competitive pressure. Table 14.1 summarises the changes in game rules during our sample period. From episodes 577 to 592, there are no multiple rounds per episode; instead, five contestants attempt to answer all of a fixed number of questions (in our sample, 25 questions) and the one with the highest score in the end becomes the winner. This is the simplest game format in our sample. Using data from these episodes, we construct individual-level panel data following individual contestants (five per episode) over 25 questions. Using the panel data, we examine the dynamics of contestants' performance over the course of the game, as the game approaches the end and the winner is revealed.

14 Over our data period 2008–2011, Korean girls' average PISA score in reading was higher than that of boys. However, the average for math was slightly higher for boys than girls over this period.

Table 14.1: Game formats

	Round 1			Round 2			Round 3	
Episode	**Knockout**	**Buzzer**	**Penalty**	**Knockout**	**Buzzer**	**Penalty**	**Buzzer**	**Penalty**
Annual								
577–592	N	Y	Y	–	–	–	–	–
593–627	N	N	N	N	N	N	Y	Y
Survival								
629–635	1	Y	N	3	N	N	Y	N
636–650	1	Y	N	3	Y	N	Y	N
651–663	1	Y	N	3	Y	Y	Y	N
664–679	2	Y	N	2	Y	Y	Y	N
681–703	2	Y	Y	2	Y	Y	Y	N
704–714	2	N	N	2	Y	Y	Y	N
715–777	2	N	N	2	Y	N	Y	N

Notes: Some episodes are not included in our sample because they are special shows or their video files are missing. In episodes 613 to 627, when no contestant obtained 500 points until Round 3, there was a final round where the best two contestants competed for 500 points.

Next, from episodes 593 to 627, each weekly show consists of three rounds, but there is no knockout over rounds; that is, five contestants remain in all three rounds. The three rounds differ simply by question type. Details are given in the top panel of Table 14.1. In each weekly show, there are five new contestants. Weekly winners are advanced to monthly championships, and monthly winners compete in annual championships. Thus, these episodes are labelled as 'Annual' in the top panel of Table 14.1.

Episodes 629 onwards are labelled as 'Survival' in the bottom panel.[15] Note that these games also consist of three rounds. In the first round, the show begins with five contestants, but one or two with the lowest scores are knocked out after the first round. In the second round, only one contestant with the highest score survives and is advanced to the final round, where they compete with the previous week's returning winner. Since the final round is fundamentally different from the others, in this chapter, we focus

15 Episode 628 was the annual championship game where only two contestants appeared. We excluded this episode from our regression sample.

on the first two rounds only.[16] Therefore, no contestant appears in more than one episode in our sample, while they may appear repeatedly over two rounds within an episode.

We focus on three main game features: fastest-finger buzzer type, a knockout and points reduction for a wrong answer (penalty).[17] These features are likely to be characterised by varying levels of stress, which earlier studies using different types of data have found affects males and females differently. For example, the exam performance of males and females is found to be affected differently by variations in future payoffs (see, for example, Attali et al. 2011; Ors et al. 2013; Morin 2015; Azmat et al. 2016).

Table 14.1 shows how episodes differ across rounds in terms of these three features of our data – fastest-finger buzzer type, a knockout and a penalty for a wrong answer. Note from the table that the game rules have changed a few times. In some shows, there was a buzzer with a buzzer press; that is, contestants were required to push a buzzer to obtain the chance to answer. There were also shows without a buzzer. In these shows, all contestants choose or write their answer on their personal screen. Also, the shows differ by whether there are any knockouts from advancing to the next round and, if so, how many are knocked out. Lastly, the shows differ by whether there is a point reduction or a penalty associated with providing the wrong answer. Other studies in an exam context have found that such penalties for a wrong answer affect women's performance more adversely than men's (see, for example, Baldiga 2014; Coffman and Klinowski 2019), while Funk and Perrone (2016) finds the opposite.

Summary statistics

Table 14.2 presents the summary statistics of the variables we use in our subsequent regression analyses. The shows typically comprise two or three rounds. In some shows, there are dropouts (those with the lowest score) after

16 In the final round, the winner from the previous week plays and their performance should be qualitatively different because there are dynamic factors such as learning and time-varying prize sizes.

17 There are some other features in specific game rules; contestants are initially given some basic points. Points differ by the difficulty of each question. For some questions, there is also a bonus gift, such as a laptop computer or a digital camera. In some shows, contestants are given one chance to pre-empt the first opportunity to answer the question. Question types are also various, including true or false, multiple-choice, and short-answer open-ended questions. In our regression analyses later, the effects of some of these features are absorbed by episode-specific fixed effects.

the first round, while other shows do not have such a feature. In Table 14.2, ignoring the details of game rules, we just present the summary statistics by round, focusing on the first two rounds (rounds 1 and 2) and by gender. For each round, we also present gender differences in columns [4] and [8].

Table 14.2: Descriptive statistics

	[1]	[2]	[3]	[4]	[5]	[6]	[7]	[8]
	All				Round 2 advances			
	All	Boys	Girls	B – G	All	Boys	Girls	B – G
Characteristics of contestants								
Girl	0.361 (0.481)	–	–	–	0.306 (0.461)	–	–	–
Age	17.388 (0.532)	17.448 (0.533)	17.281 (0.516)	0.167 [0.000]	17.415 (0.556)	17.461 (0.543)	17.294 (0.575)	0.167 [0.035]
Co-education	0.407 (0.491)	0.390 (0.488)	0.437 (0.497)	-0.047 [0.165]	0.432 (0.496)	0.416 (0.494)	0.468 (0.501)	-0.052 [0.306]
General school	0.839 (0.368)	0.826 (0.379)	0.862 (0.346)	-0.035 [0.165]	0.806 (0.396)	0.794 (0.405)	0.835 (0.373)	-0.041 [0.311]
Private school	0.542 (0.498)	0.569 (0.496)	0.495 (0.501)	0.073 [0.034]	0.555 (0.498)	0.578 (0.495)	0.504 (0.502)	0.074 [0.143]
Metropolitan	0.514 (0.500)	0.515 (0.500)	0.514 (0.501)	0.001 [0.978]	0.522 (0.500)	0.521 (0.500)	0.525 (0.501)	-0.005 [0.929]
Medium-size cities	0.394 (0.489)	0.383 (0.486)	0.415 (0.494)	-0.033 [0.334]	0.385 (0.487)	0.381 (0.486)	0.396 (0.491)	-0.015 [0.767]
Performance outcomes								
Round 1 score	1.000 (0.224)	1.020 (0.231)	0.965 (0.206)	0.055 [0.000]	1.114 (0.175)	1.127 (0.183)	1.085 (0.151)	0.042 [0.018]
Round 1 rank	3.000 (1.376)	2.904 (1.393)	3.169 (1.331)	-0.265 [0.005]	2.175 (0.948)	2.114 (0.962)	2.313 (0.903)	-0.199 [0.039]
Round 1 top 1	0.210 (0.408)	0.242 (0.429)	0.154 (0.361)	0.088 [0.002]	0.335 (0.472)	0.375 (0.485)	0.245 (0.431)	0.130 [0.007]
Round 1 top 2	0.439 (0.497)	0.468 (0.499)	0.388 (0.488)	0.080 [0.020]	0.670 (0.471)	0.695 (0.461)	0.612 (0.489)	0.084 [0.081]
Advance to Round 2	0.643 (0.479)	0.673 (0.470)	0.591 (0.492)	0.082 [0.001]	–	–	–	–
Round 2 score	–	–	–	–	1.000 (0.772)	1.060 (0.752)	0.863 (0.800)	0.197 [0.012]
N =	900	575	325	–	454	315	139	–

Notes: Standard deviations are presented in parentheses; Advance to round 200 is defined for the shows with Round 1 dropouts (episode no. ≥ 629 in Table 1, *N*=710); Age is missing for 371 contestants in the all sample and 208 for the Round 2 advances sample. Columns [4] and [8] present the gender differences in sample means and p-values in brackets.

The numbers of observations for each group are reported at the bottom of Table 14.2. We have 900 observations with usable responses from Round 1. There are five contestants in each game, and therefore our sample covers 180 games (episodes). Among these 900 contestants, 325 are girls, and 575 are boys. Note that there are more boys than girls, which we shall further discuss later. The last four columns of Table 14.2 provide details of the 454 contestants who advanced into Round 2 from Round 1, of whom 139 are girls and 315 boys. Thus, girls in Round 1 comprise 36 per cent of observations, and 31 per cent in Round 2. If this were so for our data, we would expect to see the proportion of females increasing from Round 1 to Round 2, as the boys in the left tail of the cognitive ability distribution got knocked out of the competition. But this is not what we observe. Instead, we find that girls are less likely than boys to advance to Round 2. We shall return to this issue later in our regression analysis of Round 2 performance.

Table 14.2 shows that the average age of contestants is just over 17 years.[18] Our contestants are high-school students who are usually aged 16 to 18. About 40 per cent of contestants attend co-educational schools, and 84 per cent attend the schools that are called the general-education schools in Korea (rather than special-purpose schools that are the alternative, such as science or foreign-language schools).[19] Just over half the samples attend private schools. Boys are more likely to attend private schools than girls, and the difference is statistically significant (p-value = 0.034). But private and public schools are not very different in Korea because even private schools cannot admit students selectively.[20] Most of the sample lives in metropolitan areas and medium-sized cities.

18 We have converted high-school grade to age, since contestants do not reveal their age but only their high-school grade. To do this conversion, we assumed high-school grade 1 = age 16 and so on. Note further that school grade is missing for 371 contestants (41 per cent). This is because it is up to them whether to introduce their grade or not. Because of many missing values of age, we will be careful in interpreting our results below related to age. In regression analyses, we put a value of zero when age is missing and control for age dummies (16, 17 and 18) with the missing cases as the base group.

19 Special-purpose schools are those focused on specific subjects like arts, music, science or foreign languages. Some special-purpose schools are elite schools. They are selective, while students are assigned to general-education schools based on their residence (school district). There are also vocational schools but we do not have any students from those schools in our sample.

20 Private schools in Korea are privately owned, but under the so-called 'equalisation policy' they are not very different from public schools. High schools governed by the equalisation policy receive equal government funding, charge the same fees and follow the same national curriculum. However, private schools maintain autonomy over their personnel decisions, while public schools do not (Hahn et al., 2018).

The second half of Table 14.2 presents the summary statistics of contestants' performance variables. The game is a typical quiz game. Contestants solve quizzes, and they score points when they get the answers right. We standardise the raw score for each round by dividing it by each episode-round's mean score because there are some different point systems across episodes and rounds. The results in Table 14.2 already show the gender gaps in performance between girls and boys. We find that girls score lower than boys in both rounds 1 and 2. The gap amounts to 5.5 per cent of the mean score of Round 1 and 19.7 per cent of the mean of Round 2. That is, the gap increased over rounds.

As girls score lower, their rankings are also lower. Figure 14.1 shows the average scores by gender over two rounds. The variable 'Round 1 top 1' refers to being first in Round 1, and girls are less likely than boys to be in this group. The variable 'Round 1 top 2' refers to being first or second in the first round, and again, girls are less likely to be in this group. Of the contestants advancing into Round 2, boys have a higher Round 1 score than girls, though this difference is significant only at the 10 per cent level.

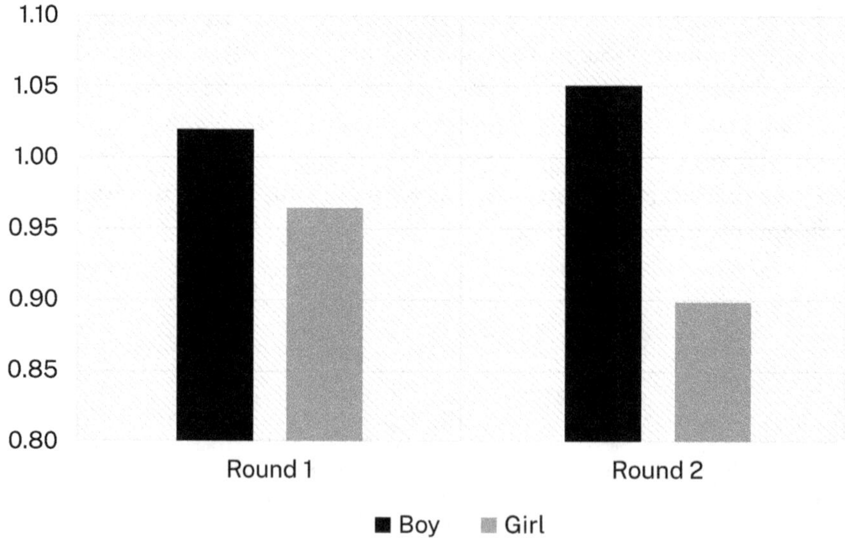

Figure 14.1: Gender differences in score between rounds 1 and 2

Note: Average standardised scores by gender and by round. Raw scores are standardised to have a mean of 1 in each round of each episode.

We present the summary statistics of Round 1 performance for those who advance to Round 2 in columns [5]–[8]. The results show that not only are boys more likely to advance to Round 2, but also that they do so with higher scores. That is, comparing girls and boys who successfully advanced to Round 2, we find boys performed better in Round 1 than girls.

We will be using these variables in subsequent regression analyses below, where we control for other factors likely to affect performance and investigate if gender gaps in performance vary across games with different rules.

But first, for the purpose of our study, it is important to ensure that contestants are randomly assigned across episodes with different rules. While our understanding is that the TV show producers did not assign contestants to episodes depending on game rules and gender differences in contestants' abilities, we nonetheless check the balancing of contestant characteristics across different game rules. Table 14.3 presents the results.

Table 14.3: Characteristics of contestants by game rules

	[1]	[2]	[3]	[4]	[5]	[6]
	No knockout	Knockout	No buzzer	Buzzer	No penalty	Penalty
Girl	0.400 (0.491)	0.350 (0.477)	0.379 (0.486)	0.342 (0.475)	0.365 (0.482)	0.346 (0.477)
Age	17.371 (0.510)	17.395 (0.542)	17.326 (0.525)	17.420 (0.534)	17.274 (0.509)	17.650 (0.491)
Co-ed	0.287 (0.454)	0.440 (0.497)	0.432 (0.496)	0.379 (0.486)	0.418 (0.494)	0.362 (0.482)
General school	0.923 (0.267)	0.816 (0.388)	0.796 (0.404)	0.886 (0.318)	0.827 (0.379)	0.886 (0.318)
Private school	0.538 (0.500)	0.543 (0.498)	0.502 (0.501)	0.586 (0.493)	0.531 (0.499)	0.584 (0.494)
Metropolitan	0.492 (0.501)	0.521 (0.500)	0.534 (0.499)	0.493 (0.501)	0.517 (0.500)	0.503 (0.501)
Medium-size cities	0.436 (0.497)	0.383 (0.486)	0.381 (0.486)	0.409 (0.492)	0.392 (0.488)	0.405 (0.492)
Observations	195	705	470	430	715	185

Notes: Sample means of contestant characteristics are presented. Standard deviations are presented in parentheses. We divide the sample by each game rule: by the knockout rule in columns [1] and [2], by the buzzer rule in [3] and [4], and by the penalty rule in [5] and [6].

We separate the sample by whether a specific rule is applied or not and present the means and standard deviations of contestant characteristics; whether or not there is knockout in columns [1] and [2], whether or not there is a buzzer in [3] and [4] and whether or not there is a penalty for a wrong answer in [5] and [6]. The most important variable for the purpose of our chapter is gender. We should check if the gender composition of contestants is systematically different depending on the game rules. In Table 14.3, we find no significant difference by any of the three game rules.

In Table 14.3, we find significant differences in some contestant characteristics by game rules. For example, we find that students in co-educational schools are more likely to be assigned to episodes with knockouts. However, we do not find any systematic patterns that might bias our estimates below. We find significant differences in general schools for all three game rules. Students in general schools are, on average, worse than those in special-purpose schools. However, the results in Table 14.3 do not show any systematic patterns such that better students are more likely to be assigned to more competitive games, and, if any, the differences are not substantial. Also, one may think that the contestant composition could be manipulated in a way to boost the viewership rating, but this is very unlikely since the broadcasting company is publicly owned, and the viewership rating is not high anyway. Therefore, we conclude that contestants are not systematically assigned to episodes with different game rules, at least with respect to their ability. But we control for all observable characteristics when we conduct our regression analyses.

Specifications and empirical findings

From our discussion to date, we summarise two broad conjectures to be addressed with regression analyses of our data. These conjectures are, first, is there a gender gap in performance in a competitive environment? And second, do girls perform worse when competitive pressure is greater? Because the rules of the game show changed considerably over the period for which we have data, we are able to estimate a number of different specifications to address these conjectures. These specifications and estimates are reported later in the chapter.

Gender gaps in Round 1

To address the first conjecture, we wish to establish whether or not there is a gender gap in performance in the quiz show. To do so, we initially use all 900 observations of data from Round 1, because all contestants participate in the first round and therefore we do not have to worry about selection by knockouts.[21] Thus, the reader should note that the estimating sample here includes all types of games, in contrast to subsequent subsections. Therefore, any estimated effect of gender from this sample is the average Round 1 effect across all game types.

We estimate a simple linear equation as follows:

(1) $S_{ij} = \beta_0 + \beta_1 Girl_{ij} + X_{ij}\gamma + \delta_j + \varepsilon_{ij}$,

where subscript *i* denotes the individual contestant and *j* the episode. The dependent variable, S_{ij}, is the standardised (Round 1) score. We divide the raw score by each episode's mean score to control for heterogeneity across episodes in the level of question difficulty or any unobservable factors that affect overall performance.[22] $Girl_{ij}$ is the indicator for whether the contestant is a girl, so β_1 captures the gender difference in the performance represented by the dependent variable.

We control for episode-specific fixed effects, δ_j, which capture any effects of episode-level unobservable factors that equally affect the five contestants in an episode.[23] Vector X_{ij} includes variables such as age, indicators for school type (general and private schools) and residential areas (metropolitan and medium-sized cities).

As mentioned earlier, we have information on the qualifying-test scores for a subset of 229 contestants. All students who apply for the game show should take the qualifying test, and they have to pass the minimum score to qualify for the show.[24] This qualifying-test score is a good control for

21 There still exists a selection problem with respect to selection into the game, which we cannot resolve without data on those applicants who failed to enter the game or unless we have some common measures by which we can compare our contestants with high-school students in general.

22 The results where we use the raw scores as the dependent variable are similar.

23 Any effects of the game rules should be subsumed by the episode-specific fixed effects. For comparison, we present the results with or without the fixed effects.

24 We do not have any knowledge about the qualifying-test scores. In our sample, the minimum is 20, so we guess that this would be the cut-off. The maximum is 44, so we also guess that the full mark would be 45. Episodes where the test scores are available are from 655 to 703, so there is not much variation in game rules. For this reason, we cannot control for the test scores when we estimate the impacts of game rules.

ability that is orthogonal to the capability to compete, because the test is taken individually in a non-tournament manner. Thus, we will also present the results after controlling for the test score to check the robustness of our estimates from the baseline specification using the full sample.

Table 14.4 reports the results from estimating equation (1), where we want to address the conjecture that there is a gender gap in contestants' performance in the game shows. Robust standard errors, clustered by episode, are presented in parentheses. Here we consistently see across different specifications that girls have a significantly lower standardised score than boys. The estimates are robust in controlling for episode-specific fixed effects in column [2]. The gender gap amounts to about 5 per cent compared to the mean score. The only other control that is statistically significant in columns [1] and [2] is attendance at a general-education school, which is associated with a decline in score, as expected (the base group is attending a selective special-purpose school).

Table 14.4: Round 1 performance

	[1]	[2]	[3]	[4]
Girl	-0.051*** (0.016)	-0.054*** (0.019)	-0.114*** (0.033)	-0.092*** (0.032)
Qualifying-test score	–	–	–	0.007** (0.003)
General school	-0.049** (0.021)	-0.063** (0.030)	-0.095** (0.040)	-0.072* (0.040)
Private school	0.007 (0.015)	0.008 (0.021)	0.037 (0.033)	0.029 (0.033)
Metropolitan	0.001 (0.024)	0.004 (0.034)	0.042 (0.050)	0.032 (0.049)
Medium-size cities	-0.004 (0.023)	-0.004 (0.033)	0.011 (0.047)	0.004 (0.047)
Constant	1.056*** (0.026)	1.076*** (0.041)	1.185*** (0.100)	0.987*** (0.108)
Episode FE	No	Yes	No	No
Observations	900	900	229	229
R^2	0.023	0.027	0.091	0.110

Notes: * 10% significance; ** 5% significance; *** 1% significance; Robust standard errors, clustered by episode, are presented in parentheses. Age dummies with missing age as the base group are included in all specifications.

In columns [3] and [4], we report the results from estimating equation (1) on the subsample of individuals for whom we have the qualifying-test score. The cost of this exercise is losing 671 observations. In column [3], while we restrict the sample to those with the qualifying-test score available, we do not control for the test score. In column [4], we additionally control for the qualifying-test score. By comparing columns [3] and [4], we can infer the impact of controlling for the proxy variable of ability. The results show that controlling for the test score decreases the size of the gender gap from -0.114 to -0.092, but the remaining gap is still significant and substantial in terms of its magnitude, about 9 per cent of the mean score. The reduction of the gender gap indicates that the gender gap we find in the game show is partially reflective of gender-specific selection or gender differences in the distribution of ability.

In summary, the estimates reported in this section support our first conjecture – that there is a gender gap in performance in this competitive environment.

Gender gaps under different game rules

As explained previously, we focus on three major game features: fastest-finger buzzer, knockouts and points reduction for a wrong answer. We focus on these features because the intensity of competition would differ depending on them. Thus, we examine whether the gender gap in performance differs by those game rules. This is an important contribution of our chapter, since it sheds some light on the underlying mechanism that contributes to gender gaps in behaviours under competition. In particular, we can address our second conjecture: do girls perform worse when competitive pressure is greater?

To investigate this, we expand equation (1) and include the interaction terms between $Girl_{ij}$ and the game rules:

(1') $S_{ij} = \beta_0 + \beta_1 Girl_{ij} + \beta_2 Girl_{ij} \times Knockout_{ij} + \beta_3 Girl_{ij} \times Buzzer_{ij} + \beta_4 Girl_{ij} \times Penalty_{ij} + X_{ij}\gamma + \delta_j + \varepsilon_{ij}$.

Our hypothesis is that girls may underperform in a more competitive environment, and all the above-mentioned rules increase the intensity of competition. For example, by estimating β_2, we test whether the gender gap gets larger (or smaller) when there is a knockout after Round 1 than when there is no knockout.

The results from estimating equation (1') are presented in Table 14.5. Column [1] presents the results without episode fixed effects. In this specification, X_{ij} contains the indicators for the game rules. Column [2] shows the results with episode fixed effects.

Table 14.5: Gender differences in Round 1 score by game type

	[1]	[2]	[3]	[4]
Girl	0.034 (0.033)	0.041 (0.041)	0.053 (0.038)	0.062 (0.046)
Interactions with girl				
Knockout	-0.044 (0.038)	-0.048 (0.047)	–	–
Buzzer	-0.111*** (0.040)	-0.122** (0.048)	–	–
Penalty	0.007 (0.051)	0.008 (0.061)	–	–
Knockout × buzzer × penalty	–	–	-0.144** (0.059)	-0.160** (0.072)
Knockout × buzzer × no penalty	–	–	-0.174*** (0.049)	-0.191*** (0.059)
Knockout × no buzzer × penalty	–	–	-0.159** (0.065)	-0.173** (0.079)
No knockout × buzzer × no penalty	–	–	-0.070 (0.045)	-0.078 (0.056)
Constant	1.043*** (0.032)	1.081*** (0.042)	1.037*** (0.036)	1.081*** (0.042)
Test result (*p*-value) for				
Girl × knockout | buzzer × no penalty	–	–	0.011	0.022
Girl × buzzer | knockout × penalty	–	–	0.839	0.877
Girl × penalty | knockout × buzzer	–	–	0.595	0.639
Controls	Yes	Yes	Yes	Yes
Episode FE	No	Yes	No	Yes
Observations	900	900	900	900
R^2	0.039	0.045	0.040	0.046

Notes: * 10% significance; ** 5% significance; *** 1% significance; Robust standard errors, clustered by episode, are presented in parentheses. Control variables in Table 14.3 are included. In columns [1] and [3], without Episode FE, game format dummies are controlled for. In column [1], the indicators for knockout, buzzer and penalty are included. In column [3], the four combination indicators are included.

The results show that, after allowing for the gender gap to vary by the game rules, the indicator for girls becomes positive, although it is not statistically significant. This means that, without any rule that potentially increases psychological pressure, girls do not perform worse than boys. The estimates are almost identical between columns [1] and [2]. We also find that girls perform worse than boys when they have to press a buzzer to obtain the right to answer. The estimate for the rule of knockout is also negative but statistically insignificant. The estimate for the penalty is insignificant and even positive.

Equation (1') assumes that the effects of the game rules are independent. However, the equation can be mis-specified. As seen in Table 14.1, the game rules were actually implemented in various combinations rather than independently. While there are three rules, we have five combinations in our sample: (knockout, buzzer, penalty) = (0,0,0), (1,1,1), (1,1,0), (1,0,1), and (0,1,0), where each element indicates whether the corresponding rule is implemented or not. Note that the rule of the buzzer was applied by itself, but the other two rules were never implemented independently. This means that the independent effect of, for example, a knockout cannot be estimated. To reflect this fact, we modify equation (1') and directly estimate the effects of the combinations of the rules. Specifically, we include the indicators for the four combinations, (1,1,1), (1,1,0), (1,0,1), and (0,1,0), after taking (0,0,0) as the base group.

The results are presented in columns [3] and [4] in Table 14.5, without and with episode fixed effects, respectively. The results again confirm that girls do not underperform than boys under lower psychological pressure. However, we find that girls perform worse than boys in all combinations but the last when only the rule of buzzer is implemented.

From the results of the interaction terms, it is possible to infer the effect of a specific rule conditional on a combination of the other two rules.[25] For example, we can infer the effect of the knockout rule, conditional on the buzzer rule being implemented but the penalty not, by subtracting the estimate for (0,1,0) from the estimate for (1,1,0). The test results are presented in the second-to-last panel in Table 14.5. We find that the conditional effect of the knockout rule is statistically significant. This suggests that a game show of the type where losing contestants are flung out of the game is associated with a greater gender gap in performance

25 We are grateful to an anonymous referee for pointing this out.

than in a game show where no one is thrown out. This is consistent with our conjecture that girls, who are typically more risk-averse than boys, face greater psychic pressure than boys in this form of the game. This choking under pressure likely explains some of the observed gender gap.[26] However, our results are limited in that we do not know whether this is totally the effect of the knockout or if the knockout rule is effective only when the buzzer rule is jointly implemented.[27] We also find that the rule of buzzer or penalty does not have any significant additional effect when the other two rules are already applied.

So far, we have found that girls generally perform worse than boys in Round 1 in terms of score, especially in settings where psychological pressure is higher. Next, we check whether the score deficit of girls is significantly large enough to affect the probability of their advancing to the next round when there is any knockout. Table 14.6 presents the results from the estimation of the linear probability model where the dependent variable is the indicator of whether the contestant successfully advances to Round 2. Similar to Table 14.5, first, we estimate the equation assuming the independent effects of the game rules. The results are presented in columns [1] and [2], without and with episode fixed effects. Then, in columns [3] and [4], we estimate the equation directly, estimating the effects of the rule combinations. Since the estimating subsample is restricted to those episodes with a knockout (705 observations), there are only the combinations from the other two rules, buzzer and penalty. Note that the base group consists of the episodes where there is the penalty rule but no buzzer rule.

In columns [1] and [2], we find that, while girls are less likely to advance to Round 2 when either the buzzer rule or the penalty rule is applied and the magnitude of the gender gap is large (ranging from 12 to 17 percentage points), these estimates are imprecisely estimated. On the other hand, in columns [3] and [4], we find that, compared to the base group (with penalty but no buzzer), the estimate for the combination of buzzer and penalty is statistically significant. Therefore, it is the effect of the buzzer,

26 Moreover, according to psychologists such as Arch (1993) and Block (1983), men are more likely to see a risky situation as a challenge to action, whereas women view it as a threat to be avoided.

27 While numerous studies show that on average girls are more risk-averse than boys (see, for example, Eckel and Grossman, 2002; Dohmen et al., 2011; Booth and Nolen, 2012a, b), this has been found to depend on the task by, for example, Filippin and Crosetto (2016). Note further that time pressure may also play a role: see Shurchkov (2012) found that males outperform females when there is time pressure, but only in tasks where males are believed to be better. However, females were found to do better in any type of task that did not imply time pressure. We are unable to distinguish between these potential mechanisms with our data.

conditional on penalty, that matters. The buzzer effect is large, decreasing the probability of girls' advancing to the next round by 29–34 percentage points. However, we do not know whether the effect is solely due to the buzzer rule or becomes significant only with the penalty rule. This is a major limitation of our setting. Also, as in Table 14.5, we try to infer the conditional effect of a specific rule. For example, we can infer the effect of the penalty conditional on the buzzer rule by comparing the two estimates. It turns out to be statistically insignificant.

Table 14.6: Probability of advancing to Round 2

	[1]	[2]	[3]	[4]
Girl	-0.026 (0.063)	-0.001 (0.080)	-0.026 (0.063)	-0.001 (0.080)
Interactions with girl				
Buzzer	-0.127 (0.095)	-0.162 (0.116)	–	–
Penalty	-0.159 (0.115)	-0.176 (0.140)	–	–
Buzzer × penalty	–	–	-0.285** (0.109)	-0.338** (0.136)
Buzzer × no penalty	–	–	-0.127 (0.095)	-0.162 (0.116)
Constant	0.720*** (0.084)	0.692*** (0.103)	0.720*** (0.084)	0.692*** (0.103)
Test result (*p*-value) for girl × penalty | buzzer	–	–	0.170	0.212
Controls	Yes	Yes	Yes	Yes
Episode FE	No	Yes	No	Yes
Observations	705	705	705	705
R^2	0.061	0.074	0.061	0.074

Notes: * 10% significance; ** 5% significance; *** 1% significance; Linear probability models estimated by OLS. Robust standard errors, clustered by episode, are presented in parentheses. The number of knockouts is controlled for. Control variables in Table 14.3 are included. In columns [1] and [3], without Episode FE, game format dummies are controlled for. In column [1], the indicators for knockout, buzzer and penalty are included. In column [3], the four combination indicators are included.

Gender gaps over rounds

Previously, we compared games under different rules that likely provoke different levels of competitive pressure. In addition, competitive pressure also varies over the course of a game. For example, it is likely to escalate as contestants advance to a higher round, or as a couple of contestants face the moment the final winner is determined. Our results for Round 1 suggested that girls may be more responsive to psychological stress than boys. This emerged from the natural experiment that we have at our disposal, arising from contestants' responses to changes in the rules of the game.

We next examine contestants' behaviour at the second stage of the game. Studies by Cai et al. (2019) and Iriberri and Rey-Biel (2019) look at gender differences in performance in two-stage competitions. Iriberri and Rey-Biel (2019) use data from a two-stage math competition in Madrid in Spain, while Cai et al. (2019) use data from the college entrance exam (Gaokao) in China, the first stage of which is a mock examination. Cai et al. (2019) find that, compared to male students, females underperformed on the highly competitive Chinese entrance exam relative to their performance in the low-stakes mock examination. They attribute this to females' relatively lower tolerance for psychological pressure as well as their weaker incentives to perform in such a high-stakes situation. Iriberri and Rey-Biel (2019) analyse two-stage elimination math contests, in which participants compete to pass from stage 1 to stage 2 and later to be among the winners. They find that the gender gap in math performance increases from stage 1 to stage 2 of a math competition. They attribute the increase in female underperformance to higher competitive pressure.

Following this literature and our Round 1 results, our conjecture is that the gender gap in performance at the second stage will be bigger than at the first, because the level of stress will be increasing as the competition proceeds. The stakes will also be increasing, as potential earnings grow. We already know from the results in Table 14.5, as well as from inspection of the means in Table 14.1, that girls are less likely than boys to advance to Round 2 and that the greater male variability hypothesis is not supported by our data. But perhaps the better girls have survived to Round 2. If so, this would drive down the gender gap and swamp the psychological stress effect.

Along this line of thought, we now estimate equation (1) for Round 2 and check if the gender gap is indeed increasing in the second round. In addition, we try to use two different specifications for robustness. First, we use the between-round score difference (Sij2 – Sij1) as the dependent variable. In this specification, we can directly compare whether girls perform relatively worse in the second round than boys (girls might perform absolutely better in Round 2, but we compare the improvements with boys' performance).

An additional specification that we use to compare girls' and boys' performance changes over rounds is to use individual-round panel data and estimate a panel-data model like the following equation:

(2) $S_{ijr} = \beta_0 + \beta_1 Girl_{ij} \times 1[r = 2] + \delta_i + \tau_{jr} + \varepsilon_{ijr}$,

where S_{ijr} is the standardised score of contestant i in round r of episode j. Note that since there are two rounds, contestants can appear in the sample up to two times. Those who are knocked out after the first round are included in the sample, but they are not actually used because of individual fixed effects.

The advantage of this specification is that we can control for any time-constant unobservable characteristics of either contestants or episodes by individual contestant-specific effects δ_i. The fixed effects absorb the gender effect in Round 1 since gender is a time-invariant characteristic, but we can capture the change of the gender effect from Round 1 to Round 2 by estimating the coefficient for the interaction term between gender and round indicators, $Girl_{ij} \times 1[r = 2]$. Also, we can control for episode-by-round fixed effects, τ_{jr}. The fixed effects should capture any unobservable effects, which are common to all contestants in each round and each episode.[28]

Table 14.7 reports estimates from an equation where the dependent variable is the Round 2 score. In column [1], we have the gender gap with no other controls. Here we see that the gender gap in performance is 20 per cent, substantially larger than the comparison of just 5.5 per cent from column [1] of Table 14.4. Thus, the gender gap in performance in Round 2 is much bigger than in Round 1. The estimate in column [2], where the other control variables are included, is similar, and that in column [3] with episode fixed effects added is even larger, being about 25 per cent. This is likely because the level of stress is increasing as the competition proceeds. This result is similar to that found by Cai et al. (2019) and Iriberri and Rey-Biel (2019).

28 The performance in Round 2 may be affected by the contestant's relative ranking in Round 1. To check this, we controlled for Round 1 ranking or the score gap from the leading contestant. The results are similar; girls still underperform than boys in Round 2.

It might be expected that strong competition in traditionally male domains (for example, mathematics, as found by Iriberri and Rey-Biel 2019) may hinder girls' performance. However, it is interesting that exposure to extreme competition in Round 2 of the quiz show also hampers girls' performance in the more gender-neutral domains (namely, history, literature, natural science, music and the arts) of our quiz show.

Table 14.7: Round 2 performance

	[1]	[2]	[3]
Round 2 score			
Girl	−0.197** (0.083)	−0.193** (0.086)	−0.258* (0.132)
Episode FE	N	N	Y
Observations	454	454	454
R-squared	0.014	0.020	0.039
Score difference			
Girl	−0.155* (0.079)	−0.155* (0.082)	−0.208* (0.126)
Episode FE	N	N	Y
Observations	454	454	454
R^2	0.009	0.016	0.042

Notes: * 10% significance; ** 5% significance; *** 1% significance; Robust standard errors, clustered by episode, are presented in parentheses. Age dummies with missing age as the base group are included in all specifications.

In Table 14.7, we also report results from estimating an equation of the form ($S_{ij}2$ – $S_{ij}1$), where the first difference allows us to difference out individual fixed effects that are likely to affect performance. This is estimated on the subsample of 454 contestants for whom we have complete data in rounds 1 and 2. Here we also find that differenced performance is significantly lower for girls than boys, again likely illustrating that the level of stress is increasing and self-confidence eroding as the competition proceeds.

The results from estimating equation (2) also show that girls perform relatively worse in the second round than in the first round compared to boys. We estimate the coefficient of the interaction term between indicators for girls and Round 2 with individual contestant fixed effects and episode-round fixed effects. The estimate is similar to those in Table 14.6. The point estimate is –0.203 (p-value = 0.047).

Gender gaps over questions

The specification in equation (2) above compares contestants' performance between rounds 1 and 2. The idea is that competitive pressure is larger in the second round. At a more micro level, competitive pressure may change within a round over questions as the game proceeds. Such a dynamic analysis can be helpful in shedding more light on contestants' behaviour under competitive pressure because we can observe individual contestants at every moment their winning probability changes.[29]

We are able to undertake play-by-play panel data estimation using data from some of the shows. As can be seen in Table 14.1, in episodes 577–592, there are no rounds or knockouts, and each show's five contestants answer all 25 questions until the end of the game. The contestant with the highest score becomes the final winner. Two of these 15 shows were special formats, and we therefore dropped those and used data from 13 of the shows. From these 13 shows, we construct individual play-by-play performance data, with a panel structure of 25 periods (questions) per contestant. This yields an estimating subsample of 1625 person-round observations. By watching all episodes from the beginning to the end, we record detailed information about all five contestants' actions and outcomes for each question: whether they successfully pressed the buzzer (that is, pressed it faster than others) and whether their answer was correct. We use one of these action/outcome variables as the dependent variable in the following regression equation.

(3) $Y_{ijt} = \beta_0 + \beta_1 Girl_{ij} + \beta_2 WP_{ijt} + \beta_3 Girl_{ij} \times WP_{ijt} + \gamma PT_{jt} + \tau_t + \delta_j + \varepsilon_{ijt}$,

where subscripts indicate individual contestant i and question number t (i.e., t-th question, from 1 to 25) in episode j. We observe individuals repeatedly in 25 questions.

We examine two outcome variables. Y_{ijt} is the indicator for whether contestant i in episode j obtains the right to answer question t or the indicator for whether contestant i in episode j obtains the right to answer question t and gets the question right. There might be multiple contestants who obtain the right to answer because the fastest one got the wrong answer, and then the next one is determined again, depending on who presses the buzzer fastest, excepting the one who got the wrong answer in the first place.

29 This can be viewed as a form of feedback, and we use the winning probability as a proxy for this. For papers that are able to use more explicit forms of feedback, see Eriksson et al. (2009) and Berger and Pope (2011), though the latter does not look at gender.

The biggest advantage of using panel data is that we can examine how contestants behave over the course of the game. In particular, we think that the most important factor contestants consider over the course of the game should be the winning probability. This is because the game is a winner-takes-all type of game, so the probability of winning the game is ultimately more important than absolute scores.[30] Therefore, unlike cross-sectional analysis using equation (1), we control for the (predicted) winning probability of each contestant at the moment of question t, WP_{ijt}.

It is obvious that the winning probability matters for contestants' behaviour or strategy, but it is not directly observed, even by the contestants themselves. We assume that contestants, like econometricians, estimate their winning probability at the moment of question t by using the probit model of the following form:

(4) $Prob(Final\ Winner_{ij}) = F(\gamma_1 Score_{ijt} + \gamma_2 SGap_{ijt} + \gamma_3 MaxPoints_{jt})$,

where the dependent variable is whether contestant i is the final winner in episode j. Explanatory variables are the contestant's own score ($Score_{ijt}$), their score gap ($SGap_{ijt}$) with the top-ranked contestant (which is zero if the contestant is top-ranked), and the maximum points available after question t ($MaxPoints_{jt}$). We estimate the model for $t \geq 2$.[31] At the beginning of the show ($t = 1$), we assume that all contestants have an equal probability of winning (0.2). Similarly, we assume the probability is one if the contestant is top-ranked and the score gap between their score and the second-ranked contestant's is greater than the maximum points available. We assume that contestants predict their winning probability by using the same probit model.

In addition to checking whether the effect of winning probability differs by gender, we include the interaction term between the winning probability (in the mean deviation form) and the indicator for girls ($Girl_{ij} \times WP_{ijt}$). We control for the fixed effect (τ_t) for the question number to capture any effects that might arise as the game approaches the end. As before, δ_j is the episode fixed effect. Since the sample is a balanced panel dataset at the individual level, we can further control for individual contestant-specific fixed effects instead of the episode fixed effect. For robustness, we will

30 However, it is possible that contestants still consider their final scores importantly because of their intrinsic motivation. Objectively, there is no difference between, for example, second place and the last place, but it might matter emotionally or socially since they are watched by friends and families.

31 The estimation results of the probit model are presented in Appendix Table A14.1.

present the results from both specifications.[32] Lastly, we control for the number of points of the question (PT_{jt}). All contestants know these points before responding. We expect that the larger the points are, the more likely contestants are to take a risk, that is, pressing the buzzer even without full confidence in their answer. Thus, the likelihood of pressing the buzzer will be higher, but the accuracy rate will be lower.[33]

We report in Table 14.8 the results of estimating equation (3) using the individual-level panel data, where there are 25 questions. Columns [1]–[3] show the results for whether an individual pressed the buzzer fastest and obtained the right to answer, and [4]–[6] the results for whether the answer was correct. For each outcome, we try three specifications: with or without control variables and with individual fixed effects. As we are using individual-level panel data where there are 25 questions, we control for question number dummies (which are similar to time variables in usual panel data) as well as episode fixed effects.

Table 14.8: Individual play-by-play performance

	[1]	[2] Buzzer	[3]	[4]	[5] Accuracy	[6]
Girl	-0.045* (0.022)	-0.045* (0.023)	–	-0.039** (0.016)	-0.038** (0.016)	–
Points	–	0.002 (0.002)	0.002 (0.002)	–	-0.002** (0.001)	-0.002 (0.002)
Winning prob.	–	0.131 (0.135)	-0.119 (0.127)	–	0.142 (0.124)	-0.238* (0.120)
Girl × winning prob.	–	-0.323* (0.167)	-0.369* (0.194)	–	-0.226* (0.109)	-0.156 (0.152)
Constant	0.290*** (0.008)	0.199*** (0.040)	0.246*** (0.065)	0.198*** (0.006)	0.217*** (0.036)	0.297*** (0.062)
Question number FE	Y	Y	Y	Y	Y	Y
Episode FE	Y	Y	–	Y	Y	–
Individual FE	–	–	Y	–	–	Y
Observations	1625	1625	1625	1625	1625	1625
R^2	0.008	0.021	0.065	0.003	0.008	0.057

Notes: * 10% significance; ** 5% significance; *** 1% significance; Robust standard errors, clustered by episode in columns [1], [2], [4] and [5] and by individual in columns [3] and [6], are presented in parentheses.

32 In the panel data analysis, we did not control for the control variables included in equation (1). They are individual-specific constant variables, such as age and school type. Instead, as a robustness check, we try to control for individual-specific fixed effects, which should absorb all the effects from those time-invariant individual characteristics.

33 We estimate Eq. (2) by the linear probability model. We also experimented with using probit or logit models, but as the results are qualitatively same, we do not report them here.

The results reveal some intriguing gender differences. First, girls are less likely to press the buzzer fastest. Column [1] shows that girls' probability of obtaining the right to answer is about 4.5 percentage points lower than boys. The estimate is robust to including control variables. In columns [2] and [3], we included the interaction term between the winning probability and the indicator for girls. The results in column [2] show that girls are less likely to press the buzzer fastest, and this tendency is more salient when their winning probability is higher. The results are robust to controlling for individual-specific fixed effects in column [3].

Columns [4]–[6] present the results for accuracy, that is, whether or not the contestant earns points. In other words, this is whether or not the contestant presses the buzzer fastest and his or her answer is correct.[34] Thus, the outcome variable is the multiplication of the probability of obtaining the right to answer and that of the answer being correct. In columns [4] and [5], we find significant gender differences; girls are less likely to earn points than boys. However, the magnitude of the estimates is absolutely smaller than that of those in columns [1] and [2], where the dependent variable is just the probability of obtaining the right to answer. Comparing the estimates for the interaction term between columns [2] and [5], we also find that the estimate in column [5] is smaller in the absolute term than that in column [2]. This means that while girls are less likely to press the buzzer fastest, the gender gap is weaker because there is a smaller gender gap in terms of accuracy. The estimate for the interaction term in column [6] is also smaller and statistically insignificant. In the results for accuracy, it is notable that accuracy is lower when the points are larger. This is probably because contestants are more likely to take a risk when the stakes are larger.

The results suggest that girls are more passive than boys, especially when they are closer to winning the game. To see this pattern in more detail from a dynamic perspective, we estimate equation (2) by restricting the sample to that closer to the end of the game gradually, that is, restricting the sample by $t \leq 1,2, \ldots, 25$. We use the same specifications as those in columns [2] and [5] in Table 14.7, where we control for episode fixed effects and present only the estimates for the gender dummy ($Girl_{ij}$) and the interaction term ($Girl_{ij} \times WP_{ijt}$). Figure 14.2 plots the point estimates and 95 per cent confidence intervals. Also for comparison, we present the estimates for the average effects from columns [2] and [5] in Table 14.7 by horizontal dashed lines.

34 In order to estimate the gender effect on accuracy per se, we need to estimate a two-stage system of equations where the selection equation for obtaining the right to answer is jointly estimated.

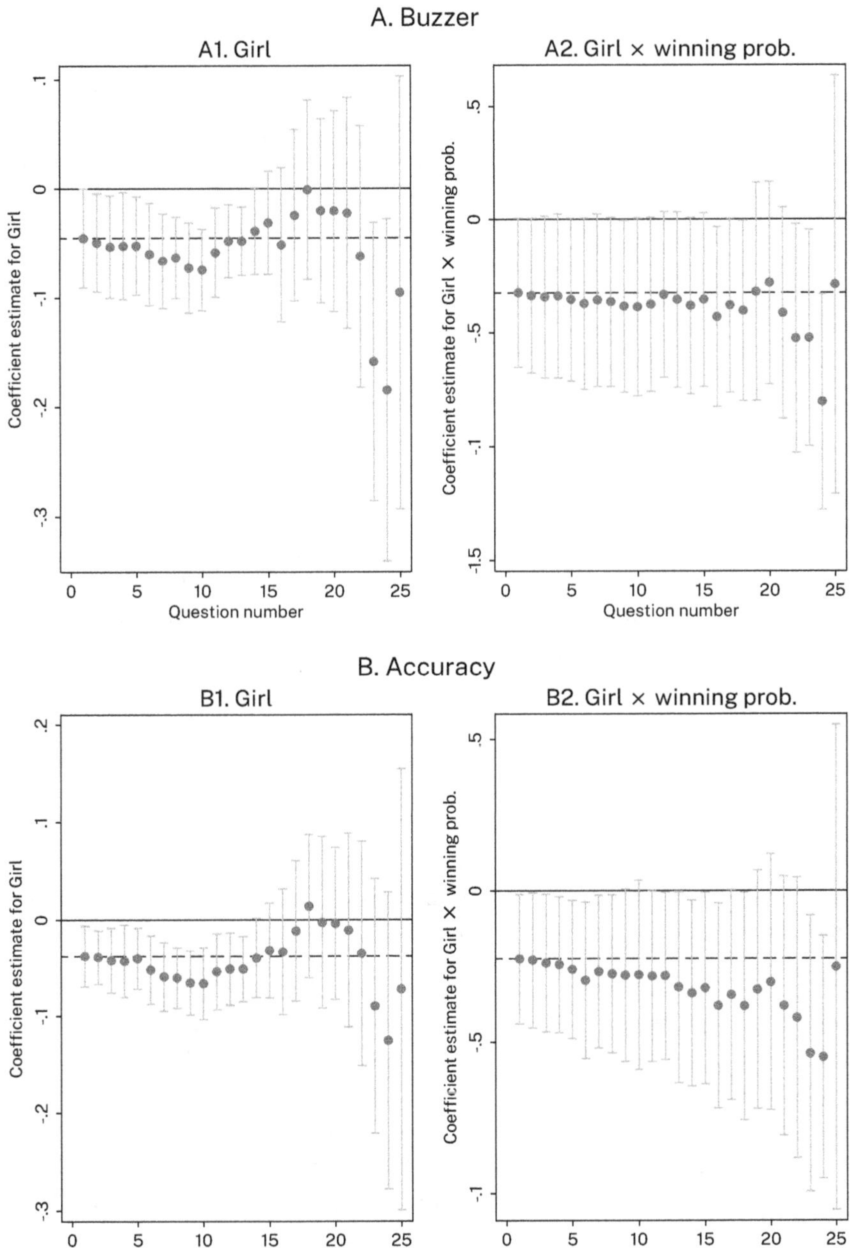

Figure 14.2: Gender differences in end-of-game behaviour

Note: The graphs are based on the estimates from equation (2) for the subsample where question number is greater than or equal to each number on the horizontal axis. The point estimates and 95 per cent confidence intervals are presented. The horizontal dashed line represents the average effect presented in columns [2] and [5] of Table 14.7.

Figure 14.2 reveals intriguing dynamics of gender differences. In particular, the female gender dummy effect improves as games wear on, but only up to around the 20th game; after this point, both buzzer-pressing and accuracy decline for girls. This suggests that girls may be losing tenacity or confidence as the end of the 25-stage game approaches, and that, as a consequence, they reduce their effort.[35] In other words, the girls are quitting too easily. The results show the dynamics of accuracy rates, and the overall trends are similar, which means that the dynamics are basically driven by the behaviour of buzzer-pressing.

Conclusions

In this chapter, we analysed performance data from a long-running Korean television quiz show, whose contestants were on average 17 years old. First, we found that while there is typically a gender gap in performance across episodes of the quiz show game, this gender gap is not found in baseline games with less competitive pressure. Second, to investigate underlying mechanisms that might explain these gender gaps, we explored how male and female performance varied under different combinations of rules of the game. We found that there are no gender gaps when stress is kept to a minimum. However, in games with particular combinations of knockout rules, there are significant gender gaps in performance. Owing to the way in which the game show was implemented, we were unable to distinguish whether this was due solely to knockouts or to the combined effect of, for example, knockout and buzzer press. Yet we were able to show the conditional effect on the gender gap in performance of particular rule combinations.

Third, we explored performance in Round 2 of the shows, where we found larger gender gaps. These are consistent with girls being increasingly hindered by psychological stress and risk aversion as the competition proceeded. Finally, we used panel data to estimate performance in the games in which players stay in for 25 questions. Here, we found that girls are less likely to respond faster even when their winning probability is higher. We also found that their probability of answering correctly is lower. These panel data results are consistent with boys' overconfidence and girls' lack of confidence.

35 An analogous effect was found by Cai et al. (2019) and Iriberri and Rey-Biel (2019), whose females' average performance dropped off at the final stage of their 2-stage competitions.

It is interesting that we have found these gender gaps in performance in Korea, whereas they have not been found in the US game shows (see Jetter and Walker 2016). This may not only be due to different cultural values between the two countries, but also because our results come from variations of a previously studied game and not from the basic format.

Finally, we consider the chief policy implication of our findings. As we noted in the Introduction, obtaining promotion and pay raises often involves competition. If women respond negatively to some forms of competition but men do not, there will be fewer women succeeding in such competitions. Our results indicate that in Korea, girls are significantly more adversely affected by certain combinations of high-stress game rules.

Acknowledgements

This chapter was first published as Booth, A.L., and Lee, J. (2021). 'Girls' and boys' performance in competitions: What we can learn from a Korean quiz show', *Journal of Economic Behavior & Organization*, 187:431–447. doi.org/10.1016/j.jebo.2021.04.031.

We would like to thank the editor and two anonymous referees, as well as Michael Jetter and seminar participants at the Korean Labor Economic Association, for their helpful comments. We also thank Jisun Kim for her excellent data work. Lee's work was supported by the Ministry of Education of the Republic of Korea and the National Research Foundation of Korea (NRF-2020S1A3A2A02104190).

References

Apicella, C.L., and Dreber, A. (2015). 'Sex differences in competitiveness: Hunter–gatherer women and girls compete less in gender-neutral and male-centric tasks', *Adaptive Human Behavior and Physiology*, 1:247–269. doi.org/10.1007/s40750-014-0015-z.

Arch, E. (1993). 'Risk-taking: A motivational basis for sex differences', *Psychological Reports*, 73(1):6–11. doi.org/10.2466/pr0.1993.73.1.3.

Attali, Y., Neeman, Z., and Schlosser, A. (2011). 'Rise to the challenge or not give a damn: Differential performance in high vs. low stakes tests'. IZA Discussion Paper No. 5693. doi.org/10.2139/ssrn.1842090.

Azmat, G., Calsamiglia, C., and Iriberri, N. (2016). 'Gender differences in response to big stakes', *Journal of the European Economic Association*, 14(6):1372–1400. doi.org/10.1111/jeea.12180.

Baldiga, K. (2014). 'Gender differences in willingness to guess', *Management Science*, 60(2):434–448. doi.org/10.1287/mnsc.2013.1776.

Berger, J., and Pope, D. (2011). 'Can losing lead to winning?', *Management Science*, 57(5):817–827. doi.org/10.1287/mnsc.1110.1328.

Block, J.H. (1983). 'Differential premises arising from differential socialization of the sexes: Some conjectures', *Child Development*, 54(6):1335–1354. doi.org/10.2307/1129799.

Booth, A.L. (2009). 'Gender and competition', *Labour Economics*, 16(6):599–606. doi.org/10.1016/j.labeco.2009.08.002.

Booth, A.L., and Nolen, P. (2012a). 'Gender differences in risk behaviour: Does nurture matter?', *The Economic Journal*, 122(558):F56–F78. doi.org/10.1111/j.1468-0297.2011.02480.x.

Booth, A.L., and Nolen, P. (2012b). 'Choosing to compete: How different are girls and boys?', *Journal of Economic Behavior & Organization*, 81(2):542–555. doi.org/10.1016/j.jebo.2011.07.018.

Booth, A., Cardona-Sosa, L., and Nolen, P. (2014). 'Gender differences in risk aversion: Do single-sex environments affect their development?', *Journal of Economic Behavior & Organization*, 99:126–154. doi.org/10.1016/j.jebo.2013.12.017.

Booth, A.L., and Yamamura, E. (2018). 'Performance in mixed-sex and single-sex competitions: What we can learn from speedboat races in Japan', *The Review of Economics and Statistics*, 100(4):581–593. doi.org/10.1162/rest_a_00715.

Booth, A.L., Fan, E., Meng, X., and Zhang, D. (2019). 'Gender differences in willingness to compete: The role of culture and institutions', *The Economic Journal*, 129(618):734–764. doi.org/10.1111/ecoj.12583.

Buser, T., Niederle, M., and Oosterbeek, H. (2014). 'Gender, competitiveness, and career choices', *The Quarterly Journal of Economics*, 129(3):1409–1447. doi.org/10.1093/qje/qju009.

Buser, T., Dreber, A., and Mollerstrom, J. (2017). 'The impact of stress on tournament entry', *Experimental Economics*, 20(2):506–530. doi.org/10.1007/s10683-016-9496-x.

Cahlíková, J., Cingl, L., and Levely, I. (2020). 'How stress affects performance and competitiveness across gender', *Management Science*, 66(8):3295–3310. doi.org/10.1287/mnsc.2019.3400.

Cai, X., Lu, Y., Pan, J., and Zhong, S. (2019). 'Gender gap under pressure: Evidence from China's national college entrance examination', *The Review of Economics and Statistics*, 101(2):249–263. doi.org/10.1162/rest_a_00749.

Choi, E.J., and Hwang, J. (2020). 'Transition of son preference: Evidence from South Korea', *Demography*, 57(2):627–652. doi.org/10.1007/s13524-020-00863-x.

Coffman, K.B., and Klinowski, D. (2019). 'The impact of penalties for wrong answers on the gender gap in test scores'. Harvard Business School Working Paper No. 19-017.

Dohmen, T., Falk, A., Huffman, D., Sunde, U., Schupp, J., and Wagner, G.G. (2011). 'Individual risk attitudes: Measurement, determinants, and behavioral consequences', *Journal of the European Economic Association*, 9(3):522–550. doi.org/10.1111/j.1542-4774.2011.01015.x

Dreber, A., von Essen, E., and Ranehill, E. (2011). 'Outrunning the gender gap – Boys and girls compete equally', *Experimental Economics*, 14(4):567–582. doi.org/10.1007/s10683-011-9282-8.

Dreber, A., von Essen, E., and Ranehill, E. (2014). 'Gender and competition in adolescence: Task matters', *Experimental Economics*, 17(1):154–172. doi.org/10.1007/s10683-013-9361-0.

Eckel, C.C., and Grossman, P.J. (2002). 'Sex differences and statistical stereotyping in attitudes toward financial risk', *Evolution and Human Behavior*, 23(4):281–295. doi.org/10.1016/S1090-5138(02)00097-1.

Eriksson, T., Poulsen, A., and Villeval, M.-C. (2009). 'Feedback and incentives: Experimental evidence', *Labour Economics*, 16(6):679–688. doi.org/10.1016/j.labeco.2009.08.006.

Filippin, A., and Crosetto, P. (2016). 'A reconsideration of gender differences in risk attitudes', *Management Science*, 62(11):3138–3160. doi.org/10.1287/mnsc.2015.2294.

Funk, P., and Perrone, H. (2016). 'Gender differences in academic performance: The role of negative marking in multiple-choice exams'. CEPR Working Paper No. DP 11716.

Gneezy, U., Niederle, M., and Rustichini, A. (2003). 'Performance in competitive environments: Gender differences', *The Quarterly Journal of Economics*, 118(3):1049–1074. doi.org/10.1162/00335530360698496.

Gneezy, U., Leonard, K.L., and List, J.A. (2009). 'Gender differences in competition: Evidence from a matrilineal and a patriarchal society', *Econometrica*, 77(5):1637–1664. doi.org/10.3982/ECTA6690.

Hahn, Y., Wang, L.C., and Yang, H.-S. (2018). 'Does greater school autonomy make a difference? Evidence from a randomized natural experiment in South Korea', *Journal of Public Economics*, 161:15–30. doi.org/10.1016/j.jpubeco.2018.03.004.

Iriberri, N., and Rey-Biel, P. (2019). 'Competitive pressure widens the gender gap in performance: Evidence from a two-stage competition in mathematics', *The Economic Journal*, 129(620):1863–1893. doi.org/10.1111/ecoj.12617.

Irwing, P., and Lynn, R. (2005). 'Sex differences in means and variability on the progressive matrices in university students: A meta-analysis', *British Journal of Psychology*, 96(4):505–524. doi.org/10.1348/000712605X53542.

Jetter, M., and Walker, J.K. (2016). 'Gender in jeopardy! The role of opponent gender in high-stakes competition'. IZA Discussion Paper No. 9669. doi.org/10.2139/ssrn.2725030.

Jetter, M., and Walker, J.K. (2017). 'Anchoring in financial decision-making: Evidence from *Jeopardy!*', *Journal of Economic Behavior & Organization*, 141: 164–176. doi.org/10.1016/j.jebo.2017.07.006.

Khachatryan, K., Dreber, A., von Essen, E., and Ranehill, E. (2015). 'Gender and preferences at a young age: Evidence from Armenia', *Journal of Economic Behavior & Organization*, 118:318–332. doi.org/10.1016/j.jebo.2015.02.021.

Koellinger, P., Minniti, M., and Schade, C. (2013). 'Gender differences in entrepreneurial propensity', *Oxford Bulletin of Economics and Statistics*, 75(2): 213–234. doi.org/10.1111/j.1468-0084.2011.00689.x.

Lee, J. (2008). 'Sibling size and investment in children's education: An Asian instrument', *Journal of Population Economics*, 21:855–875. doi.org/10.1007/s00148-006-0124-5.

Lindberg, S.M., Hyde, J.S., Petersen, J.L., and Linn, M.C. (2010). 'New trends in gender and mathematics performance: A meta-analysis', *Psychological Bulletin*, 136(6):1123–1135. doi.org/10.1037/a0021276.

Morin, L.-P. (2015). 'Do men and women respond differently to competition? Evidence from a major education reform', *Journal of Labor Economics*, 33(2): 443–491. doi.org/10.1086/678519.

Niederle, M., and Vesterlund, L. (2007). 'Do women shy away from competition? Do men compete too much?', *The Quarterly Journal of Economics*, 122(3):1067–1101. doi.org/10.1162/qjec.122.3.1067

Niederle, M., and Vesterlund, L. (2011). 'Gender and competition', *Annual Review of Economics*, 3:601–630. doi.org/10.1146/annurev-economics-111809-125122.

OECD. (2017). 'The pursuit of gender equality: An uphill battle'. OECD Publishing, Paris. doi.org/10.1787/9789264281318-en.

Ors, E., Palomino, F., and Peyrache, E. (2013). 'Performance gender gap: Does competition matter?', *Journal of Labor Economics*, 31(3):443–499. doi.org/10.1086/669331.

Säve-Söderbergh, J., and Lindquist, G.S. (2017). 'Children do not behave like adults: Gender gaps in performance and risk taking in a random social context in the high-stakes game shows Jeopardy and Junior Jeopardy', *The Economic Journal*, 127(603):1665–1692. doi.org/10.1111/ecoj.12355.

Shurchkov, O. (2012). 'Under pressure: Gender differences in output quality and quantity under competition and time constraints', *Journal of the European Economic Association*, 10(5):1189–1213. doi.org/10.1111/j.1542-4774.2012.01084.x.

Appendix

Table A14.1: Winning probability

	[1] First	[2] Last
Score	0.007*** (0.001)	0.011*** (0.001)
Score gap	-0.008*** (0.001)	-0.002** (0.001)
Max points	0.000 (0.000)	0.000 (0.000)
Constant	-2.342*** (0.505)	-1.702*** (0.491)
Observations	1560	1560

Notes: ** 5% significance; *** 1% significance; probit model; marginal effects.

Afterword and acknowledgements

Uneven Rewards has presented 14 of my papers written over the past four decades of my working life. Some are with co-authors, others are single-authored. The collection is also a partial tour through the evolution of economic thinking about the labour market and ways of obtaining data to evaluate labour policy.

In selecting which of my papers to include in this volume, I deliberately avoided papers that are mainly theoretical, with the exception of Chapter 1, which was about collective action and the free rider problem. This is a topic that has always intrigued me, and that will continue to do so, for collective action is of ever-growing importance, since human beings need to engage in pre-emptive collective action to prevent us from causing our own extinction.

While I have heard some academic colleagues talk about the free rider problem with regard to their co-authors, I have never found this to be a problem. My co-authors are my friends and remain so, and I am grateful for their enthusiastic support in providing permissions to reproduce our work in this volume.

I wrote and published a total of seven papers with my University of Essex friend and colleague, Patrick Nolen, who passed away unexpectedly from COVID-19 in October 2020. Our very first joint paper – about gender, cultural influences and economically relevant preferences – appears as Chapter 10 in this volume. Patrick is remembered with great affection by those who knew him, and his intellect, humour and lively presence are sadly missed.

I would like to thank Andrew Kennedy of Crawford School of Public Policy, ANU, who invited me to be part of the *Global Thinkers Series*, an initiative of the Public Policy Editorial Board at ANU Press. As I noted in the introduction, that this volume will be open access is one of the reasons that I accepted his invitation. I would also like to thank Bruce Chapman for his enthusiastic support for this collection, and the staff at the ANU Press for their careful editing and beautiful cover design. Thanks also to Tim Hatton, who always takes a great interest in whatever I work on and is ever willing to discuss a wide variety of research issues.

Canberra
September 2025

www.ingramcontent.com/pod-product-compliance
Lightning Source LLC
LaVergne TN
LVHW010952100826
845153LV00002B/206

* 9 7 8 1 7 6 0 4 6 7 2 9 6 *